THE PHILOSOPHY OF JÜRGEN HABERMAS

The Philosophy of Jürgen Habermas

A Critical Introduction

UWE STEINHOFF

TRANSLATED BY KARSTEN SCHÖLLNER

OXFORD
UNIVERSITY PRESS

OXFORD
UNIVERSITY PRESS

Great Clarendon Street, Oxford ox2 6dp
Oxford University Press is a department of the University of Oxford.
It furthers the University's objective of excellence in research, scholarship,
and education by publishing worldwide in

Oxford New York

Auckland Cape Town Dar es Salaam Hong Kong Karachi
Kuala Lumpur Madrid Melbourne Mexico City Nairobi
New Delhi Shanghai Taipei Toronto

With offices in

Argentina Austria Brazil Chile Czech Republic France Greece
Guatemala Hungary Italy Japan Poland Portugal Singapore
South Korea Switzerland Thailand Turkey Ukraine Vietnam

Oxford is a registered trade mark of Oxford University Press
in the UK and in certain other countries

Published in the United States
by Oxford University Press Inc., New York

British Library Cataloguing in Publication Data
Library of Congress Cataloging-in-Publication Data
Steinhoff, Uwe.
The philosophy of Jürgen Habermas : a critical introduction / Uwe Steinhoff;
translated by Karsten Schöllner.
p. cm.
"This book is an abridged English version of my study Kritik der kommunikativen Rationalität:
Eine Darstellung und Kritik der kommunikationstheoretischen Philosophie von Jürgen Habermas
und Karl-Otto Apel (Paderborn: Mentis, 2006)" – Pref.
ISBN 978-0-19-954780-7
1. Critical theory. 2. Rationalism. 3. Habermas, Jürgen – Criticism and interpretation. I. Schöllner,
Karsten. II. Steinhoff, Uwe. Kritik der kommunikativen Rationalität. III. Title.
HM480.S742 2009
193—dc22
2008053820

Typeset by SPI Publisher Services, Pondicherry, India
Printed in the UK by the MPG Books Group

ISBN 9780199547807

3 5 7 9 10 8 6 4 2

A mis amigos de Buenos Aires

Preface

This book is an abridged English version of my study *Kritik der kommunika-tiven Rationalität: Eine Darstellung und Kritik der kommunikationstheoretischen Philosophie von Jürgen Habermas und Karl-Otto Apel* (Paderborn: Mentis, 2006). For this English version I omitted those parts of my analysis of Apel's philosophy that are not important for understanding Habermas. Quite a few parts of Apel's philosophy, however, are indispensable for understanding Habermas—overlook-ing this fact is quite common in the Anglo-Saxon literature on Habermas and leads to misinterpretations. I hope to correct some of these misinterpretations here.

When quoting Habermas (or Apel) I use so far as possible the existing English translations of the original texts. Unfortunately, the translations of some of Habermas's expressions are somewhat awkward, the most awkward probably being the rendering of "verständigungsorientiertes Handeln" as "action oriented towards reaching understanding". I thought long about replacing this translation throughout the text with an alternative one but finally decided against it. One reason is that it is not that easy to come up with a better translation; the other reason is that not using the more or less canonical translations might confuse readers. Nevertheless, outside of the quotations, for the sake of brevity I some-times use "understanding-oriented" for "verständigungsorientiert" and "success-oriented" for "erfolgsorientiert". I also kept the translations of sentences like "Du sollst nicht töten" as "You should not kill" (instead of "You ought not to kill"). The reader should bear in mind that the "should" in these sentences is meant to rep-resent a normative imperative and not prudential advice. Where necessary, I have corrected, amended or commented on existing translations to make it clear what Habermas is really saying. On these occasions I have also provided the reference to the original texts.

The present work does not examine all of Habermas's writings. It does not deal with his older attempt at an epistemological justification of communicative rationality, which Habermas abandoned long ago and replaced with a linguistic approach. Nor does it deal with his more or less political interventions in current issues, his criticism of liberal eugenics or his recent—remarkably reactionary and anti-Enlightenment—apologetics of religion. Rather, this book describes, analy-ses and criticizes what Habermas is most famous for: his so-called critical theory of communicative action and rationality, which starts with an interpretation of speech-acts, develops a communicative concept of rationality, analyses the ten-sions between "system" and "lifeworld", negotiates a path through discourse ethics and culminates in a "discourse theory of law and democracy". This monumental theory has had a significant impact not only on philosophy, but also, among other disciplines, on psychology, sociology and the political sciences. While it is cer-tainly not universal in scope, it is still far more ambitious than any other present-day Western philosophy and might well merit Habermas the title of being the last system-builder in Western philosophy. The term "system" is in fact decisive. Everything hangs together in Habermas's philosophy of communicative rationality. It is impossible—although, unfortunately, it is attempted all too often—to understand, for example, Habermas's theory of law and democracy without understanding the foundations it is built upon, that is, without understanding discourse ethics and, more fundamental still, the theory of communicative action. It is my hope that the present work will contribute significantly to a more thorough, precise and also more critical understanding of Habermas's philosophy.

Hong Kong
September 2008

Acknowledgements

Section 2.4 is an expanded English version of "Die Begründung der Konsenstheorie. Über das fehlende Fundament der Diskursethik", *Logos*, Neue Folge 3, pp. 191–210. Section 3.3.3 is the revised English version of "Probleme der Legitimation des demokratischen Rechtsstaats", *Rechtstheorie* 27, pp. 79–105. The Appendix is the English version of "Habermas' relativistische und dezisionistische Wende", *Aufklärung und Kritik* 9(2), pp. 61–8.

I thank Karsten Schöllner for translating the present work from German, and Michael James for copy-editing it.

Contents

Introduction

The philosophy of Jürgen Habermas purports to be keeper of the flame for the Enlightenment and guardian of an emphatic, "uncurtailed" concept of reason. It opposes both the *postmodern critique of reason*, which it regards in light of the "project of modernity" as self-contradictory and defeatist, and so-called *scientism*, which allegedly cedes normative questions to the purview of irrational decision-making in taking its standards of rationality from the natural sciences and the Weberian concept of purposive rationality. (By "scientism" Habermas and his philosophical companion and comrade-in-arms of many years, Karl-Otto Apel, mean the ideas above all of critical rationalists, but also those of most proponents of analytic philosophy, particularly of analytic metaethics.) Habermas's philosophy presents itself as a *critical theory of society*, emphasizes its *scientific rigour* and also claims to withstand the test of interdisciplinary and even empirical research.

It is hardly surprising that a philosophy such as this—a school of philosophy, ultimately—is one of the most frequently discussed at present. First, it inevitably attracts much sharp criticism, since both postmodernists and advocates of scientism see it as the defender of a chimaera and an obstacle to the true work of enlightenment, which, as such, has to shed light on itself and its own limits. Thus, for the postmodernists it is a typical expression of modernity's insupportable pretensions and its blindness to differences in its attempt to impose itself everywhere with a false claim to universal validity. For the proponents of "scientism", on the other hand, the Habermasian philosophy represents a *regression* to the period preceding more recent accomplishments of modernity. Moreover, orthodox Marxists have their own reasons for taking issue with this philosophy, as do adherents of the older critical theory with this younger version of it. The list of its adversaries could go on indefinitely.

Second, it touches upon what for many are very painful old wounds, and, to continue the metaphor, promises to soothe them.

Habermas's programme—whereby his older attempt at an *epistemological* justification of communicative rationality, which according to general opinion has clearly failed, is superseded by a *linguistic* approach[1]—is perhaps best introduced in his own words:

In this work I have tried to introduce a theory of communicative action that clarifies the normative foundations of a critical theory of society. The theory of communicative action is meant to provide an alternative to the philosophy of history on which earlier critical theory still relied, but which is no longer tenable. It is intended as a framework within which interdisciplinary research on the selective pattern of capitalist modernization can be taken up once again.[2]

Such a programme certainly has its appeal. And Apel, whose transcendental–pragmatic philosophy has provided the indispensable groundwork for Habermas's universal pragmatics, also touches the nerve of our time, or at least *a* nerve, and provokes considerable interest when he diagnoses the following problem—and then offers a solution in the form of discourse ethics as the "macro-ethics of humanity on the finite Earth"[3]:

> On the one hand, the need for a universal ethics, i.e. one that is binding for human society as a whole, was never so urgent as now—a time which is characterized by a globally uniform civilization produced by the technological consequences of science. On the other hand, the philosophical task of rationally grounding a general ethics never seems to have been so difficult as it is in the scientific age. This is because in our time the notion of intersubjective validity is also prejudged by science, namely by the scientistic notion of normatively neutral or value-free "objectivity".[4]

Yet drawing up a programme is one thing, carrying it out another. How do the proponents of this discourse ethics—a term I apply equally to the core of both Habermas's and Apel's theoretical constructs and which in the following is meant as a catch-all term for Habermas, Apel and their philosophical allies—actually proceed?

According to Habermas—and it is with his philosophy that the present work is concerned, even if, in order to understand it better, it will be necessary to examine certain central elements of the Apelian transcendental pragmatics that Habermas enlists—the problem described above cannot be solved with recourse to a mere *purposive rationality*, since, as we have just seen, precisely this conception of rationality is a *component* of the problem (see also Section 2.1). Instead, Habermas considers it necessary to have recourse to an "uncurtailed", "*communicative rationality*"—meaning a rationality conceived in terms of consensus, thus able to secure intersubjective validity, and understood from the outset as *discursive*. Elucidating this concept and trying to show that it cannot be traced back to purposive rationality (Section 1.2) take Habermas on a path through his theory of communicative action to an attempt to demonstrate that the conditions of rationality of this communicative action can be explicated only by a theory of argumentation or, more precisely, a discourse theory (Section 1.3).

This theory of a discursive rationality, then, accommodates the conception of a *universalistic morality of reason* (Section 2.1). Here it is necessary first to characterize more precisely this discursive rationality, which gives rise to the problem of identifying individual norms of discourse. Habermas essentially borrows the transcendental pragmatics developed by Apel, without sharing the latter's aspirations to final justification and transcendental status (Section 2.1). According to this conception, norms of discourse and "presuppositions of argumentation" cannot be disputed without so-called performative contradictions, such that to demonstrate that such a contradiction obtains is to identify just such a presupposition. Apel and his students claim to arrive at a *final justification* of norms of discourse in this manner. They understand these norms as directly moral in nature and count among them the norm-justifying principles U and D that underpin discourse ethics (Section 2.2).[5] Habermas rejects the conception of norms of discourse as directly moral norms (Section 2.2.2.3). Instead he seeks to *derive* the principles U and D from the norms of discourse (Section 2.3). (This is just as problematic as the more direct transcendental–pragmatic version, which makes the consensus or discourse theory of truth advocated by Habermas and Apel significant for discourse ethics as a possible solution to the problem (Section 2.4).) Finally, Habermas tries to explain how the norms of action justified according to the principle U under idealized conditions could possibly be rationally applied to real situations (Section 2.5).

Habermas attempts to make the theory of communicative action and discourse ethics fruitful beyond the strictly ethical and moral field and, conversely, to find confirmation of it in empirical theories (Chapter 3). Here he draws on research in psychology (Section 3.1) and on the process of socio-cultural evolution (Section 3.2) as well as on political and sociological questions wherein the desired "critical theory of society" is to assume concrete form.

The present study is both a detailed exposition and a rigorous critique. It aims to explicate and critique Habermas's argumentation step by step, from beginning to end. Where Habermas's argumentative transitions or those of other proponents of discourse ethics are not sufficiently explicit or simply absent, this study will attempt to make the theory as strong as possible by filling in the gaps with considerations and textual quotations taken from the theory itself. (Should this approach be rejected, then the gaps remain, which is a problem for the theory under analysis and not for the analysis itself.) Despite the rich body of literature on this subject, a *comprehensive* examination at this level of detail is in my opinion still lacking.[6] Yet it is necessary for a proper understanding and precise assessment of a philosophy that begins microscopically with the interpretation of speech acts and then after a long journey ends (provisionally) in macroscopic and monumental fashion with a "discourse theory of law and democracy".

1

"Communicative" versus Purposive Rationality

Proponents of discourse ethics seek to develop a conception of "communicative" or "discursive" rationality. Here I will use the two terms as synonyms, even though lately Habermas, following Apel, distinguishes "communicative" rationality from "discursive" rationality:

> Since argumentative practices are, so to speak, a reflexive form of communicative action, the justificatory rationality embodied in discourse [="discursive rationality"] does indeed rest to a certain extent on the communicative rationality embodied in everyday action; nonetheless, communicative rationality remains on a level with epistemic and teleological rationality. Communicative rationality does not constitute the *overarching* structure of rationality but rather one of three core structures that are, however, interwoven with one another by way of the discursive rationality that emerges out of communicative rationality.[1]

However, in the "Theory of Communicative Action" communicative rationality *is* this discursive rationality:

> The rationality inherent in this practice [of communicative action] is seen in the fact that a communicatively achieved agreement must be based *in the end* on reasons. And the rationality of those who participate in this communicative practice is determined by whether, if necessary, they could, *under suitable circumstances*, provide reasons for their expressions. Thus the rationality proper to the communicative practice of everyday life points to the practice of argumentation as a court of appeal that makes it possible to continue communicative action with other means when disagreements can no longer be repaired with everyday routines and yet are not to be settled by the direct or strategic use of force. For this reason I believe that the concept of communicative rationality, which refers to an unclarified systematic interconnection of universal validity claims, can be adequately explicated only in terms of a theory of argumentation.[2]

If the concept of communicative rationality can find explication only in a theory of argumentation—rather than, for example, in a simple theory of communicative action—then communicative rationality *is* a rationality of argumentation, that is, a *discursive rationality*. This does not imply that the distinction more recently drawn by Habermas is false—quite the contrary. Rather, it is the approach taken in the "Theory of Communicative Action" and elsewhere that is false when, instead of construing communicative rationality directly from the conditions of rationality of communicative action itself, the theory turns to the conditions of rationality of the *linguistic mediation* of communicative action. This linguistic mediation is understood as being *oriented to reaching understanding,* and its conditions of rationality are then in turn explicated with recourse to the concept of the *discursive* "redeemability" of claims. The motive behind this approach has remained the same: whether we say that communicative rationality finds explication in a theory of argumentation, or that "the justificatory rationality embodied in discourse does indeed rest to a certain extent on the communicative rationality embodied in everyday action", both formulations belie the mistaken attempt to fabricate some kind of essential connection between the rationality "proper to" communicative action and the rationality "proper to" discourse. Yet discourse rationality does not provide the explication of the (conditions of) rationality of communicative action, nor does it "rest on" it, either "to a certain extent" or at all. This chapter will provide a detailed demonstration of this argument, among other things. However, my concern here is a preliminary *terminological* clarification to avoid confusion. In what follows I will be using the term "communicative rationality" as Habermas did in the "Theory of Communicative Action"—and thus in accordance with its use in secondary literature as well, which should be a relief to the reader. This concept of communicative rationality corresponds to Apel's concept of discursive rationality. In general I will prefer the term "communicative rationality".

Proponents of discourse ethics aim to contrast and superordinate this *communicative rationality* to purposive rationality. In so doing they hope not to reduce purposive rationality to communicative rationality but rather to show that communicative rationality is the more comprehensive or "more integrative" rationality, and ultimately is authoritative in deciding the areas to which strategic rationality may be legitimately applied. In short, communicative rationality is to exercise ultimate authority over legitimacy.

In what follows I will first examine whether the project of delimiting so-called communicative rationality from purposive rationality has any hope of success (1.1).

I will then turn to Habermas's attempt at this delimitation. Central to this attempt is the distinction between action oriented towards success and action oriented towards reaching understanding (1.2).

Finally it will be necessary to examine in detail how exactly the "rationality proper to the communicative practice of everyday life", that is, the communicative rationality purportedly distinguishable from purposive rationality, "points to the practice of argumentation as a court of appeal" and how far this court's jurisdiction extends. That is, we will need to examine how—and if—starting from so-called communicative rationality we can arrive at a discourse theory of rationality, and whether the communicative rationality "explicated" by this discourse theory can in fact be accorded the status of primacy (over purposive rationality) that discourse ethics claims for it (1.3).

1.1. THE UNRIVALLED STATUS OF PURPOSIVE RATIONALITY

A person can *rationally* lay a cement floor in his or her garage—for example, not painting himself or herself into a corner and having to walk over the wet cement after smoothing it—without his or her *action* being a rational one. Of course, laying cement is an action; but there is a difference between evaluating the *way* in which a thing is done and evaluating the *action itself*. If he or she continues to lay cement matter-of-factly even though someone has just thrown at him or her what is clearly recognizable as a grenade, then the way he or she executes the particular task, that is, laying cement, may still be rational, but this action itself is not; he or she is not acting rationally (on the assumption of relatively normal interests on his or her part). One could say—and this accords with our ordinary use of language—that someone *performs* an action *in a rational manner*, which means pursuing a *particular goal* in a rational manner (which does not imply being "in rational pursuit" of that goal) whenever the agent is convinced with good reason that the manner in which he or she is proceeding is effective and adequate, in other words *efficient*. In this case the agent's action satisfies the criterion of *instrumental rationality*. Yet *that* the agent performs the action, effectively or otherwise, can still be *irrational*. The standard of *purposive rationality* is decisive here; and it is in orientation to purposive rationality that the agent will weigh a particular end, such as laying cement, against other ends, as well as against means and side-effects, and come to the conclusion that it would be better to forget about laying cement and leave the garage.

And this is the question we need to ask about "communicative rationality": does it raise the same claim as purposive rationality? The latter claims to supply the standard for the rationality of actions. Thus, is "communicative rationality" a standard for the rationality of actions or merely, like the rationality of laying cement, a standard for the rationality of *how* to perform certain actions— and actions of a specific type, that is, "communicative" or "discursive" actions? Proponents of discourse ethics claim that the concept of communicative rationality—allegedly in contrast to purposive rationality—represents an *"uncurtailed concept of reason"*,[3] and yet the examples with which Habermas seeks to explicate this concept are all examples of *instrumental* reason, if even this.

We will return to these particulars later. Here we may raise the issue of the possible consequences of this distinction. If "communicative rationality" is merely a standard for the rationality of *how* to perform "communicative" or "discursive" actions, it is not at all in a position to recommend itself in comparison with purposive rationality, since according to this reading the rules of communicative rationality consist simply in those rules a person has to follow in order to communicate effectively, that is, in a way that will achieve the goal of reaching understanding. These rules could be traced back to instrumental rationality, which also means, as Karl-Heinz Ilting has already argued in his critique of Apel, that they would be merely *hypothetical* imperatives: one has to follow them *if* one wants to communicate effectively.[4] Thus communicative rationality would be conceptually and practically subordinate to purposive rationality—conceptually, because communicative rationality is then nothing more than purposive rationality *under the assumption of the goal of communication as an unconditional end*. To borrow a phrase from Habermas, communicative rationality is in that case just a *derivative* of purposive rationality and not the other way around. And practically, because the question of *whether* it is rational in a particular situation to effectively communicate (or enter into a discourse) can be answered only according to the principles of purposive rationality.

But the first reading, according to which "communicative rationality" is a standard for the rationality of actions (and not only of the *way* they are performed), also shows "communicative rationality" in a poor light, since it is hardly possible that we could have two different concepts of the rationality of actions. And the thought that some obscure concept of "communicative rationality" could hold up against Weber's concept of purposive rationality seems a priori implausible as long as we look closely at Weber's definition without letting our judgement be coloured by the common bias that it is "instrumental". Weber's definition, famously, is:

Action is purposive-rational [*zweckrational*] when it is oriented to ends, means, and secondary results. This involves rationally *weighing* the relations of means to ends, the relations of ends to secondary consequences, and finally the relative importance of different possible ends. Determination of action *either* in affectual *or* traditional terms is thus incompatible with this type.[5]

Of course, there are certain flaws in this definition. What does "rationally weighing" mean, particularly if we consider conditions where time is scarce and a decision has to be made? Naturally we do not have to weigh all possible ends, means and secondary consequences against each other. There is a level of epistemic effort that is itself irrational. Thus, this weighing process (which in some circumstances could be very brief) does not necessarily need to identify and analyse various *concrete* means and secondary results or other ends that might be in opposition to the particular action; it is rather the *categories* "ends", "means" (or, to put it better, "ways of realizing the end") and "secondary results" that the decision-making process has to *orient* itself to, even if this is only to ascertain that one of these categories does not require any *further* consideration in a concrete situation.

I would therefore like to suggest the following definition:

A person's action is rational precisely when the person has evaluated the action under the categories of ends, ways of realizing these ends, and side effects with at least as much epistemic ambition as the person has confirmed to be opportune at the time of the action.

Before this definition could serve a criterial function, we would have to clarify what it means to confirm something as opportune. However, for present purposes the definition is sufficient,[6] namely, to illustrate the following:

If a philosopher makes the claim that someone could be acting rationally without acting in accordance with purposive rationality (and for Weber value-oriented rationality was only a preliminary stage to true rationality, that is, purposive rationality, and not on equal terms with it), then this philosopher necessarily has to adopt one of the following two positions:

(1) A person's action can be rational even if the person has not evaluated the action under the categories of ends, ways of realizing these ends, and side-effects with at least as much epistemic ambition as the person has confirmed to be opportune (i.e. in the person's best interest) at the time of the action.

If we keep in mind that people can of course have not just egoistic interests but also interests aimed at the well-being of others—and it is the disregard of this circumstance that makes the critique of big bad purposive rationality and its allegedly egoistic and calculating nature so popular and so cheap, a moralizing attack on a straw man—then it is hard to avoid the conclusion that statement (1) is contradictory. Whoever accepts this claim either does not understand the meaning of the word "rational" or is ignoring it in the interest of false labelling.

The second alternative is to claim the following:

(2) A person's action is not rational if the person has not evaluated the action under the categories of ends, ways of realizing these ends, and side-effects with at least as much epistemic ambition as the person has confirmed to be opportune at the time of the action, but there is at least one *additional* aspect that could bear on the process of weighing ends, ways of realizing these ends, and side-effects.

Now, this claim is false. What further aspect could there be? One might be inclined to answer: morality. Of course one can take morality into account. One can account for the economy and aesthetics and environmental protection and one's fellow citizens, and all of this can readily be subsumed under the concepts of ends, means (in the sense of ways of realizing these ends) and side-effects. The concepts of means, ends and side-effects cover everything that is at all worthy of consideration. There simply is no fourth aspect.

Furthermore, I would like to point out that this definition of a purposively rational action does not exclude actions that were evaluated with a greater epistemic effort than appears to be opportune for the agent in the given situation. Of course, as mentioned, this effort would then itself be irrational—just as entering into discourses and large-scale discussions is rather irrational in most situations.

It is furthermore unclear what one could possibly object to in Weber's claim that purposive rationality is nothing other than the rationality of action per se. If the concept of communicative rationality presents itself at the same level of abstraction as, for example, cement-laying rationality, then actions are not subject to the standard of communicative rationality *as such* but only a *certain type* of action would be subject to this standard (or, to be more precise: the way actions of this type are performed is subject to this standard). And in this case an action can be communicatively rational without being *rational* (because an action can be instrumentally rational without being rational, that is, purposively rational). On the other hand, if the concept of communicative rationality claims to be at the same level of abstraction as purposive rationality—that is, if it claims to assess the rationality of actions as such—this claim also implies that rational action requires either *more* or *less* than the rational weighing of ends, means and side-effects. This claim contradicts the meaning of the term "rational"—the claim is false. There is no way out of this dilemma, and thus the attempt to identify a "communicative rationality" different from purposive rationality but equal or even superordinate to it is futile.

1.2. HABERMAS'S ATTEMPT TO DISTINGUISH COMMUNICATIVE RATIONALITY FROM PURPOSIVE RATIONALITY

Is this diagnosis confirmed by an examination of the particulars of Habermas's attempt to carry out his project?

If we take into consideration the most grievous objection that Habermas has to field, we could sketch the path that Habermas's endeavour takes as follows:

At the very beginning of the *Theory of Communicative Action*, under the heading "Rationality—A Preliminary Specification", Habermas, while claiming to provide an analysis of the usage of the word "rational", tries to define the two types of rationality by distinguishing between acts of assertion (oriented to reaching understanding) and so-called teleological action: whereas teleological action aims at *success*, assertion, in contrast, aims at *truth*. Later Habermas distinguishes other actions besides assertions from teleological actions, which leads to a general distinction between actions *oriented to reaching understanding* and actions *oriented towards success*.

According to Habermas, the rationality of both assertions and teleological actions is measured against the justifiability of the "validity claims" in question. However, he argues that the conditions of rationality are not the same for teleological actions and assertions, and evidently he believes that these differences in the *conditions* of rationality allow a distinction between two *concepts* of rationality.[7] Thus the analysis of the conditions of rationality of action oriented to reach understanding leads him to the concept of communicative rationality.

Naturally, the decisive objection to Habermas's endeavour to distinguish understanding-oriented action from success-oriented action—and thus communicative rationality from purposive rationality—is that the former can be traced back to the latter. This objection can be raised at two levels.

First, it could be argued that Habermas's paradigm of action oriented towards reaching understanding, namely, communicative action, is simply a sub-class of success-oriented action, which would make the illocutionary (=understanding-oriented) speech acts that mediate communicative actions likewise success-oriented. Thus Habermas takes great pains to distinguish communicative action from success-oriented action—which, in the context of social interactions, he calls strategic action.

Second, one can always point out that, even *without* being embedded in success-oriented communicative action, speech acts oriented towards reaching understanding are directly success-oriented, quite simply because the illocutionary goal of reaching understanding is still a *goal*. Anyone wishing to communicate understandably obviously wants to *succeed* in communicating understandably. Habermas also tries to mobilize counter-arguments to this objection.

1.2.1. Habermas's Explication(s) of the Concept of Rationality

Let us start then by examining Habermas's attempts to explicate the concept of rationality. In the first round we will look primarily at those arguments that

Habermas provides for the thesis that so-called success-oriented actions and (understanding-oriented) assertions are categorically distinct from one another (and thus not reducible to one another) (1.2.1.1). Subsequently we will turn to the definitions themselves that Habermas provides for those purportedly different conditions of rationality for the allegedly different types of rationality, and we will investigate whether they are correct as well as whether, correct or not, they do in fact reflect the categorical distinction that Habermas wishes to draw (1.2.1.2).

1.2.1.1. Actions Oriented towards Success vs. Assertions (Oriented towards Reaching Understanding)

"The close relation between knowledge and rationality", according to Habermas, "suggests that the rationality of an expression depends on the reliability of the knowledge embodied in it." This is a non-sequitur.[8] However, it is not so important for the course of the argument. Habermas continues:

Consider two paradigmatic cases: an assertion with which A expresses a belief with a communicative intention and a goal-directed intervention in the world with which B pursues a specific end. Both embody fallible knowledge; both are attempts that can go wrong. Both expressions, the speech act and the teleological action, can be criticized. A hearer can contest the *truth* of the assertion made by A; an observer can dispute the anticipated *success* of the action taken by B.[9]

By desiring us to see these two types of action (and "action" is the proper heading, not "expression") as criticizable from fundamentally distinct points of view— here under the aspect of truth, there under the aspect of success—Habermas tries, right from the start, to frame matters so as to set a course for the distinction between different types of rationality. But the two actions can in fact be criticized from the same point of view. Whoever expresses something "with a communicative intention" *intends something*. Communication, for example: he at least intends to be understood. His end is to be understood. The attempt to achieve this end with the speech act can go wrong, as Habermas says. Yet "the attempt went wrong" is synonymous with "the attempt did not *succeed*". And of course a speech act can be criticized for its lack of success—just like what Habermas calls a "goal-directed intervention in the world".

Conversely, Habermas tells us:

The effectiveness of an action stands in internal relation to the truth of the conditional prognoses implied by the plan or rule of action.[10]

Thus we can also criticize a non-linguistic action for the falsity of its underlying prognosis. Here one could object that what is criticized as false in a propositional sense is not *the action itself*, whereas the *assertion* itself is criticized as false in a propositional sense; so that there is a difference here. Aside from the rather questionable relevance of this objection, it is also incorrect. It is based on a confusion caused by linguistic ambiguity. The word "assertion" refers to an *act* of assertion on the one hand and that which *is* asserted on the other hand. An assertion *qua speech act* cannot be true or false, as Habermas himself knows very well.[11] Thus he writes that A "makes a truth claim for the asserted *proposition p*".[12] In other words, the assertion qua speech act cannot be criticized as false in a propositional sense any more than a non-linguistic action can. The criticism "that is false" can only ever pertain to what is *connected* with the assertions and/or actions—with the proposition it conveys or with the underlying prognosis.

Of course, there is also a prognosis underlying the assertion. This means that the criticism "that is false" can refer to two different things: to the prognosis and to the asserted proposition. But this does not represent a fundamental distinction between "goal-directed actions" and assertions either. If I mail a letter containing some kind of message, then of course, just like an assertion, this act can be criticized first for the falsity of the conditional prognosis, second, along with this, for its ineffectiveness and third for the falsity of the message I included.

In short, the profound distinction Habermas would like to see between assertions and "goal-directed interventions" is not there. Not only can "goal-directed actions" be criticized under the same aspects as assertions, but there are also goal-directed actions that serve the same goal as assertions, namely, communication. Sending a letter or broadcasting a television programme or shooting a flame-gun *are* all examples of this sort of action, just like assertions. This means that the distinction Habermas seeks between purposive rationality and "communicative rationality" either fails to capture anything, or else comes down to the distinction between a general description and one of its subsets, like any other distinction between purposive rationality per se and one of the forms it can assume when applied to an end posited as absolute (e.g. as applied to laying cement). Habermas's own definitions confirm this quite clearly:

…the rationality of an action is proportionate not to whether the state actually occurring in the world as a result of the action coincides with the intended state and satisfies the corresponding conditions of success, but rather to whether the actor has *achieved* this result on the basis of the deliberately selected and implemented means (or, in accurately perceived circumstances, could normally have done so).[13]

The rationality of the use of language oriented toward reaching understanding… depends on whether the speech acts are sufficiently comprehensible and acceptable for the speaker to achieve illocutionary success with them (or for him to be able to do so in normal circumstances).[14]

It is hard to miss the fact that this second definition is simply an *application* of the first, more general definition to the concrete case of the use of language oriented towards reaching understanding—nothing more. Thus even Habermas's own definitions hold that the rationality of the use of language oriented towards reaching understanding is measured against the *same* criterion as the rationality of teleological success-oriented action.

Moreover, even if speech acts could be distinguished from other actions as Habermas would like to, that is, by means of different validity claims—which is not the case—it would still be very far from clear what this has to do with different types of rationality or different standards of rationality, since criticizing an

assertion as *false*, for example, is not equivalent to criticizing it as *irrational*. As I
see it, it is Habermas's strategy here to generate this connection by using the concept of claims and by suggesting a certain analogy to "goal-oriented intervention".
At the same time he involves the concept of justification, which naturally already
has an internal connection with rationality:

> In both cases the critic refers to claims that the subjects necessarily attach to their expres-
> sions insofar as they are intended as assertions or as goal-directed actions. This necessity is
> of a conceptual nature. For *A* does not make an assertion unless he makes a truth claim for
> the asserted proposition *p* and therewith indicates his conviction that his statement can, if
> necessary, be *justified* [*begründet*]. And *B* does not perform a goal-directed action, that is, he
> does not want to accomplish an end by it unless he regards the action planned as promising
> and therewith indicates his conviction that, in the given circumstance, his choice of means
> can if necessary be *justified* [*begründet*].[15]

Here Habermas seeks to profit from the unproblematic and uncontested thesis
that the rationality of "goal-oriented actions" assumes a choice of means aimed
at effectiveness. (Where Habermas errs, however, is in *reducing* the rationality of
actions to just this.) He then attributes a *claim* not only to speakers in reference to
the propositions they assert but also to actors in reference to the assumed effectiveness of the means. The analogy suggested here is this: when the rationality of
goal-oriented actions rests on the justifiability of their specific claim, namely, the
claim of effectiveness, then the rationality of assertions will probably rest on the
justifiability of their claim to *truth*. Thus here we find one reason, among others,
why Habermas places such a high value on the concept of the claim; without this,
the analogy would look quite different, namely: when the rationality of a goal-
oriented action rests on the justifiability of its effectiveness, the rationality of an
assertion, too, will probably rest on the justifiability of its effectiveness.

I have just argued that "goal-oriented actions" and assertions can both be criticized under precisely the same aspects. In our context now this means: if "goal-
oriented actions" involve a claim to effectiveness, then so do assertions. They
involve the claim, as Habermas puts it, of being "sufficiently comprehensible and
acceptable for the speaker to achieve illocutionary success with them (or for him
to be able to do so in normal circumstances)".[16] In fact, however, the situation
is even more unfortunate for Habermas: an agent does not attach the *claim* to a
justifiable choice of means to his or her action. If I fumble around for the night
lamp in the dark and alone; if then, in an illumination-oriented attitude (which,
along with the understanding-oriented attitude, belongs to the larger class of
success-oriented attitudes) I flick the switch to turn the lamp on, it is quite off-
topic to speak of "raising claims". I certainly *suppose* the effectiveness of flicking
the light-switch—and even if I only make an *attempt*, I suppose that the attempt
is worthwhile in one way or another. But as long as no other person is present
whom I assure: "you can count on me, with this carefully considered action I will
certainly succeed in making light", then "claim" is a bad choice of word; this is not
how we use the term. Thus this brings us back to my more correct formulation of
the analogy, which is much less favourable to Habermas.

There are additional gaps in the argument worth mentioning. *Even if* an agent were to raise a claim, why must it be a claim to a justifi*able* choice of means— meaning, as Habermas uses the term "justifiable",[17] a choice of means that can be justified to *others*? If B holds an action to be promising, it follows at most that B considers the choice of means *justified*, that she considers herself to have good reasons for holding these means to be effective. She could, however, be entirely convinced—and there are no "conceptual necessities" of any sort that speak against this—that she is unable to justify this choice of means to *others*. Habermas's thesis that agents have to assume the justifiability of their choice of means remains itself unjustified.

This also applies to the curious reduction of the rationality of action to the justifiability of the effectiveness of means to an already given end. Habermas himself writes:

With his assertion, *A* makes reference to something that *in fact occurs* in the objective world; with his purposive activity, *B* makes reference to something that *should occur* in the objective world. In doing so both raise *claims* with their symbolic expressions…[18]

Now, as long as we assume that B in fact does raise claims with her action, and if moreover we recognize that she of course makes reference to something that *should* occur, then at least *one* claim she raises is this: that a particular something *should* be, that is, that the goal she pursues *should* be achieved. But then obviously an action could be criticized not only for its ineffectiveness but also for its intended goal. Thus the rationality serving as the critical standard for actions would not at all be the curtailed, purely instrumental "rationality" of action of Jürgen Habermas, but rather the purposive rationality of Max Weber.

In addition, Habermas continually emphasizes how *three* validity claims are raised in connection with each speech act, and thus with assertions as well: not only a truth-claim but also claims to rightness and to truthfulness or sincerity.[19] While these claims may perhaps not come into conflict within what Habermas calls communicative action, they certainly do outside of it. Moreover, ascertaining the rationality of an assertion requires deliberation, and once again it is purposive rationality that would seem to suggest itself as the standard for this process of deliberation. If Habermas intends to describe the rationality of assertions only *within* the assumptions of communicative action—and it seems to me that he cannot quite decide on this point, or at least the language he uses is not consistent—then the comparison with the rationality of so-called goal-oriented actions is misleading, since then, as already mentioned, these two rationalities are not situated at the same level of abstraction. More precisely, the one rationality, that of understanding-oriented speech acts, is then just a specific application of the other. If we follow this reading we end up with a communicative rationality that is not *demarcated* from purposive rationality, but rather *dependent* on it.

In summary: Habermas claims that success-oriented actions and assertions (oriented towards reaching understanding) can be criticized under the aspects of their effectiveness/ineffectiveness in the one case and their truth/falsity in the other; whereby this criticism refers to a *validity claim*. Habermas then presumes that the rationality of a success-oriented action depends on the justifiability (towards others) of its specific validity claim—the claim to effectiveness—and that, analogous to this, the rationality of an assertion likewise depends on the justifiability of *its* validity claim, namely, the claim to truth. He then infers from the fundamental difference between these two validity claims to an equally fundamental categorical difference between the conditions of rationality of (understanding-oriented) assertions and those of success-oriented actions. The following objections, among others, suggest themselves. First, success-oriented actions and assertions can be criticized under precisely the same aspects. In particular (understanding-oriented) assertions can also be criticized under the aspect of their effectiveness. There is no relevant difference here between understanding-oriented assertions and success-oriented actions; rather, understanding-oriented actions *are* success-oriented, as are illumination-oriented flickings of light-switches. Second, normally we do not raise any *claims* with success-oriented actions. We *assume* the effectiveness of our own success-oriented actions, but we by no means have to *claim* this in front of others. For this reason alone the rationality of a success-oriented action cannot be found in the justifiability of its claim to others. Its rationality consists rather in the justification of a certain assumption for oneself. Third, the rationality of an *assertion* likewise does not consist in the justifiability of its possible claim to truth. It is one thing to reject the truth-claim of an assertion and another to criticize it as irrational. The truth of an assertion can be justifiable to others without the assertion being rational—it could, for example, under certain circumstances be wildly irrational to tell the truth, even a truth justifiable to others. Even if there were only a single case of this—although there are clearly countless such cases—it would be enough to falsify Habermas's contention that the rationality of an assertion depends on the justifiability of its truth-claim. Thus Habermas's argumentation is invalid.

1.2.1.2. Habermas's Definitions of Rationality

So far I have been attacking Habermas's concept of rationality by undermining its ostensible argumentative and explicative pillars; now it is time for a frontal assault on Habermas's definition of rationality. It reads as follows:

> Thus assertions and goal-directed actions are the more rational the better the claim (to propositional truth or to efficiency) that is connected with them can be justified [*begründet*]. Correspondingly, we use the expression "rational" as a disposition predicate for persons from whom such expressions can be expected, especially in difficult situations.[20]

Does this definition stand up to scrutiny?

To begin with "goal-directed actions": let us assume that someone receives a phone call that he cannot make head or tail of; he has no idea who the caller is, what motivations the caller has or what relation the caller could have to him, and a voice says: "Destroy your furniture post-haste!" Upon hearing this the man so instructed starts fires throughout the house, in the optimally justified conviction that this is an effective method for destroying his furniture. Most people would describe this man's action of effectively destroying his furniture in this context as "crazy" or "entirely irrational", since they are well aware that the rationality of an action includes not least of all the rationality of the motivations behind it; yet, according to Habermas's definition above, the action is simply "rational". This sort of definition of rationality clearly conflicts with our use of language.

This entirely unsuited characterization of rational action, in blatant contradiction to our use of language, is not a mere lapse on Habermas's part. He continues to speak this way. Thus we read:

Action has a teleological structure, for every action-intention aims at the realization of a set goal. Once again, the rationality of an action is proportionate not to whether the state actually occurring in the world as a result of the action coincides with the intended state and satisfies the corresponding conditions of success, but rather to whether the actor has *achieved* this result on the basis of the deliberately selected and implemented means (or, in accurately perceived circumstances, could normally have done so). A successful actor has acted rationally only if he (i) knows why he was successful (or why he could have realized the set goal in normal circumstances) and if (ii) this knowledge motivates the actor (at least in part) in such a way that he carries out his action for reasons that can at the same time explain its possible success.[21]

Again we can recall the counter-example of the man who destroys his furniture at the behest of a prankster on the telephone. An action is not yet rational when the reasons the agent gives for the action explain their possible *success*; for an action to be rational, these reasons have to justify the action itself and thus justify not just the choice of means but also the choice of end.

For all that Habermas likes to speak of the "curtailed" conception of rationality, it is his own conception that is curtailed. Habermas curtails the rationality of actions to mere *instrumental* rationality—which would never occur to a proponent of purposive rationality. This curtailed rationality, however, describes not the actual rationality of an action but only its hypothetical rationality, which obtains only *on condition* of the unqualified desirability of realizing a certain goal. An action that is rational only in the instrumental sense is as much a kind of rational action as a paper tiger is a kind of tiger. An instrumentally rational action is one that *would* be rational *if* a rational weighing of goals, means and side-effects led to the goal pursued. In other words, instrumentally rational actions are rational only if they also happen to be purposively rational. In addition, Habermas's definition would still be false even in the limited terms of instrumental rationality, that is, in terms of the rational choice of means for a *pre-set* goal, because, contrary to his definition, a successful agent can act rationally even if he does *not* know and is mistaken about why he was successful (or why he would have been able to realize his goal under ordinary circumstances). For someone to rationally choose means, it is sufficient that, as Anglo-Saxon epistemologists say, he has fulfilled his *epistemic obligations.*[22] One can be obligated only to things that are within one's possibilities. Thus if an agent thoroughly considers the question of which means are suited to realizing a certain goal, carefully studies the options and consequently forms a solidly founded judgement according to the best of his knowledge and understanding that the means M is the best suited, there is clearly not the slightest reason to call the action of this agent irrational when he uses these means, regardless of whether his error was due to faulty perception or anything else—as long as it was not due to a lack of epistemic *rationality* in his deliberative process. For it is quite logical that a person acts with instrumental rationality when he or she selects the means for a given goal *rationally*, which also means "*with a view* to expediency" (though not by itself "*de facto* expedient"). Rationality does not imply infallibility, or even infallibility given "appropriate perception". Making a rational choice means choosing in a rational manner, by means of a process of rational deliberation and examination. To demand more would be irrational (since this demand quite evidently fails to make sense).

Thus Habermas's definition of "goal-directed action" is incorrect in several respects.

Let us now move on to his characterization of the rationality of assertions.

To say that an action is rational, whether a speech act such as an assertion or any other kind of act, means nothing more or less than to say that it is rational *to perform* that action. A trip to New York is rational if it is rational to travel to New York. The assertion "Frank is truly a considerate and warm-hearted guy" is rational when it is rational to assert: "Frank is truly a considerate and warm-hearted guy." If Frank is a very powerful man who credibly assures me that he will shoot me dead if I do not tell everyone I meet that he truly is a considerate and warm-hearted guy, and if furthermore my life is dear to me and upon thoroughly weighing the circumstances it appears rational to me to assert that Frank is truly a considerate and warm-hearted guy, than the assertion *is* rational, entirely independently of whether "the claim (to propositional truth…) that is connected with [it]" can be justified. In other words, the justification of the assertion has nothing to do with the justification of what it asserts, or with the thesis or proposition that it states.

Furthermore, Habermas could have seen this himself if he had only generalized what he himself says about expressions "which appear with the claim to truthfulness or sincerity" (indeed, why only this kind of expression?):

In many situations an actor has good reason to conceal his experiences from others or to mislead someone with whom he is interacting about his "true" experiences. In such cases he is not raising a claim to truthfulness but at most simulating one while behaving strategically. Expressions of this kind cannot be objectively criticized because of their insincerity; they are to be judged rather according to their intended results as more or less effective. Expressive manifestations can be appraised on the basis of their sincerity only in the context of communication aimed at reaching understanding.[23]

Quite apart from the fact that it is not the *claim* to sincerity that gets simulated here (as is at best the case with certain jokes, for example) but the *sincerity* itself, there are obviously many situations where an actor also has good reasons to misrepresent matters of the "objective world", that is, to lie with his assertions and not just with so-called expressive manifestations. There is no difference between these two kinds of utterance in this respect: it is only in the context of communication aimed at reaching understanding, if at all, that the rationality of an assertion is determined by its truth (or, more accurately, by the actor's attempt to fulfil the truth claim) or even by its justifiability. With regard to the point about justifiability, one might at first perhaps wish to object that precisely a lie seems to be more rational *as* lie the more "watertight" it is; so a liar would do well to come up with some matching arguments for the lie that he could use to "patch it up" if push comes to shove. However, this of course does not apply to all situations (such as when there is no time to plan these things) and also does not agree with Habermas's use of the term *begründen* (=to justify or "to ground"), as will shortly become clear. As he uses the term, nothing can be *justified* with lies.[24] So we can stick to the statement that the rationality of an assertion cannot be determined by the justifiability of the truth of its propositional content outside of a situation aimed at communicative understanding. This also means that the rationality of persons cannot be determined by the justifiability of what they assert.

How does this look *within* a situation aimed at communicative understanding? With regard to the communicative use of speech acts Habermas explains:

> With his speech act, the speaker pursues his aim of reaching understanding with a hearer about something. This illocutionary aim, as we will refer to it, is two-tiered: the speech act is first of all supposed to be understood by the hearer and then—so far as possible—accepted. The rationality of the use of language oriented toward reaching understanding then depends on whether the speech acts are sufficiently comprehensible and acceptable for the speaker to achieve illocutionary success with them (or for him to be able to do so in normal circumstances).[25]

Of course, here one could reiterate the same criticism that, as we saw above, can be levelled against Habermas's characterization of the rationality of action even if we are charitable enough to read it as a characterization of instrumental "rationality"; namely, that the rationality of the speech acts of the speaker who aims at reaching understanding do not in any way depend on whether they are comprehensible and acceptable or whether the speaker achieves illocutionary success with them or would be able to under normal circumstances. It depends solely on whether the speaker *is rationally justified in assuming* that the speech acts will achieve illocutionary success. Accordingly Habermas errs when, still leaning on the idea of justifi*ability*, he goes on to argue:

> Once again, we do not call only valid speech acts rational but rather all comprehensible speech acts for which the speaker can take on a *credible* warranty in the given circumstances to the effect that the validity claims raised could, if necessary, be vindicated discursively.[26]

For one thing, it is possible in certain circumstances for a person to take on a credible "warranty" (a real warranty ruling out all fallibility could of course never be credible) for the discursive justifiability of a statement even when it is *not* in fact discursively justifiable. Moreover, it is already sufficient anyway, at least in the case of an assertion, if the speaker takes on a sincere and credible "warranty" for the truth of his or her assertion, that is, it suffices to produce the assertion in such a way that it is credible. It is entirely possible for speech acts to be credible that I would be unable to justify if they were called into doubt—such as a speech act of the form:

"Yesterday I was at home alone." Since I clearly have no witnesses for the correctness of my statement and would also be unable to provide any otherwise telling evidence, I can hardly justify my statement. It would not even make sense to ask for a justification. However, the statement is nonetheless quite believable. One seldom sees simple observations get called into question. They are believed because the "warranty" for their truth (and not their justifiability) that the speaker takes on is credible. Moreover, as we have already seen in consequence of Habermas's erroneous characterization of the rational choice of means or speech acts, speech acts can very well be rational even if the speaker cannot even provide a credible guarantee of *truth* to the hearer.

I would like to illustrate this and show how contrary Habermas's definition of rational understanding-oriented assertions is to our use of language with the following example. At a party I find myself talking with a group of people, and the conversation turns to insects. Since I, who am not a biologist, only recently read about it in a standard reference work on ants, I say—purely oriented to reaching understanding, incidentally—"Yes, insects are pretty impressive. For example, the African Marathon ant can travel over 40 km without any food or water"; to which someone responds, "I rather doubt that." I respond by appealing to the reasons for my assertion: "It's true, I read that yesterday in the renowned work by Prof. Amoisius." Whereupon my conversational partners—as it turns out, a group of ant researchers nominated for the Nobel Prize—explain to me: "It has been proven that Prof. Amoisius was mistaken, at least on that point. There were a series of studies that unequivocally disproved his claim." And upon hearing this I am convinced that my assertion is false.

Moreover, my assertion was not only false but it also failed to meet the conditions that Habermas upholds for the *rationality* of an assertion: that is, I could not provide my listeners with any credible warranty for either the truth or the justifiability of my assertion and thus I was not in a position "to convince my conversation partners of the truth of my statement and bring about a rationally motivated agreement". To the contrary, it is the experts who could claim every warranty for disagreeing with my assertion. Nonetheless, it would not occur to any competent speaker to describe my assertion as "not rational". For of course it is a given that in using language in orientation to reaching understanding I am rationally justified in believing the information that I read about ants in a modern standard reference work on ants, and in repeating it to others with corresponding assertions. I am justified in doing this because I have *good reasons* for my belief in the correctness of the information and for my assertion.

An action, whether a speech act or any other kind of act, is rational when there are good reasons for it. Is this not what Habermas says, too? Now, at one point he does in fact say it:

We can summarize the above as follows: Rationality is understood to be a disposition of speaking and acting subjects that is expressed in modes of behaviour for which there are good reasons or grounds.[27]

This is an incorrect summary on Habermas's part of his own contentions, in that he is guilty of a conflation—unintentional, or strategic?—without which his "discourse fetishism" would be unthinkable. He conflates being *justified* with being *justifiable to others.* If aliens were to "beam" me to their planet in another galaxy without anyone else noticing, and then "beam" me back shortly thereafter, then *for me* the thesis that aliens exist would be a very well-justified thesis, without my being able to justify it to others; they would think that I was a little under the weather. In other words, having good reasons for something, and being able to justify something to others, are two different things. Thus Habermas is simply incorrect when he says (I quote again):

For *A* does not make an assertion unless he makes a truth claim for the asserted proposition *p* and therewith indicates his conviction that his statement can, if necessary, be defended. And *B* does not perform a goal-directed action, that is, he does not want to accomplish an end by it unless he regards the actions planned as promising and therewith indicates his conviction that, in the given circumstance, his choice of means can if necessary be *justified* [*begründet*].[28]

It is correct to say: A does not make an assertion unless he thereby expresses (sincerely or insincerely) that he has *good reasons* for his assertion. (The same holds for a "goal-oriented action".) It is a contradiction to say "I just saw a pigeon land on the balcony for a second and then fly off" and then, upon critical questioning, "no, I do not have any reasons to believe in the correctness of my assertion." Saying this would retroactively nullify the "assertion" as an assertion, and it could no longer be recognized as such by the other person. However, it is *not* a contradiction to say "I just saw a pigeon land on the balcony for a second and then fly off" and upon critical questioning to say "no, I'm sorry, I can't justify the correctness of this assertion to you, *of course* I don't have any proof, I don't take photos of those kinds of things. You'll just have to believe me." This is very much an assertion, and, in contrast to the first example, a credible assertion, at least in so far as one has no reason to doubt the credibility of the speaker—and often we do not have any reason to. Of course, the speaker could try to justify *his credibility* (which is often impossible), but this justification is different from the justification of the assertion.

We can summarize our results so far as follows:

Habermas's explication of the concept of rationality is untenable. In fact it evinces a certain carelessness of analysis to reduce the rationality of so-called goal-oriented actions to instrumental rationality. It is likewise false to tie the rationality of assertions, understood as speech acts, to the justifiability of their *propositional content.* In fact their rationality, like the rationality of all other actions, is set by the standard of purposive rationality. If we presuppose the goal of reaching understanding, then the rationality of speech acts is determined according to instrumental rationality, a derivative of purposive rationality. Furthermore, it is mistaken to locate the rationality of actions and speech acts in their justifiability to speakers/listeners and thus to bind them to certain practices of "discursive redemption". An agent's action is rational when it is *justified for the agent* (whereby to preclude any misunderstandings we should note that this "for" is relativist but not subjectivist, that is, for something to be justified for someone it is not sufficient that the person *holds* it to be justified). However, whether or not the action is justifiable to others (or even justifiable as justified for the agent) is irrelevant. Thus all explications of rationality offered by Habermas have been refuted—including his explication of the rational conditions of speech oriented towards reaching understanding. The concept of rationality upheld by discourse ethics lacks any foundation.

1.2.2. The Failure of All Arguments against the Reducibility of Understanding-oriented Action to Success-oriented Action

We have seen that both understanding-oriented assertions and illumination-oriented flickings of switches are equally success-oriented and that the very same concept of rationality is applicable to both, namely, that of purposive rationality.

Habermas does not want to yield to the very evident fact that the orientation to understanding can be subsumed under the orientation towards success and that *all* actions are success-oriented; yet on the other hand—it is simply too blatantly clear—he cannot entirely resist it either. Thus Habermas's arguments in his defence are downright contradictory on this point. He concedes that a "teleological structure"[29] is fundamental to *all* actions and that "at a general level, *all* actions, linguistic and non-linguistic ones, can be conceived of as goal-oriented activity."[30] Nonetheless—and this is less comprehensible—even though every action is directed towards goals, that is, purposes, according to Habermas not every action is a purposive action. Here one can respond that the thesis *that there are actions aimed at purposes that are not purposive actions* is contradictory. There have to be errors concealed in Habermas's argumentation in support of this thesis.

In the following section we will look at this argumentation using the example of the concept of communicative action that is so central to Habermas's social theory. With this model of action Habermas intends to analyse "the linguistic mechanism of coordinating action by way of the illocutionary binding (or bonding) effect of speech acts"[31] and explain "how social order is possible".[32] With this approach he hopes to set himself apart from explanatory models that take strategic action as their fundamental concept. According to Habermas, these models fail to explain "how contexts of interaction that emerge solely from the reciprocal exertion of influence upon one another of success-oriented actors can establish themselves as stable orders".[33] Now, one might think that the genesis of social order allegedly exemplified by communicative action (the coordination of action through the binding effects of understanding-oriented speech acts) could be set off from the attempt to explain social order as the result of the reciprocal influences of success-oriented action only if communicative action were not *itself* a success-oriented endeavour. For then clearly the coordination of action achieved in communicative action would ultimately be the result of success-oriented interactions.

Yet Habermas (in the meantime) quite plainly refers to communicative action as purposive action.[34] Nevertheless, it is held to be distinguishable from strategic action. The criterion of distinction is supposed to be that in communicative action the action is coordinated by producing understanding, and because of this the orientation towards one's own success is allegedly not "primary" in communicative action. This would not help us identify a communicative rationality distinct from purposive rationality, since, as purposive action, communicative action is of course still subject to the standards of purposive rationality. But quite apart from this consideration, the distinction falls apart, for two reasons. First, as we will see, the concept of strategic action does not rule out the possibility of coordinating action through reaching understanding; thus communicative action is just a form of strategic action and the communicative agent is in fact primarily oriented towards his or her own success. Second, *reaching understanding* is—although Habermas resolutely denies this—*itself* a purposive action, as we have already seen. In Section 1.2.2.2 I will discuss the quite curious arguments with which Habermas seeks to evade this negative result and to deny understanding-oriented use of language its character of purposiveness.

1.2.2.1. The Failure of All Arguments against the Reducibility of Communicative Action to Strategic Action

Two preliminary conceptual clarifications are necessary to preclude potential misunderstandings.

1. Here I use the term "goal-directed actions" for all actions aimed at a goal. Whether or not this goal is external to the action is irrelevant. For of course actions that serve as an end in themselves are still ends or goals. If I raise my right arm simply for the sake of raising my right arm, this is a goal-directed action; the goal is simply to raise my right arm.

   A goal-*directed* action—and there are no other types of action—is not necessarily purposively rational. Seen in light of purposive rationality it could be entirely irrational.

2. The term "strategic action" is not used here or by Habermas as it is used in ordinary language. When someone feigns love and wants only sex, then in ordinary language (although a rather embellished vein of ordinary language) we would speak of strategic action. Concerning strategic action in this sense, Habermas's claims that strategic action can be guided only by "egocentric calculations of success" (which we will examine shortly) would be *prima facie* plausible. However, with strategic action Habermas means *goal-directed social action*, and I will show that Habermas's claims regarding this type of action are an over-generalization. Strategic action in the sense intended here *can* be egocentric, but it can also be altruistic. As we will see, the *very same* holds for communicative action as well.

What is strategic action, and what is communicative action?

It is not entirely clear in all of Habermas's characterizations of communicative action where the *definition* ends and the *theory* about it begins; that is, it is not always clear *what* exactly is included in the definition of communicative action. On occasion it is solely the condition "that participants carry out their plans cooperatively in an action situation defined in common" that is said to be constitutive of communicative action.[35] This definition—which I will occasionally refer to as communicative action *in a broad sense*—dominates the secondary literature on Habermas, particularly as the two most prominent of Habermas's characterizations of communicative action (which I will quote shortly) could be interpreted in this way—although they are not without ambiguity.

In the most clear and thorough definition of communicative action, however, Habermas is by no means satisfied with this one condition, nor with the reference to actions oriented towards reaching understanding; rather, he writes that, in the case of communicative action, action is coordinated via the "binding and bonding effects (*Bindungseffekte*) of speech act offers" and furthermore that "the way in which linguistic processes of reaching understanding function as a mechanism for coordinating action is that the participants in interaction agree about the validity claimed for their speech acts."[36] In fact this definition of communicative action is the definitive one, as is confirmed by other text passages.[37] However, *there is nothing* that could meet this definition, since it is not possible to coordinate action the way Habermas describes.[38] In other words: *communicative action in its true and strict sense does not exist.*

This result is obviously devastating for Habermas's theory, but perhaps it might still be possible to infer the conditions of communicative rationality from the *concept* of communicative action. After all, the conditions of strategic rationality could also be specified even if there were no strategic action for whatever reason. However, if communicative action, whether existent or not, can conceptually be subsumed under strategic action, then we still lack a communicative rationality that can be opposed to strategic rationality. How does Habermas draw the required distinction?

> The teleological model of action is expanded to a *strategic* model when there can enter into the agent's calculation of success the anticipation of decisions on the part of at least one additional goal-directed actor. This model is often interpreted in utilitarian terms; the actor is supposed to choose and calculate means and ends from the standpoint of maximizing utility or expectations of utility.[39]

Habermas then distinguishes strategic action thus defined from "communicative action" as follows:

> By contrast, I shall speak of *communicative* action whenever the actions of the agents involved are coordinated not through egocentric calculations of success but through acts of reaching understanding. In communicative action participants are not primarily oriented to their own individual successes; they pursue their individual goals under the condition that they can harmonize their plans of action on the basis of common situation definitions.[40]

And elsewhere, in contrasting different types of action, namely, strategic, norm-regulated, dramaturgic and "communicative" action, he writes:

> In all cases the teleological structure of action is presupposed, inasmuch as the capacity for goal-directed action is ascribed to actors, as well as an interest in carrying out their plans of action. But only the strategic model of action *rests content* with an explication of the features of action oriented directly to success; whereas the other models of action

specify conditions under which the actor pursues his goals—conditions of legitimacy, of self-presentation, or of agreement arrived at in communication, under which alter can "link up" his actions with those of ego.[41]

Already we can see that the distinction between communicative action and strategic action is *irrelevant* to the attempt to establish a rationality distinct from the purposive rationality applicable to purposive action; since strategic action, norm-regulated action, expressive or dramaturgic action and communicative action are all types of action wherein "the teleological structure of action is presupposed", they are all evidently directed at goals and hence are purposive activities. Consequently the actions corresponding to these types of action are rational if and only if they are *purposively rational*.

Habermas could succeed in defusing this objection only by the great feat of showing that an action aimed at a goal somehow, bafflingly, is *not* necessarily a purposive action. As mentioned, he does in fact dabble in this sort of logical and semantic equivalent of squaring the circle; and, as also mentioned and as we will see in the next section, he fails in this.

Ironically, Habermas's explanations of the alleged distinction between communicative action and strategic action quoted above not only betray the fact that both kinds of action are cases of purposive activity; they also, in direct contrast to Habermas's intentions, betray the fact that communicative action *can be subsumed under strategic action*.

The treacherous words here are the italicized "*rests content*". It should be clear that a definition A that rests content with the specification of fewer characteristics is for this reason broader and more comprehensive—that is, has broader application—than a definition B that names additional conditions that an object defined by B has to fulfil besides those specified by A. Thus logically whatever falls under the second definition can also be subsumed under the first. If we define an elephant as a large land mammal with a long trunk, then this definition also includes the consensus-oriented elephant, which has to fulfil the further condition of consensus-orientation. A consensus-oriented elephant is an elephant, even if not every elephant is consensus-oriented. And since, as Habermas correctly notes, the definition of strategic action is so modest and economical, it is comprehensive enough that it easily subsumes communicative action under its definition as well.

At this point it is already becoming clear that Habermas's attempts to distinguish communicative action from strategic action are implausible from the very outset. They prove to be baseless on the face of it, even before one goes into details. Nonetheless in the following I intend to examine the details of these attempts. I will begin with the examination of the particular condition that according to Habermas communicative action is subject to, and subsequently will consider Habermas's efforts to represent communicative action as not primarily success-oriented and distinct from the purported egocentrism of strategic action.

What, then, should we think of the central characterization that in communicative action the participants pursue their individual goals *under the condition* "that they can harmonize their plans of action on the basis of common situation definitions"?[42]

It depends on how we interpret the word "condition". If it is meant as in "the workers will work only under the condition that they are given ownership of some of the means of production", then Habermas's characterization of communicative action cannot be satisfied, and there is no communicative action. If, however, it is meant in the sense of a *framing* condition, in the sense of "circumstances", then communicative action is an unexceptional form of goal-directed action.

Let us start with the first case. In this sense of condition, the statement that "in communicative action participants pursue their individual goals under the condition that they can harmonize their plans of action" means "in communicative action the following holds: if the participants cannot harmonize their plans of action, they do *not* pursue their individual goals." Well: what then *do* they do? Do they die on the spot? Or pass out? For they would have to do—or rather, they would have to suffer—one of these two things for them to *not* pursue their individual goals whenever they cannot harmonize their plans of action. In a waking state one always follows certain individual goals, even in just sitting still and meditating; in this case the goal is just this, to sit still and meditate. This in turn means that the participants *cannot* place their participation under the condition stated, since this condition expresses an intention; thus, *in* realizing this intention and ceasing to pursue their individual goals they falsify it, since realizing an intention *is* successfully pursuing a goal. Even if we were to allow them this one goal as a kind of exception, this would still mean that those acting communicatively would have to prefer resigning themselves entirely through either death or coma to pursuing their individual goals without the hope of consensus. This is not rational.

According to the second possible interpretation, "in communicative action participants pursue their individual goals under the condition that they can harmonize their plans of action" simply means "in communicative action the participants pursue their individual goals in circumstances in which they can harmonize their plans of action." Habermas has a rather unfortunate penchant for misplaced modal verbs. That people *can* harmonize their plans of action does not mean that they do. Thus this definition, taken literally, is also compatible with modes of action in which the participants bash each other's skulls in. In the interest of charitable interpretation one may wish to cross out this modal verb "can". The remaining definition can then be simplified to: "in communicative action participants harmonize their plans of action." And in fact Habermas occasionally has recourse to similarly unequivocal formulations, above all in responding to critics who want more clarity:

I use the term *communicative action* for that form of social interaction in which the plans of action of different actors are co-ordinated through an exchange of communicative acts, that is, through a use of language (or of corresponding extra-verbal expressions) orientated towards reaching understanding.[43]

But if this is all that Habermas intends to say, why did he not say it so simply and understandably from the very beginning? This relates to Habermas's intent to incorporate a normative element into communicative action from the very beginning—hence all the talk of the "condition" that communicative action is subject to. Elsewhere he says explicitly that this is the condition "under which all participants in the interaction *may* pursue their own plans".[44] I have already demonstrated that such a normative interpretation of "condition", namely, condition as (self-) obligation or (self-) commitment, is untenable, at least as a *limitation* on behaviour. The version of communicative action under discussion here, that is, communicative action as action under the coordination of plans of action, is not untenable; rather, it is banal and takes us nowhere. For it is quite clear that this sort of coordination of plans of action by no means has to necessarily contrast with purposive rationality and strategic action. Rather, it *often* contrasts with these: that is, opting for communicative action is often simply foolhardy and irrational, as it is whenever not doing so would bring certain advantages that upon careful consideration one values more than communicative action. On the other hand, it is on occasion very clever and flawlessly rational, which of course means: purposively rational.

These concerns about the possible compatibility between communicative action and purposively rational action in certain contexts have already been brought to bear against Habermas, by Michael Baurmann among others.[45] Habermas refers to him with the remark:

Other critics also support their arguments by referring to the fact that, here as there [in the strategic as well as in the communicative model of action], a teleological structure of action is presupposed; however, they identify the pursuit of illocutionary aims without reservations (as is envisaged in the model of communicative action) and the pursuit of perlocutionary aims through the agency of illocutionary successes already achieved with the egocentric pursuit of one's own interests and aims permissible in the model of teleological or strategic action, and this leads to one model merging with the other. Such an identification is impermissible, even if the description of both cases is based on the same teleological language game of end-setting actors who pursue goals, achieve results and trigger off effects. For the illocutionary "ends" of reaching understanding cannot be defined without referring to the linguistic means of understanding: the medium of language and the telos of reaching understanding intrinsic to it reciprocally constitute each other.[46]

When Habermas sets "ends" in scare-quotes in connection with the word "illocutionary", he in fact implies that these are *not really* ends after all—just as I occasionally suggest, by putting "communicative rationality" in scare-quotes, that this is not *really* a form of rationality, as it is either a second-rate forgery of instrumental rationality or else mere fantasy. This will hardly have escaped the reader's notice. In Habermas's case, however, it will be unclear to everyone—including to himself (otherwise he could have used a different choice of words)—what prodigious entities these illocutionary "ends" are supposed to be if they are not really ends. As it concerns his "illocutionary 'ends'" he is apparently unable to offer any alternative to the words "end" or "goal" and their synonyms. Why this is the case is quite clear.

I will return to the discussion of Habermas's untenable views about illocutionary acts and ends later. For now I would just like to note that Baurmann by no means *identifies* "the pursuit of illocutionary aims without reservations" with "the egocentric pursuit of one's own interests and aims permissible in the model of teleological or strategic action"; rather, Baurmann correctly observes that purposive action is not necessarily egocentric, and thus *subsumes* rational communicative action under purposive action.

We should also note that Habermas's response to Baurmann quoted above, however correct or incorrect it may be, is one thing for certain: irrelevant. For here Baurmann was not concerned to trace *illocutionary acts* back to purposive rationality (although he correctly claims that this is possible as well) but rather to trace *communicative action* back to purposive action in certain contexts. In certain contexts this reducibility *is* clearly given. Moreover, in all those contexts where it is not given we can easily trace communicative action back to plain irrationality.

Communicative action has this in common with other types of action. If, incidentally, we wish to begin as Habermas does by incomprehensibly distinguishing types of action according to *which conditions they are subject to*, regardless of how we interpret the word "condition", we end up with considerably more types of action than those four that Habermas prefers to discuss. For example, hopping-on-one-leg action. According to Habermas, the agents engaging in communicative action pursue "their individual goals under the condition that they can harmonize their plans of action on the basis of common situation definitions".[47] Similarly, the agents engaging in hopping-on-one-leg action pursue their individual goals under the condition that they hop on one leg. These agents are free to pursue such individual goals as getting a pedicure, writing an article or performing heart surgery— as long as they do it hopping on one leg. This might have aesthetic appeal, but is it rational? Similarly one could ask about communicative action: if the police are discussing with a kidnapper ways of delivering the ransom money, would they truly be acting rationally if they were to *harmonize* their plans of action with the kidnapper without illocutionary reservation—such as the plan to catch him?

Thus, communicative action can be irrational. Of course, it can also be rational—purposively rational. This is quite evident, and thus Habermas's insistence to the contrary is nothing but dogmatism.

Habermas himself refers to game theory as an example of his theory of strategic action and approvingly quotes Otfried Höffe's explanation:

The rationality criterion of game theory refers not to the choice of individual moves but to the choice of strategies. Stated in the form of a maxim for decision, the basic pattern runs as follows: "Choose the strategy which, in the framework of the rules of the game and in view of your opponents, promises to bring the greatest success."[48]

Now, as mentioned, it is evident that there will be situations in which, in the framework of the rules of the game (and even where there are no rules) and in view of the opponents, the most salient strategy to maximize utility is communicative action in so far as communicative action is possible. This is one of the results of game theory. When Habermas questions whether communicative action can also be purposively rational—when he disputes the claim that there is in principle no necessary incompatibility here—then he also has to question whether there could be a situation in which communicative action promises the actor more success. One might wonder how this could be thought to be a recommendation of communicative action.

Moreover, it is psychologically impossible for someone to knowingly choose an action that promises the *less* "success", as communicative action does according to Habermas. Occasionally this is claimed to be possible under the banner of "weakness of will". I believe first of all that this is a false description of the phenomenon of "weakness of will". For it is, I repeat, psychologically as well as conceptually entirely impossible for someone to consciously choose an action that promises less *success* than an alternative action. Second, once again, it would be a questionable recommendation of communicative action if it were conceivable only as the product of weakness of will. Thus Habermas's attempt to introduce communicative rationality as a form of rationality independent of purposive or strategic action misfires.

Andreas Dorschel, who came to this same conclusion, is of the opinion that the distinction is *nonetheless* "intuitively quite plausible". Intuitions can lead us astray, and I find it difficult to even relate to this intuition of his. He summarizes his ambivalent stance as follows:

A suitable theoretical conception of this prima facie plausible typology including criteria remains desideratum.[49]

If we consider that here we are dealing with *analytic* criteria and not with *epistemic* criteria, then this means that Dorschel finds a distinction prima facie "plausible" even though he admittedly does not know what it consists in. This should give us pause. However, he then tries to illustrate his intuition that the "opposition between 'success-orientation' and 'orientation towards reaching understanding'" contains a "useful insight" with an example:

When it comes to ascertaining the truth of an assertion, then in a certain sense...it is not rational conduct to insist that the result of the examination has to orient itself around the fact that a negative result would bring certain financial advantages. The rationality that notably lacks in such an insistence cannot be purposive rationality, since the demand is nothing other than the expression of a purposively rational consideration. An orientation of action around this rationality—however one would like to label it in contrast to purposive rationality—seems to rule out rejecting something one has seen to be true and correct by appealing to the negative impact that the determination of its truth and correctness would have for one's own success. In this sense, not "success-orientation" per se but the unconditional insistence on reaching one's own success is in fact incompatible with the aim of reaching an understanding about something with others...(—unless, nota bene, just *this* was the *only* success that was ever at stake; then it could also be pursued *unconditionally*, because, collapsing into the goal of reaching understanding, it could never come into conflict with this).[50]

How is it the expression of a purposively rational consideration if someone tries to achieve the goal of reaching an understanding with others that a certain assertion is false by appealing to the fact that this would bring financial advantage to himself or herself or to others? It is *not* purposively rational, since here the person is imagined to choose a means that is clearly entirely unsuited to achieving the goal set. The "rationality that notably lacks in such an insistence", namely, the insistence that others hold a certain assertion to be false because they or oneself would then receive money, is very much a case of purposive rationality. And the imperative not to let money decide *when it comes to ascertaining the truth*, that is, *when* finding out whether or not a certain statement is true *is the goal*, is simply a hypothetical imperative: a demand of instrumental rationality. Thus I cannot agree with Dorschel when, appealing to this admittedly very illuminating example, he claims that we can still "find sufficient meaning in the concept of orientation toward reaching understanding…to make the necessity to distinguish communicative actions from strategic actions at least prima facie plausible".[51] It is by no means a "necessity" to categorically *distinguish* a type of action A from the type of action B that includes it rather than subsuming the one under the other—rather, it is an error, even prima facie.

It does not look any more promising for Habermas's attempt to attribute special moral significance to communicative action and to distinguish it from strategic action as not being primarily success-oriented or not subject to the ruthless sway of so-called egocentric calculations of success.

First of all it bears repeating that it is not only psychologically but also conceptually impossible for someone not to be primarily oriented towards his or her own success. Action is intentional, that is, intending something, that is, directed towards achieving goals, that is, success-oriented. If my behaviour is not oriented towards *my* success (the concept "success" should of course not be understood in terms of careerism) but rather towards Frank's success, then my behaviour, if we can even call it this, is certainly not my *action*. It could be the case that Frank has planted electrodes into my brain by means of which he can override my will and control my body.

Of course, I can make others' goals *my own*, even Frank's goals. Thus in this way I can work for others' success—even primarily, *in a certain sense*, in so far as I simply would like Frank to have success and thus work (quite strategically) to ensure that he has it, whatever (in certain limits) this success may consist in. Yet in a sense that is important for the theory of action—in the motivational sense—Frank's success is *secondary* for me. I strive for Frank's success only because I see a success *for me* in Frank having success. If I did not see a success for me in this, I clearly could not strive for Frank's success. I *cannot* act otherwise.

Thus it is conceptually necessary that the actions of a person are oriented towards his or her own success; and "communicative action", if it is action at all, is no exception.

As far as "egocentrism" is concerned, Baumann also showed that the attempt to link egocentrism to strategic action per se is misleading.[52] It is telling that Habermas does not go into Baumann's arguments individually. In any case it is easy to see that Baumann is right. The agent in Kant's dilemma, who decides based on his conscience to save an innocent victim of persecution and thus from death by lying, is acting strategically but not egocentrically. If the commander of a concentration camp tells a group of 10 prisoners that they can choose 1 candidate from among them to die, or else 5 of them will be killed, and the prisoners start to consider this; and one of them, A, knowing of the others' altruism, persuades them with lies to pick *him or her*, claiming that due to a fatal illness he or she does not have long to live anyway—then this is strategic conduct in Habermas's sense of the term. In his concept of strategic action Habermas assumes "at least two goal-directed acting subjects who achieve their ends by way of an orientation to, and influence on, the decisions of other actors".[53] A reckons with the others' altruism from the outset; he or she anticipates that, if he or she were to tell the truth, the others would rule against taking him or her as victim. Thus he or she uses lies to influence the others' decision. Thus, this is an example of strategic action. Yet we could not call it egocentric! Of course this martyr also acts in accordance with his or her own interests; otherwise, as mentioned, he or she has not acted at all. But it can be in a person's interests to preserve others' interests, and not just due to financially compensated lobbyism, but because the interests of others, and these others themselves, are valuable to him or her. A person can have altruistic interests.

Conversely, communicative action can also be very egocentric. Habermas himself rejects the notion:

that communicative actors may not *also* be oriented each to his own success

and he continues:

but in the framework of communicative action, they can attain a sought after goal only through successfully arriving at an understanding; reaching understanding is decisive for the coordination of their actions.[54]

But then reaching understanding, as Habermas himself says, only has "the instrumental role of serving as a mechanism for coordinating individual actions."[55] This shows, for one thing, that reaching understanding and communicative action can be evaluated from the viewpoint of purposive rationality. Communicative action is simply an instrument (and thus the individual success orientation is *primary* and the understanding orientation *secondary*, and not the other way around as Habermas claims). Habermas writes:

This illocutionary success is relevant to the interaction inasmuch as it establishes between speaker and hearer an interpersonal relation that is effective for coordination ...[56]

So the coordinating function of speech acts lies in their illocutionary success, thus ultimately in their illocutionary force, of which Habermas says:

The illocutionary force of a speech act consists in its capacity to move a hearer to act under the premise that the commitment signalled by the speaker is seriously meant ...[57]

In other words, communicative action looks something like this: in communicative action the agents are after their own success. However, they can achieve this only through a linguistically mediated coordination of their actions with the actions of others. This coordination for the sake of achieving their ends proceeds such that the agents mutually and quite sincerely move each other to act under the premise, that is, under the expectation that they are ready to observe the commitments that they enter into with their speech acts. This means that in communicative action the participants pursue their goals by using their interactive partners' lack of reservation, that is, their readiness to observe their illocutionary commitments, to coordinate action, thus ultimately making use of this readiness as a means and framing condition in the achievement of their goals. We should add that the agents in communicative action of course also make use of their knowledge of the physical world. Without twisting the formulation too much, one can clearly say of communicative action, according to Habermas's own explanations of it, that it is determined by "expectations as to the behavior of objects in the environment and of other human beings; these expectations are used as 'conditions' or 'means' for the attainment of the actor's own rationally pursued and calculated ends." This is the formulation that Weber uses. It is one of Weber's definitions of purposive rationality.[58]

Since communicative action is only an instrument for achieving one's own goals, the communicative agents as such could be indifferent to each other. One does not necessarily communicate with them for their sake but rather for one's own sake—one simply has to when one wishes to have success. A communicative agent could say, for example (and could even say it in front of the others given a sufficient position of power and self-confidence):

The plans of action and interests of my partners in interaction do not matter to me at all. As far as I'm concerned they can all go to ruin. Unfortunately, right now we're all in the same boat. Since we can only accomplish this together, I have to reach an understanding with them and they have to reach an understanding with me. If the situation should change, I will do everything to get rid of these obnoxious people.

Communicative action does not protect against egocentrism.

Moreover, two brothers can also come to an agreement to bash in their aunt's skull in her sleep while fully oriented towards reaching understanding. When they sneak into her room at night, where, because she is sleeping, she is not a partner in interaction but rather merely the object of their brotherly interaction, and they mediate their actions with understanding-oriented speech acts such as "Pull the cover away!" and "Hit her!", this is an instance of communicative action, according to Habermas's own definition. Murder, dropping atomic bombs on major metropolises, even genocide under certain conditions, could be examples of communicative action.

If one were to try to get around this—which Habermas does not—by revising communicative action to require the coordination of action not only among participants but also among all *affected*, then communicative action would become practically impossible. Why? Supposing I want to cook something with a friend: we have communicatively decided on a recipe. Have we? If we want to make something vegetarian, the butchers are affected by our decision, since then the share of our money that would have gone to one of them goes to the greengrocer. Thus we have to coordinate our decision with the butchers—with the butchers, plural, since clearly our decision to buy from butcher A would affect all other butchers as much as our original decision to make something vegetarian. Of course, our decision to cook *at all* affects all restaurant owners. In short it is quite clearly impossible to coordinate one's actions with all the affected. Thus one may not read the word "participants" as "affected" in the definition of communicative action— since it is supposed to be a practice of *everyday life*. Thus it remains the case that murder, dropping atomic bombs on major cities, and genocide can be examples of communicative action—examples of just that sort of action on which Habermas founds his moral justification programme.

To conclude our discussion of communicative action, we should add that Habermas occasionally denies his own procedure in defining communicative action. Thus, in response to the objection of Erling Skjeis[59] that his concept of communicative action collapses into an intentionalist theory, he writes:

I define communicative action purely by structural properties, not by subjective ones (such as the intentions and attitudes of the participants).[60]

This claim contradicts his own definitions. I quote the central definition again:

By contrast, I shall speak of *communicative* action whenever the actions of the agents involved are coordinated not through egocentric calculations of success but through acts of reaching understanding. In communicative action participants are not primarily oriented to their own individual successes; they pursue their individual goals under the condition that they can harmonize their plans of action on the basis of common situation definitions.[61]

Clearly this refers to the goals and plans of action, and hence to something subjective. However, Habermas also believes without any doubt that communicative action can also be defined *solely* as being "coordinated…through acts of reaching understanding". (Later I will show that this is erroneous and that communicative action *by no means* has to be mediated by "acts of reaching understanding", that is, by illocutionary acts—unless we write this into the definition, with accordingly disagreeable consequences. We will see, moreover, that Habermas more generally cannot make his speech act theory and its emphasis on reaching understanding through validity claims at all fruitful for a theory of consensual coordination of action, and thus that the true "core" of the theory of communicative action is in fact merely illusory.[62]) Yet, even if he were in a position to do this, it would not help him very much, since Habermas says about acts of reaching understanding:

An attempt to reach understanding with the help of speech acts succeeds when the speaker reaches his or her illocutionary goal in Austin's sense of the word.[63]

The goals of a speaker are, after all, the goals of a speaker, and thus quite evidently belong to the realm of the subjective. The goals of a speaker are his or her intentions. Since Habermas defines illocutionary acts only in terms of illocutionary goals and can define them only in this way, he also defines communicative action in terms of something subjective. We can see this again reflected in the following definition:

I have called the type of interactions in which *all* participants harmonize their individual plans of action with one another and thus pursue their illocutionary aims *without reservation* "communicative action".[64]

Reservations (which Habermas, moreover, understands as deceptive *intentions*[65]) are subjective.

Moreover, the "justification" that Habermas offers for his claim that he defines communicative action solely in terms of structural characteristics is quite telling in its perversity. He writes:

Only on this basis can I assume, in the case of perlocutions, that the instrumental attitude of someone who only seemingly meets the conditions of communicative action (at first) remains unrecognized to the other, who sincerely fulfils these suppositions. An agent's concealed intention is intermeshed with the *structure* of consent-oriented action.[66]

First of all, his dichotomy between subjective characteristics and structural characteristics leads us astray, since there are structural characteristics that are also subjective, simply because there are structures that are subjective. The structure of a person's preferences, for example, is one such subjective structure. Since Habermas implies an opposition here, he has to mean non-subjective structures when he speaks of "structure". Now, the subjective is by definition that to which the subject has privileged access, which means that the subjective of a subject is in principle not equally accessible to everyone. In contrast, it has to hold of the non-subjective that it is in principle equally accessible to everyone. But this is precisely contrary to what Habermas suggests in his justification. If communicative action were defined in terms of non-subjective structural characteristics, then it would be entirely *inexplicable* how it could escape one participant's notice that the other is *not* acting communicatively and thus that no communicative action really obtains. This would have to be clearly visible in the structures. If, on the other hand, we were to define communicative action in terms of the attitudes and intentions of the participants, then it is quite easy to explain how it could escape someone's notice that the other is not fulfilling the conditions of communicative action—precisely *because* these conditions are subjective (and thus not equally accessible to others).

Furthermore, in his justification Habermas adduces the case where the *structures* of communicative action obtain although the speaker only seems to fulfil the conditions of communicative action, that is, she does *not fulfil* them. (That these structures obtain is how Habermas "explains" the possibility of not noticing the speaker's instrumental attitude.) Now, based on the general rules of logic, communicative action can hardly be defined in terms of its structure if despite this structure obtaining *communicative action* does not obtain. In brief: Habermas's explanation is, as he himself said of Skjei's objection, "not particularly convincing".[67]

Since Habermas places so much weight on the "structure" of communicative action, one would like to know what this structure actually consists in. In his article against Skjei he says relatively little about this, and what he does say merely repeats precisely that type of contradiction that we have just seen. Thus for example he claims: "...the structure of consent-oriented action presupposes sincerity in all participants."[68] If this really were the case, then how could the structure of consent-oriented action obtain *without* the participants' sincerity? Apparently we are dealing here not so much with a structural presupposition after all, but rather, as we have seen, with a *definitional* requirement.

Elsewhere Habermas provides the following explanation—which I quote here at length because its recourse to the "structure" of communicative action is at the same time one more attempt to somehow distinguish communicative from success-oriented action (and also not quite distinguish it):

> Of course, even in communicative action, the teleologically structured sequences of action of the individual actors pervade the processes of reaching understanding; it is, after all, the purposive activities of the participants in interaction that are linked up with one another via the medium of language. However, the linguistic medium can fulfill this linking-up function only if it *interrupts* the plans of action—each respectively monitored in terms of the actor's own success—and temporarily changes the mode of action. This communicative coordination [*Schaltung*] by way of speech acts performed unreservedly subjects the action orientations and action courses—egocentrically geared toward the requirements of each actor involved—to the structural constraints of an intersubjectively shared language. These constraints force the actors to change their perspective: they must shift perspective from the objectivating attitude of an actor oriented toward success who wants to realize some purpose in the world, to the performative attitude of a speaker who wants to reach understanding with a second person with regard to something in the world. Without this switch to the conditions for the use of language oriented toward reaching understanding, the actors would be denied access to the potential inherent in the binding and bonding energies of language.[69]

First of all, here (as in the other passages where Habermas speaks of the structure of communicative action) we do not find any answer to the question of what exactly this structure consists in. The structure of an object may in fact, among other things, *lead* to the constraint x, but the structure is not *the same thing* as this constraint. As long as Habermas does not precisely explain what the relevant structure of an intersubjectively shared language is supposed to be, we cannot know whether those constraints Habermas speaks of do in fact follow from this structure (Habermas could be in error here), nor whether they have anything to do with any particular structure at all. Thus Habermas offers us only the empty word "structure", and whether this bears any content remains to be demonstrated.

We can see its lack of content in the fact that it is incorrect to say that the constraints of an intersubjectively shared language force a perspective shift towards the performative attitude. After all, *strategic* linguistic action is also linguistic action, that is, it makes use of an intersubjectively shared language. Habermas defines strategic action among other things precisely in terms of the absence of the performative attitude.[70] Thus, the use of an intersubjectively shared language obviously does *not* force us to assume a performative attitude. The "structural constraints" Habermas speaks of are not to be found.

Is it at least true of the communicative coordination by way of speech acts performed unreservedly that it requires subjects to assume a performative attitude and abandon egocentrism? As we saw above, strategic action can be altruistic, and, conversely, communicative action can be quite egocentric. In the next section we will see (and can draw support for this from Apel) that strategic action can also occur in a performative attitude. However, it is still correct that the coordination of action by means of speech acts performed unreservedly involves the attitude (performative or otherwise) or, to put it better, the will of a speaker to reach an understanding about something. However, it is not in any relevant sense *forced*. For an event B (such as a shift in attitude) to be forced by a cause A (the mysterious powers of a "structure", for example), it is necessary for A to precede B in time. This is a precondition of causality. Hopping on one leg does not force me to hop on one leg, rather it *consists* in hopping on one leg. Likewise the unreservedness of coordination consists in the unreservedness of this coordination; this unreservedness is just the understanding-oriented attitude of a speaker. In other words, the alleged "structural constraints" that Habermas speaks of are in reality nothing other than definitional conditions. "Unreserved communication is unreserved communication" is how Habermas's insights into structural constraints can be summarized.

As regards the intriguing "interruption theory", if someone wishes to hang a picture on the wall and is already holding it there with the nail through the eyelet, and then puts aside the picture and the nail because he or she has forgotten the hammer and starts to search for it—then he or she has not *interrupted* his or her orientation to his or her goal of hanging the picture, but rather *on the basis* of this orientation he or she is looking for the hammer. Using a means to an end does not "interrupt" one's plans of action, it is part of the plan of action. Since the medium of language has this linking-up *function*, the function of coordinating action to reach a set goal, the use of the medium of language is not an interruption of the pursuit of this goal but part and parcel of it—and thus part of an orientation to success. It would be an interruption only if the agent took up the hammer not to drive the nail into the wall but to make music by banging some pots; or if the agent spoke not to coordinate action but just to have a nice chat about something.

Moreover, hammers also have structures (such as the relative length of the head and handle as well as the surface structure), and thus we can illustrate how Habermas's theses under discussion here alternate between triviality and nonsense with the following theory of hammering action:

Of course, even in hammering action, the teleologically structured sequences of action of the individual actor pervade the processes of hammering; it is, after all, the purposes of the actor that are to be realised via the medium of hammering. However, the hammer as medium can fulfil this function only if it *interrupts* the plans of action—each respectively monitored in terms of the actor's own success—and temporarily changes the mode of action. This hammering shift by way of hammering acts performed unreservedly subjects the action orientation and action course—egocentrically geared toward the requirements of the actor—to the structural constraints of a hammer. These constraints force the actor to change his perspective: he must shift perspective from the objectivating attitude of an actor oriented toward success who wants to realize some purpose in the world, to the hammering attitude of an actor who wants to adapt to the requirements a hammer imposes concerning its use with respect to something in the world. Without this switch to the conditions for the use of a hammer, the actor would be denied access to the potential inherent in the hammering energy of a hammer.

In summary:

Habermas's own formulations already show clearly—even if unwittingly—that strategic action *encompasses* communicative action, i.e., communicative action is only a particular form of strategic action. If we understand communicative action as action in which the agents coordinate their plans with each other without reservations (the stronger reading, according to which the agents in communicative action pursue their interests only under the condition that they can coordinate their interests with each other, makes communicative action conceptually self-contradictory), then we can easily find contexts in which communicative action is purposively and strategically rational, along with other contexts in which it is clearly irrational since it is not purposively rational.

Furthermore, Habermas's attempt to associate strategic action with egocentrism is as inapt as his attempt to associate communicative action with morality or altruism. There are strategic actions that are altruistic, just as there are communicative actions that are egocentric, depraved and criminal.

Also unfounded is Habermas's claim to have defined communicative action in terms of structural characteristics. His own definitions, and even the formulations that he uses to reinterpret or, in other words, disavow them, all contradict this claim. And of course those "structural constraints of an intersubjectively shared language" that he attributes to communicative action in his "interruption thesis" also apply to linguistically mediated strategic action.

Thus we can conclude that this second approach to distinguishing between purposive rationality and a so-called communicative rationality, namely, by means of a distinction between success-oriented or strategic action on the one hand and communicative action on the other, also fails.

1.2.2.2. The Case of Speech Acts

Thus, illocutionary acts can be traced back to success orientation precisely when they are used in communicative action, since, as we saw, communicative action is *itself* success-oriented. As mentioned, Habermas himself disputes the interpretation "that communicative actors may not *also* be oriented each to his own success",[71] rather, he sees "the process of reaching understanding" in "the instrumental role of serving as a mechanism for coordinating individual actions".[72] Thus it is rather off-putting when in another passage, and contrary to his other definitions of communicative action, Habermas attributes to communicative action "those linguistically mediated interactions in which all participants pursue illocutionary aims, and *only* illocutionary aims".[73] Elsewhere Habermas had more realistically allowed for "the pursuit of illocutionary aims without reservations...and the pursuit of perlocutionary aims through the agency of illocutionary successes already achieved" in communicative action.[74] If illocutionary acts are to take on an instrumental role in the coordination of actions, and if these actions themselves serve some other goals—and Habermas explicitly describes communicative action and "the carrying out of communicatively harmonized plans of action" as "purposive activities"[75]—then communicative agents do not pursue *only illocutionary aims,* but rather also goals such as that of building a house together in coordination (or something of this sort).

What if, however, in so far as this is at all possible, we were to consider illocutionary speech acts outside of those contexts in which they are means to an external goal? Then the question arises—and Habermas poses this question without realizing that one first has to prise these illocutionary acts out of their instrumental contexts such as those of communicative action—as to whether the pursuit of *merely* illocutionary goals is success-oriented. If not, then maybe here we will have found the context or object for which the conditions of rationality "are of a different calibre than the conditions for the rationality of successful purposive activity".[76] I had to burst this bubble earlier in my brief discussion of Habermas's response to Baurmann's objection. For if someone, for example, a speaker, has a goal, even an illocutionary goal, then he wants to achieve this goal. If he did not want this, then he would not have this goal. Success in pursuit of a goal consists in achieving this goal, and Habermas himself continually speaks of "illocutionary success".[77] Thus if someone wants to achieve a goal, this *means* quite simply that he wants to be successful in the pursuit of this goal. And if someone wants to be successful in the pursuit of a goal—otherwise he would not pursue that goal in the first place—then he is evidently success-oriented.

Habermas does not overlook these logical and analytic connections entirely, since after all he remarks: "Certainly, at a general level, *all* actions, linguistic or non-linguistic ones, can be conceived of as goal-oriented activity." Unfortunately, this holds not only at this "general" level but at every level, or, to put it better: this has nothing to do with any levels at all, and thus Habermas is mistaken when he continues:

However, as soon as we wish to differentiate between *action oriented toward reaching understanding* and *purposive activity*, we must heed the fact that the teleological language game in which actors pursue goals, are successful, and produce results takes on a different meaning in the theory of language than it does in the theory of action—the same basic concepts are interpreted in different ways.[78]

Now, if we wish to distinguish Indian elephants from elephants, we must heed the fact that this distinction cannot be an *opposition*, since Indian elephants are after all elephants, and understanding-oriented action is doubtlessly a purposive activity and is thus subject to the standards of rationality for purposive action. Someone who desires not to concede this might lapse into arbitrary conceptual definitions to advance an argument that certainly cannot be justified in a rational and proper conceptual explication. Thus Habermas writes:

For our present purposes, it suffices [this formulation is revealing] to describe purposive activity in a general way as a goal-oriented and causally effective intervention in the objective world....Underlying the plan of action here is an interpretation of the situation in which the goal of action is determined (a) independently of the means of intervention (b) as a state to be brought about causally (c) in the objective world.[79]

This "general way" of description is, however, incorrect. For "purposive activity", as the word clearly signals to each competent speaker, simply describes an activity that is aimed at a purpose, a goal. The (a)s, (b)s and (c)s that Habermas so meticulously lists are the product of convenient fantasy.

If, however, just *for the sake of argument, counter*factually, we were to assume that Habermas's definition of "purposive activity" were correct, would Habermas's new attempt to find actions that are not purposive actions be successful? To answer this question we should more closely examine how Habermas proceeds. He writes:

> If we conceive of a speech act as a means whose end is reaching understanding [*als Mittel zum Zwecke der Verständigung*] and divide up the general aim of reaching understanding into the subcategories of, first, the aim that the hearer should understand the meaning of what is said and, second, the aim that she should recognize the validity of the utterance, then the description of how the speaker can pursue these aims does not fulfill any of the three conditions mentioned above.

And he continues:

> *a.* Illocutionary goals cannot be defined independently of the linguistic means of reaching understanding. Grammatical utterances do not constitute instruments for reaching under-standing in the same way as, for example, the operations carried out by a cook constitute means for producing enjoyable meals. Rather, the medium of natural language and the telos of reaching understanding [*das Telos der Verständigung*] interpret one another reciprocally: the one cannot be explained without recourse to the other.[80]

All of these statements are inapt. Let us start with the last one. What is a telos of reaching understanding [*Telos der Verständigung*]? The German *Verständigung* (which is actually best translated as "communication" and not as "reaching under-standing") can describe a process of more or less successful communication or its result. Otherwise one also uses the expression in the sense of "agreement", such as "the parties came to an understanding". However, here "agreement" in fact means *compromise*; thus it would be simply false to claim, as Habermas does, that *Verständigung* also means mutual agreement in the more demanding Habermasian sense. Let us look past this. What is the telos of reaching under-standing? "Telos", as we know, means "goal". The telos of "reaching understand-ing" in the full-fledged Habermasian sense means reaching mutual agreement. This is a flawless reconstruction of how we should understand "telos of reaching understanding", and my explanation did not involve any reference to the medium of natural language.

Yet Habermas might mean more than this; he might mean that one cannot *achieve* the goal of reaching understanding without using the natural language as a medium, a means. Of course this is also unfounded. If I am out taking a walk with someone who earnestly desires to take a short-cut through a certain meadow and I think this a bad idea, I can just as well move him or her to come to an understand-ing with me using a sentence of justification as I can by gently taking his or her head in my hands and pointing it in the direction of the agitated and unfriendly-looking bull he or she had failed to notice—and unlike pointing with my finger, this would not be a sign, that is, a "non-verbal speech act". Whereupon my friend, instead of responding to my "validity claims" with a "yes" of natural language, says not a word but simply returns to the normal path with me arm-in-arm, entirely consensually—thus without any recourse to natural language.

And the cook? Since Habermas emphasizes that illocutionary goals cannot be defined independently of the means of reaching understanding, he is apparently of the opinion that, in contrast, the cook's goal to prepare enjoyable meals can very well be defined independently of his cooking operations. Now, *if* we conceive of speech acts as means for the goal of reaching understanding and define this goal as Habermas does, then illocutionary goals cannot in fact be defined independently of the linguistic means of reaching understanding. According to Habermas, it is part of the illocutionary goal among other things that the hearer understands the meaning of *what was said*, that is, of the speech act in question. In other words, the illocutionary goal that the speaker pursues in executing the speech act is that *this very speech act* be understood and accepted. Thus the definition of the goal of a speech act, that is, of a certain means, refers to this very means. (As we will see shortly, the downright trivial circumstance that illocutionary goals cannot be defined without reference to speech acts does not mean that they cannot be achieved without speech acts.) However, these sorts of goals that involve the reference to certain means can readily be defined for the art of cooking. The *illoculinary* goal, let us say, of a certain concrete operation in cooking consists in *this very* operation leading to a certain enjoyable meal of a determinate amount. Obviously, then, illoculinary goals per definition cannot be defined without reference to the means of cooking. Yet the general goal of cooking, namely, making enjoyable meals, can be. The industrial production of enjoyable meals is also possible and would not be considered cooking. The same holds for the general and standard goal of speech acts, namely, the goal of *communication* in the broadest sense. Why do I say to someone, for example, "It's raining"? If someone were to ask me: "Why did you perform this speech act?", I would certainly not answer: "Because I wanted him to understand it and accept it as valid", but rather: "Because I wanted to let him know that it's raining." After all, if I were to learn that the person understands only German, I would simply choose another speech act: "*Es regnet.*" The goal of expressing something or letting someone know something that I pursue with my speech act can be defined and achieved entirely independently of a particular speech act. I can even pursue it without any speech acts at all, as in the case with the bull.

Of course, I cannot define the *standard goal of illocutionary acts* in Habermas's sense independently of these acts, since according to Habermas illocutionary acts are those acts in which illocutionary goals are pursued:

Acts of this kind [such as threats, for example]—acts that have become independent as perlocutionary acts—are not illocutionary acts at all, for they are not aimed at the rationally motivated position of an addressee.[81]

However, if I define illoculinary acts as those in which illoculinary goals are pursued, then the illoculinary acts lack nothing in this regard compared with illocutionary acts.

We can see, then, that Habermas arrives at his ostensibly profound distinction between a purposive activity such as cooking and an activity such as reaching understanding with the help, not of astute philosophical analyses of language, but rather of arbitrary definitions. These definitions can equally well be applied to cooking, torturing, waging war and the art of manicuring to get the same results—all of these activities being, according to Habermas, very much purposive activities. The illoculinary goals of cooking, the martialary goals of waging war, manicurinary goals of manicure and the propagandary goals of propaganda can all be defined such that all of these goals cannot be defined independently of the means with which they are achieved (and, in the case of propagandary goals, these could even be linguistic means). Thus, despite his assurances to the contrary, speech acts, understood in the Habermasian sense as illocutionary acts, fall under his a, b, c-definition of purposive activity just as well or just as poorly as acts that he considers true purposive actions. Once again there is no basic difference between speech acts and other purposive actions. The goals of most speech acts in the most common sense of the term, namely, those performed with normal goals rather than illocutionary ones, can without the slightest difficulty be defined independently of the means of achieving them. Again there is no difference.

Above I mentioned parenthetically that illocutionary goals cannot be defined without reference to speech acts, but can nevertheless easily be achieved without them. If, for example, I say to someone who has a good command of English but is not familiar with the word "roll-on deodorant": "Buy a roll-on deodorant please!", then she will not understand this speech act, at least not sufficiently. "What is that?", she asks. It is still my illocutionary goal that she understand this speech act; but the speech act itself has proven ineffectual as a means. What can I do? I could, for example, imitate the movements of using roll-on deodorant, sniff very demonstratively at my armpits and make an exaggerated expression of delight. This is also not a conventional sign and a use not of language but rather of imagination and acting ability; however, if the other person is of average intelligence, I will have achieved my illocutionary goal in this way. In other words, I will have reached my goal that a certain speech act be understood without using this speech act or any other speech act as a means. If someone were to object here—somewhat digressively—that the speech act in question had at least been uttered and thus was a means of reaching the goal *together* with my acting performance, this is as if one were to say that the means to reach my goal that someone sees the hippopotamus behind them include not just my agitated pointing in that direction but also the hippopotamus itself. This is not how we speak, at least not reasonably. Accordingly, in my example the illocutionary goal was definitely achieved without any *linguistic* means of reaching understanding.

Here, incidentally, there is no analogy to illoculinary goals. I can make an incomprehensible speech act understandable after the fact, but I cannot make an act that failed to provide a certain type and exact amount of an enjoyable meal successful after the fact. Illoculinary goals not only cannot be defined without reference to certain means, they also cannot be achieved without recourse to these certain means.

Let us now turn to Habermas's exposition of point (b):

The speaker cannot intend the aim of reaching understanding as something that is to be brought about causally, because the kind of illocutionary success that goes beyond mere understanding of what is said depends on the hearer's rationally motivated agreement. The hearer must, as it were, of her own free will give approval to agreement on a given matter by recognizing (the validity of) a criticizable validity claim. Illocutionary goals can be attained only cooperatively; they are not, unlike causally produced effects, at the disposal of the individual participant in communication. A speaker cannot attribute illocutionary success *to himself* in the same way that someone acting purposively is able to attribute to himself the result of his intervention in the nexus of innerworldly processes.[82]

First, the speaker has to at least *bring about* his or her illocutionary success with his or her speech acts. This is clear above all when she tries to add support and plausibility to a speech act she has already performed with further justifications. If she did not intend any effect, she could dispense with all justification and leave the matter to chance. However, she does not do this. Rather, she intervenes, she in fact tries to bring something about on the part of the hearer. Now, to talk of an acausal effect is as much patent nonsense as talk of round triangles. "Effects have causes" is an analytically true sentence; it follows from the meaning of the word "effect" that an effect is produced by a cause. Thus, as long as the speaker has the intention to achieve or realize an illocutionary success (and Habermas uses these words as well), which means to *bring something about*, then she has no other option than to intend this success as something to be brought about causally. Of course, Habermas could always decide that whatever brings about the understanding is no longer to be called "cause", just as he would prefer not to call the goal of reaching understanding a "goal" at all. Yet causes, goals and tables are causes, goals and tables, even when Habermas refuses to call them such.

Thus what Habermas intends to prove—that the speaker could not intend to bring about the goal causally or as something to be brought about causally—is already conceptually self-contradictory. Nonetheless, let us take a look at the other theses with which Habermas intends to justify the status of illocutionary goals as removed from causality.

According to Habermas, the "illocutionary success...depends on the hearer's rationally motivated agreement."[83] Yet precisely this speaks in *favour* of the causal realizability of illocutionary success. Rationally motivated agreement is agreement motivated by reasons. Yet it is an "ancient—and commonsense—position that rationalization is a species of causal explanation".[84] Our common sense tells us, and rightly so, that reasons are causes.[85] The burden of proof is on Habermas, although he fails to cope with it.

Of course this should not be seen as arguing that there is no difference between justification and force or compulsion. Rather, it is meant only to demonstrate that this difference is not to be found in a distinction between causality and acausality. We can see this from another perspective if we consider what the success of a compulsive measure such as a threat depends on. According to Habermas a threat can never be a justification or even an illocutionary act at all; and it fails when the person being threatened believes that the threatening person lacks the means to enforce it. In that case "the hearer contests the reasons that were supposed to motivate her to act in the manner predicted by S [the person making the threat]".[86] The acceptance of these reasons that the success of a threat depends on cannot therefore be enforced any more easily than the acceptance of an illocutionary act and the reasons that it depends on. Thus if the agreement to an illocutionary act, the recognition of the validity claims raised with this act, is "brought about acausally" (whatever this might mean), then this holds equally for the recognition of the claims to the means of enforcement raised with a threat. Moreover, this would still be the case even if it were true that illocutionary acts "rely on general, addressee-independent reasons that could convince anyone".[87] This is, however, not true. Most illocutionary acts, such as those with which communicatively acting house-builders or treasure-seekers on the high seas coordinate their actions, can produce agreement only in so far as they all share a goal, that is, the *reward* for the efforts (and is this not an *empirical* motivation in Habermas's sense of the term?). The reason offered in support of the illocutionary speech act "We have to risk shipwreck", namely, "Otherwise the others will get there first", might convince the treasure-seekers, but it would hardly convince everyone.

Incidentally, a post-metaphysical thinker like Habermas would have to concede that mental states are produced by physical states, namely, brain states (even if they cannot readily be identified with these). Physical states, however, as Habermas would agree, are physically caused. Now, the path from the utterance of a speech act to the agreement with it can also be described with physical concepts: the speech act causes sound waves, these cause vibrations on the eardrum, which cause certain electro-chemical processes in the brain and thus rational agreement. (Even if Habermas believed that justification does not take a physical path, but rather transports itself and its hearer into a transcendental realm of rationality, that, so to speak, instead of traversing the air it takes a short cut through a Habermasian hyperspace—Habermas does speak of the "extramundane"[88]—even then the effect achieved, as effect, is, I repeat, conceptually necessarily causal. Of course, there is no transcendental realm of any sort.) Even justifications, understood as justifying speech acts, ultimately bring about rational agreement through physical processes. This does not undermine rationality; the assumption of the contrary thesis does.

According to Habermas, the approval "of her own free will" cannot be produced causally either. Not only can we reply by repeating the same arguments from the previous paragraph here, but we could also doubt whether the agreement of a hearer, such as the agreement with a justification, really does occur of his or her own free will. After all, Habermas speaks of the "forceless *force* of the better argument".[89] It is precisely when considering rational arguments that one is no longer free to decide which ones one accepts and which not. This non-freedom does not mean an epistemic obligation, but rather an *unavoidability*: one cannot believe whatever one chooses; one does not *decide* to find x convincing, but rather one finds it convincing whether or not one wants to.[90]

Here one might respond that the hearer is nonetheless not truly *forced* to agree. This is correct. But not everything that proceeds otherwise than by force is for that reason alone done as a result of free will. Certain things just happen automatically, reflexively, vegetatively, in any case independently of my will. As Bernard Williams rightly noted, one cannot "just so", from one moment to the next, believe an argument or hold it to be valid based on a decision.[91] Thus the categories of free will and compulsion are out of place here.

But could this not present us with a difference from what Habermas calls "purposive activity"? Could the difference not consist in the fact that agreement, even if it does not occur of one's own free will in the true sense of the term, nonetheless cannot be compelled by force? Now, trust, famously, also cannot be won by force. One cannot point a weapon at someone and say "trust me or I'll shoot you", and then expect this strategy to work. Nonetheless, and this is also well known, one can in some circumstances most certainly win the trust of someone with strategic action and purposive activities. One could have the targeted person mugged by accomplices and then come to the "rescue" with scenes of daring kung-fu action from a Bruce Lee movie. Or, in a more mundane version, one could return the wallet still full of cash. The use of fighting techniques in saving a mugging victim and the return of the wallet are not speech acts but rather purposive activities that one can perform mutely. Thus, with purposive activities one can bring about things (such as winning someone's trust) that one cannot force. These activities are no different from speech acts in this regard.

Moreover, it would change nothing about this situation if one now tried to combine the rationality argument and the agreement argument in the objection that one cannot *rationally* win trust in the way described. This objection is false. If someone continually risks his life to save mine, even without saying a word, and is constantly returning my wallet even if he could have used the money himself, and stands loyally by my side in a crisis, then it is highly rational of me to trust this person (as long as there are no indications of anything suspicious about him).

For Habermas the condition of freely given cooperation is also incompatible with causation.[92] Here we could object that at the level of mere agreement there is no cooperation of any kind. We can repeat the same arguments here that I used above against the idea of agreement out of free will. If a hearer considers the argument of a speaker and believes it, this is not the expression of a decision but rather a cognitive automatism, an unavoidability. We can hardly speak of "cooperation" here.

Cooperation can of course be necessary at another level. Before this cognitive automatism can provide a result independently of the *immediate* will of the person considering the argument, it is necessary *that* the person consider the argument. The person can wilfully refuse to do so (which, incidentally, is not per se irrational). However, this is not a gain for Habermas. Since every instance of cooperation depends on the will, and the will can in principle be compelled by force, every instance of cooperation, even the act of taking an argument into consideration, can be compelled by force. The intractable sceptic, for example, who out of an irrational fear of landing in performative self-contradictions has been obstinately refusing to put himself in an argumentative situation (this is Habermas's picture of the sceptic) could after all be held at gunpoint and told: "If you don't start to argue with us sincerely, to critically scrutinize our theses and deliberate about them rationally—and as you know, we have the means to find out if you really are—we will have to resort to rather unfortunate sanctions." Thus whatever cooperation might be necessary for speech acts can also in principle be compelled by force just as much as the cooperation of the slaves who built the pyramids. Once again there is no difference between speech acts and purposive activities.

So we can conclude that illocutionary goals are states to be brought about causally. In this regard they are not distinct from purposive activities. Those properties that Habermas adduces to demonstrate the distinctiveness of understanding-oriented action cannot be found in this kind of action or else can be seen equally in the classic purposive activities in the Habermasian sense.

Readers who might have felt that my talk of "Habermasian hyperspace" was a polemical exaggeration might change their mind in view of Habermas's explanations of point (c):

Finally, from the perspective of the participants, the process of communication and the result to which this is supposed to lead do not constitute innerworldly states. Persons acting purposively encounter one another solely as entities in the world, despite the freedom of choice they mutually attribute to each other; they are accessible for one another only as objects or opponents. Speaker and hearer, by contrast, adopt a performative attitude in which they encounter one another as members of the intersubjectively shared lifeworld of their linguistic community, that is, in the second person. In reaching an understanding with one another about something in the world, the illocutionary aims they pursue reside, from their perspective, beyond the world to which they can refer in the objectivating attitude of an observer and in which they can intervene purposively. To this extent, they also remain in a transmundane position for one another.[93]

Habermas speaks here of things that are supposedly not innerworldly, but rather *beyond*; and of the "transmundane". In the *Theory of Communicative Action* he also talks in the same context of the "extramundane".[94] These explanations by Habermas are anything but post-metaphysical.

To remove any doubt: of course I, too, do not believe that a process of communication is an innerworldly state; not because it is not innerworldly, but because a process is not a state. Since a process of communication, as mentioned above, is ultimately a physical process, it is certainly innerworldly. It is no less innerworldly from the perspective of the participants; in fact, it is not at all clear what it would even *mean* to say that the participants readily outsource the process of communication to a place beyond the world—how do they do this? What is going on in their minds when they do? And where does Habermas actually *demonstrate* that the participants in the process of communication imagine the process and themselves outside of the objective world?

Perhaps the following example may help to show that the participants in a process of communication do not believe themselves departed from the world. If I call out to someone I see on the street: "Look out, a car!", then I do not believe that he or she is transmundane or extramundane or that the car will pass through him or her like a ghost; rather, I assume that my communicative partner is a physical object that cannot exist in the same spot at the same time as another physical object. In fact this is one of the motivations for my warning; otherwise I would not worry about it. Another motivation is that I also see him or her as a *subject*, as an end in himself, and thus I assume that he wants to live. Seeing someone as a physical object does not in any way exclude seeing him or her as subject at the same time. Moreover, I in fact yell in his or her direction rather than organizing a séance.

Those sentinels of hermeneutic endeavour unaware that even authors have certain commitments might now claim that Habermas "didn't mean it *that* way", but rather wanted to underline the various attitudes in which agents can meet each other. Now, if it was said a certain way but not meant that way, then it is just rhetoric.

Moreover, Habermas seems to *actually* distinguish the objective world (the only one there is) from the subjective and social world. It is important to him that he does not, like Popper, just mean different sectors of the *same* world (which would be reasonable), but in fact *different worlds*.[95] If these different "worlds" were in fact different *worlds*, then one might assume that the objects of the one could hardly have an impact on objects of the other. But they can. One can exert a chemical, that is, physical influence on one's feelings, that is, one's subjective world, with pills, that is, physical objects. And norms can influence and even regulate the movements of physical objects, such as cars in traffic. In other words, a legal norm is just as much a part of the objective world as a stone and an emotional impulse. Habermas himself conceives the objective world "as the correlate of the totality of true propositions".[96] One can clearly make true or false propositions about personal feelings just as much as one can about the existence of social norms and physical objects. Habermas, moreover, has never once even tried to lend any plausibility to his assertions to the contrary.

As far as the question of *attitudes* is concerned, and the manner in which we encounter people, it is simply incorrect to say that in purposive activities or strategic action we encounter others only as mere objects or as opponents. I made it clear above that strategic action in no way excludes altruistic motives or seeing others as persons. I can do something *for* another (and thus see him or her as subject). In strategic action, whether linguistically mediated or not, one can encounter the others in the second-person mode.

Incidentally, as Apel remarks against Habermas, this also holds even if we put aside altruistic contexts. Apel writes:

In fact I find it false, for example, to equate the rationality of *strategic* action with that of *social engineering*, which does in fact divide people into subjects and mere objects of nomological explanations or prognoses and thus objects of administration and planning. In my view we could instead say that the basic difficulty of all social technology—the difficulty of self-fulfilling and self-destroying prophecy—demonstrates precisely that point at which social technology turns to *economic-strategic* or *political-strategic interaction* between the social engineers and their human "objects"...

These examples also show that the rationality of strategic action is in principle not a rationality of the *subject-object relation* but rather of *interaction*—often even a rationality of *linguistic communication*—between *subjects*; and this despite the fact that the subjects of strategic interaction actually do attempt to instrumentalize each other within their frameworks of utility calculation...[97]

Of course, I do not share the opinion that strategic action necessarily implies instrumentalization. However, I do very much share the opinion that one also encounters others as subjects in instrumentalizing and authentically egocentric strategic interactions.

Thus Habermas's demarcation of speech acts from purposive activities also proves to be illusory in terms of attitudes as well.

Our discussion of the points (a), (b) and (c) has shown that Habermas's attempt to distinguish speech acts from purposive activities fails even if we assume that with purposive activities the goal of action is determined "(a) independently of the means of intervention (b) as a state to be brought about causally (c) in the objective world". We should recall here that this assumption was counterfactual and that it is ultimately irrelevant whether purposive activities satisfy these conditions. Purposive activity is activity aimed at a purpose, a goal. Teleological action is action that is teleological. It is, in fact, just this simple. This makes it rather disconcerting when Habermas's definitions of purposive and teleological action evince profound confusions and are in consequence thoroughly false. To take just one of the many examples of this:

Since Aristotle the concept of *teleological action* has been at the center of the philosophical theory of action. The actor attains an end or brings about the occurrence of a desired state by choosing means that have promise of being successful in the given situation and applying them in a suitable manner. The central concept is that of a *decision* among alternative courses of action, with a view to the realization of an end, guided by maxims, and based on an interpretation of the situation.[98]

Regarding the first and second sentence, one does not have to apply the means "in a suitable manner" in order to act teleologically. If Bob wants to shoot Bill and grabs the pistol, but unfortunately for him grabs it the wrong way around and pulls the trigger, he has obviously *not* applied the means, that is, the pistol, "in a suitable manner". Nonetheless, his use of the weapon is without doubt an example of purposive action. Moreover, the means does not have to "have promise of being successful", at least when this means anything more than "subjectively promising". Concerning the third sentence, it is rather bizarre to take decision as the central concept. Clearly the concept of *telos*, of *goal*, is the central concept for teleological action. Furthermore, teleological action by no means requires guidance by maxims. It is called teleological action, not deontological action.

Elsewhere Habermas varies the definition so that the focus is on "an *action plan* based on an *interpretation of the situation* and aiming at the realization of a goal, enabling a *choice* to be made between *alternative actions*".[99] Now, action alternatives are not given in *an* action plan, singular—what would the alternative be?—but in action *plans*, *goals*, and, in so far as the action is not an end in itself, *means*. Moreover, the existence of actions that are ends in themselves speaks against the central role of the action plan. If I want to raise my right arm, then the raising of this arm is the goal of my action, it is itself an end. There was an *intention* underlying the raising of my arm, but, in view of the primitivity, the simplicity of the action—a *basic action*[100]—it would be quite an exaggeration to speak of an underlying action plan.

Despite its falsity, the definition just considered—which continually recurs throughout Habermas's writing in diverse variations and thus can be seen as more definitive than the ad hoc a, b, c definition—shares one aspect with the definition that I proposed as correct, namely, that it quite reasonably declines to say anything about certain things. To wit:

In contrast to Habermas's (a), (b), (c) definition, it says, firstly, nothing about the relation of the means to the *determination* of the end of action. Secondly, the word "causal" does not occur, nor any synonym. Thirdly, the definition says nothing about "which world" (whatever that is supposed to mean) the goal of action is located in or which attitude the agents encounter each other in. In other words, whether the goal of action is determined independently of the intervening means; whether the goal is brought about causally, acausally, magically, metaphysically, subphysically, illocutionarily, perlocutionarily, revolutionarily or parasitically; whether it is found in the first, second or third world, in hyperspace or in the Platonic realm of the ideas; whether the agents encounter each other as first, second or third persons, ghosts, objects or divinities in objectifying, performative, pejorative or perverted attitudes—for Habermas's own definitions of teleological action that are less oriented towards proving the thesis, all this is irrelevant to the question of whether an action is purposive activity. Thus Habermas's defences of the points (a), (b) and (c) discussed above are not only false; they are irrelevant.

We can summarize the results of Section 1.2 as follows: both understanding-oriented speech acts—whether or not embedded in communicative action—and communicative action itself are *success-oriented*, as is all action. Thus the same standard of rationality that applies to communicative action and speech acts oriented towards reaching understanding applies also to root canal treatments, hammering nails, sending letters, murdering rich aunts, deceiving one's opponents and all other actions—namely, the standard of purposive rationality. Habermas's "communicative rationality" is either one particular case of instrumental rationality—just as the rationality of laying cement is—and thus it does not serve as a standard of rationality for actions as actions but rather only for the way that actions of a certain type are executed—or else it is simply a phantasm. Purposive rationality remains the sole standard for the rationality of actions.

1.3. FROM ACTION ORIENTED TOWARDS REACHING UNDERSTANDING TO A DISCOURSE THEORY OF RATIONALITY

We have already seen that the proponents of discourse ethics fail in their attempt to single out a communicative rationality that cannot be traced back to purposive rationality. At the centre of this critique was Habermas's distinction between action oriented towards success and action oriented towards reaching understanding, or more specifically between strategic action and communicative action. The following will examine in greater detail the implications that Habermas wants to draw from the distinction and whether these implications stand up to scrutiny.

Habermas would like to arrive at a conception of discursive reason, of reason in which justification is intersubjective and requires one to be able to move *others*[101] to rational acceptance of one's own "validity claims". "What grounding [*Begründung* = justification] means, can be explained only in connection with the conditions for discursively redeeming validity claims."[102] To put it concisely, justification is equated with justifi*ability* to others, which of course explains the particular significance assumed by the notion of consensus.

Above (1.2.1) I criticized Habermas for tying the rationality of what he calls purposive activities to their justifi*ability* in the first chapter of the *Theory of Communicative Action*. In his later writings this is no longer his intention, or at least, as we saw, his definitions are no longer formulated this way. However, concerning the rationality of *speech acts oriented toward reaching understanding*, which stem from the equally understanding-oriented communicative action, he continues to uphold the equation of rational with justifiable and thus the close internal connection to argumentative practice,[103] about which he says in his *Theory of Communicative Action*:

Thus the rationality proper to the communicative practice of everyday life points to the practice of argumentation as a court of appeal that makes it possible to continue communicative action with other means when disagreements can no longer be repaired with everyday routines and yet are not to be settled by the direct or strategic use of force.[104]

Here we already have a reference to discourse *ethics*.

Of course, the question arises *how* exactly the (instrumental) rationality proper to the communicative practice of everyday life points to the practice of argumentation and thus to *discourse*, and moreover whether this "pointing to" allows for the far-reaching conclusions desired. It seems that what would have to be demonstrated for the Habermasian theory is *that a communicative, that is, understanding-oriented practice of everyday life is rational if and only if a speaker can justify to others the speech acts she performs in this practice and thus in principle can consensually redeem his or her "validity claims"*.

Sometimes Habermas characterizes the rationality of understanding-oriented speech acts in this way, and sometimes not. I have the impression that it is not entirely clear to Habermas that only the validity of this characterization, if anything, could serve as the bridge from communicative action to the assumption that it is the "consensus-fitness" ["*Konsensfähigkeit*"] of a norm, that is, its ability to find unanimous acceptance in practical discourse, that proves it to be *rational*. And this assumption is of course indispensable if, like Habermas, one claims to describe discourse ethics as a *morality of reason* [*Vernunftmoral*], that is, if one claims that the observance of moral norms (that are discourse-ethically justified) is *rational*. However, if Habermas does not support the argument I proposed here based on my judgement that it is suggested by at least *one* textual passage, then he does not have any argument.

The text passage I refer to is a footnote more precisely specifying the following formulation, which Habermas uses again and again but which is nonetheless not sufficient to "point to" discourse:

An assertion can be called rational only if the speaker satisfies the conditions necessary to achieve the illocutionary goal of reaching an understanding about something in the world with at least one other participant in communication.[105]

And the decisive commentary in the footnote reads:

A speaker who makes an assertion has to have a "reserve supply" of good reasons at his disposal in order to be able, if necessary, to convince his conversation partners of the truth of his statement and bring about a rationally motivated agreement.[106]

If *this* were true, then it would also be correct to say that "the rationality proper to the communicative practice of everyday life" points to argumentative discourse, in the quite precise sense explicated in this footnote.

Nonetheless, this still leaves the *status* of this communicative or discursive rationality open at best. For if these conditions of rationality are a valid standard only in "contexts of communication",[107] then this rationality is simply one application of *instrumental* rationality.

However, precisely this is the case, such that one wonders how it even occurred to the proponents of discourse ethics to try to extend a domain-specific rationality, on the same level as other domain-specific rationalities such as cement-laying rationality or dental-care rationality, beyond its proper domain.

The improper extension of this rationality occurs in two steps.

First it is implicitly assumed that the conditions of rationality for speech acts oriented towards reaching understanding are the same as those for practical discourses. Yet since understanding-oriented speech acts and practical discourses do not have the same goals—the former aim at reaching understanding (in the Habermasian sense), the latter aim either at clarifying practical questions ("What should we do?", "Which norms are valid?", "What is just?", "What is moral?") or, which is not the same, at resolving conflicts of action—this assumption is by no means self-evident. Moreover, I have already pointed out that the proponents of discourse ethics are mistaken even about the conditions of rationality for understanding-oriented speech acts.

The second step in this extension is to claim in terms of a generally Kantian morality of reason that it is *rational* to *observe* outside of discourse that which was justified as morally correct within practical discourse. Habermas concedes that, according to ordinary language use, "when we act immorally, we are not necessarily behaving irrationally", but argues that this means only that "our way of using language can no longer serve as an unbiased witness."[108] (Whereupon we might wonder who is an "unbiased witness"—Habermas himself?)

In the following I will first show that the path is blocked that would lead from communicative action or speech acts oriented towards reaching understanding to a discourse theory of rationality. To this end I will only have to recall certain errors in Habermas's characterization of the conditions of rationality of understanding-oriented speech acts that have already been criticized above (1.3.1). I will also directly criticize the theory itself. (Moreover, the reader should bear in mind that a discourse theory of *rationality* is not identical to a discourse theory of truth and correctness. Arguments for the one are not necessarily arguments for the other. The proponents of discourse ethics seem to me to overlook this.) I will refute the extension of understanding-oriented rationality in both steps (1.3.2).

Finally, I will examine whether Habermas succeeds in consolidating his discussions of speech act theory, the theory of action and the theory of rationality into any kind of coherent whole or whether they form an unconnected and perhaps contradictory assemblage of prop pieces (1.3.3).

1.3.1. On the Alleged Link with the Practice of Argumentation

Why does "the rationality proper to the communicative practice of everyday life" not point to the practice of argumentation, to discourse, as a court of appeal? We have already seen the answer: given the assumed goal of reaching understanding, for an assertion oriented towards reaching understanding to be instrumentally rational nothing more is required than that the speaker *have good reasons to assume* that he or she will reach the intended understanding with this speech act. (To recall, in Habermas's sense of "reaching understanding", an assertion oriented towards reaching understanding means an assertion that a speaker utters without reservation and with the intention that it be understood and accepted.) It is *not* necessary that the speaker have a "reserve supply" of convincing reasons with which in fact to be able to generate rationally motivated agreement.

The following weaker definition from Habermas is also incorrect, aside from the fact that it is too weak anyway to *equate* rationality with discursive redeemability, which discourse ethics would need to do in order to be a rational morality:

Once again, we do not call only valid speech acts rational but rather all comprehensible speech acts for which the speaker can take on a *credible* warranty in the given circumstances to the effect that the validity claims raised could, if necessary, be vindicated discursively.[109]

We have already seen the fallaciousness both of the stronger characterization of the instrumental rationality of understanding-oriented speech acts and of this weaker version. We saw this in the example of the cocktail party where I make an assertion about "marathon ants" that was rationally based on the reasonably considered evidence available to me, yet where I lacked any reserve supply of good reasons and could not take on any credible *warranty* for my hearers of having this supply of reasons. (We have also seen already that these characterizations are particularly fallacious as characterizations of rationality in general rather than merely instrumental rationality, which I would like to recall here to preclude the misunderstanding that I might be just *arbitrarily* situating communicative rationality within instrumental rationality. We have seen that "communicative rationality" is at base purely instrumental; for just this reason—which we will discuss shortly—the question arises *how* it could be used as a standard beyond its original domain, if at all.)

To make it short and sweet: an assertion aiming at reaching understanding is instrumentally rational when the speaker has good reasons to assume that he or she will reach the illocutionary goal with that assertion. The speaker does not have to be able to discursively redeem the assertion, or take on a credible (if possibly faulty) warranty that it can be vindicated, or be able to justify the assertion *at all*, since success can also be achieved without such justifiability. For example, this holds of assertions like "Yesterday at home alone I read a story by Borges", which could be justified only under rather far-fetched circumstances but still have illocutionary success simply due to the credibility of the speaker (which according to Habermas is not discursively redeemable[110]). Thus "the rationality proper to the communicative practice of everyday life" points to reasons, not to discourse.

Moreover, even if "the rationality proper to the communicative practice of everyday life" were to point to discourse, why should this discourse be subject to the same conditions as a practical discourse? By "communicative practice of everyday life" Habermas means communicative action, which according to him is characterized among other things by the use of illocutionary acts without reservation to coordinate action. The illocutionary goal of these illocutionary acts is that they be understood and accepted; and for Habermas these acts being "accepted" means, in this context, "*rationally* accepted". (Otherwise there would be still a second insurmountable obstacle on the path from speech acts oriented towards reaching understanding to *the practice of argumentation* as an alleged court of appeal.)

The speech act of one person succeeds only if the other accepts the offer contained in it by taking (however implicitly) a "yes" or "no" position on a validity claim that is in principle criticizable. Both ego, who raises a validity claim with his utterance, and alter, who recognizes or rejects it, base their decision on potential grounds or reasons.[111]

Yet the speech acts with which we deliver moral judgements or endorse norms do not fit this picture very well. Statements such as "Jessica is a completely morally depraved person", "Frank is a repugnant, egocentric scumbag", "Pornography should be absolutely forbidden, that goes without saying", "Homosexuality is unnatural", "You must do your duty", "We have to keep pushing democratization forward", "The dignity of man is unassailable", etc. by no means aim at rational acceptance. As Charles Stevenson showed in his astute analysis,[112] they are often a mix of the expression of one's own feelings and attitudes and an attempt to induce these feelings and attitudes on the part of others. This does not mean—and Stevenson emphasized this quite emphatically, although cognitivist critics tend to overlook it—that one could not *also* provide reasons for these speech acts. But these speech acts cannot be reduced to their cognitive content, and, more importantly, their *rational acceptance* is by no means necessary for their *success*. Acceptance does not have to rest on reasons; it can also be achieved through other kinds of influence. Thus speech acts of this sort by no means point towards argumentative discourse as a court of appeal, but rather as *one* means alongside others to support these speech acts.

1.3.2. The Claims of a Discourse Theory of Rationality

After thus severing the chain of arguments towards a discourse theory at several points, we should now turn to this theory itself. First I will refute the claim that norms that satisfy the discourse principle D or the rule of argumentation U allegedly at work in discourse are *justified*. I will refute this claim on purely epistemological grounds without recourse to an appeal to our moral intuitions (1.3.2.1). However, even if norms satisfying the discourse principle D were justified, it would not yet be rationally justified to *follow* them, since morality and rationality are not to be conflated (1.3.2.2).

1.3.2.1. On the Differences between Justifiable, Valid, and Justified Norms

According to Habermas the moral principle (U) "performs the role of a rule of argumentation...for justifying moral judgments",[113] such as norms. The principle states:

Every valid norm must satisfy the condition that the consequences and side effects its *general* observance can be anticipated to have for the satisfaction of the interests of *each* could be freely accepted by *all* affected (and be preferred to those of known alternative possibilities for regulation).[114]

The principle of discourse ethics (D) to be derived from this stipulates:

Only those norms can claim to be valid that meet (or could meet) with the approval of all affected in their capacity as participants in a practical discourse.[115]

This formulates a condition for the validity of a norm—a condition clearly tied to discourse. However, a *valid* norm is not a *justified* norm, just as a true proposition is not necessarily a justified proposition. Habermas himself also refers to practical discourse as "a procedure for testing the validity of norms that are being proposed and hypothetically considered for adoption".[116] Now, a litmus test is a procedure for determining whether a liquid is acid or base. If this procedure is carried out by interested parties and the litmus paper colours red, then the proposition that the liquid is acidic is well justified. However, this procedure has to actually be carried out to arrive at this justification of the proposition. The mere fact of a colouring of the litmus paper does not justify the proposition as long as it is not known to the people themselves. There could in fact be other indications, if less reliable ones, that justify the negation of the proposition. Of course, the same holds for the norms allegedly justif*iable* by the moral principle of discourse ethics: norms that contradict these could also be justified.

Here one could question whether these norms are truly justified—meaning rationally justified—if they were not tested with the most reliable procedure. Is it not irrational to believe something that one could not have believed after using the more reliable and equally accessible procedure?

Aside from the fact that we could rather strongly doubt (more precisely, we can rule it out) that practical discourse with its improbable idealizations is accessible and thus can assume the function of a true criterion,[117] the rationality of a belief depends not just on the epistemic ambitiousness of the process of forming that belief but also on the rationality of this process as an action. A simple example: if a person on the street sees a dog that looks like a dachshund, then the opinion of this person, based on a brief glance, is entirely rational. A brief glance is by no means the most effective method; there is a margin of error that other procedures would have been able to reduce. For example, this person could have *thoroughly* examined the dog while consulting reference works of canine science; the person could have gone so far as to carry out a genetic analysis. Although these sorts of procedure would doubtless have been more reliable, we would not hesitate to call a person's opinion that something is a dachshund justified based on a brief glance. How thorough and ambitious the epistemic process has to be for us to call the resulting belief justified depends on the importance of the question, as we saw in this example. One could now say that the question of a norm's validity is more important than the question of a certain dog's breed. That may be so, but the question of which norms are valid and which are not valid is certainly not infinitely important. Scrutinizing the validity of norms is not the point of life.

Perhaps the proponents of discourse ethics would even concede that an opinion does not have to be formed with the most epistemically effective procedure possible in order to be rational. They do not offer any clear statement on this, since the point does not seem to have occurred to them. If, however, they do concede this point, then they should bear in mind that it limits the critical potential of discourse ethics (in so far as it has any such potential), since due to the circumstance just described certain societal norms that are invalid according to discourse-ethical opinion cannot be refuted as unjustified based solely on this invalidity (which discourse ethicists have allegedly noticed). The favoured accusation of irrationalism (which as always has considerable rhetorical force) would have to be used more sparingly, at least in communication "without reservation". Invalid norms could be very much justified.

Of course, we should distinguish between justification in the sense of being justified on the one hand and justification in the sense of a justifying proposition or a justifying speech act on the other hand. If the person A in our example with the dachshund hears from another person B: "That's not a dachshund, because dachshunds have differently shaped ears", then the because-clause is a justification for the preceding thesis. However, as long as the addressee of this justification does not examine the dachshund's ears more closely and conclude that they in fact could not be the ears of a dachshund, the thesis, as already explained, is not justified for the addressee. Nonetheless, the justification could be *valid*. As Christoph Lumer explains, "valid"—like "sharp" when said of a knife—is a qualitative predicate that describes the functional capacity of a certain object. "Sharp" characterizes the functional *capacity* of knives, "valid" that of arguments. A knife does not have to be actually used for it to be sharp; it only has to cut well *if* used appropriately, where "appropriately" means something like "according to its 'instructions for use' or users' manual". Of course, speaking of "instructions for use" makes more immediate sense in reference to an electric drill. We do not expect an electric drill without batteries to function when it is not plugged into a socket, that is, when it is not used in accordance with its instructions for use. That it fails to function under these circumstances does not mean that it is not *capable* of functioning, that is, that it is out of order in some way. In just the same way an argument is valid for an addressee if its epistemically rational appraisal by the hearer *would* convince him or her.[118]

Applying this to discourse ethics, one could ask whether U or the principle D derived from it could be used in the form of a valid argument. The following general form seems reasonable:

The norm N is valid because it would be freely accepted by all affected in a practical discourse.

This argument would be valid for its addressee if he or she would be convinced by it upon appropriate appraisal. But what would an appropriate appraisal consist in? In carrying out a practical discourse? If this were the case then this argument would have no practical value, since according to discourse ethics one can convince oneself of the validity of a norm *directly* in practical discourse. All of the participants in a practical discourse are allegedly already of the opinion, and necessarily so, that a norm is valid if it meets with general approval in practical discourse. Thus one would no longer need the argument in the first place; it would be redundant.

Fine, one might say; this proves only that the principles U and D are practically, politically, societally, ethically and philosophically without value, but it does not change anything about the possibility of their *validity* as arguments. Robert Alexy, whose "theory of practical discourse" Habermas has referred to approvingly, writes:

The discussion of moral philosophy carried out within the institution of academia, without external pressure on the decisions and carried out in principle without personal limits across generations, comes closest to the model proposed with these rules [of practical discourse, U.S.][119]

However, in the discourse that "comes closest" to practical discourse (and in which we are participating right now), the principles U and D of discourse ethics have generated very little force of conviction. This does not exactly speak in favour of their validity. One might respond that this discourse still only comes close to the true, ideal practical discourse and is not identical with it. This response backfires, however. For if Alexy concedes "the unfulfillable quality of ideal conditions"[120] and thus the factual impossibility of carrying out a true practical discourse, this no longer implies only the valuelessness of the principles U and D in all the respects mentioned above, but their invalidity as arguments as well.

We had said, after all, that for an electric drill to be capable of functioning it has to function under the appropriate conditions specified in the instructions for use. We need to add the trivial qualification that of course conditions *that cannot be fulfilled* have no place in the instructions for use. We would not deny the functional capacity of an electric drill just because it has no electricity at the moment—because, for example, it is lying unused in the toolbox or we find ourselves in a situation without electricity. But what about an electric drill that requires an amount of electricity greater than the total energy of the universe to function?

It is clear that such an object is not only not a functionally capable electric drill, it is in fact not an electric drill at all. It is garbage or at best a reliquary or a work of art. Similarly, an "argument" that can convince only under conditions that cannot be produced (which is quite convenient, incidentally, since it guarantees protection against falsification) is *not* an argument, and certainly not a valid one, but rather just a noise.

If to escape this result one could finally bring oneself to accept a practically feasible appraisal of the discourse-ethical argument as sufficient, then we can no longer explain how it is that those appraisals (not least of all critiques) that the argument was subjected to should not have been sufficiently ambitious. If they were sufficient, then it is proven that the discourse-ethical argument at the very least has no universal validity. (To avoid *this* result, one would have to escalate to the assumption that the opponents of discourse ethics are all irrational. This sort of manoeuvre disqualifies itself.)

Thus far we have seen that for a norm (or a thesis) to be justified it is not necessary that it meets or would meet with general agreement in a discourse. Besides, general agreement in a discourse is not sufficient for this. Furthermore, the claim that a norm would receive general agreement in discourse is either not any sort of argument for the rightness of the norm at all, or else, at the very least, not a universally valid argument. To put it briefly, the conditions of rationality of norms and theses are certainly not to be found in discourse.

1.3.2.2. On the Difference between the Justified Status of a Norm and the Rationality of Its Observance

Yet even if precisely those norms that would find general agreement in a practical discourse were rational or justified (which is not the case), it does not follow from this that it is rational to *observe* such norms. According to Habermas practical discourses concern which "norms of action ought to be adopted [*in Kraft gesetzt*, which means something like socially accepted and sanctioned—though not necessarily legally]".[121] But of course it can be rational for an agent to agree to a certain norm and even to quite fervently work in support of it, while at the same time it could be equally rational for him or her to occasionally violate the norm, depending on how it serves his or her interests. This is sufficiently well-known as the free-rider problem.

However, as already mentioned, Habermas in fact argues that it *cannot* be rational to (knowingly) violate valid moral norms; and, as also already mentioned, this contradicts our use of language. To brush this fact aside with the remark: "But then, of course, our way of using language can no longer serve as an unbiased witness",[122] is dogmatic. Habermas does admittedly provide additional arguments, including a direct argument based on the "cognitive claim" of moral judgements (1.3.2.2.1) as well as an indirect argument that claims a priority of communicative action over strategic action and aims to derive from this a priority of the one type of rationality over the other (1.3.2.2.2). These arguments do not allay this dogmatism in any way, since one can fall for them in the first place only by ignoring our language use, which shows us from the outset that these arguments *cannot* be correct.

Let us take a closer look at this.

1.3.2.2.1. On the Difference Between "Cognitive Claims" and Claims to Rationality

Habermas writes:

On the contrary, our practices of criticizing immoral actions and of disputing moral questions by appealing to reasons suggest rather that we associate a cognitive claim with moral judgments.[123]

So what? A bank robber also associates a cognitive claim with the thesis that bank robbing is *illegal*—it by no means follows from this that he finds it irrational to rob banks. Likewise the bank robber could easily be of the opinion that robbing banks is *immoral* and provide reasons for this opinion; but this does not yet mean that he finds it irrational to rob banks. Quite possibly he will hold up the nearest bank with a bad conscience, but not in doubt of his own rationality—only of his morality. In short, associating a cognitive claim with the assertion of a norm's moral or legal validity is not the same thing as asserting the *rationality* of observing the norm. Habermas should listen to our use of language more closely.

In general Habermas's theories about reasons and justifications all show a rather one-sided inclination towards moralism, which is not especially rational. Thus he claims:

A valid moral judgment does indeed *signify* [*bedeutet*] in addition an obligation to act accordingly, and to this extent every normative validity claim has rationally motivating force grounded in reasons....the insightful addressee then knows he has no good reason to act *otherwise*.[124]

Again, it by no means follows from obligation to action x that it is rational to do x. The phrase "to this extent" marks the statement as a non-sequitur. It does not even follow from the "motivating force grounded in reasons" of a moral judgement that it is rational to act accordingly. For the "motivating force grounded in reasons" of a moral judgement could be opposed by the motivating force grounded in reasons of a prudential judgement. Someone who cares at all about both morality and about his finances, and who knows that a certain action is morally right but would have financially disastrous consequences for him, has reasons to perform the action as well as reasons not to. Accordingly, someone is not irrational merely because he or she acts differently than *certain* reasons (i.e. moral reasons) suggest; rather, the person has to act differently than suggested after *rationally weighing* the various reasons. Habermas's assumption that moral reasons have primacy over non-moral reasons in practical questions is just this: an assumption.

1.3.2.2.2. The Alleged Primacy of Communicative Action over Strategic Action
This assumption corresponds to the other assumption, namely, that communicative action has primacy over strategic action.[125] Since the idea is obviously to derive the (rational) primacy of morality ultimately from this alleged primacy of communicative action, and since the primacy of morality is, as we saw, an illusion, one can assume the invalidity of the arguments on which Habermas intends to base the primacy of communicative action.

The three arguments are the "parasitism" argument (1.3.2.2.2.1), an argument from the theory of meaning (1.3.2.2.2.2) and the argument that communicative action evinces "stronger implications of rationality" than strategic action (1.3.2.2.2.3).

1.3.2.2.2.1. The "Parasitism" Argument Habermas formulates his parasitism argument as follows:

The elementary speech act can serve as a model for consent-formation not itself arising from success-oriented action only if the use of language oriented towards reaching understanding may be viewed as the original mode of use of language, to which consequence-oriented use of language and indirect understanding (giving to understand) stand in a parasitic relation.... This is exactly what a detailed investigation of the illocutionary forces and the perlocutionary effects of speech acts can show. Speech acts can only serve the perlocutionary aim of influencing the hearer if they are suitable for achieving illocutionary aims. If the hearer did not understand what the speaker said, even a speaker acting strategically could not stimulate a hearer to behave in the desired way with the help of communicative acts. To this extent, consequence-oriented use of language is not an original mode of language use, but the subsumption of speech acts serving illocutionary aims under the conditions of success-oriented action.[126]

This argumentation is quite astonishing.[127] Firstly, it is more suited to downgrading the status of language use *oriented towards reaching understanding* than that of its strategic use. If "consequence-oriented use of language is…the subsumption of speech acts serving illocutionary aims under the conditions of success-oriented action", then it is in fact *these speech acts serving illocutionary aims* that are subsumed, *subordinated*, namely, *under* the conditions of success-oriented action. Of course, they are thereby placed under the standard of purposive rationality, that is, this standard remains *superordinate* and ultimately decisive. This is a point for it, not against it.

We can also see how unimpressive the "original" status of understanding-oriented language use would be (if it were true) from the following analogy: a heart surgeon relies on adequate support from others, including for example the proper anaesthetization of the patient, without which he cannot operate. Thus heart surgery is not an original activity, but rather the subsumption of activities serving other aims such as anaesthesia, disinfecting scalpels, mopping the surgeon's forehead, etc., under the conditions of heart-surgical action. What does this tell us about the status of mopping foreheads in comparison with heart surgery?

Thus it is clear that Habermas's parasitism argument for the justification of the primacy of language use oriented towards reaching understanding is irrelevant. Moreover, it is incorrect.

Firstly, speech acts by no means necessarily have to be understood in order to influence the hearer.[128] If I want to intimidate someone it can be enough if I direct a loud and aggressive flurry of speech acts at him or her that he or she cannot understand because he or she does not speak the language. In fact this circumstance might even increase the intimidating effect. If on the other hand I want to influence someone by means of his or her understanding of the speech acts used, then it is analytically true that he or she has to understand the speech acts for this purpose. However, it is still false to claim that these speech acts have to be "suitable for achieving illocutionary aims", since the illocutionary aim according to Habermas does not just consist in being understood but also in achieving rational consensus. Yet, if I have the intention of using a speech act with the perlocutionary aim of insulting the hearer, I might perform the speech act: "You're a stupid pig and your mother's a whore." I strongly doubt that there is any danger of reaching the illocutionary goal of a free consensus concerning the validity claims raised. It is more likely that the other abstains from taking a "yes position" vis-à-vis this statement. Thus this speech act is absolutely unsuited to reaching illocutionary goals. Moreover, this holds not just for these sorts of drastic insult but also for simple lies and all other speech acts that are not without reservations, that is, for *all* strategic speech acts, since according to Habermas these strategic speech acts cannot bring about *rational* consensus.[129] However, it is this rational consensus that the illocutionary goal consists in.[130] Thus Habermas's claim, namely:

Speech acts can only serve the perlocutionary aim of influencing the hearer if they are suitable for achieving illocutionary aims[131]

is contradictory.

Thus there is no "perlocutionary parasitism" exploiting speech acts serving illocutionary aims for its own dark purposes (as parasites do). Perlocutionary acts (in the sense of acts of non-argumentative influence) cannot be performed with the help of illocutionary acts, at least not according to the theories that Habermas commits to elsewhere.

Besides this impossible parasitism, might not another kind of parasitism be possible? Elsewhere Habermas mentions the example of a speaker

who wants to persuade [*überreden*] his audience of something…perhaps because in the given situation he lacks convincing arguments. Such nonpublic perlocutionary effects can be achieved only parasitically, namely, on condition that the speaker feigns the intention of *unreservedly* pursuing his illocutionary aims and leaves the hearer in the dark as to his actual violation of the presuppositions of action oriented toward reaching understanding.[132]

First of all: this strategic use of language is not "parasitic" on the communicative *use of language*—the latter use of language does *not* occur here, after all—but rather on the audience's *belief* that they are addressees of argumentation. It is this belief that the speaker uses for his goals. If the audience did not have this belief, the speaker could not achieve his goals. The fact that the communicative use of language is parasitic on the belief *in itself* (i.e. in the communicative use of language), whereas the strategic use of language is parasitic on the belief *in another use of language* (namely, in the communicative one), does not change anything about the fact that the strategic use of language is not parasitic on the communicative *use of language*; rather, it underscores this fact. Belief is not use of language. The illocutionary use of language is just as parasitic on this belief—which, incidentally, is induced *strategically*, as we will see—as is the perlocutionary use; here we cannot uncover any primacy of one over the other.

Second of all: it is not even correct that we can persuade people only if they do not know that we are trying to persuade them of something. Habermas's assumption to the contrary could be better attuned to realities. The game of seduction is one example of an attempt at persuasion that the hearer sees through but that can nonetheless be successful.

Habermas himself concedes that there is such a manifestly strategic use of language, one that is recognized by the hearer as such. These sorts of strategic speech acts can be successful without the speech act even being parasitic on the hearer's belief that he or she is the addressee of an illocutionary act. Insults are one particularly conspicuous example of this. However, Habermas claims that even insults and other so-called perlocutions "require successful illocutionary acts as their vehicle".[133] We have already seen that this is false. "You're a pig" works fine without any such vehicle, as do threats, since acts "of this kind—acts that have become independent as perlocutionary acts—are not illocutionary acts at all, for they are not aimed at the rationally motivated position of an addressee".[134] Quite. And since they have become independent, they are not parasitic.

But, one might respond here, can we not at least hold the following:

> In manifestly strategic action, illocutionarily weakened speech acts, if they are to be comprehensible, continue to refer to the meaning they owe to a use of language that is antecedently habitualized and originally oriented toward reaching understanding.[135]

Thus Habermas is of the opinion that we have to first learn a language as used in its orientation towards reaching understanding. Habermas also mentions this astonishing view in support of his pragmatic theory of meaning[136] (which, as we will see, is also false). However, in his more insightful moments Habermas realizes that, for example,

> demands in the course of ontogeny are initially learned as simple imperatives reinforced by sanctions and only at a later date as normatively "backed-up" imperatives.[137]

So demands oriented towards reaching understanding seem to be parasitic *on the strategic use of language*, in the sense of "parasitism" just discussed.

Furthermore, it is not any different with language as a whole. We do not learn language in interactions oriented towards reaching understanding; at least I doubt whether mothers who hold a bottle in front of their two-year-olds and say "here's the bottle, here's the bottle...(etc.)" are pursuing the illocutionary goal that their children acknowledge the claims to sincerity, truth and normative rightness tied to the speech act. The infant could hardly have mastered these concepts. The mothers want to teach their children the language; they also simply have fun talking to them. There are, first and foremost, no illocutionary goals involved. And when the child is old enough to understand the relevant exhortations, and does not speak "properly", then it is told "Speak properly!" often with a threatening tone of voice. And, if ultimately the child is dragged to the speech therapist, no one asks if he or she consents.

Moreover, even if the strategic use of language were parasitic on interactions oriented towards reaching understanding in the sense of "parasitism" at issue here, that is, in the sense that one has to have already taken part in these interactions (perhaps during one's acquisition of the language) in order to be able to speak strategically, it is still quite clear that one has to have performed purposive activities at some point in order to be able to speak at all. For we can speak only as long as we live; and if we stopped eating—and feeding ourselves is a purposive activity in Habermas's sense of purposive activities that are truly purposive (and we know that for Habermas there are purposive activities that are not really purposive)— then we would die relatively soon thereafter. And then it would be over with speaking, whether strategically or in orientation towards reaching understanding. Thus speech oriented towards reaching understanding is parasitic on purposive activities, whereas these non-linguistic activities are in no way parasitic on action oriented towards reaching understanding, never mind speech. Accordingly, the primacy of speech acts (or any act) oriented towards reaching understanding can hardly be made plausible with recourse to Habermas's idiosyncratic theory that the "symbolic reproduction" of society can be accomplished *only* through communicative action.[138] This thesis is false.[139] Moreover, symbolic reproduction is clearly not possible without material reproduction, whereas material reproduction is possible without symbolic reproduction (the boy raised by wolves cannot achieve "symbolic reproduction" in Habermas's sense of the term, but clearly can still live regardless). Here we again see the primacy of purposive activities and thus the primacy of purposive rationality.

So the strategic use of language is by no means parasitic on the use of language oriented towards reaching understanding.

How do things look with the converse? We have already seen that we do not learn our native language in interactions oriented towards reaching understanding.[140] And it strikes me as impossible to learn a second language exclusively in such understanding-oriented interactions. However, I will not continue to pursue this; I am much more interested in the question of whether the understanding-oriented use of language is parasitic in Habermas's central sense of parasitism, according to which one action is parasitic on another when it is *subordinated* to another, or is used for the purpose of the other. Let us put the question to Habermas. According to him,

we must take into consideration that not only do illocutions appear in strategic-action contexts, but perlocutions appear in contexts of communicative action as well. Cooperative interpretive processes run through different phases. In the initial phase participants are normally handicapped by the fact that their interpretations do not overlap sufficiently for the purpose of coordinating actions. In this phase participants have either to shift to the level of metacommmunication or to employ means of indirectly achieving understanding. Coming indirectly to an understanding proceeds according to the model of intentionalist semantics. Through perlocutionary effects, the speaker gives the hearer something to understand which he cannot (yet) directly communicate. In this phase, then, the perlocutionary acts have to be embedded in contexts of communicative action. These strategic *elements* within a use of language oriented to reaching understanding can be distinguished from strategic *actions* through the fact that the entire sequence of a stretch of talk stands—on the part of all participants—under the presuppositions of communicative action.[141]

This last sentence needs to be corrected, as a look at the previous sentences makes clear. Strategic elements are presumably so called because they are elements that are strategic. These elements *are* perlocutionary acts, Habermas tells us. I assume, furthermore, that perloctionary acts are so called because they are acts, that is, actions. If the strategic elements are strategic and, moreover, are *identical* with the perlocutionary acts, then, following the well-known Leibniz' law that "two" identical things have the same properties, we can conclude that the perlocutionary acts of which we speak share all properties with the strategic elements they are identical with, including the property of being strategic. It follows, Habermas's protestations to the contrary notwithstanding, that we are dealing here with strategic actions.

As regards this indirect achievement of understanding by the use of strategic actions, Habermas summarizes the explanation quoted above by saying that it "remains *subordinated* to the aim of communicative action".[142] If Habermas had not already italicized the word "subordinated", I would have done so myself, since this emphasis practically makes any further explanation superfluous as long as we recall that central meaning of "original"—and thus that of its counterpart, "parasitic"—that concerns us here:

If the hearer did not understand what the speaker said, even a speaker acting strategically could not stimulate a hearer to behave in the desired way with the help of communicative acts. To this extent, consequence-oriented use of language is not an original mode of language use, but the subsumption of speech acts serving illocutionary aims under the conditions of success-oriented action.[143]

According to Habermas, a use of language B that is subsumed under a use of language A, *that is, subordinated* to it, is the *original* use of language, and thus the other is *parasitic*. (Unless Habermas would say: "What's sauce for the goose is not yet sauce for the gander.")

So let us summarize Habermas's statements and, making use of Leibniz' law of identity, draw the logical conclusions:

"Normally", Habermas writes, contexts of communicative action depend on subordinating acts of reaching understanding indirectly, that is, strategic actions, to their goals. For if it were not possible for the speaker to give "the hearer something to understand which he cannot (yet) directly communicate", then the very state of affairs in which "interpretations…overlap sufficiently for the purpose of coordinating actions" could not arise, that is, the state in which reaching understanding directly, and thus a communicative use of language, is first possible. Thus the use of language oriented towards reaching understanding is not an original use of language but rather the subsumption of speech acts that serve perlocutionary aims under the conditions of action oriented towards reaching understanding.

This is "normally" so for the relation between strategic use of language and the use of language oriented towards reaching understanding. Now, not all means of "achieving understanding", that is, of communication (*Verständigung*) (in the ordinary sense of the word, not its Habermasian, consensus-driven sense) are linguistic in nature. One can also communicate something to another person with a facial expression. Sometimes one pulls another person's leg as a joke. In some variations of this one keeps a straight face while saying something that the hearer might register with astonishment. If one kept up the straight face, the other person might possibly never realize that it is just a joke—and so the desired effect, laughter let us say, would not come about. Thus, one eventually starts to grin, and with this comes the other's relieved laughter. However, the converse would not be considered a good idea: to hop around scratching oneself like an ape with a silly grin when one intends to say something serious. *That* an assertion is meant seriously has to be *communicated* by the appropriate facial expression—in this case a relatively normal one. One might think that I could of course just directly state that I mean the assertion seriously. I could say this, but it would not be understood this way if I said it with a broad grin and eyebrows moving up and down in Groucho Marx style. In this case one would tend to see my speech act as an ironic reference to the simple-mindedness of certain philosophers of language. In written language this dependence on the means of indirect, non-linguistic communication is also ubiquitous. There is, after all, a reason why business correspondence is not typed on pages that were ripped out of a four-colour Donald Duck comic; if it were it would hardly be taken seriously, but rather summarily thrown into the waste-paper basket. In short, these sorts of non-linguistic means of communication first generate the "seriousness value" (serious/unserious) with which a speaker wishes his or her speech act to be understood. This is not just a general rule, but is *always* the case: *the "consequence-oriented achievement of understanding", that is, consequence-oriented communication, is the original mode of communication, to which the communicative use of language in the Habermasian sense relates parasitically.*

1.3.2.2.2.2. The Argument from the Theory of Meaning Habermas's following thesis could be interpreted as an additional argument for the primacy of action oriented towards reaching understanding:

Reaching understanding is the inherent telos of human speech.[144]

By "reaching understanding", as we have seen, Habermas means not just the understanding of meaning but the reaching of a consensus.

In the meantime Habermas has conceded, particularly in light of speech acts specific to quarrels, such as insults, that:

Indeed, the assumption that linguistic communication aims fundamentally at agreement seems completely counterintuitive...[145]

Yet the emphasis here is on "seems". For while Habermas's revisions concede that perlocutions at the level of action do not aim at consensus, at another level, a higher and ultimate level as it were, consensus still remains the standard of success even for perlocutions, and thus Habermas continues to adhere to his "pragmatic theory of meaning", if in revised form, as we will see. This theory presents us with the same connection between justification and discourse that we have already encountered and that I refuted. Now, however, the connection is not made primarily in terms of the *performance* of a speech act, but in terms of *understanding*. Habermas writes:

> Previously, I had presumed that the acceptability of speech acts depends on the knowledge of reasons that (a) justify an illocutionary success and (b) can rationally motivate an agreement between speaker and hearer. I now have to revise this formulation in view of my differentiation within the concept of reaching understanding, and in view of the status of speech acts such as insults and threats.
>
> ad a) To understand a speech act is to know the conditions for the illocutionary or perlocutionary success that the speaker can achieve with it (with this, we take account of perlocutions whose success, however, presupposes comprehension of the illocutionary act employed in a given case.
>
> ad b) One knows the conditions for illocutionary or perlocutionary success of a speech act when one knows the kinds of actor-independent or actor-relative reasons with which the speaker could vindicate her validity claim discursively....
>
> Even perlocutions, which ride on the backs of illocutionary acts, can be criticized from the point of view of the truth of the assumptions implied in a given case (about conditions for context-dependent perlocutionary effects).[146]

We have already seen that perlocutions by no means assume an understanding of the particular illocutionary act used.[147] Habermas himself concedes a few sentences later that "perlocutions *as such* do not represent illocutionary acts." This "as such" presumably means "as perlocutions". But since he italicized "as such", he must think that there are no perlocutions that exist only as such, that is, as perlocutions, but rather that they also exist as—as what, really? As *illocutions*, perhaps? Since otherwise for Habermas illocutionary acts are by definition not perlocutions, it would seem that the non-goal-like goals are not the only sign of conceptual contradictions in Habermas's argumentation for his theory.

Let us look closer at Habermas's pragmatic theory of meaning. We can see that agreement is given a central role in the original point (b). Habermas's statements in "ad b)" represent not so much a retreat from this as its *Aufhebung*. Nonetheless, at this level there can no longer be any claim of primacy of the use of language oriented towards reaching understanding, since the conditions of perlocutionary success might be recognized in discourse, but they do not *lie in* or *refer* to discourse. In fact, as Habermas himself knows,[148] a speaker can also achieve perlocutionary success even if he or she himself or herself is unaware of any reasons with which he or she could discursively vindicate his or her "claim" that the perlocution will be successful.

Additionally, Habermas's pragmatic theory of meaning is false.[149]

Let us assume that I am playing the quiz-game "Guess the Speech Act" with Habermas. For this purpose I tell Habermas what kind of reasons a speaker could use to discursively vindicate the validity claims for a speech act S. Habermas now has the task of guessing the speech act. And now the clue: the kind of reasons includes both moral reasons and reasons based on existing conventions. The candidate is to volunteer an answer when he has found out what the speech act is.

The moral should be clear. If the type of reasons is too general, then one can use them to vindicate practically any speech act, and thus they no longer distinguish one speech act from another.

If, on the other hand, the type is too specific, then it will turn out that the speaker can also understand a speech act without knowing the kind of reasons with which one could vindicate or "redeem" the validity claims of the speech act discursively. If a secretary is of the opinion that the validity claim of the speech act uttered by his or her boss, "Please bring me a coffee", can be discursively vindicated only with reasons referring to the clauses of his or her employment contract, but then, in discourse, unfortunately comes round to the opinion (which he or she would have rejected previous to the discourse) that his or her boss is entitled to such a demand based solely on his status as boss and general custom, this does not in any way mean that he or she had previously not understood the speech act. He or she had understood the speech act very well—and had rejected it for precisely this reason—even when he or she did *not* know or even suspect that his or her boss would be able to discursively vindicate his or her validity claim with arguments concerning the relation between the roles of boss and secretary. How is one supposed to know precisely, *previous* to discourse, that which one recognizes only in or *after* discourse? If we could know this so precisely beforehand, then discourse would be superfluous and not as epistemically significant an institution as Habermas constantly claims.

Thus Habermas is caught in an irreparable dilemma: knowledge of the general kind of reasons that could vindicate the validity claims of a speech act is not sufficient to understand the speech act. (This is indeed so evident that Habermas's vague talk of "kinds of reasons" can hardly be accorded the status of a *theory*.) And knowledge of some more specific kind of reasons that could vindicate the speech act is not necessary.

Moreover, this knowledge of the more specific kind of reasons is also not sufficient. Not even knowledge of the *exact* reasons is sufficient. The following example should make this clear:

Let us suppose that I am on the telephone with the ticket office of a theatre and would like to know whether any tickets are still available for today's show. I could say: "I would like to know if there are still tickets for this evening." This is an expressive utterance, the utterance of a wish. I could also say: "Are there still tickets for this evening?" That is a question; whereas "Please tell me if there are still tickets for this evening" is a mixture of request and imperative. Thus we have three different speech acts here; and yet there is absolutely no reason to suppose that the reasons "with which the speaker could vindicate her validity claim discursively" should vary between them. In fact we can plausibly assume that the reasons are identical (e.g. "I spoke politely, and the people in the ticket office are there to provide information"). Thus it appears that one has not yet understood a speech act even if one knows the *exact* reasons with which the speaker could discursively vindicate his or her validity claims, since these reasons can be used to vindicate the validity claims of *diverse* speech acts.

Moreover, Habermas makes the rather strong claim that understanding a speech act *means* knowing the conditions of its success—that is, according to Habermas, the kind of reasons with which the speaker can vindicate his or her validity claims. In other words, for Habermas, understanding a speech act *consists* in this knowledge. We have already seen that Habermas's pragmatic "theory" of meaning leads to an inescapable dilemma (or, rather, trilemma). Now it has also led us into an inescapable circle. This circle becomes clear if we ask how exactly the speaker is supposed to arrive at this knowledge of the reasons that could vindicate the validity claims of the speech act, the knowledge that is allegedly necessary for its understanding. Let us suppose that someone says to me: "Close the window!" If this speech act is a command, then the reasons that could vindicate its validity claims discursively are quite different than in the case where it is merely a request. (The reasons do in fact vary between requests and commands. However, they did not vary between the speech acts in my theatre example.) In the first case, I would of course want to know the reasons that could bring the other person to assume he is in a position to command me at all. So: how am I supposed to understand the speech act? This is no easy matter, since this understanding has to include the knowledge of *what sort of speech act it is*—command or request (or joke, lyrical rendition, philosophical example, etc.). Yet to know what sort of speech act it is, I have to know, according to Habermas, with which reasons the speaker could discursively vindicate the validity claims tied to the speech act. But what these reasons are depends on what kind of speech act it is. To know that, I would have to know the reasons with which the speaker…etc. Habermas's pragmatic "theory" of meaning entails the impossibility of understanding speech acts. Yet since, as we know, it is most certainly possible to understand speech acts, we can infer backwards to the falsity of Habermas's "theory".

1.3.2.2.2.3. The Argument from the Stronger "Implications of Rationality" and "Ontological Presuppositions" of Communicative Action Habermas mounts a third argument to demonstrate the superior rationality of communicative action over strategic action. In this argument, communicative action has not just the whole world behind it; it has three worlds behind it. But we had best let Habermas explain this himself:

At first glance, only the teleological concept of action seems to open up an aspect of the rationality of action.…That this appearance is deceiving becomes evident when we represent to ourselves the "ontological"—in the broad sense—presuppositions that are, as a matter of conceptual necessity, connected with these models of action. In the sequence teleological, normative, dramaturgical, the presuppositions not only become increasingly complex; they reveal at the same time stronger and stronger implications of rationality.

(a) The concept of teleological action presupposes relations between an actor and a world of existing states of affairs.…

With regard to ontological presuppositions, we can classify *teleological* action as a concept that presupposes *one* world, namely the objective world. The same holds for the concept of *strategic action*.[150]

I will skip over normative and dramaturgical action and come to the essential point:

Only the communicative model of action presupposes language as a medium of uncurtailed communication whereby speakers and hearers, out of the context of their preinterpreted lifeworld, refer simultaneously to things in the objective, social, and subjective worlds in order to negotiate common definitions of the situation.[151]

However, the brazen assumption "the more worlds, the more rationality" (under the principle "quantity becomes quality") is anything but self-evident; hence it would need to be actually substantiated by an analysis of language use. This also holds for the other points Habermas introduces with the claim that they imply a higher rationality of communicative action. Why do they imply a higher *rationality*? Habermas does not give us any arguments for this of any sort. His thesis that those bizarre "ontological presuppositions" he ascribes to communicative action imply a greater rationality lacks all justification whatsoever. And as shown by the conceptual explications I offered against the Habermasian postulates and shored up with illustrative examples, the thesis is also false.

Aside from their irrelevance, those characteristics and structures that Habermas introduces as the alleged expression of a superior, "uncurtailed" rationality of communicative action are either de facto absent from communicative action or else have an equal or greater presence in strategic action. And wherever we do see Habermas ascribe a characteristic to communicative action that, coincidentally, turns out to be relevant to the question of rationality, its relevance is purely negative—it shows a want of reflectivity in communicative action.

Let us take a closer look at all this. First, as to the "worlds": I have already shown that Habermas does not wish this talk of three worlds to be understood metaphorically as various regions within *the one world*; he means it literally.[152] I cannot see anything rational about this multiple ontomania. Models of action that presuppose three times as many worlds as there are do not inspire particular confidence.

But let us be charitable and act as if these world concepts were meant metaphorically. What should we think of Habermas's claim that the concept of strategic action "presupposes *one* world, namely the objective world"? Not so much; particularly as Habermas follows just this claim with the words:

Here we start with [*gehen aus von*] at least two goal-directed acting subjects who achieve their ends by way of an orientation to, and influence on, the decisions of other actors.[153]

Goals and ends are subjective. Thus Habermas's own definition of the concept of "strategic action" presupposes more than just *one world*. And since Habermas also characterizes strategic action as "social action",[154] it would be interesting to know how an action could succeed in being a social action without any connection to the social world.[155]

At this point one could try to locate the "one-sidedness" of strategic action not in the *object* of reference but in the *type* of relation. Thus one might claim that strategic action admittedly relates to all three worlds, but *only in an objectifying manner*. We have already seen that Habermas occasionally argues in a similar vein—just as we have seen, with confirmation from Apel, that these arguments are false.[156]

Furthermore, Habermas's aversion to objectifications, at least in the context of his theory of rationality, is rather off-putting. It would hardly be a sign of unrivalled rationality to view one's goals exclusively in an expressive attitude rather than occasionally reconsidering them and reviewing their appropriateness—and this is at least *one* meaning of "objectify". Moreover, it is by no means irrational or immoral to make humans the object of research.

This also holds even if we grant that Habermas has a concept of objectification that is stronger than the Kantian one (whereby Apel's criticism was aimed at precisely this stronger conception). Then objectification would not mean just making something an epistemic object, but also that in cognizing subjects we abstract from their subjective side. Habermas writes:

On the level of scientific discourse, however, there is a tendency to delimit the object domains of, for example, psychology or sociology, by neglecting their hermeneutic dimensions, in such a way that the components of the subjective or the social world are naturalistically assimilated to physical entities or to observable behavior. In each case they are made into components of the objective world, inherently accessible only in the objectivating attitude; that is, they are forced into the basic conceptual framework of physicalism or behaviorism. As opposed to this naturalistic reduction, the point here is only to defend non-objectivistic approaches in psychology and the social sciences.[157]

The words "forced" and "reduction" show that Habermas has little regard for this kind of objectification. Yet it should be noted that the behavioural therapy based on Skinner's behaviouristic theory of learning has proven significantly more effective than Freud's hermeneutic method. If one wishes to rid oneself of a phobia and if one were able to accomplish this by adopting a sufficiently objectifying attitude to the phobia—that is, not interpreting it hermeneutically as a symbolic structure for eight years or more, but rather treating it as a physiological malfunction and erasing it chemically with an injection—why should one not do this? This situation calls for a simple rational weighing of goals, means and side-effects against each other. It might turn out, then, that the objectifying attitude towards the social or subjective world is the rational one in a certain situation. Aside from all this, Habermas's theory of communicative action—despite its strange dabbling in system theory—seems to me to be a hermeneutic reduction. There are good reasons to prefer naturalistic "reductions"—which, moreover, are seldom reductions, but rather entirely legitimate viewpoints, whose value can be measured by their results—to fruitless hermeneutic reductions.

Now, according to Habermas there is yet another type of "world relation", namely, the relation *via validity claims*. Habermas thinks that it is *only* in communicative action—or, more precisely, in communicative speech acts—that the *three* validity claims of sincerity, truth and normative rightness are all raised.

With this model of action we are supposing that participants in interaction can now mobilize the rationality potential—which according to our previous analysis resides in the actor's three relations to the world—expressly for the cooperatively pursued goal of reaching understanding. If we leave to one side the wellformedness of the symbolic expressions employed, an actor who is oriented to understanding in this sense must raise at least three validity claims with his utterance, namely:

1. That the statement made is true (or that the existential presuppositions of the propositional content mentioned are in fact satisfied);

2. That the speech act is right with respect to the existing normative context (or that the normative context that it is supposed to satisfy is itself legitimate); and

3. That the manifest intention of the speaker is meant as it is expressed.[158]

He even declares the raising of these validity claims constitutive of communicative action:

Only those speech acts with which speakers connect criticizable validity claims are constitutive of communicative action.[159]

And elsewhere he writes:

Announcements and imperatives do not aim at agreement (in the strict sense). Nonetheless, they move within the horizon of a mutual understanding based on validity claims and thus still within the domain of communicative rationality.[160]

In light of how much value Habermas places on the following claim:

But communicative action designates a type of interaction that is *coordinated through* speech acts and does *not coincide with* them,[161]

one might wonder why communicative action is suddenly *constituted* by those speech acts connected with criticizable validity claims, thus seeming to in fact coincide with them. This does not fit very well with Habermas's other definitions of communicative action. But maybe all he means here is that communicative action is precisely that action that is *coordinated* by such speech acts. Yet, as I have already shown, this thesis also does not very well fit the definition of communicative action as action wherein the participants harmonize their plans of action; one might note that utterances such as "Turn on the gas" or "Smash that Jew's skull in" or a command to perpetrate genocide are imperatives and commands, too, and as such, according to Habermas, operate "within the domain of communicative rationality". Though I have shown that genocide could also be carried out in agreement with all participants, the Holocaust is not one example of this. Yet if it is no longer decisive that the participants *assent* (in the sense of free and unforced agreement) to the speech acts with which the actions are coordinated, but only that these speech acts *raise* the *claim* to sincerity, rightness and truth, then the Holocaust counts as an example of communicative action. This is so even if this claim is made without reservation, i.e., sincerely, which Habermas does not even call for here. And if lack of reservation is made a condition, then still a great number of the crimes committed in the Holocaust count as communicative action.

Let us now bring these parenthetical remarks about Habermas's definitional efforts and the ensuing consequences for an allegedly superior morality of communicative action to a close and return to our examination of the "implications of rationality". Now, even if it were *only* communicative action that raises all three validity claims, this does not make communicative action more rational. I have already shown that an action such as the reaching towards a light-switch when alone does not need to be bound up with any "claims" (or even to be able to be bound to these claims) to be rational.

Moreover, *all* actions, including perlocutionary speech acts, are criticizable under *all* possible aspects.[162] Anyone who thinks otherwise should name me a speech act, and I will be happy to criticize it under all possible aspects (or at least under the three aspects favoured by Habermas).

Habermas himself even concedes that threats, for example, can be "challenged…from the two points of view of the lack of truthfulness of the declaration of intention and the lack of truth of the existential presupposition". He illustrates this with the following examples:

You don't really mean what you are saying.

and

You don't have anything you can use against me.[163]

Now in my opinion it is not too hard to see that one could also say: it is immoral of you to threaten me. Interestingly, Habermas does not see this. He would rather dispute the "context" than the moral rightness.

I would like to quote his explanations of this in their entirety, since apart from illustrating the point at issue they also provide an occasion to clear up two other typical terminological confusions of universal pragmatics. Habermas writes:

In addition, the context presupposed by the speaker, within which (4) first becomes a threat for a specific addressee, can also be contested:

(4''') You can't threaten me with that—he has already known it for a long time.

In such a case the speech act is not strictly speaking *contested*; rather it is simply explained why the intended effect will not occur and why the perlocution remains *ineffective*. Only illocutionary acts that can be *valid* or *invalid* may be contested.

(However, perlocutions of this kind can be re-embedded in a normative context in a secondary way because, of course, the condemnation of misdemeanors in a moral or a legal sense appeals to a normative background consensus and to this extent, despite its pejorative connotation, is directed toward agreement. For this reason, such *normatively embedded* reproaches—unlike actions that do not really aim to say anything but, in saying something, aim to offend someone—can be rejected on the basis of reasons. Something similar to what holds for moral reproaches, condemnations, and so on also holds, for example, for legal threats of punishment; due to the legitimating background consensus about the norms of punishment themselves, the threatened punishment is regarded as a consequence of a legal system for which agreement is presupposed.)[164]

I fully concede that it is not the speech act that is contested in the case of a threat. Speech acts, like all other *actions*, cannot be contested as a matter of principle. We do not say "I contest your question" or "I contest your request" or "I contest your greeting." Whoever talks this way is no *competent* speaker. Although we do say "I would contest that" in response to another's point and in this way "contest an assertion", this is due to the ambiguity of the word "assertion". For this word means—primarily, it seems to me—the *proposition asserted*. When we are asked "What did he say?", we say: "He said *that*…", thus describing a proposition, not an action. The same holds for questions, incidentally; "What was his question?", "His question was *whether...*"—also a proposition. *Asking* a question is a speech act, *giving* a promise is a speech act, *making* an assertion is a speech act—promises, questions and assertions, however, are *not* speech acts, but rather propositions in certain roles. Of course, for the sake of brevity we could *call* the speech act with which a question is posed "question" rather than "asking a question", as I have done here. But then, of course—as Habermas very much intends—we are speaking of acts; and these cannot be *contested* at all.

Moreover, we do not say "Your greeting is valid." Or "Your insult is valid." Speech acts cannot be valid or invalid.[165] Habermas needs this talk of validity, however, to give the impression that everything coheres as it should in his concept of communicative action. In fact, he imposes upon the concepts of truth, sincerity and normative rightness a misused abstraction and then calls this "integration".

However, the decisive point is that a threat does not have to be a normatively "embedded" threat to be criticized (not "contested") with reasons. Rather, the statement: "Your repugnant threat does not even have the veneer of a legitimate appeal to a background consensus and is a pure, undisguised act of violence" *is* already a justified criticism of a threat under the aspect of normative rightness. And the statement "Your speech act was not meant to say anything of substance, you just wanted to insult me" is already a justified criticism of a speech act. Thus Habermas's claims are false, and we can conclude that, just like communicative speech acts, strategic speech acts can be criticized under all three aspects.

To be sure, Habermas claims that the criticizability of an utterance depends on the claims it raises; thus we might also suppose him to think that an utterance that can be criticized under the aspect of rightness must necessarily raise a rightness *claim*. In a comparison of assertions and "goal-directed interventions" he writes: "In both cases the critic refers to claims..."[166] Yet we have seen that speech acts do not necessarily need to raise any claims in order to be criticizable; the two things have nothing to do with each other (and the three claims under discussion here have for their part nothing essentially to do with rationality). Incidentally, here we see another failed attempt on Habermas's part to produce an "internal relation". (And Habermas does after all suggest that the rationality-enhancing "complexity" of communicative action unfolds or manifests the most diverse sorts of "internal relations".[167])

On the one hand, this result is unfortunate for Habermas's "integrative" ambitions. On the other hand, one might say: okay, strategic action may be criticizable under precisely the same three aspects as communicative action, but it does not raise all three *claims*.

In fact strategic speech acts do not *necessarily* raise all three claims. And purposively rational speech acts—that is, rational strategic speech acts—raise these claims only when it is reasonable to do so, whereas communicative action raises these claims even when it is not reasonable. However, it is also evident that one *can* raise all three claims with an insult, and typically one does—naturally without aiming at agreement. If I call someone a "pig", then in the case that the appropriateness for this speech act is called into question by a third party I can explicitly *claim* to be entitled to the speech act. This does not prevent me from at the same time saying to the target of my insult, "I don't care one bit whether you or anyone else agree that I was entitled to this insult, you pig" (and this relates back to the "link to argumentative discourse" under a different aspect). One can obviously raise a claim without having to place any particular value on reaching agreement. This also holds for the claim of sincerity. In the case of *this* claim—in contrast to the claim to rightness—one would certainly want it to be affirmed by the *insulted person*, and accordingly one would insist on this and explicitly claim that one sincerely means it; but whether this claim is recognized by a third party could be a matter of indifference. We can of course also raise truth claims with insults, for example, as concerns their existential presuppositions, as Habermas himself concedes.

Incidentally, it is not at all the case, as Habermas thinks it is, that one can raise truth claims only with perlocutions in so far as the existential presuppositions of the speech act are concerned; one could also raise a truth claim as to the propositional content of the perlocution. It is quite easy to make this point by borrowing the argument Habermas uses to demonstrate "cognitive claims". We might recall:

On the contrary, our practices of criticizing immoral actions and of disputing moral questions by appealing to reasons suggest rather that we associate a cognitive claim with moral judgments.[168]

Now, our practices (and here by "our" I do not mean to include those who speak only in an elaborate code) of disputing with reasons about questions such as, for example, whether someone is a "pig" ("Why am *I* a pig? *You* started this fight!") speaks to the fact that we connect a cognitive claim to insults of this type. And since this sort of discussion is not concerned with the question of whether a norm is right, but rather with the question of whether a certain property (that of being a "pig") holds for a certain object, we are dealing here with a claim to truth. Moreover, this shows, contrary to Habermas's belief, that truth claims are by no means necessarily directed at "discursive vindication" or agreement; and this is not restricted to those truth claims raised with insults.

We can conclude that all three validity claims can be raised with strategic action as they can with communicative action. Unlike in the case of communicative action, which according to Habermas raises *exactly* three validity claims, we can raise *additional* claims with strategic actions if we so choose; for example, the claim to a high aesthetic quality of the speech act or the claim to earn an entry in the Guinness Book of World Records for the loudest volume. If it seems strategically reasonable to an agent acting strategically to raise these claims, then she raises them. And five validity claims are, quite simply, *more* than three.

Thus strategic action can relate to at least as many regions of the world in at least as many ways with at least as many validity claims as communicative action.

Moving now from relations to the world to relations to language, we will also find that strategic action can take at least as many *functions of language* into consideration as communicative action does. Habermas thinks otherwise:

The one-sidedness of the first three concepts of language can be seen in the fact that the corresponding types of communication singled out by them prove to be limit cases of communicative action: *first*, the indirect communication of those who have only the realization of their own end in view; *second*, the consensual action of those who simply actualize an already existing normative agreement; and *third*, presentation of self in relation to an audience. In each case only one function of language is thematized: the release of perlocutionary effects, the establishment of interpersonal relations, and the expression of subjective experiences. By contrast, the communicative model of action...takes all the functions of language equally into consideration.[169]

As we know, insincere speech acts, like perlocutions, are disallowed in the use of language oriented towards reaching understanding. However, language can also serve the function of misleading, insulting, persuading, singing to earn money, using speech-sensitive computer programmes and alarm clocks, etc. Strategic action can make use of all of these options; communicative action cannot. Moreover, strategic action does not in any way exclude the use of language to reach understanding, since this use can also be strategically rational. In fact, as we have seen, communicative action *is* a form of strategic action—at least if we read Habermas's definition of "communicative action" in a way that allows for the very existence of the definiendum. In short, it is not strategic action where the one-sidedness is to be found.

After this counting up of worlds, world relations and functions of language, Habermas continues his rebuke of strategic action and praise for communicative action with the claim that the former is not reflective enough:

For the communicative model of action, language is relevant only from the pragmatic viewpoint that speakers, in employing sentences with an orientation to reaching understanding, take up relations to the world, not only directly as in teleological, normatively regulated, or dramaturgical action, but in a reflective way. Speakers integrate the three formal world-concepts, which appear in the other models of action either singly or in pairs, into a system and presuppose this system in common as a framework of interpretations within which they can reach an understanding. They no longer relate *straightaway* to something in the objective, social, or subjective worlds; instead they relativize their utterances against the possibility that their validity will be contested by other actors.[170]

The word "reflective" can be read in the sense of "reflexive" or in the sense of "well-considered". (However, it cannot be used, as Habermas seems to think, as the opposite of "direct". The opposite of "reflective" is "unreflective".) Habermas would not dispute the fact that strategic action is reflective (at least purposively rational strategic action); in fact he himself says that the agent acting strategically reckons. So Habermas must mean the word in the sense of "reflexive". What does this reflexivity consist in? In the way that agents take up their relations to the world. However, there is nothing particularly reflexive in the mere integration of formal concepts of worlds per se. Thus we should rather look for this reflexivity in the agents' relativizing "their utterances against the possibility that their validity will be contested by other actors". Habermas continues:

Reaching an understanding functions as a mechanism for coordinating actions only through the participants in interaction coming to an agreement concerning the claimed *validity* of their utterances, that is, through intersubjectively recognizing the *validity claims* they reciprocally raise.[171]

If I understand this right, this is the reflexivity in question: someone says something and then relates back to it, mediated by criticism or agreement, either in revising it, I suppose, to increase the likelihood of consent, or else, in so far as agreement has already been achieved, checking off his speech act as "accepted". And the indirectness Habermas speaks of comes into play when action is made dependent on this agreement. As we know, agents acting communicatively pursue

their individual goals under the condition that they can harmonize their plans of action on the basis of common situation definitions.[172]

In light of such a refined system of finely tuned feedback loops in communicative action, one might anxiously ask: can strategic action really keep up?

I think so. We should not forget that we are discussing points here that Habermas treats under the moniker "implications of rationality". We can assume, then, that an indirect relation to problems is particularly rational for Habermas. I cannot share his view. If I see a car coming towards me on the wrong side of the street, it is rational for me to relate to it *directly* and swerve out of the way, rather than reaching for my mobile and discussing the problem with the communicative community. Moreover, a model of action that declares language to be relevant *only* under the aspect of taking up "relations to the world" *in orientation towards reaching understanding,* turns a blind eye to all other aspects and neglects to ask whether another use of language might not be appropriate in a certain situation strikes me as anything but reflective and reflexive (if these terms are interpreted in a way that is somewhat more relevant to a theory of rationality). It seems, in fact, rather preoccupied and close-minded. Furthermore, agents acting strategically also relativize their actions—that is, against their effectiveness. They do not conceive of their actions as absolute or unconditional but rather are ready to learn from failures in order to perform other, more promising actions. And finally, agents acting strategically can of course also act indirectly when necessary. Agents acting communicatively do this even when it is foolish.

Thus, Habermas's thesis that the "presuppositions" of communicative action, including "ontological" presuppositions and above all linguistic ones, present stronger "implications of rationality" than the presuppositions of strategic action is false. Incidentally, our critique of this thesis and the arguments deployed against it also refute the claim that communicative action involves a higher degree of *complexity* than strategic action (although of course a higher degree of complexity does not necessarily imply a higher rationality).

1.3.3. Integration or Confusion?

Aside from the issue of *higher* complexity, a further question arises. Does Habermas succeed *at all* in bringing the various strands of his theory of language and speech acts together into one *complex,* unified under the concept of communicative action? Or does he leave us with a mere collection of loose ends? After all, Habermas sees his concept of communicative rationality as connecting to "ancient conceptions of *logos*",[173] and both language and the idea of a harmonious synthesis are central to the concept of logos. Moreover, Habermas explicitly ascribes an "integrative role"[174] to his communicative rationality—here under the heading of "discourse rationality".[175]

So: do Habermas's considerations of speech act theory cohere harmoniously?

Let us look at how Habermas tries to tie these strands together. I have already quoted this explanation of his:

Reaching an understanding functions as a mechanism for coordinating actions only through the participants in interaction coming to an agreement concerning the claimed *validity* of their utterances, that is, through intersubjectively recognizing the *validity claims* they reciprocally raise.[176]

And as he explains in greater detail:

Thus the speaker claims truth for statements or existential presuppositions, rightness for legitimately regulated actions and their normative context, and truthfulness or sincerity for the manifestation of subjective experiences. We can easily recognize therein the three relations of actor to world presupposed *by the social scientist* in the previously analysed concepts of action; but in the concept of communicative action they are ascribed to the perspectives of *the speakers and hearers themselves*. It is the actors themselves who seek consensus and measure it against truth, rightness, and sincerity, that is, against the "fit" or "misfit" between the speech act, on the one hand, and the three worlds to which the actor takes up relations with his utterance, on the other.[177]

First of all, as we already discussed, utterances cannot be valid. Thus it would be hard to come to an agreement about the validity of utterances. These sorts of attempt would make no sense. Someone might object here that this is merely a terminological problem; one could define the term "validity" such that it pertains to speech acts that measure up to the three validity claims favoured by Habermas. One could do this, of course; but since it flies in the face of our use of language and is hence ideally suited to sow confusion, it should be avoided. However, the decisive point is this: in order to capture what Habermas means by validity, our philosopher of language *first has to introduce* just such a concept. He does not, by any stretch of the imagination, take it from our "communicative practice of everyday life". And the fact that there is no concept in our communicative practice of everyday life for the phenomenon that Habermas wishes to term "validity" is, in my view, a clear indication that this phenomenon does not play any particularly significant role for competent speakers in the communicative practice of everyday life. Most likely it is not even registered. In other words, contrary to his claim, Habermas's arguments on this point have relatively little to do with the communicative practice of everyday life.

This suspicion is confirmed if we do what Habermas would rather avoid, namely, look at suitable examples.

A father says to his son: "Lie over my knee, I'm going to spank you!" It is quite evident that the son can recognize the sincerity, legitimacy and the truth of the existential presuppositions of this speech act without being in agreement with the father's request. We can easily imagine the father adding further speech acts to this and asking: "Are you in agreement with this, my son?" For the son's sake we would hope that he says "No" at this point. However, this particular son is, unfortunately, "without reservations", as Habermas calls it, that is, honest to the point of simple-mindedness, and the father is a devout reader of the "Theory of Communicative Action". So the father continues, asking:

"Do you not believe that my demand is *legitimate*?"

Because of how he has been socialized, the son answers:

"Of course, as my father you are entitled to make that sort of demand."
"Do you not believe that my demand and its utterance were *sincere*?"
"Quite the contrary. Unfortunately, it was quite certainly sincere."
"Do you doubt the *existential presuppositions* of the speech act?"
"Of course not, I know that you have a knee and I have a backside."

"Fine, then", says the father, "since there is a consensus as to the truth, rightness and sincerity of the speech act, you *are* in agreement. How nice that we could clear this up in our unreserved discourse." And then he grabs hold of the son, lays him over his knee and starts spanking him.

This is *agreement* according to the theory of communicative action—which also lays claim to be a *critical* theory.

An example similar to the demand to accept a beating can be constructed with declarations of war—and I will leave it to the reader to envision this in detail. And any women who receives marriage proposals from a universal-pragmatic philosopher should be counselled to think it over several times before she unreservedly recognizes its truth, sincerity and legitimacy; otherwise there might be a misunderstanding.

It should be clear enough by now that a consensus about the validity claims of *speech acts* is not sufficient for an agreement about the *matter* addressed by speech acts.

The following example shows that such a consensus is also not necessary. Frank asks Julie if he should call the theatre and reserve two tickets for the play. She responds: "First of all, you don't care whether I say yes or no. You're just going to reserve tickets anyway, and then say that we might as well go now that we have tickets reserved. So, secondly, I find it mean and hypocritical of you to even ask. Besides, thirdly, it would be a miracle if there are still any tickets left. But it doesn't cost anything to ask. So here, call!" And with these words she hands him the local weekly with the telephone number of the theatre. In short, Julie does not recognize any single one of the validity claims of Frank's speech act (and Frank does not need to recognize any of her validity claims), yet despite this she comes to an agreement with Frank about the matter at issue in the speech act and about the coordination of their actions. Habermas's thesis:

Reaching an understanding functions as a mechanism for coordinating actions only through the participants in interaction coming to an agreement concerning the claimed *validity* of their utterances, that is, through intersubjectively recognizing the *validity claims* they reciprocally raise

is false.

With the failure of this thesis, which is the core of the theory of communicative action, *the entire theory collapses into itself.* Reaching an understanding [*Verständigung*], which Habermas considers "to be a process of reaching agreement [*Einigung*] among speaking and acting subjects",[178] functions flawlessly without any agreement about the validity of speech acts.

Moreover, it functions even without *illocutionary* acts—in Habermas's sense of the term. This entirely contradicts Habermas's assumption; as he writes:

What we mean by reaching understanding [and the understanding-oriented attitude] has to be clarified *solely* in connection with illocutionary acts.[179]

We have seen earlier[180] and again just now that this has very little to do with reality. Yet Habermas needs to bring illocutionary acts and goals together with communicative action. So he writes:

Thus I count as communicative action those linguistically mediated interactions in which all participants pursue illocutionary aims, and *only* illocutionary aims.[181]

We have already noted that Habermas himself was forced to retract this "and *only*".[182] Thus the following reformulation suggests itself:

Linguistically mediated interactions that are coordinated by all participants solely through the pursuit of illocutionary (and not perlocutionary) aims constitute communicative action.

As mentioned, this is Habermas's authoritative definition, whereas his "popular" definition, as we might call it, mentions only the condition "that participants carry out their plans cooperatively in an action situation defined in common".[183] Communicative action in its true, strict sense does not exist. The coordination of action through illocutionary acts in the way Habermas describes is impossible. Moreover, it is not even true that one necessarily pursues illocutionary aims in acting cooperatively—no matter how the "linguistic mechanism of coordinating action" might function. The illocutionary aim is simply that the speech act be understood and its validity claims recognized (which, as Habermas explicitly states, does *not* hold for imperatives and announcements, *even though* they are still supposed to operate "within the domain of communicative rationality"). Thus, when a speaker pursues illocutionary goals with an assertion, she has to want the assertion to be (rationally) accepted as true. But why should someone want this in communicative action, understood as action concerned with the cooperative coordination of action—especially when, as we saw, illocutionary successes are by no means necessary for this? Let us consider the following situation: I call a friend of mine and say: "I just looked in the weekly paper, the concert we wanted to go to doesn't happen until next week." "No, no, I saw that too, and I asked the organizers. The concert is tonight, it's a misprint in the paper." "Oh, thank God." My assertion that the concert happens a week later was rejected, but not to my dismay, clearly. It is simply incorrect to claim here that I had performed this speech act with the aim of it being accepted. Of course I wanted it to be accepted as true *if* my friend were not better informed. However, this is a *different* aim than the one Habermas terms *illocutionary*. Moreover, I certainly wanted my assertion to be *rejected* in the case where she *did* have better information. Habermas himself concedes this, since he places value on the notion that speakers in communicative action "relativize their utterances against the possibility that their validity will be contested by other actors".[184] To put it succinctly, *no* illocutionary aims are pursued in communicative action, understood as action in which action plans are coordinated cooperatively.

They are not usually pursued outside of communicative action either. Even when, in non-communicative action, I have an interest in the other person accepting a statement as true—as in the case of lying, for example—it does not have to matter to me at all whether this acceptance is *rational*. In general we can say that Habermas's extremely unorthodox—not to say outlandish—definition of illocutionary acts has the result that most examples of those types of speech act that would normally be considered illocutionary, such as questions, assertions, promises, declarations of love and requests, are *no longer* illocutionary acts. If I ask someone what time it is, I do not care if the person tells me the time *rationally* or because, through some irrational mental processes, he considers himself the god Chronos. I am interested in the time, not in the mental processes of the other person. And if I were asking not for the sake of learning what time it is but as a tactic to approach the other person, then I might be quite delighted if the answer was not given rationally but rather, to use Weber's terms, affectively. Also, the everyday use of the other speech acts listed—which Habermas supposedly wishes to "reconstruct"—are by no means directed towards rational acceptance of the speech act. *Acceptance*, whether rational or not, is entirely sufficient, and often we do not even aim for this, but just want to be understood.

Dietmar Köveker claims that Habermas has drawn the "consistent conclusion"[185] from "the" theory of speech acts and from the difficulties of treating perlocutions with this argument: "Acts of this kind—acts that have become independent as perlocutionary acts—*are not illocutionary acts at all*, for they are not aimed at the rationally motivated position of an addressee."[186] To this we can respond that neither is it consistent, nor does it have anything to do with "the" theory of speech acts, but rather only with Habermas's distorted version of the theory. The conclusion is not consistent because, while one is not normally aiming at a rationally motivated position with a threat such as "Your money or your life!", one *can* be. Someone who intends to prove this could confront a subject with this threat, "Your money or your life!", while directing a rationality detector at the subject in order to document the results, with the precise intention of moving the subject to *rationally* give up his money. And of course it is in no way irrational—which, incidentally, Apel points out in response to Habermas[187]—to prefer to give up one's money upon being threatened with a drawn weapon rather than losing one's life. So this threat would then count as an illocutionary act. And Habermas's "theory" of speech acts is distorted because with assertions, promises, requests and other speech acts that are normally considered illocutionary we typically do *not* just aim at rationally motivated positions, but rather at quite different things. Accordingly, for Habermas speech acts such as requests, assertions, questions, etc. would no longer be illocutionary acts per se—rather, only a few *examples* of these types of speech acts would count as illocutionary acts. Thus Habermas's speech act theory is not even capable of correctly identifying its own object—the speech act.

To summarize the results of the first chapter:

The project of demarcating a so-called communicative rationality from purposive rationality had already proven to be implausible in its basic approach, and this has been entirely confirmed upon examination of the details of this project. The so-called speech acts oriented towards reaching understanding can be traced back to success-oriented actions, communicative action can be traced back to strategic action, and discourse is also a goal-oriented activity. Thus discourse, communicative action and action oriented towards reaching understanding are subject to the standard of *purposive rationality*. The rules that make the *way of performing* these various actions rational are the rules of *instrumental rationality*, which is in turn a derivative of purposive rationality.

Moreover, Habermas would not have succeeded in working out a discourse theory of rationality even if he had been able to make a categorical distinction between strategic action (or success-oriented action) and communicative action (or action oriented towards reaching understanding) plausible. The rationality allegedly inherent in communicative action does *not* point to discourse, and the transition to a theory of discursive rationality is not possible. Furthermore, Habermas fails to make the primacy of communicative action over strategic action plausible. There is a primacy here, but it is the reverse of what Habermas thinks—the primacy is on the side of strategic action and thus, again, of purposive rationality. Finally, Habermas also fails to bring together his various theoretical arguments about speech acts, action and rationality into a coherent whole. It remains a mere contradictory aggregation of prop pieces; a *theory* of communicative action is nowhere to be found.

2

The Justification of Discourse Ethics

The exponents of discourse ethics build their justificatory programme for morality based on so-called communicative reason. However, as the previous chapter aimed to show, this is not a sustainable foundation.

According to Habermas, practical discourses concern the question of "whether norms of action ought to be adopted".[1] This question can be read in a number of ways: first of all in the sense of whether it is *rational* to adopt certain norms of action N. If this is the question, it should be noted that enacting norms is an action—as is settling "conflicts of action by consensual means", which Habermas also counts as an end of practical discourse.[2] However, as we saw earlier, actions are ultimately subject to the standards of purposive rationality. Thus the rationality of enacting norms simply cannot be gauged from the standard of communicative rationality, just as it cannot be held subject to standards of dental hygiene rationality or cement processing rationality.

The question quoted above could of course also be read as the question of whether adopting certain norms of action N is *moral*. In fact, Habermas says elsewhere that practical discourse relates to "a procedure for testing the validity of norms that are being proposed and hypothetically considered for adoption".[3] Here the concern is to justify, not an action, but a *thesis*, namely, that a certain norm is moral or valid. The standard for the justification of theses is neither purposive rationality nor communicative rationality but rather *epistemic* rationality. However, as we saw earlier,[4] a thesis can be epistemically justified without first having been tested and declared good in a discourse or by so-called communicative rationality.

Of course, the rationality of *action* comes into play once more in the question of whether it is rational to actually follow a moral or valid norm. Here again this falls under the jurisdiction of purposive rationality and not so-called communicative rationality.

Thus before we even start to approach the real core of the discourse-ethical programme of justifying morality, we already see that it can only misfire in relying on the concept of communicative rationality.

Here I will begin by following the structure of Habermas's "Discourse Ethics—Notes on a Program of Philosophical Justification".[5] In his "Preliminary Remarks" Habermas tries to motivate his cognitivist position generally and thus to secure the initial plausibility of his goal of justifying morality. He then comes to his actual procedure: with recourse to Apel's transcendental–pragmatic method—that is, by using the argument from performative self-contradiction—Habermas means to identify the norms of discourse always already implicitly recognized. However, in contrast to Apel he does not see them as immediately moral in nature and does not count among them the norm-justifying principles U and D. Rather, he claims that the principle U can be *derived* from these discursive norms, and from this in turn can be derived the basic principle D of discourse ethics, according to which only those norms are valid that find or could find acceptance in a practical discourse. (Habermas has never actually carried out this derivation.) And finally Habermas, who does not share Apel's thesis of the uncircumventable and untranscendable (*unhintergehbar*) nature of discourse, tries to demonstrate the practical impossibility of evading the obligations of discourse-ethical principles with his thesis of the uncircumventable nature of "the communicative practice of everyday life"—a thesis that Apel for his part does not share.

Thus, I will turn my attention first to the preliminary considerations behind Habermas's discourse ethics (2.1). Subsequently I will examine Apel's method of justification, including its claim to final justification and to the uncircumventable status of discourse (2.2). Then we will deal with Habermas's attempt to derive the principles U and D from the rules of discourse (2.3). Since this derivation is just as problematic as Apel's more direct take on the issue, the consensus- or discourse-theory of truth and validity will become relevant as a possible alternative approach to justification for discourse ethics, and thus, deviating from the course of Habermas's treatment in "Discourse Ethics—Notes on a Program of Philosophical Justification", it will be subject to closer examination here (2.4). It will also be imperative to take a closer look at the additional difficulty of how the norms of action that are justified according to principle U under idealized conditions are to be applied to *real* situations (2.5).

2.1. HABERMAS'S PRELIMINARY CONSIDERATIONS

In my introductory remarks here I once more drew attention to the fact that neither the justification of theories nor that of norms has any relation to communicative rationality or discourse. However, Habermas even claims—since, like Apel, he continually conflates justification and validity—that the conditions for the *validity* of norms and moral judgements are to be found in practical discourse. For Habermas this is not true of theoretical judgements. To take an example: the conditions of validity—that is, of the truth—of the judgement that there is no life on Jupiter are to be sought not in discourse but on Jupiter. If there is life on Jupiter, the judgement is true; otherwise it is false. How discourses are constituted, whether they exist and how validity claims are redeemed is irrelevant.

As concerns practical judgements, this is allegedly a quite different affair, and so Habermas declares it the aim of his preliminary remarks that:

It will become clear why philosophical ethics, unlike epistemology, for example, can readily assume the form of a special theory of argumentation.[6]

In his view, echoing the need for "some canon or other of induction" in theoretical discourse, an "analogous bridging principle is needed for practical discourse". Thus, it seems to him that

all studies of the logic of moral argumentation end up having to introduce a moral principle as a rule of argumentation that has a function equivalent to the principle of induction in the discourse of the empirical sciences.[7]

Leaving aside for the moment the question of this bridging principle, we can begin with a look at Habermas's argumentation for the first thesis: that philosophical ethics can "readily" assume the form of a special theory of argumentation. The argument runs as follows:

But if in the long run the social currency of a norm depends on its being accepted as valid in the group to which it is addressed and if this recognition is based in turn on the expectation that the corresponding claim to validity can be redeemed with reasons, it follows that there is a connection between the "existence" of norms and the anticipated justifiability of the corresponding "ought" statements, a connection for which there is no parallel in the ontic sphere. While there is an internal connection between the existence of states of affairs and the truth of assertoric statements, there is no inner connection between the existence of states of affairs and the *expectation*, held by a certain group of people, that such statements can be justified. This difference may also explain why, when we ask what makes valid moral judgments possible [*Bedingungen der Gültigkeit von moralischen Normen*, which also, less "transcendentally" and foremost, means the conditions *under which* moral judgments are valid], we are compelled to proceed *directly* to a logic of practical discourse, whereas determining the conditions for the validity of empirical judgments requires analysis in terms of epistemology and the philosophy of science, an analysis that is, at least initially, independent of a logic of theoretical discourse.[8]

As we will see here, this argument's two premises are incorrect and its conclusion irrelevant. Concerning the first premise Habermas himself concedes:

Typically, rationally motivated assent will be combined with empirical *acquiescence*, effected by weapons or goods, to form a belief in legitimacy whose component parts are difficult to isolate.

Certainly, it is his own faith in legitimacy speaking when he continues:

Such alloys are interesting in that they indicate that a positivistic enactment of norms is not sufficient to secure their *lasting* social acceptance. Enduring acceptance [*Durchsetzung*, which means that the norm is actually obeyed] of a norm *also* depends on whether, in a given context of tradition, reasons for obedience can be mobilized, reasons that suffice to make the corresponding validity claim at least appear justified in the eyes of those concerned.[9]

I would have seen these "alloys" as indicating precisely the opposite, but it also strikes me that we do not need indications when we have proof. The claims to legitimacy of the governments of Poland or East Germany under Soviet socialism were not felt to be "justified" in the slightest by the great majority of their citizens, even when these states continually claimed as much in their propaganda—and were confirmed in this, as we can see, by Habermas's "critical theory". After all, these states did *last* for a time (and I assume that Habermas would not interpret "lasting" as "lasting forever"). Their collapse lay not so much in the erosion of some conviction of their legitimacy—for then they would have had to collapse decades earlier, which, in contradiction to Habermas's theory, they did not do—but rather in the erosion of a significant piece of the means of repression in the form of the Red Army. With these means those in power were obviously able to uphold the order they desired without having to rely upon the population's belief in the legitimacy of this order.

If at this point someone who had been a victim of the propaganda of these states were to object that I do not have any real empirical evidence for the lack of support that I claim these states encountered in the populace—which, by the way, despite the lack of representative surveys, is false—we could refer them to examples of more closely contained social spaces that have been investigated with the greatest accuracy of method. Hans Haferkamp, who also holds this thesis of Habermas to be false, observes:

> On the level of organizations, institutions such as military units, mental hospitals, and prisons are perfectly able to coordinate behaviour effectively without the slightest attempt being made to generate the agreement of their members. Such institutions prove to be extremely stable; mutinies, revolts and insurrections should not be overestimated...[10]

When there are palpable punishments for transgressions of the norms and when the surveillance is effective enough, the likelihood that those subject to these norms will obey even those that they find illegitimate is certainly not inconsiderable. This should not be particularly surprising.

As for the second premise of Habermas's argument, the recognition of a norm is based only on the belief in the rightness of this norm and not on the expectation "that the corresponding claim to validity can be redeemed with reasons". Among certain people such an expectation may be a precondition for the recognition of the norm, but this is by no means the normal case. Many follow norms without so much as wasting a moment's thought on the question of whether any of them can ultimately be justified. They follow these norms simply because "one" just follows these norms or because "one" just "knows" that these norms are right.

Furthermore, someone could even recognize a norm while expecting it to be incapable of justification. Thus according to Keuth, there can be "*no 'good reasons' to find a norm correct in a cognitive sense*", but there could very well be "*'good reasons' to accept a norm*, for instance when the consequences of following it furthers one's needs or the needs of others".[11]

Here the "good reasons" to accept a norm would be those of purely purposive rationality. However, one could even have *moral* reasons to recognize a norm and hold these reasons to be correct in a *cognitive* sense, without thereby finding the *norm itself* to be correct. Thus in the Middle Ages there was debate as to whether the good—whatever it may be—is what God wants or whether the good is independent of God's will and God demands it because it is good. Someone convinced of the former could believe something to the effect that God had issued just any norms, for example, in order to separate those who are devoted to his will in obedience to these norms from those who are not. This sort of believer would live with the expectation that God says to him in heaven—in discourse—something along these lines: "These particular norms just occurred to me. I could have chosen other norms. The norms in themselves are completely meaningless." This believer would recognize the norms even though he does not believe that their claim to rightness (which God does not pretend to in the first place) can be justified. It is right *to follow* these norms, because God has issued them; the norms themselves are neither right nor wrong.

From these two unfounded premises (namely that "in the long run the social currency of a norm depends on its being accepted as valid in the group to which it is addressed" and that "this recognition is based in turn on the expectation that the corresponding claim to validity can be redeemed with reasons") Habermas then draws an irrelevant conclusion: irrelevant, because the conclusion, the "it follows" clause, claims a relation only between the *actual social currency* of a norm and the *expectation* of its justifiability, and not between the *validity* of a norm and its *actual justifiability*. Thus Habermas's further conclusion—that the question as to the conditions of *validity* of moral judgements compels us to proceed to a logic of practical discourse (instead of, for example, "practical expectations") and does so "directly" and "readily"—is a hasty leap.

However, Habermas seems to have his eye on an additional route to practical discourse. Thus he commends Stephen Toulmin:

Toulmin abandons the semantic analysis of expressions and sentences, focusing instead on the issue of the mode in which normative propositions are justified, the *form of the arguments* adduced in defending or rejecting norms and commands, and the criteria for good reasons that motivate us, by dint of insight, to recognize demands as moral obligations. "What kinds of things make a conclusion worthy of belief?" With this query Toulmin makes the transition to the level of a theory of argumentation.[12]

But this argument also fails to manage the transition to *validity*. There could easily be good reasons for a certain opinion without this opinion being *true*. Accordingly there could also be good reasons for assuming the validity of a norm without the norm itself being valid. Habermas has the habit of overlooking this distinction between validity and justification, and so he over-hastily *identifies* what one *should* do with what one has *reasons* for doing.

In defence of this questionable identification Habermas makes an equally questionable appeal to what he calls P. F. Strawson's "linguistic phenomenology of ethical consciousness". Its purpose is "to open [one's] eyes...to [one's] own everyday moral intuitions".[13] However, Habermas describes Strawson's position in terms that artificially squeeze it into the straitjacket of the theory of communicative action. Habermas claims, for example, and with an air[14] of innocently repeating an observation of Strawson's:

As long as moral philosophy concerns itself with clarifying the everyday intuitions into which we are socialized, it must be able to adopt, at least virtually, the attitude of someone who participates in the communicative practice of everyday life.[15]

Strawson says nothing of the sort. In fact, he does not even say that these intuitions can be examined only in the non-objective attitude. He does not take any position at all on this methodological question. And even if he had said that we can elucidate these moral intuitions only from the non-objective stance, still the "communicative practice of everyday life" is not the only alternative to this objective attitude. Habermas believes it is; Apel, as we saw, does not share this belief, and with good reason.[16]

In the present context this point is not particularly interesting, except in so far as it shows the rather off-putting way that Habermas appropriates a "famous essay"[17] for his own purposes. But let us turn now to the identity thesis mentioned above:

...indignation and reproaches directed against the violation of a norm must in the last analysis be based on a cognitive foundation. The person who makes such a reproach believes that the perpetrator may be able to justify himself by, for example, rejecting as unjustified the normative expectations to which the indignant party is appealing. To say that I *ought* to do something means that I *have reasons* for doing it.[18]

Habermas imputes even this observation to Strawson. Strawson makes no such observation.

Someone who reproaches another person for having infringed a norm means first and foremost, not that the accused may be able to justify himself, but rather quite clearly and simply *that the accused has infringed a norm and should not have done so.*

Furthermore it is an unsubstantiated claim that the statement that I ought to do something *means* that I have reasons for doing it. This does not hold even if we keep in mind that obviously *good* reasons are what is meant.[19] Someone could have good reasons for killing his rich aunt (if he stands to inherit her money) but it does not follow from this that he *ought to* kill his aunt. What might be *rational* for a person and what that person *ought to* do are two different questions.

However, Habermas qualifies this himself:

One would misconceive the nature of these reasons, however, were one to reduce the question What ought I to do? to a question of mere prudence or expediency.[20]

If Habermas already understands this, why does he first make the obviously false claim: "To say that I ought to do something means that I have reasons for doing it"? Why does he not say right away (which would still be false): "To say that I ought to do something means that I have reasons of the sort XY for doing it"? The answer is quite simple: Habermas aims to justify a rational ethics.[21] And a rational ethics (in any case one that is based on Kant, as discourse ethics is) subsumes the moral under the rational as a subset of the latter, where it does not go so far as to identify them. Yet it supposedly does subsume the moral under the rational not as a matter of definition, but with the aim of *showing* that the morality of an action implies its rationality, and the immorality of an action its irrationality. But then this rational ethics cannot simply mark off certain reasons as privileged from the very beginning while discounting others as irrelevant.

Now it is also clear that it can be at the same time both rational *and* immoral to kill one's aunt for her inheritance. And this makes it apparent that a rational ethics is implausible. We have already witnessed Habermas's prevarications in action, dogmatically brushing aside ordinary language and using idiosyncratic postulations.[22] It is not necessary to go into this again here.

Furthermore it would still be incorrect to claim: "To say that I ought to do something means that I have *moral* reasons for doing it." One ought to follow laws, after all; in any case this is what the lawgivers want. And when judges sentence anti-nuclear activists who blockade missile bases, despite recognizing the *moral* admissibility of the blockade, they judge simply that the law commands one to refrain from such blockades, that from the standpoint of the law the activists *ought to* refrain from them. And the judges justify their sentences with *legal* reasons. A look at the ordinary use of language shows us that morality does not have a monopoly on ought-statements. If something is morally imperative, then one ought to do it, but clearly the reverse is not true: that everything one ought to do is *morally* imperative. Thus to say that one ought to do something does not mean having moral reasons to do it.

But if something is *morally* imperative, does this not at least mean, ultimately, having moral reasons to do it? Not at all. First of all, one does not necessarily need to have reasons for it to be the case that one should do something. That a person *has* reasons implies that he *knows* about them. If we say about Frank something like: "Frank has good reasons to believe that Jasmine is not going to come", this statement implies the additional statement: "Frank believes that Jasmine is not going to come, for good reasons." Someone who has good reasons to believe something knows about these reasons. To express the situation where Frank *does not* know of these reasons suggesting that Jasmine will not come, although the reasons are plainly clear, one would have to say something like: "He *would have* good reasons to believe that she is not going to come." He would have them just in the case where he rationally takes notice of them. But since he does not rationally take notice of these reasons, he does not in fact *have* the reasons. Now it is clear that ignorance not only does not absolve one from punishment, but also—at least in many conceptions of morality, if not most—does not absolve one from *ought*, from the obligations of morality. In my view slavery was immoral in antiquity even if the slave-owners, due to insufficient thought on the matter, due to their irrationality, did not *know* of any of the moral reasons and thus de facto did not *have* reasons to find it immoral or to stop it.

In addition, one could easily take the position—and I do take this position— that slavery in antiquity (or wherever) and the associated wrongs such as torture and rape were immoral even if the slave-owners came to the conclusion, based on *rational* considerations, that slavery and the behaviours associated with it were morally beyond reproach. And it is quite possible that they did in fact come to this conclusion based on rational considerations. To rule out this possibility would only be to evince one's blindness to the enormous differences between the epistemic situation of that time and ours in the present day.

Here someone might object that you cannot *reproach* someone with having done something that he *rationally* holds to be right. But why not? Sundry theologians in the Middle Ages spoke of reason as a "harlot", which was not meant as a compliment to its moral reputation. If someone through rational consideration came to the conclusion that one does not have to believe in God and so one does not have to follow certain commandments supposedly issued by Him, these theologians would nonetheless find this conclusion reprehensible along with the possibly ensuing non-compliance with certain norms. And if they found the considerations that led to this to be rational, they would see in this further only confirmation of the abjectness of reason itself. They would proclaim it as a moral imperative not to let oneself be seduced by the harlot reason, but rather to remain steadfast in faith. Of course one could argue for the position that you cannot reproach someone for behaviour that the person rationally finds to be morally right—that it *is not* immoral to do something that one rationally thinks is moral. But then this is a concrete moral position and not a *meta*ethical position about the meaning of "moral". For obviously it is not hard to recognize the position of our anti-rationalist theologians as an example of a moral position, such that we would have a hard time accusing these theologians of not having understood what "morally imperative" *means*. And, to bring up one last example, one can also see this in the sentence: "The moral imperative to respect human rights also holds for dictators; unfortunately, a dictator who does not share this moral opinion has no reason whatsoever to hold himself to it." The point of this sentence is not to repeat what was said earlier, namely, that it can also be rational for someone to act contrary to morality, that moral reasons are not necessarily sufficient reasons for action. The point here is rather that one could question whether a moral imperative necessarily involves *any* reasons for action *at all* for a particular person. Our sentence here, in contrast to sentences like "The bachelor's wife is a hair-dresser" or "corpses lead dangerous lives" or "the cube is round", is not contradictory, as every competent speaker can easily see for himself or herself. Even something's being "morally imperative" does not *mean* "having moral reasons to do something".

I would hope that this brief foray into linguistic phenomenology will open the eyes of discourse ethicists to our everyday linguistic intuitions. These intuitions refute the alleged connection between the concepts of "ought" and "reasons" and thus prove erroneous Habermas's thesis that "philosophical ethics…can readily assume the form of a special theory of argumentation."[23]

Furthermore, philosophical ethics could not assume this form even if it were the case, which it is not, that saying one "ought to do something" meant that one "has reasons to do it". For it is quite apparent that the question posed by Toulmin that Habermas so lauds—"What kinds of things make a conclusion worthy of belief?"—does not offer a transition to the level of a theory of *argumentation*, but instead to the level of *epistemology*, which, as is well known, concerns among other things the question of when a belief is justified. "Good reasons" do not have to be arguments given to us by *others* in a practical discourse or with which we could convince *others* in a practical discourse. A conclusion is "worthy of belief" for a person P if the conclusion *is justified for P*; it is not necessary for the conclusion to be justifiable by P to others.[24]

To be sure, there could be circumstances in which a practical discourse is in fact the only procedure for the formation of belief that is epistemically exacting enough. But what these circumstances are is itself an epistemological question. And since the epistemic effort necessary also depends on the time available and the urgency of the actions in question, and yet Habermas hitches his practical discourse to the goal of the consensus and participation of all persons affected, it should be clear enough that there is no path leading to the principles U and D that he advocates. A norm is certainly not justified for someone only when it accords with U or D.

This threat of a transition to epistemology—a transition that certainly suggests itself here—is one that Habermas is very much aware of, and this is why he insists so emphatically that "when we ask what makes valid moral judgments possible, we are compelled to proceed *directly* to a logic of practical discourse."[25] We have seen that this thesis is unfounded, whereas its negation is not.

The transition to epistemology would also pose a threat to Habermas, given his intentions, because in the intensive backlighting of epistemology practical judgements can appear rather threadbare and above all lacking in *truth value*. Habermas is aware of this effect:

The intuitionist attempt to grasp moral truths was doomed to failure because normative statements cannot be verified or falsified; that is, they cannot be tested in the same way as descriptive statements. In view of this, and given the mentioned presupposition ["that truth or the validity of descriptive propositions, and it alone, determines the sense in which a statement, any statement, is accepted as valid"], the alternative is a wholesale rejection of the idea that practical questions admit of truth.[26]

Yet Habermas certainly aims to attain a cognitivist position, and he explains:

The noncognitivist position relies primarily on two arguments: first, the fact that disputes about basic moral principles ordinarily do not issue in agreement, and second, the failure, discussed above, of all attempts to explain what it might mean for normative propositions to be true…The first argument loses its force if we can name a principle that makes agreement in moral argumentation possible in principle. The second argument fails if we give up the premise that normative sentences, to the extent to which they are connected with validity claims at all, can be valid or invalid only in the sense of propositional truth.[27]

Let us first look at Habermas's response to the second objection. The question arises as to whether we can really give up the above-mentioned premise as simply as all that. What is the alternative validity claim supposed to be?

Habermas claims in fact to be able to make out a claim of normative rightness here that is only *analogous* to the truth claim[28] and thus distinct from it, since these two claims "occupy different 'positions' in the communicative practice of everyday life". He tries to demonstrate this by pointing to alleged "asymmetries" that emerge, as he acknowledges, only if "we look at the matter more closely".[29] Habermas offers two examples:

(a) One ought not to kill anybody.

(a') It is commanded not to kill anybody.

And he explains:

A norm may be formulated in a statement like (a), but this act of formulating it, i.e., of writing a sentence, *need not* itself by [sic!] conceived of as a speech act, that is, as something other than the impersonal expression of the norm. Statements such as (a) are commands that we can address *secondarily* in one way or another through speech acts. This has no equivalent in the domain of facts.…Unlike sentences (a) and (a'), descriptive statements such as "Iron is magnetic" or "It is the case that iron is magnetic" cannot be expressed or used independently of the illocutionary role of a certain type of speech act if they are to retain their assertoric power.

We can account for this asymmetry by saying that claims to truth reside *only* in speech acts, whereas the locus of normative claims to validity is primarily in norms and only derivatively in speech acts.[30]

These remarks are incorrect.[31] They would still be incorrect even if they were not asserted by Habermas or otherwise embedded in speech acts, but rather printed out by a computer by some random process. A proposition obviously has assertoric force, that is, it *says* or states something and can be true or false, even *without* being used in a speech act.[32] Both sentences above about iron are, incidentally, entirely correct.

Habermas also discovers a further "asymmetry".

While there is an unequivocal relation between existing states of affairs and true propositions about them, the "existence" or social currency of norms says nothing about whether the norms are valid.[33]

This is not an asymmetry. Rather, Habermas does not compare norms and propositions on the same level, in the same respect, and thus makes a category error. The error can be repeated the other way around:

While there is an unequivocal relation between valid norms and true propositions about them, the actual "belief in" or social currency of descriptive statements says nothing about whether the statements are valid.

If in his comparisons Habermas refrained from category mistakes, which seem almost intentional, he would find that a norm N is valid when the statement "N is valid" is true, and that a state of affairs S exists when the statement "The state of affairs S exists" is true. Thus Habermas's response to the second objection of noncognitivists fails. Judgements such as "It is morally imperative not to kill", if they assert any cognitive validity claim at all, assert a truth claim, since there is no other claim to rightness apart from this. And as Habermas knows well, the question of the truth conditions of a judgement certainly does not allow any direct transition to a logic of practical discourse.

Let us now turn to Habermas's response to the first objection. It is somewhat difficult to take this at all seriously. If the predicate "makes agreement in moral argumentation possible in principle" applies to a principle if it makes agreement in moral argumentation possible in so far as it *would* be generally accepted, then this predicate can be applied, for example, to the principle RR: "Precisely those norms are valid that the leader of the National Democratic Party of Germany (NPD) party approves of"—as well as to many hundreds of other principles. However, the principle U would not be among these. For while there are of course certain norms that the leader of the NPD approves of, it is completely unrealistic to assume that there is *any* moral norm that would satisfy the condition that

all affected can *freely* accept the consequences and the side effects that the *general* observance of a controversial norm can be expected to have for the satisfaction of the interests of *each individual*.[34]

The interests of five billion people, one might think, can hardly all be brought under one roof—after all, among these five billion are rapists, torturers, dictators, child molesters, dealers in torture instruments, politicians on the boards of arms companies, workers in arms companies, shareholders in arms companies, the suppressed, the tortured, victims of rape, molested children, etc. The idea of reaching a consensus here is entirely illusory.[35]

Furthermore, and this is decisive, the non-cognitivist does not point to the "fact" that there is no principle that would issue in agreement *if* it were generally accepted, but rather that there is no such principle that *is* in fact generally accepted. And this does not exactly lose its force with the naming of a principle, U, that is *not* generally accepted.

Astonishingly, however, Habermas claims, as already mentioned, that it is *necessary* to introduce this sort of (purportedly) consensus-building moral principle in practical discourse. Why is this necessary? It is not even clear if this makes *sense*. However, Habermas goes on:

In what follows, I presuppose that a theory of argumentation must take the form of an "informal logic," because it is impossible to *force* agreement on theoretical and moral-practical issues either by means of deduction or on the basis of empirical evidence. To the degree to which arguments are deductively valid, i.e., compelling in terms of logical inference, they reveal nothing substantively new. To the degree to which arguments do have substantive content, they are based on experiences and needs/wants that are open to various intepretations [sic!] in the light of changing theories using changing systems of description. Such experiences and needs/wants thus fail to offer an *ultimate* basis for argumentation.

In theoretical discourse the gap between particular observations and general hypotheses is bridged by some canon or other of induction. An analogous bridging principle is needed for practical discourse. Accordingly, all studies of the logic of moral argumentation end up having to introduce a moral principle as a rule of argumentation that has a function equivalent to the principle of induction in the discourse of the empirical sciences.[36]

The introduction of a moral principle—say, U—is to be made plausible here with an analogy to induction, the value of which is hardly in dispute. The following quotation makes this even clearer:

Induction serves as a bridging principle to justify the logically discontinuous transition from a finite number of singular propositions (data) to a universal proposition (hypothesis); universalization serves as a bridging principle to justify the transition from descriptive indications (about the consequences and side effects of the application of the norm for the satisfaction of generally accepted needs) to the norm.[37]

However, the analogy attempted by Habermas here between U and the "principle of induction" is anything but plausible if one takes a look at the considerable differences. In doing so I will assume that Habermas, who after all does not *name* either any actual canon of induction or the principle of induction itself,[38] is proceeding in his role of a "reconstructive" philosopher continually concerned to uncover "implicit knowledge of rules"; thus that by the "principle of induction" he understands not its *formulation* but rather something that, while in need of being made explicit, is "always already" at our disposal in our know-how.

Here we have already found one of the decisive differences. The principle of induction, in contrast to U, does not first have to be introduced. It is already there. The community of researchers, and people in general, already practise induction without having to wait for some philosopher to offer a principle of induction.

In fact this would not even be possible. Another conspicuous difference between U and the so-called principle of induction is that we have a clear formulation of U and none for the principle of induction. The difficulties involved in formulating the latter principle are demonstrated to particularly striking effect in Nelson Goodman's famous investigations of the problem of induction.[39] Goodman goes to work constructively on the problems he sees and yet ultimately he is unable to provide any formulation of the principle of induction (nor does he claim to). A formulation of this sort simply does not exist, and it strikes me as a very plausible assumption that it *cannot* exist.

Despite this—or possibly because of this—all people practise induction in more or less the same way, whereas people by no means infer from descriptive indications to the validity or invalidity of norms in more or less the same way. It is not difficult to make out this difference in comparing theoretical and practical discourses. People find it significantly easier to come to an agreement about purely theoretical questions than about moral ones. Natural scientists by and large adhere to the same scientific theories but in no way do they adhere by and large to the same moral norms and principles. This is true also of moral philosophers.

Moreover, many people do not use any kind of bridging principle to justify a norm in the sense of inferring from the consequences and side effects of the norm to its validity. They can also justify them as God-given. Even when someone does infer from the consequences and side effects of a norm to its validity or invalidity, he does not necessarily have to do this in terms of universalization. He could equally well say, for example, that these consequences and side effects harm Aryans and are *for that reason* morally wrong. Some people use the one moral bridging principle to justify norms, other people use the other principle, and still others do not need any. Clearly, however, all people make use of essentially the same principle of induction to justify hypotheses. (It would be better to say: everyone proceeds in approximately the same way, since one does not necessarily have to buy into the thesis of "implicit rule-knowledge" either in induction or in language use.)

Furthermore the principle of induction secures only a transition, roughly speaking, from data to hypotheses. It is not at all the job of this principle to bring about this bizarre transition from *is* to *ought*—which is the true purpose of U, although this fact is neatly hushed up by Habermas.[40] Furthermore it is certainly not the function of the principle of induction (rather it is a side effect at most) to generate *agreement*. It is in fact a bridging principle, but it is not a rule of argumentation, at least not if "argumentation" is meant as argumentation with *others*, that is, as *discourse*. U on the other hand is very much supposed to be a rule of argumentation, according to Habermas. But of course he is mistaken in this, since there is no actual mention of argumentation in the principle U.[41] And so the attempted analogy with the principle of induction has the effect here of making this argumentation-logical interpretation, contrary to Habermas's intentions, appear even more absurd.

The function of the principle of induction is, to be sure, not exhausted in merely leading from data to hypotheses. The formulations that try to put "our" principle into words as we really use it can also be called principles of induction. These principles have been discarded, since they did not work. That does not however mean that they did not lead from data to hypotheses—this they can do with no problem. They simply do not lead us to the correct or at least approximately correct hypotheses. In other words, the principle of induction has the function of leading us to truth. And we can use this function as the measure of any tentatively proposed alternative principle of induction (and of our own as well).

What can we use as the measure of Habermas's moral principle? It is supposed to lead to consensus. This it fails to do, even when it is accepted. A whole slew of other principles do found consensus when accepted. Then what standard of measure do we have? If the moral principle is *analogous* to the principle of induction, as Habermas claims, and the principle of induction can be measured according to whether it leads to valid hypotheses, then the moral principle should be measurable according to whether it leads to valid norms. But it cannot be measured this way, since it *defines* the validity of norms, as do various other moral principles.

Since Habermas now claims: "To the degree to which arguments are deductively valid, that is, compelling in terms of logical inference, they reveal nothing substantively new", it should be pointed out to him that, under the supposition of principle U, the inference from "descriptive indications (about the consequences and side effects of the application of the norm for the satisfaction of generally accepted needs)" to the validity or invalidity of a norm is *logically compelling*, and thus U cannot uncover anything essentially new, and hence *is not a bridging principle*. Induction, in contrast, is not anything that can be presupposed in inferences as a premise, but rather is a non-explicable *inferential practice* (and not even so much as a *rule* of inference). There is not even anything we derive *from* the principle of induction—whereas something is very much derived *from* the principle U—but rather we derive things *with* the principle of induction. Although perhaps even this is incorrect and we would do better to say: the "principle" of induction consists in the transition from singular propositions to hypotheses. Clearly Habermas's attempted analogy is made out of thin air.

But to return to the question of a standard of measure for U: if the moral principle U *defines* what moral means, the question arises as to how such a moral principle could itself be justified as the right one in the first place (which is different from justifying it as sanctioned by reasons of our—obviously disreputable—purposive rationality). In fact it should already be clear by now that this is impossible. Of course this problem also holds in an abstract sense for the principle of induction as well, but at the level of practice the problem does not *pose* itself, since in practice we do not really ask ourselves if we should use "green" or Goodman's "grue" for purposes of induction. In practice there is no dispute about which principle of induction is correct. The case of morality is clearly different. Furthermore, in the case of induction, as we saw, it is at least possible to explain what its *validity* consists in without *begging the question*. This is obviously not the case with the moral principle U—which makes the "principle" look very much like an arbitrary nominal definition.[42] Habermas and Apel naturally respond to this objection by claiming that we *have no choice* but to "implicitly recognize" U in practical discourse. Given that in practical discourse, that is, in discourse about moral questions and questions of normative rightness and legitimacy, countless different moral principles are used and upheld by various groups and individuals, this claim indicates a loss of connection to reality. U is neither explicitly nor implicitly generally recognized, whether through the practical approach of the participants in the discourse or in the intuitions of their "innermost hearts"—unless, of course, one defines "practical discourse" such that this can only be a discourse in which U is recognized. However, these sorts of arbitrary definition do not provide justification of anything.

To summarize: Habermas's claim to find an analogy between the principle of induction and the moral principle is unfounded. And since the moral principle plays nothing like an equivalent role in practical discourse to the one the principle of induction plays in theoretical discourse, one can see no reason why a justificatory programme for morality should insist on the justification of just this sort of principle, the value of which is extraordinarily doubtful. In doing so the justificatory programme puts its own value very much in doubt.

Thus Habermas fails to generate even a certain initial plausibility for his justificatory programme, which he sees as the justification of a moral principle interpreted as a rule of argumentation.

This is no different when it comes to the choice of the specific candidate for this kind of justification. What would recommend U in particular as the object of this justification?

On the one hand Habermas seems to see an argument for a generalization principle like U in the supposed convergence of cognitivist ethics:

All variants of cognitivist ethics take their bearings from the basic intuition contained in Kant's categorical imperative.... The moral principle is so conceived as to exclude as invalid any norm that could not meet with the qualified assent of all who are or might be affected by it.[43]

Here we should start by noting that argumentation rules are not necessarily bound to a cognitivist claim to validity. Imagine that the king, in order to steer the recently unbridled discourse back onto a more conservative course, commands: "From now on, only those norms are to be recognized in practical discourses and arguments that do not dispute my position as ruler ordained by God." What we have here is clearly a rule of argumentation, and yet it obviously does not have to be bound to any cognitivist claim to validity. This could even be a kingdom where there are only non-cognitivists and it does not even occur to anyone to associate norms with a cognitive claim (which does not rule out arguing with reasons about which norms should be enacted or not enacted for instrumental purposes). So since argumentation rules could easily be given a non-cognitivist interpretation, there is no particular reason to have recourse only to exclusively *cognitivist* intuitions in looking for argumentation rules. Rather, this seems to be a simple case of bias.

Furthermore we do not get very much mileage out of this convergence of the variants of cognitivist ethics. The ethical systems of Judaism, Christianity and Islam are also cognitivist, but they make no mention of these intuitions. These ethical systems are rather concerned with *God's* assent. And the ethics of natural rights—which plays a much larger de facto role in our Western culture than the idea of the categorical imperative—is cognitivist, but without sharing Kant's intuition.

At another point Habermas argues using the idea of impartiality and claims:

> True impartiality pertains only to that standpoint from which one can generalize precisely those norms that can count on universal assent because they perceptibly embody an interest common to all affected.[44]

But this is also incorrect. If there were some kind of objective procedure for justifying norms—and this is what Habermas claims—then the norms thus justified would already be impartial based solely on their being *objectively* justified and thus earning intersubjective recognition. To be impartial, a norm by no means has to do justice to the interests of all people; it may very well encroach on the murderous interests of a murderer and is not reliant on his agreement (and a balance of the various interests is clearly not always possible). What it may not do is encroach on the interests of a certain person P only because it is the person P. Only here do we have something that is necessarily partial.

Our examination of Habermas's preliminary considerations on the form of his justificatory programme for morality can be summarized as follows:

Habermas did *not* succeed in showing why philosophical ethics can assume the form of a special theory of argumentation, or why the principle U in an ethics thus conceived should or even can take on the role of the decisive rule of argumentation.

First, Habermas's central argument for his thesis derives a conclusion that is irrelevant to the question from two false premises: the social currency of a norm does *not* in the long run depend on its "being accepted as valid in the group to which it is addressed", and the recognition of a norm is *not* necessarily based on "the expectation that the corresponding claim to validity can be redeemed with reasons"; rather, and this is quite different, it is based on the belief that it is *worthy of recognition*. Even if Habermas's premises were correct, his conclusion that "there is a connection between the 'existence' of norms and the anticipated justifiability of the corresponding 'ought' statements" misses the point, since Habermas would have to establish a connection between the *validity* of norms and their actual *justifiability*. His argumentation does not contribute in the slightest to accomplishing this.

Second, his further argument that "to say that I ought to do something" *means* "that I have good reasons to do it" is incorrect. It is already incorrect simply because there can be good reasons to do something immoral. Furthermore, even the claim that "to say that I ought to do something" means "that I have moral reasons to do it" is unfounded, since of course one *ought* also to conduct oneself as the law demands, and the reasons that judges give as to why according to law one ought to act in such and such a manner are legal reasons. The word "ought" does not have a specifically moral sense but rather expresses in general the imperative nature of an action—who or what makes it imperative is an open question. And finally, one does not necessarily have to *have* good reasons for it to be true that one ought to do something. It is *not* self-contradictory to say: "He came through rational considerations to the conclusion that it is not immoral to disregard God's commandments; nonetheless it was immoral of him to do this and to let himself be seduced by the harlot reason in the first place." Since this is not a self-contradictory sentence, it follows that to say that "I ought to do something" or even that "morally I ought to do something" does not mean having moral *reasons* to do something.

Third, *even if* "to say I ought to do something" meant "having (moral) reasons to do it", this still does not allow for a transition to the level of a theory of argumentation, but rather only to that of epistemology. For as we saw, someone could have good reasons to believe something or to do something without having good *arguments* with which he could justify his beliefs or his actions to others, let alone arguments that already stem from such a discourse with others. The theory of argumentation is irrelevant for the clarification of what good reasons are. Furthermore Habermas's appropriation of a cognitive status for norms is unjustified under the epistemological premise that the *truth* claim is the only cognitive claim. Habermas's attempt to show, using purported asymmetries between assertoric sentences and normative sentences, that norms have a claim to rightness merely *analogous* to the truth claim also fails. The alleged asymmetries do not exist, and Habermas's critique of non-cognitivism does not do justice to it in the slightest.

Fourth, even if philosophical ethics had to assume the form of a special theory of argumentation, namely, a theory of practical discourse, this by no means leads to the necessity of introducing a moral principle supposedly functioning as a rule of argumentation and a bridging principle for the justification of norms. Such moral principles already exist, and any additional such principle would just be one more principle and would be just as incapable of serving the required purpose of generating agreement as any of the competing moral principles. Incidentally, U, in contrast to many other moral principles, would not be capable of this even *if* it were generally recognized. Furthermore it is entirely unclear how it could be *justified* as valid. In fact, it is not even clear what this validity would even consist in.

Fifth, even if the logic of practical discourse did point to *one* such moral principle functioning as a rule of argumentation, just as, supposedly, the logic of theoretical discourse does to the principle of induction, it remains unclear why it would be U, of all things. Apart from the already mentioned incapacity of U to fulfil the role ascribed to it of generating agreement, there is in addition no such analogy between U and the principle of induction. In fact, *U is not a bridging principle*, and it is questionable whether U is even a *rule of argumentation* at all, since there is no mention of argumentations and their organization in U. U is not the expression of a philosophical insight, but rather the expression of a moral (and possibly ideological) attitude that has no more of a privileged epistemic status than any other moralities and ideologies similarly heralded with truth claims.

2.2. IN SEARCH OF SUITABLE NORMS OF DISCOURSE AND PRESUPPOSITIONS OF ARGUMENTATION

Although by this point we have already seen the implausibility of the notion of discourse ethics that a morality can be extracted from norms of discourse one way or another, we should take a look at how the proponents of discourse ethics set out to identify these very norms.

2.2.1. Methods of Identifying Norms of Discourse

On the one hand, one could examine empirically which norms are in fact observed in discourses, particularly in practical discourses. Of course, in doing so one would have to first clarify what exactly is meant by the term "practical discourse", and one would have to avoid already *defining* practical discourse as the adherence to certain norms, since then one could save oneself the trouble of the empirical examination. However, it seems reasonable to define practical discourses among other things in terms of their *ends or goals*. Various ends make an appearance in discourse ethics. Discourse is sometimes pictured as an activity meant to settle conflicts of action, at other times as an activity meant to answer the question of which norms ought to be adopted, and at yet other times as a means of answering the *different* question of which norms are valid.[45]

But if one is already setting *ends*, then of course an instrumental or technical justification of the discourse norms readily suggests itself. Norms justified in this way would simply be those one can rationally assume to be best suited to reaching the stated end.

Robert Alexy has advanced certain objections to the technical means of justification.[46] For one, he says, "then the end itself would have to be justified". However that is not at all the case at this point, where we are concerned with finding only norms of discourse (and not the scope of their normative validity). When the *question* is which norms of discourse are best suited to a certain end (whereby, incidentally, it would be a sign of rationality to occasionally entertain other possible means besides discourse), then to answer this question we certainly do not need to justify the end itself. Alexy himself says: "The rules of rational practical discourse are norms for the justification of norms."[47] With this he sets an end (the second of the alternatives mentioned above). He does not justify this end in the slightest and does not feel obliged to do so. Furthermore Alexy sees it as a problem "that mutually incompatible norms [could be] proposed as means". Why this is a problem is not clear to me. The incompatible norms would after all be associated with different rule systems, and among these one would choose precisely that system from which one can rationally expect the best results. If both systems are equally good, so much the better. Finally, Alexy says that the "state characterized as an end" could already be defined by the adherence to certain norms. Where is the problem here? Why should something not be an end in itself? Aside from this, in the particular case where one uses discourse norms to justify moral norms, the discourse norms are by no means ends in themselves.

Apel and Habermas essentially dispense with these two methods, which probably, contrary to their assurances, has to do with the fact that one simply cannot get to the rules preferred by Habermas and Apel with these methods of justification. Thus these two methods—incidentally, the only rational ones—are also the best suited to criticize the norms of discourse (mis)identified by Apel and Habermas. Later on I will do just this. For now the question arises as to which method Apel and Habermas themselves use.

Alexy calls it the "universal–pragmatic justification" of norms of discourse. Since this "method" stems more from Apel than from Habermas, here I would like to stick with the label "transcendental–pragmatic". This method consists in "showing that the validity of certain rules is a condition of the possibility of linguistic communication".[48] In fact Apel in particular is concerned primarily with the condition of the possibility of *serious argumentation*. Several objections can be made to this method of justification. First of all, if the *validity* of certain rules is a condition of the possibility of linguistic communication or, more precisely, of argumentation, then *practically* one does not have to care about them one way or the other; either they hold or they do not. In the latter case argumentation would simply be impossible even if one were to follow the norms, and in the former case it would be possible even if one did not follow them. So I presume that Alexy means their *observance*—or, in the case of certain norms, the *assumption of their observance* (Habermas) or their *recognition* (Apel)—as a condition of the possibility of linguistic communication. In this case what we have here is simply a *technical* rule that says: for the purpose of allowing linguistic communication, the observance (recognition, etc.) of this or that norm is necessary. And then the transcendental– or universal–pragmatic justification boils down to a simple *technical* justification—a fact overlooked by Alexy. The rules of discourse may admittedly present a special type of technical rule, but baking recipes are also a special type of technical rule. Besides, this transcendental–pragmatic justification does not suffice for the purpose that Alexy is also interested in, namely, identifying the norms of discourse for the justification of moral norms. For the adherence to those rules that make up the conditions of possibility for linguistic communication is *necessary* (this is what it means to speak of a "condition of possibility", if it is to mean anything at all) for conducting a practical discourse, but not at all *sufficient*. Since Apel wants to extract moral norms directly from these necessary rules, this objection does not affect him so much. However, Habermas's alleged *derivation* of a *moral* principle (U) from these supposedly necessary rules works only under the supposition that the adherence to these rules or at least the assumption of adherence to them *constitutes* a rational practical discourse. This supposition is unfounded, and thus whatever one might have logically derived from these rules cannot be a sufficient but rather at most a necessary condition of practical reason.

2.2.2. Transcendental Pragmatics

2.2.2.1. *Apel's Notion of Final Justification and Its Untenability*

Apel would like to "transform" the Kantian question of the conditions of the possibility of knowledge by removing it from the framework of the philosophy of consciousness and placing it in that of the philosophy of language, more precisely, in that of *pragmatics*.[49] In this way he believes himself capable of dealing with the *problem of final justification*, whereby he conflates without further ado the *transcendental question* of the *conditions of the possibility of intersubjectively valid critique*[50] with the epistemic problem of reaching undoubtable certainty.[51] Thus he speaks of the "transcendental identity of truth and certainty".[52]

But transcendentality and infallibility are two different things. Albert always used to ask Apel why particular convictions about transcendental issues are actually supposed to be *immune to revision*.[53] Apel seems not to understand this question. Not only does he hold the two things to be identical (like the morning star and the evening star), he even seems unable to make the conceptual distinction between them. Thus he explains:

When one reflects on the conditions of possibility of proposing hypotheses, one comes to different insights that cannot sensibly be referred to as "hypotheses".[54]

If this is meant as a statement about the German or English language and not Apel's private language, it is false.

We also have to note the linguistic confusions on Apel's part when he speaks of the "transcendental–reflective alternatives to the either *empirical* or *logical–analytical* insights" and claims that

in this context we have to remember that so far not a single specifically *philosophical* thesis has been traceable back to an *empirical* or *logical-analytical* insight. Thus the position of logical empiricism, for example, that there could only be either logical-analytical or empirical truths, cannot itself be called "logical-analytical" or "empirical".[55]

This dichotomy between analytical and empirical truths—whether one dreams up a third alternative or not—strikes me as inappropriate. If analytic truths, or, to put it better, analytic sentences are thought to be those that are true based on their meaning alone, then empirical sentences would have to be those that are true based on their meaning *and* the empirical evidence, that is, experience. But how can a sentence *be* true on the *basis* of experience? Experience can be deceiving. That is, experience cannot be the *ratio essendi* for the truth of a sentence or the ground of its *validity* (unless it is a sentence *about* experience) but rather only the *ratio cognoscendi*. But if an empirical sentence is defined as one that can be recognized as true with the aid of experience, then it is not clear how these kinds of sentence could be contrasted to analytic sentences. Then are analytical sentences those that can be recognized as true through mere analysis (of their meaning) without any recourse to experience? How is this supposed to be possible? To understand that "circles are round" is analytic, I have to be *familiar* with the meaning of the terms "circle" and "round", and I know this due to my linguistic socialization, which occurred via my own eyes and ears. I *experienced* the meaning of these words. Even if I simply stipulate a definition and define charbles as tables with chairs on top of them, I can still recognize the truth of the sentence "charbles are tables with chairs on top of them" only if I correctly remember the nominal definition (which itself cannot be true or false but only practical or impractical). But this presupposes having *perceived* that I stipulated this nominal definition. This is not a given. One could program a computer to continually produce new definitions. Programming it to keep an internal record of what it does is something else above and beyond this and presupposes that it *registers* its activity. And this is where the empirical information comes into play. *Inner* perception is also *empirical* perception. *All* insights that people normally can come to, including those of mathematics, are empirical in the sense that is relevant here, namely, *won* through experience. This is itself an empirical insight, and "normally" means here that other ways of arriving at insights are entirely conceivable. It could happen that knowledge is simply intuitive—and really intuitive, literally arising from nothing and not, say, mediated by chains of association that themselves have an empirical foundation.[56] Reflective insights, however, are of necessity won empirically through inner experience even if the *ground of their validity* is supposed to be a priori.

Apel, however, proceeds by *hastily imputing the a priori status of the grounds of validity of transcendental judgements onto their grounds of knowledge*. To put it more concretely: he conflates the status of the *ratio essendi*, or of the reasons for the validity of intersubjectively valid critique and of science or of the understanding of meaning, with the status of the *ratio cognoscendi* that is to generate our insights into the correctness of the alleged reasons of being or validity in the first place. And he gives a name to this mix-up: "final justification".

Let us now look more concretely at this conflation and at some of the other fundamental difficulties of this "final justification" project, which has already shown itself to be futile even prior to a consideration of the details. In particular let us look at how Apel claims to uncover the *"uncriticisable foundations of argumentation"*.[57] This requires us to isolate the *two* steps that, as mentioned, Apel does not distinguish very clearly: first the demonstration/identification of a *criterion of transcendentality*, as I would like to call it, and second its successful *application*, which, since it pertains to a *final* justification, can consist only in *producing infallible, absolute certain evidence* that a candidate for transcendentality (such as the purported "presuppositions of argumentation") also *satisfies* this criterion with certainty.

Apel gives us the following criterion:

> If I cannot dispute something without current self-contradiction [*aktuellen Selbstwider-
> spruch*] and at the same time cannot justify it deductively without formal-logical peti-
> tio principii, than it counts as one of the transcendental–pragmatic presuppositions of
> argumentation that one has to have always already recognized if the language game of
> argumentation is to retain its *sense or meaning* [*Sinn*]. Thus one could also call this tran-
> scendental–pragmatic type of argument the *final justification from the conditions of sense/
> meaning* [*sinnkritische Form der Letztbegründung*].[58]

It is interesting that Apel thinks he has already proposed a form of final justification here, since those less far-seeing people such as Albert[59] or Gethmann or
Hegselmann[60] would perhaps demand some *further* justifications with the following questions:

(a) How is one supposed to know, and with certainty, that this criterion is the
    right one? Should we not have to somehow find justification for this, in fact,
    infallible justification?

(b) How is one supposed to know, and with certainty, that something in fact cannot
    be disputed without self-contradiction and cannot be justified without a formal–
    logical *petitio principii*? Would it not be possible for us to deceive ourselves in
    predicating of a candidate for transcendentality that it satisfies this criterion?

The attempt to answer these kinds of question or, as Apel tends to do, to portray
them as mistaken and senseless necessarily brings us to the *epistemological* level.
And it is only on this level, and not on the level of the criterion for *transcendentality*, that Apel's attempt to reach absolute certainty makes any sense.

At this point we should turn to this epistemological level. Even before considering the details of Apel's and Kuhlmann's attempts to prove that certain rules
and presuppositions of argumentation have the status of final justification, we can
raise two fundamental objections to every attempt at such final justification, using
the so-called Munchhausen Trilemma and the principle of fallibility.

If we cannot dismiss questions such as (a) and (b), then we obviously find ourselves in Albert's Munchhausen Trilemma,

> which arises when one looks for a certain foundation for knowledge. One is compelled
> to choose between an infinite regress, circular argumentation, or a discontinuation of the
> procedure, which involves suspending the principle of sufficient reason, so that the search
> for this certainty proves futile.[61]

It would be better to say here: if we dismiss these questions, we already find ourselves within dogmatism. In his dispute with Albert, however, Apel claims that this
viewpoint is justified only if "one understands the trilemma strictly logically, that
is, under the old POPPER-esque assumption that sentences can only be justified
by other sentences". And he adds:

> It is simply dogmatic to claim that for each justification one has to go even further back
> to further justifications. It could be that there are certainties behind which one cannot go
> any further back. This is just what I claim, that there are "uncircumventable" certainties.

And my claim is this: if you go back to yourself, to the claim that you yourself are making in actu, then you are thrown back upon those certainties that you cannot dispute without self-contradiction.[62]

Now Albert does not claim that for each justification one has to go back to a further justification; rather, he claims just the opposite, that we could also do without this by, for example, deciding on a circular argument or a dogma. This view does not strike me as in any sense dogmatic (and Albert does not claim that he could not be mistaken about this view); rather it is quite apparently (but not infallibly) correct. This is proven by the two questions (a) and (b) above. Concerning (a), Apel implies that Gethmann and Hegselmann are asking for a deduction of the principle of final justification from another principle. "But this kind of critique misses the point of transcendental pragmatics", he assures us.[63] But maybe it is *Apel* who misses the point of Gethmann's and Hegselmann's argument: when Apel forgoes deriving the criterion of final justification from another principle, only two other options remain; either he simply does not justify it or he justifies it using the criterion of final justification itself. This would be question-begging. Now Apel, who opts for question-begging, would reply emphatically: it *cannot* be avoided. But even if this were so, if question-begging cannot be avoided, it is still question-begging, and a "justification" that commits the fallacy of question-begging, whether in the form of a derivation, demonstration or anything else, is no justification at all. So the criterion of final justification is (*finally*) unjustified.[64]

Furthermore, it is true on the one hand that the criterion of final justification cannot be *finally* justified without *petitio principii* (and thus necessarily remains finally *un*justified) as long as it is the sole criterion of final justification (which Apel assumes is the case). On the other hand, however, there is no logical reason that would preclude a *simple* (not final) justification of the criterion of final justification if it were valid in the first place. Here one could object that the criterion of final justification, if Apel is right that it has to be presupposed in all argumentation, cannot be justified *without* being presupposed. However, for Apel "presupposition" means a rather obscure "implicit recognition".[65] But the necessity of a logical or methodical circle in proving the criterion of final justification does not at all follow from the (alleged) necessity of the "implicit recognition" of this criterion. If I argue for the infallibility of a computer by saying that it answered the question of its infallibility with "yes" (and Apel argues similarly for the infallibility of his transcendental–reflective insights), then my argument is logically circular and the way I arrived at my answer to the question is methodically circular—thus my argument is invalid. But if I argue for the computer's infallibility with the argument that God himself confirmed this by appearing personally and announcing this, then my argument is clearly still not circular even if I have believed, imputed or "implicitly recognised" the computer's infallibility without interruption in the course of my argumentation. Implicit recognition has absolutely nothing to do with circularity[66]—which has escaped the attention of the transcendental–pragmatic philosophers. Thus it is unacceptable but quite telling that they nonetheless offer us nothing but circular arguments and dogmatic pronouncements for the "justification" of this criterion.

As concerns point (b), that is, the question of how one is supposed to know with certainty that something cannot be disputed without self-contradiction or justified without the logical fallacy of question-begging, we will see below that due to a whole slew of possibilities of error one of course *cannot* know this with absolute certainty. One possibility of error, that of the faulty *explication* of the so-called operational knowledge [*Handlungswissen*], is acknowledged by Apel.[67] This also spells the failure of the programme of final justification, despite Apel's insistence to the contrary.

2.2.2.2. The "Identification/Demonstration" of Presuppositions of Argumentation and the "Execution" of Final Justification

So there is no absolute certainty. We now wish to take a closer look at the transcendental–pragmatic philosophers' attempt to find it. In doing so we will be able to find additional confirmation of what we had found above based on more general considerations, namely, that transcendental pragmatics is unable to deliver any final justification. Additionally we will see that the "procedure" for "identifying" or "discovering" [*aufweisen*] presuppositions of argumentation through the "demonstration" [*Nachweis*] of performative self-contradictions—which Habermas also attempts—does not demonstrate or identify anything, but rather overhastily and dogmatically *declares* exactly those norms to be presuppositions that suit the proponents of discourse ethics.

We will start with a look at the efforts of transcendental–pragmatic philosophers to answer the question (b) mentioned above (how is one supposed to know, and with certainty, that something in fact cannot be disputed without self-contradiction and cannot be justified without the logical error of question-begging?) and in this way—in vain—to demonstrate rules or presuppositions of argumentation. First, using the example of Kuhlmann, we will consider the attempt to provide final justification for the *validity* of presuppositions of argumentation *generally*, whatever they may be (2.2.2.2.1). Subsequently we will look at Apel's and Kuhlmann's efforts to demonstrate *specific* presuppositions of argumentation and offer final justification for them (2.2.2.2.2). Finally we will return to question (a), which reads: how is one supposed to know, and with certainty, that this criterion is the right one? Should we not have to somehow find justification for this, in fact, infallible justification? In this context the criterion of final justification will then be examined as to its basic logical consistency (2.2.2.2.3).

2.2.2.2.1. Kuhlmann's Futile Attempt at a Final Justification for the Validity of the Presuppositions of Argumentation

According to Kuhlmann, things that satisfy the formula of final justification are

not circumventable or transcendable for us *at all*. It holds with absolute certainty and can be relied on as a secure and unconditional basis for further (conditional) justifications.[68]

This secure basis is, as we already know, supposed to consist in presuppositions and rules of argumentation. But how can one *infallibly* show them to be "uncircumventable", as furnished with final justification?

Kuhlmann admits that this is not possible from within the "theoretical attitude".[69] Thus he asks us to adopt a different attitude, another method besides theoretical reflection—namely, that of *strict reflection*. He explains it as follows:

> He [the reflecting subject; U.S.] has to doubt as radically as possible, he has to mobilize doubt that is not even real yet, that is merely possible. On the one hand he is not permitted to forget that a regress in justification and the Munchhausen trilemma that radical doubt entangles him in only present him with a real problem because he supposes it to be true and certain that he can meaningfully doubt in the first place, i.e. that he has operational knowledge. Ultimately he has to bring both sides together: in the position of the currently doubting subject he has to conceive the certainty that he is in fact meaningfully doubting as a basis of his universal doubt, he has to see his trust in his operational knowledge as the foundation of his abysmal mistrust in every alleged item of knowledge.[70]

Kuhlmann defines this rather interesting "testing procedure" such that the results are already *biased*. For despite his assurance to the contrary Kuhlmann does not want to let his certainty become so entirely radical. The "currently doubting subject" in this procedure is supposed to *not* doubt, but rather *presuppose*, that he assumes with certainty his ability to meaningfully doubt and that this means having operational knowledge. In other words: whoever uses this procedure can *by definition* arrive only at the outcome that he has assumed something as certain and that he has operational knowledge—no matter how matters really stand. For whoever does not arrive at the outcome favoured by the procedure has—by definition—not used this procedure.

Thus this procedure is not suited for final justification, since one is entitled to ask why one should accept such a biased procedure as a valid standard. One could just as well request of those who do not believe in the Easter bunny the following strictly reflective test procedure for the existence of Easter bunnies:

> The strictly reflective subject is not permitted to forget that he can only ask about the possibility of the Easter bunny because he supposes it to be true and certain that the Easter bunny, as patron saint and condition of the possibility of questioning, actually exists. In the position of the currently doubting subject he has to conceive the certainty that the Easter bunny exists as a basis of his universal doubt, he has to see his trust in the existence of the Easter bunny as the foundation of his abysmal mistrust in every alleged item of existence.

Thus whenever someone forgets this point in reflecting and accordingly disputes the existence of the Easter bunny, he simply has not reflected strictly, by definition. But this surely speaks against "strict reflection" and not in favour of it. Kuhlmann's procedure has not the slightest thing in common with reflection, rationality, critique and doubt; the invitation to use this procedure is an invitation to autosuggestion.[71]

Kuhlmann has obviously succeeded in this. We see this clearly when he carries out his argument for final justification. He means to show here that the claim "the rules of argumentation do not hold for me" (= p) is necessarily false. And Kuhlmann describes the performance of this argument as follows:

When we recognize (p) as an argument, i.e. as an expression formed and uttered by me (the speaker of [p]) according to rules of argumentation—if we necessarily recognize this as long as we are examining whether (p) can be upheld, then in raising this to conscious-ness we have already solved the problem. For it turns out that the validity of the rules of argumentation is only really disputed by me (such that it would make sense to examine the truth of the claim under dispute) if I at the same time recognize the rules of argumentation. Thus (p) proves to be false, even necessarily false. The validity of the rules of argumentation cannot be meaningfully disputed.[72]

This argument has been subject to various lines of criticism that we will return to later. However, one criticism that has been overlooked so far but that is quite reveal-ing of the blinkers that narrowly restrict this "strict reflection" is the following:

Kuhlmann sees the law of non-contradiction (which for Kuhlmann also includes performative contradictions) as a rule of argumentation.[73] If one opens one's eyes, as strict reflection supposedly calls for, one can see the following: in proposing (p) as an argument, according to Kuhlmann's thesis the speaker involves himself in a contradiction. This means, however, that (p) is an argument *even though* there is a contradiction, and thus what we have here is a *violation of the rules of argumenta-tion* that contradictions are to be avoided. Short and sweet: obviously the speaker is also able to argue *without* following the rules of argumentation and thus is per-fectly correct in asserting the statement (p) that Kuhlmann disapproves of: "The rules of argumentation do not hold for me."

This conclusion of course holds only under the assumption that the validity of rules of argumentation consists in the *necessity* of following them when one wants to argue. This assumption certainly fits what one would ordinarily understand as the validity of rules of argumentation and fits what is implied by Kuhlmann's statement that having recognized something as an argument means having recog-nized it as "an expression formed and uttered...according to rules of argumen-tation". If the rules of argumentation were not constitutive of argumentation, Kuhlmann's statement would be false. However, in this sense of validity the rule of argumentation that Kuhlmann so emphasizes, namely, the law of performative non-contradiction, would clearly not hold—as was shown by our reflection here, which may not be "strict" but is for that reason all the more stringent. And if this is the case with such a central rule, we have no reason to suppose it will be any different with the other rules of argumentation.

Every attempt to prevent strict reflection from backfiring and coming back to hurt transcendental pragmatics in the way shown above ends up declawing "strict reflection." Thus, to name just one possibility, Kuhlmann cannot simply insist that the law of non-contradiction is a constitutive rule of argumentation such that fail-ure to adhere to it makes argument impossible. In this case (p) would no longer be an argument, since (p) violates this rule. But if (p) is not an argument, then there is of course no performative contradiction at work when a speaker repudiates the rules of argumentation, (p) being conceived merely as a "dismissive stance".[74] But then clearly there would no longer be any performative contradictions in argu-ing. Yet performative contradictions are the criterion that the transcendental–pragmatic philosophers want to use to demonstrate rules of argumentation and provide them with final justification. This would then no longer be possible, and transcendental pragmatics comes to an end.

To avoid this consequence, one could of course fall back on the option of no longer seeing the law of (performative) non-contradiction as a rule of argumentation. However, this would bring several disadvantages. On the one hand the transcendental–pragmatic philosophers have already introduced it as a rule of argumentation with final justification.[75] It casts the entire enterprise of final justification in a poor light if one concedes the error of things today that one had claimed to be ultimately justified and certain yesterday. Furthermore it is precisely the emergence of a contradiction in disputing a rule that they want to use to demonstrate final justification. But when the law of (performative) non-contradiction is not a rule of argumentation but rather, let us say, an idiosyncratic predilection, just a "quirk" of transcendental–pragmatic philosophers, then what is this contradiction concerning "uncircumventable presuppositions" supposed to prove? Nothing.

A more attractive alternative by far for Kuhlmann would be to argue that one does not necessarily have to *comply* with the rules of argumentation, but one has to *recognize* them. This is the line taken by Habermas, who argues that at least certain rules of argumentation do not need to be factually complied with in arguing.[76] However, this contradicts Kuhlmann's claim, made in his strict reflection, that an argument is an expression "formed and uttered according to rules of argumentation". One can form and utter an expression according to the rules of argumentation only when one complies with these rules in doing so. Praising and glorifying them is not enough.

There is in my opinion nothing left for Kuhlmann besides these two alternatives. And in fact, like Apel, he talks continually about the *recognition* of these rules of argumentation more than he does about compliance with them. If Kuhlmann chooses this alternative (i.e. recognition), then we have already established the preliminary result that the assumption that Kuhlmann "raises to consciousness" in his strict reflection, namely, his assumption that only those things can be arguments that are formed in compliance with the rules of argumentation, is false. Thus strict reflection is clearly—even in the hands of a recognized authority like Kuhlmann—a highly unreliable and wholly fallible enterprise.

The emphasis on recognition rather than compliance has further disagreeable consequences for final justification. If the sentence "I recognize these rules" is not meant in the sense of "I will conform to these rules, i.e. I will comply with them", then it is tantamount to saying "I consider these rules to be valid." The question arises here as to what could possibly be meant by the "validity" of rules of argumentation. Normally one would assume that the validity of rules of argumentation means that one has to comply with them if one wants to engage in argument. But we have seen that this is not necessarily the case—for example, in the case of the central rule of the law of performative non-contradiction. Yet Kuhlmann and Apel see the rules of argumentation as *moral* norms. Accordingly their validity would be moral in nature. But the moral validity of rules of argumentation could not be demonstrated with Kuhlmann's "strict reflection" even if this were able to demonstrate that one in fact *recognizes* the rules of argumentation (as moral rules) in arguing. For whether a norm is recognized is one thing; whether it is valid is another. I will return to this point later.

Furthermore, strict reflection can by no means prove that someone recognizes the rules of argumentation. Kuhlmann had claimed: "For it turns out that the validity of the rules of argumentation is only really disputed by me...if I at the same time recognize the rules of argumentation." This does not "turn out" to be the case at all. For someone to carry out a certain action, such as turning on a radio, he simply has to carry out the action, to turn on the radio. He does not have to find the action morally right or practicable or aesthetically appealing. Accordingly, for a speaker to argue he simply has to argue. Even if he does follow certain rules or even (in case they are constitutive) has to follow them, nothing about this would stop him from finding them morally reprehensible or unsuitable for the goal of finding the truth that Kuhlmann ascribes to argumentation.[77] So Albert is entirely correct when he remarks that the question of whether someone recognizes certain rules of argumentation in arguing can be only empirically determined.[78] Kuhlmann dismissed this objection with the remark that someone who does not recognize the rules of argumentation is not arguing.[79] This is correct only if—and all this would have to be proven instead of merely presupposed—there are in fact rules of argumentation, and "recognition" is meant as compliance with them, and this is also constitutive of argumentation. We saw that strict reflection and transcendental pragmatics self-destruct under this reading. If "recognition" is meant as "holding valid" (or something similar, just not compliance with constitutive rules), then Kuhlmann's answer to Albert is wrong.

How does the situation look with the empirical data? Well, clearly not good, since in light of them Kuhlmann is compelled to slightly relativize his thesis of recognition:

This does not mean that it is impossible not to in fact recognize the norms, to decide against recognizing them and to act accordingly. That there are these sorts of decisions, that there are deliberate violations of these norms, that cannot reasonably be doubted. Rather it means that it is impossible to establish a position from which one can dispute the validity of the norms, from which one can decide against recognizing the norms, *such that a cogent argument* against the validity of these norms *could result*, i.e. such that this possibility would be able to say something about the objective logical validity of the moral principle.[80]

Against this we should note that the fact—which, as we saw above, the transcendental–pragmatic philosophers are unable to reasonably deny—that one can argue without complying with the norms favoured by Kuhlmann and Apel, for example, without the law of performative non-contradiction, also speaks strongly against the "objective logical validity" of these norms as rules of argumentation. And the validity of these norms as *moral* norms is supposed to follow from their validity as uncircumventable, that is, as norms of argumentation whose recognition is *necessary*.[81] This is, after all, the entire point of the transcendental–pragmatic justification of norms. So this also speaks against the "objective logical validity" of the alleged principle of morality. For if it is possible to not recognize these norms, then their recognition is not necessary and the inference to their validity is false.

Thus the factual non-recognition of these norms is quite clearly a cogent argument against their validity.

Kuhlmann thus has to rely on the notion of their necessary recognition. At the same time he is not entirely able to deny that it is possible to not recognize rules of argumentation, particularly those that Kuhlmann suggests to us. So he says that here we have to "reckon with *two levels*":

There is the level of presuppositions to argumentation, which are more or less implicitly made, assumed, known. It holds of this level that the norms of communicative ethics are always already *necessarily* recognized. They cannot not be recognized by the subject of norms.—On the other hand there is the level of the explicit decisions in favour of these norms or against them, for or against alternatives of action. This is the level at which the opening question of ethics, "what should we do?" is raised, and it is in regard to what happens or should happen at this level that the philosophers propose normative ethics.[82]

Happily, Kuhlmann himself sees the puzzling thing about this "solution", namely, that it can be "claimed that it is difficult to understand, according to this construction with its two levels, what a subject of norms who explicitly decides against recognizing N3 despite the necessary recognition of N3 is actually supposed to be recognizing—what this subject wants in this case, what he always already necessarily wills, or what he explicitly wills now".[83] On the other hand this formulation is directed at obscuring the full extent of the problem wherever possible. To begin with: what is meant by "decision"? Let us assume that for a certain person it is necessary for whatever reasons not to travel to London. This means that it would be impossible for him to travel to London. Nonetheless the person in question could naturally *decide* to travel to London. He would simply never be able to put this decision into practice. Kuhlmann's formulation here gives the impression that the transcendental–pragmatic argument works similarly: someone cannot fail to recognize the rules of argumentation, but he can—possibly, if he has not yet come to understand the necessity of their recognition—decide not to recognize them, although without being able to put this decision into practice. This would not really be so difficult to understand; at the very least there seems to be no logical contradiction here. However, the real problem does harbour a contradiction.

This norm N3, to stay with the example, reads:

When we are seriously interested in solving a practical problem, a problem concerning—as we can now say *in general*—the justification of norms of action, goals, needs, and interests, and particularly in the case of a conflict between the claims of the participants of a communicative community, then we have to work towards a solution that every member of the unrestricted communicative community can agree to, towards a reasonable practical consensus.[84]

I hold this norm to be wrong, morally reprehensible and profoundly naive. Hitler could certainly not have agreed to Georg Elser's attempted assassination of him, not even under "ideal conditions of communication"—which speaks in favour of the attempted assassination and not, as would follow from N3, against it. Furthermore, since *ought* implies *can*, and since a "reasonable" consensus on practical questions such as which norms to implement or to keep, a consensus reached—according to Kuhlmann's interpretation of "reasonable"—without compulsion and only through argumentation, is *impossible* among the five billion residents of Earth,[85] N3 is quite clearly invalid. This is in any case my firm conviction. In other words, I have not just decided against recognizing N3, but it is quite simply the case that I *do not in fact recognize* N3.

We can prove this to Kuhlmann using his own theory: "...a speech act or an argumentative move is always precisely that speech act or that argumentative move that it is declared to be in the corresponding performative statement or in the corresponding operational knowledge."[86] So now I would like to performatively execute the following speech act:

"I hereby deny the norm N3 my recognition."

Thanks to the performative verb, I have hereby quite unequivocally denied the norm my recognition. Since recognition and the denial of recognition are mutually exclusive, it is proven that I do not recognize N3.

If Kuhlmann nonetheless still insists that I do recognize it, although I obviously do not recognize it (and in light of my clear position on N3 this *is* obvious), then Kuhlmann is also unable to eliminate the *logical contradiction* with his theory of two levels—or only at the cost of throwing out the baby with the bathwater: the necessity of recognizing x means that the non-recognition of x is an impossibility. But if it is possible not to recognize x on the explicit level, then this *is* possible and thus recognition of x is not necessary.

One could avoid this by making the claim of necessity less general and restricting it from the very outset to the implicit level (whatever this means). In this case one would claim only that it is necessary for each speaker to recognize N3 *at the implicit level*. And the formulation of Kuhlmann's theory of levels makes it sound like this strategy. Nonetheless, a logical contradiction remains so long as this recognition remains identical on both levels. For one can *express* recognition of x explicitly in a certain way while at the same time implicitly, that is, through one's behaviour, expressing non-recognition; yet only one of the two communicative acts, either the explicit one or the implicit one, can express the *true* stance to x. One cannot recognize and at the same time not recognize something in the same way with the same type of recognition. To avoid this contradiction, one would have to interpret implicit and explicit recognition as different *types* of recognition instead of different "levels" at which the same type of recognition can be found. But then Kuhlmann would be faced with the rather difficult task of explaining how we are supposed to imagine someone who finds a norm wrong, immoral and fatuous nonetheless "implicitly recognizing" it.

These considerations show that Kuhlmann's efforts to dispel the difficulties in understanding his position necessarily fail. Thus Kuhlmann does not even address the decisive difficulty when he says:

We can understand, for example, that A knows what he should do (what he actually wills qua rational being), but at that moment wills something else, even that A wills the contradiction (or if we prefer: the error). Further this situation will certainly be familiar to some of my readers, as it is to me, from introspection. From this perspective one can understand very well what it means to decide in favour of the bad with a bad conscience...[87]

Here Kuhlmann tries without further ceremony to paint this difficulty as a version of the Socratic paradox in order to draw the conclusion he wishes, namely, that "this argument cannot be brought against transcendental–pragmatic communicative ethics in particular."[88] This attempt is, however, misleading, since our problem here is by no means that people "faced with the possibility of the better option, consciously decide for the worse".[89] Rather I find N3 bad, and in rejecting N3 I have a good conscience; and it can be assumed that most people who reject Kuhlmann's rules of argumentation also have a good conscience about it. Thus it is something else entirely that Kuhlmann would have to make plausible here, something he does not even dare to suggest. He would have to show that it is easily comprehensible from introspection how we could sincerely and emphatically repudiate a norm, explicitly deny it our recognition and consider it invalid, wrong, foolish, ridiculous and outrageous, while *still* at the same time recognizing it. Clearly Kuhlmann can hardly succeed in this; this situation represents a conceptual impossibility, an absurdity that can find no corresponding phenomenon in reality. But concepts without intuitions are empty. In other words, whenever the transcendental–pragmatic philosophers talk about "implicit recognition", they convey no semantic content whatsoever and produce mere noises. The transcendental–pragmatic concept of "implicit recognition" is meaningless.

Thus we have established so far that Kuhlmann's argument for final justification is untenable. This argument has not even been used to justify any *concrete* norms or to even try to justify any, but rather was meant to prove only that *the* rules of argumentation—whatever they may be—are necessarily valid and recognized. If the argument for final justification already fails at this level, it is clear that it certainly cannot deliver a final justification of any particular concrete norms. Although our discussion of N3 has already shown this, we will continue to assess this problem under different aspects.

Kuhlmann himself also seems to lose faith in his argument when it comes to the identification of concrete norms. For in the "Reflective Final Justification" portion of his book, which is supposed to accomplish this (although he mentions strict reflection in his discussion of methodology),[90] he does not make use of the "strictly reflective argument". In fact here he relies on theoretical reflections that he otherwise holds to be insufficient, and on certain rhetorical manoeuvres that he has meanwhile given a central prominence,[91] the curious features of which we will find occasion to discuss below.

2.2.2.2.2. How to Provide Final Justification for Specific Presuppositions of Argumentation? Apel's Dogmatic "Reflections" and Kuhlmann's Contrived "Dialogues"

Now we should take a look at how Apel claims to be able to identify and provide final justification for sundry presuppositions of argumentation using strict reflection.

…when I reflect on what I cannot dispute as a presupposition (a nomological or existential presupposition) of my act of arguing upon pain of a *performative self-contradiction*… [,] I can *discover*, as Descartes himself already suggested, the *self-evidence* of the necessary

coincidence of my thinking or arguing and my existence—discover in the light of the performative self-contradiction to be avoided: "I hereby think (or claim) that I do not exist."
The reflection on this "clash" between the *proposition asserted* and the *act of performing its
assertion* shows me in this case that my existence and the knowledge of my existence are
included in the very act of performative assertion.

And it is precisely in this sense that every active participant in argument can discover
their having already recognized Habermas's four validity claims and the possibility in principle of redeeming these claims by reaching *consensus* in argument...In redeeming the normative claim to rightness the one arguing can now, in my view, discover it in light of this
criterion as a certainty—contrary to the opinion of Alfred Berlich—that with every sincere
act of argumentation he has already recognized the *equal status* of all members of an ideal
communicative community in principle. That is, each individual element of this necessary
presupposition can be shown to be indisputable in light of an already recognized principle
of performative consistency.[92]

This procedure is fruitless.

First of all, my existence is not one of the necessary presuppositions of argumentation. For most people certainly argue without presupposing my existence.
They might presuppose *their* existence, but Apel's procedure aims to uncover universally valid presuppositions necessarily assumed by *everyone*. Yet apparently in
place of this they offer mere idiosyncrasies. Thus, as in the case of Kuhlmann, we
see here as well that the "procedure" of transcendental reflection in no way allows
an inference from oneself to others.

What is wrong with this "procedure"? Well, first of all the "clash" at issue here
is difficult to see as one between the proposition asserted and the *act* of performing its assertion. If I assert "I am asserting nothing", then the proposition asserted
in fact does contradict the *act* of its assertion—*in* my asserting this proposition,
with the *act* of assertion I do the opposite of what I assert. The situation looks
very different when I assert: "I have not recognised the equal status in principle of all communicative partners." For at the most I have recognized the equal
status in principle of all communicative partners *during* my act of assertion, on
the assumption that I have done so at all. The proposition asserted in no way
contradicts the *act* of its assertion, but rather what I "implicitly recognize" *during* execution of the act, namely, the presuppositions of argument. But a *presupposition* of argument is not an *act* of argumentation, and a presupposition
of argumentation is always a presupposition *that* something is the case, that is,
it is a *proposition*. Otherwise Apel would be unable to speak of *knowledge*, and
Kuhlmann would be unable to claim that a *theory* of argumentation is implicit in
operative knowledge.[93]

Of course, we could also look at the *act* of presupposing—instead of the presuppositions, that is, the propositions presupposed. But the *act* of presupposing only
contradicts the proposition mentioned above, "I have not *recognized* the equal status in principle of all communicative partners" (and there is only a contradiction
here if we understand "recognized" to mean "implicitly recognized", that is in the
sense of "(implicitly) presupposed"). It does not contradict the statement Apel
declares to be "performatively self-contradictory" in arguing that the discourse

norms *themselves* and not just their recognition cannot be disputed without per-formative contradiction, namely, the statement: "It is not the case that one *ought to* recognize the equal status in principle of the members of an ideal communicative community." This presupposition does not tell us anything about the *act* of presup-posing, about the *act* of recognition, and thus cannot be in contradiction with it. There would be a contradiction only to the purportedly presupposed *proposition:* "One ought to recognize the equal status in principle of the members of an ideal communicative community." In other words, Apel's, Kuhlmann's and Habermas's claim that one can dispute the presuppositions of argumentation only upon pain of a *pragmatic, performative* self-contradiction is false. The contradictions "uncov-ered" by our proponents of discourse ethics are all *propositional* contradictions in so far as they exist at all. To be sure, we could *call* the contradiction between an explicitly claimed proposition and the proposition "implicitly recognized" in its assertion in the form of a presupposition of argumentation a "performative self-contradiction"—but that would only be a further instance of false labelling.

Of course, for false labelling to be successful one needs not just a label but some-thing to put it on. In this case we would need a contradiction—namely, the one between the presupposition of argumentation and the proposition asserted. The second is easy to get, but where do we find the first? Apel's characterization of the transcendental–reflective procedure claims to be able to answer this question—but it never delivers on this claim. In order to be able to reflect upon this "clash" one would first have to find it. This presupposes our ability to find a presupposition of argumentation that contradicts the proposition in question. But how to identify the presuppositions of argumentation is precisely the question. The indication that the "clash" consists in a performative self-contradiction does not bring us any further, since for Apel, due to this false labelling, a performative self-contradiction *is* nothing more than a contradiction between an asserted proposition and a presupposition implicitly recognized in its assertion. How we can discover this contradiction, how-ever, is once again the problem at issue. Thus Apel ends up chasing his own tail.[94]

Yet maybe this clash is just something that one *registers* when one is entangled in a performative self-contradiction, as its epiphenomenal by-product, so to speak—and with Apel it *sounds* like this. (This by itself—although not just this—would make the procedure empirical through and through, as empirical as a stomach ache.) But how is this supposed to be possible? Apel also characterizes the presup-positions of argumentation as "operative knowledge".[95] Thus it corresponds to our knowledge of the rules of grammar. Now it is a very idiosyncratic notion that a competent speaker of English—who at the same time has no particular knowledge of the *theory* of grammar (the *formulation* of certain rules)—feels a certain "clash", an experience of dissonance, when he says, "In simple present tense the verb 'to do' is not required as an auxiliary verb to express negation." A clash would occur only if he *breaks* this rule and says, for example, "I smoke not", but not when he merely *disputes* the rule. Thus the idea that one could "demonstrate" any grammatical or pragmatic rules by trying to dispute them and then seeing if one feels a "clash" is without any foundation.

Furthermore, how is one supposed to know that a certain clash does demonstrate a contradiction to the universal presuppositions of argumentation? It is not surprising—in fact it is predictable—that someone like Apel, who does not so much implicitly assume the alleged presuppositions of argument as much as he simply believes in them and is convinced of them, will feel a "clash" when he *disputes* them—especially when he *wants* to find them without fail and thus could easily become the victim of autosuggestion. Of course, a committed Nazi will also feel this sort of clash when he disputes the Führer principle. These "clashes", these experiences of dissonance, may point to certain attitudes, convictions and biases of the person who has them; they are hardly suited for demonstrating universally valid, necessary presuppositions of argumentation. It is clearly not possible to find any criteria with which one could recognize, on reflection, that a certain experience of a "clash" points to universal and necessary presuppositions of argumentation and not to just any particular and contingent assumptions and convictions.

Apel is not perturbed by any of these questions, if only because he never asks them of himself. Instead, a page later he again emphatically assures us—without providing any evidence—that his procedure works very well and can be used to demonstrate certain rules of argumentation, such as those already mentioned in the previous quotation. And he writes:

To see this, one only has to—sure enough—engage sincerely in methodical reflection in the sense mentioned; and of course no-one can be forced to do this.[96]

With this claim we have arrived at the real heart of the Apelian method. The "methodological reflection" is not in itself a source of bias, it is simply inadequate, for the reasons discussed above. But the *use* Apel makes of this "methodological reflection", the *way* he resorts to it in his argumentation, corresponds to just that entirely unacceptable element of bias that we already saw in connection with Kuhlmann's description of strict reflection: whoever fails to "discover" the norms heralded by Apel has not sincerely engaged in the procedure. Nor, according to Apel, has one in that case seriously taken up the transcendental question: "What do I have to presuppose to be valid in order for my current argumentative action—question, claim, conclusion, call for confirmation or dissent—to *make sense?*", which supposedly first "makes room" for the decisive "evidence".[97] And so Apel, who attributes to the "results" of his "procedure" a status beyond logical–analytic or empirical insights (and, as mentioned above, logical–analytic insights are empirical, they are just not synthetic), also does not shy away from claiming the following about Albert:

As long as he does not seriously *engage* in this—that is, in the serious scrutiny of the transcendental-reflective alternatives to either *empirical* or *logical-analytic* insights—one cannot take seriously his recent claim that he has no objection to the programme of a transcendental epistemology.[98]

In other words, Apel is simply accusing Albert of insincerity.

But it is not only a cursed fallibilist such as Albert, but even honest-to-goodness Kantian transcendental philosophers (have even *these* failed to seriously engage in the "transcendental-reflective alternatives"?) who fall victim to Apel's infallible verdicts, although here in more psychological, less moralistic tones; among other things, they are naïve.

To appropriately evaluate Apel's verdict we will have to step back a little. The objection is that, even if we can ascertain certain of our argumentative presuppositions through reflection, their universality (rather than their socio-cultural particularity) can be demonstrated only through (fallible) empirical investigations, such as by "proving the presupposed rules through interrogation of 'native speakers'".[99] Apel responds to this as follows:

(A) The reference to [the] fact that under certain socio-cultural conditions, discourse norms can not be explicitly acknowledged, is totally irrelevant to our context; for it concerns only the question of whether the normative presuppositions in question are necessarily implicit in an *adequate concept of argumentation*. Here the suspicion of a *petitio principii* could be raised, because, it could be objected, it concerns precisely the attainment, above all, of an adequate concept of argumentation through an empirical investigation.

(B) Nevertheless, this objection offers us the opportunity to answer appropriately from the point of view of transcendental–pragmatics. The answer would be something like: an adequate concept of argumentation, concerning its necessary conditions, can only be attained through *strict transcendental reflection*; for example, through the following reflection: for us it is unthinkable to comprehend the methodical sense of the proposed empirical procedure of proof without already presupposing the four validity claims and their essentially possible discursive validation or invalidation. With this it is patently demonstrated that the mentioned presuppositions of argumentation as such are *for everyone* who argues uncircumventable, untranscendable (*nichthintergehbar*) and inasmuch, undebatable, unquestionable.[100]

Now the objection treated here by Apel says precisely that the circumstance that something important—such as comprehending the sense of the proposed empirical procedure—is inconceivable *for us* unless we make certain presuppositions of argumentation, does not show that this is inconceivable for *everyone* without these presuppositions, thus making them universal. Apel's "strict transcendental reflection"—namely, the thought that, if something important for us is inconceivable without certain presuppositions, this shows that it is inconceivable *for everyone* without these presuppositions—simply *repeats* the thesis that the objection targets, and is thus not a counter-argument but rather an expression of the incapacity to respond reasonably to objections. The "appropriate" answer "from the point of view of transcendental–pragmatics" is thus nothing but dogmatic insistence.

At the conference where this objection was raised, Apel's response was longer,[101] and yet apparently no more convincing for transcendental philosophers. So Apel complains:

…nowadays the orthodox Kantians are in my opinion very far removed from a radical application of the *method of transcendental reflection*. The objection under discussion, for example, was raised by a renowned transcendental philosopher, and it made sense to all of the conference participants, including all of the transcendental philosophers present. The main reason why the transcendental philosophers conduct themselves de facto like naïve empiricists could in my opinion be traced back to the fact that they are fixated on Kant's *epistemological* question and have hardly considered the possibility of applying Kant's transcendental question in *strict reflection* to one's own conditions of argumentation. Of course they are also unused to the presumption [*Zumutung*] of finding *public linguistic argument* and thus *normative presuppositions of a contrafactually anticipated ideal communicative community* within their own *thinking*.[102]

"Presumption" is the perfect word choice. Elsewhere Apel explains how the sentence "the current king of France is bald" cannot be considered meaningful, since due to its failure to satisfy the "existential presuppositions" in the proposition being asserted it cannot be true or false.[103] Now the sentence is very much meaningful, even if its existential presuppositions are not satisfied; after all, this also holds for the existential presuppositions of sentences about phlogiston, and of course these are also meaningful, even if in error. However, if Apel considers these sentences meaningless, then he has to explain how it could make sense—and make *pragmatic* sense, and the transcendental–*pragmatic* philosopher has to ultimately be concerned with pragmatic sense—to respond to the question "*Are there* 'normative presuppositions of a contrafactually anticipated ideal communicative community' within thinking?" with the demand: "*Find* them!" "Look and see" would be a more sensible suggestion. Yet Apel does not advise the transcendental philosophers to first look and see, but rather presumes that they simply have to kindly go and find those presuppositions. This puts him in line with Kuhlmann's strict reflection as a "test procedure", the results of which are already known before the test is conducted.

Fascinatingly, Apel thinks—along with Kuhlmann and contrary to Habermas— that this *must* be so. And he refers to a "*a* transcendental–pragmatically decisive argument" (which is the only one he provides):

If it were possible to *empirically* assess the *general and necessary presuppositions of argumentation*, then it would also have to be possible that these presuppositions are falsified and at the same time presupposed as valid.[104]

Apel does not provide any further explication of this "decisive" argument. Evidently he assumes that the then-clause cannot possibly be true and thus that the conditional clause has to be false. However, this argument has certain weaknesses.

It is odd when a presupposition is falsified—and this is done by epistemological subjects—while at the same time these very same epistemological subjects continue to presuppose its validity. An epistemological subject, one would think, cannot simultaneously see a presupposition as falsified *and* presuppose it as valid. However, *that just this is possible* is elsewhere *one of the decisive transcendental– pragmatic theses*.[105] If Apel has in the meantime come to understand that this transcendental–pragmatic thesis is false, then this is to be applauded, but it hardly offers a suitable defence of his philosophy.

Furthermore, even if we cannot empirically *falsify* a presupposition, this does not mean that we cannot empirically *assess* it. This sort of assessment would always turn out positive for the presuppositions of argumentation—not because they are necessarily *true*, but because we necessarily *hold* them to be true. This does not make such assessment superfluous or less "meaningful", as Apel claims in all seriousness,[106] since a negative result concerning a purported presupposition of argumentation would after all show that it is not in fact a presupposition of argumentation.

This now brings us to the decisive fallibilistic insight that this transcendental–pragmatic argument is also false and betrays certain confusions. This is because what is at stake here is not the empirical assessment of the presuppositions themselves, that is the assessment of their correctness, but rather the empirical appraisal of the question whether presuppositions are *made* and, if so, which. And there is no hint in Apel's decisive counter-argument—which instead seems to miss the topic entirely—as to why it should be impossible to falsify answers (i.e. transcendental–pragmatic ones) to *this* question. Of course they can be empirically falsified. In fact this is just what has happened. Several philosophers, including myself, have reflected upon what it is that they cannot dispute on pain of a performative self-contradiction. And those philosophers who do not happen to be proponents of transcendental pragmatics ascertained that they do *not* recognize several if not all of the presuppositions of argumentation mentioned by Apel and his followers. I myself, for example, accept none of the rules of argumentation mentioned by Apel so far. Thus Apel's thesis that the presuppositions are universally and necessarily recognized in arguing is empirically false.

So clearly the thesis that one can demonstrate the truth or falsehood of statements about all of those things allegedly presupposed by participants in argument only by means of fallible, empirical investigations such as "proving the presupposed rules through interrogation of 'native speakers'" is not at all "extremely implausible", as Apel claims,[107] but rather entirely correct. Furthermore, it is not even quite clear which alternatives Apel is able to offer. For "transcendental" or "strict reflection", that is, the "reflective *test of consistency* in the sense of the attempt to dispute the claimed presupposition without performative self-contradiction" is no alternative. This becomes clear when Apel himself—apparently to counter the very natural suspicion of dogmatism—assures us of the following:

> Of course *every possible opponent* is eligible for this test; more precisely: each and every person—and this includes a sufficiently well-educated Papuan—who is able to share the problem with the proponent, namely the question of the necessary presuppositions of argumentation. All others cannot be partners but only "objects of theory" in the argumentative discourse.[108]

How, we would like to ask—except for Apel, who clearly does not share *this* question—are we to ascertain which result this Papuan will come to *without* empirical evidence? This could hardly happen with Apel's strict reflection (which, incidentally, would also be nothing more than an empirical procedure once we cleanse it of its biases), since as a declared expert in transcendental philosophy Apel should know that *reflection* in the sense of *being cast back upon oneself*, in the sense of the reflection on what one has already recognized,[109] cannot possibly work with regard to others, even if it works *for* the others themselves: I can reflect back only on myself, I cannot reflect *back* upon others. In other words, Apel can at most reflect upon *his* presuppositions of argumentation, not those of others. He can only determine *their* presuppositions of argumentation empirically, through the interrogation of "native speakers". And if the native speakers discover different presuppositions of argumentation from Apel's, then at first it is just his word against theirs. But not entirely. For the number of philosophers and other native speakers who claim not to recognize the presuppositions favoured by Apel far outnumber those who claim that they do. And this makes the testimony of transcendental pragmatics somewhat less plausible than that of UFO sightings or haunted houses, since after all those reporting about hauntings or UFOs typically do not claim that there are UFOs and ghosts wherever we are looking. If we ask a UFO spotter why it is that we have yet to see a UFO ourselves, he can obviously answer that it is most likely simply because no UFO has ever flown by us. They are rare, after all. With Apel the case is different: he claims that *whoever* reflects makes presuppositions of argumentation of a certain kind while doing so. But then why is it not everyone who reflects that sees them, but only Apel and some of his followers?

These sorts of question and argument will not have any effect on Apel, with his continual admonitions to have insight. Instead he prefers to complain that the recognition of the presuppositions of argumentation he has supposedly discovered "unfortunately is empirically not self-evident even among philosophers".[110] Apparently every tester is eligible for Apel, but not every test result. Not for a moment does it occur to him that this lack of recognition could be an indication of the falsity and error of his "discoveries". Instead, as we saw, in the face of disagreeable results of reflection he resorts to attacking the people behind them and accusing them of non-compliance, insincerity, lack of effort, "naivety" and short-sightedness—even though one of the purported rules of discourse calls for recognizing others as argumentative partners with equal status. Apel clearly feels himself not to be bound by this rule, explaining instead that the necessity of recognizing the presuppositions in question "is testified [*bezeugen*] *in actu* by all those who argue seriously", even—for what does it matter to Apel what others say—"even were they to affirm the opposite".[111] So Apel does everything correctly in "transcendental reflection", and when others arrive at different results then *they* must have done something wrong. This seems to be clear to him from the very beginning, otherwise he would be unable to brush aside the results of others' reflection so easily. Then he would have to *justify* the claim that they are false, and, moreover, not only with recourse to his *own* reflections, since their correctness is just what the reflection of the others puts into question. In fact what he does is no more or less than to incessantly repeat the results of his own reflection and declare them as the only sacred and true revelation, while declaring the results of others—with an arrogant and circular reference to *his* infallible revelation—as the products of character flaws or a lack of competence. Apel evidently holds himself to be the chosen one among the philosophers and the representative of the ideal communicative community on Earth.[112] He demonstrates this in spectacular fashion through his *way* of philosophizing, even when he *claims* something different for cosmetic reasons.

Accordingly, Apel's dogmatism and the overbearing presumptuousness of his "proofs" have been criticized again and again. In light of this criticism it is very much out of place for Apel to label the reproach made against him that he puts into the concept of argumentation only what he wants to get out of it later the "standard argument against transcendental pragmatics" (although of course this argument—depending on the context—is *also* raised), and to rebut it with the claim that the transcendental–pragmatic procedure works using the "demonstration of a contradiction that…*shows itself* when in dialogue (argumentative discourse) the proponent of a proposition can be brought to reflect on the presuppositions of his current act of arguing".[113] The standard objection is rather that Apel simply ignores the circumstance that at this point something entirely *different* reveals itself from what he claims and that he dogmatically *posits* that the things he favours do reveal themselves here, otherwise one must be doing something wrong (e.g. not truly reflecting on an act of *argumentation*, an objection with which Apel at last does seem to resort to a fittingly idiosyncratic definition of "argumentation").

It would seem that Apel is so blinded by his own dogma and so incorrigibly convinced of the conclusiveness of his procedure that he is no longer capable of entertaining the possibility that the "disbelief" of his opponents, *despite* their earnest and sincere reflection on possible presuppositions of argumentation, arises simply because this reflection reveals something *different* from what Apel wants to see. Instead, as mentioned, he prefers to accuse his opponents of non-compliance, insincerity or lack of real effort. The alleged discourse-ethical recognition of argumentative partners is replaced by sectarian strategies of immunization and projection.

In his dispute with Kuhlmann, Albert accurately describes the structure of his procedure thus:

K has recognized some rules, which we can call K-rules. O disputes the validity of these rules for himself with the O-thesis. K now produces an interpretation that embeds the O-thesis within a context that presupposes the validity of the K-rules. Now K has no difficulties drawing the conclusion that there is a contradiction, such that O could not reasonably dispute the validity of the K-rules—carried out with an air of these K-rules being somehow sacrosanct and thus their validity established.

Why should it not be allowed to enquire into the *justification* of the K-rules or to *doubt* the validity of these rules? Should something be out of the question from the outset because K is convinced of its validity and thus is allowed to expect that O *has* to *implicitly* agree with him even if he *explicitly* disputes this? The author [Kuhlmann; U.S.], who otherwise is so quick to find instances of question-begging among the critics of transcendental pragmatics, has evidently accomplished a veritable specimen of this here.[114]

Following Albert, this argument against Apel's and Kuhlmann's "proof procedure" has also been raised by Keuth, Peter Rohs and Arno Ros. The latter spoke quite tellingly, as mentioned, of "interpretive hauteur".[115]

With reference to Ros, Gerhard Schönrich finds that this argument ignores "the status of the argumentative situation".[116] In fact it is Schönrich who misunderstands the status of Ros's objection, which he calls the "argument from particularity", since it has nothing to do with "particularity" and furthermore does not in any way rely on any particular assumptions concerning the status of the argumentative situation. Since Schönrich evidently was not convinced by Ros's own example, I would like now to make the following basic point clear once and for all (and this is basically a summary of Keuth's very commendable recipe *"Wie letztbegründet man seine Forderungen?"* or "How to provide final justification for one's claims"[117]):

Schönrich, Apel and Kuhlmann, like everyone else, necessarily make the argumentative presupposition R while arguing, namely, that *everything* is fallible and nothing capable of final justification. Schönrich, Apel and Kuhlmann will of course dispute this, but, being a transcendental–pragmatist with intimate knowledge of what others suppose in arguing, this fails to impress me. For it is clear that Schönrich, Apel and Kuhlmann entangle themselves in self-contradictions with their acts of disputing, since they have, without doubt, implicitly presupposed R in doing so—which, as I already said, is one of the presuppositions of argumentation (of which I have assured myself in transcendental reflection). It could be that all three of them, failing to see this, continue to insist that despite strict reflection they fail to discover any imputation of the presupposition when they argue; the hypothesis that one *has* to assume R would thus be false. However, considering this, one of course cannot "take seriously", as Apel puts it, the claim of Apel, Kuhlmann and Schönrich to have sincerely engaged in strict reflection; for if they had, they would of course have discovered that they always already assume R in arguing. For in arguing one just does always presuppose R, as these three prove every time they try to dispute it and become entangled in performative self-contradictions, which I know because I have assured myself of the argumentative presupposition R in transcendental reflection. So they presuppose R. "Anyone who does not appreciate or accept this", to quote again from Apel, "is automatically excluded from the discussion."[118]—This argumentation is an exact copy of the method by which the transcendental–pragmatic philosophers "argue". Maybe now, despite his rather broad conception of philosophy, Schönrich can understand somewhat better why Ros feels that he has to protest against the consideration of Apel's "procedure" as "a particularly commendable form of philosophical argument".[119]

In addition, this procedure does not become any more commendable in dialogue form. Kuhlmann does provide an allegedly strictly reflective dialogue meant as a refutation of the argument mentioned. Before turning to this example, we should first more precisely clarify what it is that Kuhlmann sees as a strictly reflective dialogue.

It is characteristic of this dialogue that we see a back-and-forth between two levels that are normally held separate, the level at which the topic at hand is being spoken about and the level at which the communication or argumentation is spoken about. This second level pertains to operative knowledge about arguing. The topics here are rules of the game, procedural regulations, what counts as what, etc.—This gets negotiated without the dialogue parties abandoning their position and stance as dialogue partners. This means that what they discuss on the level of metacommunication they discuss as players who come to agreements about currently valid rules, moves and problems during the game without leaving the game itself, that is, without taking on the distanced position of theorists of communication. This is the idea behind *strict reflection*.[120]

The decisive formulation here is "without taking on the distanced position of theorists of communication", since everything that Kuhlmann describes here can be undertaken from the theoretical stance, for example, by a distanced theorist of communication. There is absolutely no reason why two communicative theorists in conversation should not also be able to theorize about their particular conversation with a continual shifting of levels. So where is the difference here? Kuhlmann answers this with the help of a "typical" dialogue that is meant to clarify "the difference between *theoretical* and *strict* reflection".[121] The telling aspect of this dialogue is less the rather naïve justifications of the protagonist of transcendental pragmatics than the dramatic circumstance that the opponent cannot get a word in edgewise.[122] This is quite "typical" of "strict reflection"—which fundamentally biases the result of its application.

If one does not adopt these transcendental–pragmatic biases as one's own, it quickly becomes clear that the merits Kuhlmann claims of dialogues marked by a continual shifting of levels and by metacommunicative reflectivity are simply not there. Directly after the longer quotation above Kuhlmann describes these as follows:

It is important to note that at the level of metacommunication, the level at which operative knowledge is mobilized, a level at which questions and problems can certainly arise, thus at which one can definitely desire to know something, that at this level long or unending research processes are not possible and not provided for, at least not with regard to the presuppositions whose imputation or non-imputation are relevant for the reaction of the argumentative partner....Argumentative processes are our means of clarifying whatever is problematic. If in normal situations they were to continually entangle us in non-trivial problems such that we were unable to know without research processes how we are to respond to the moves of the other party, then they would not be a suitable means for this. Thus there can be no long research processes about what happens in such a case. But there can be deft maieutic dialogues, which, however have to lead to an elimination of the problem after only a few steps.[123]

This argumentation is staggering. To clarify its structure somewhat, I would like to furnish the argumentative schema with a different content by way of contrast:

Surgical intervention is a means of solving certain health problems of the patient. Now, there are long-running research projects into what the surgeon is to look out for in these operations, in particular how one is to react to certain complications that arise in the patient. But all this takes too long for the alternative physician K.—despite regular publication of the provisional results. And K. now has the idea to speed things up and clarify the matter once and for all. He recommends to the researchers that they switch from the theoretical level, such as the precise observation and evaluation of as many data on operations as possible, to the *strict* level, that is, to research the operations *while* one is *taking part* in the operations

oneself *as doctor*. At this level, the level of the operation itself—or, better still, just as problems are arising—long or unending research processes are in fact not possible and not provided for. And K. concludes from this that any medical deliberations under these conditions
will "have to lead to an elimination of the problem after only a few steps".—Needless to
mention the rather high opportunity costs of our alternative physician's strict medical reflection, such as those deaths that might have been avoided by a less original procedure. The
same holds true of the opportunity costs of Kuhlmann's strict reflection in his philosophy of
language—namely, an entirely avoidable lack of knowledge.

What is "important to see" in Kuhlmann's opinion are in fact *theoretical* assumptions, mere *hypotheses*, on the correctness of which those particular qualities that
Kuhlmann ascribes to his "strict reflection" *depend*. These hypotheses themselves
probably have to be "assumed to be certain" during strict reflection, entirely in line
with the prejudicial mechanism we have already become familiar with. Yet reasonable people will not assume them to be certain. So the notion that the assumptions
of a speaker are "relevant to the reactions of the argumentative partner" is not
accurate. When we ask "how do you *mean* that?", we are asking not about presuppositions but about intentions. Thus the metacommunication that Kuhlmann
champions does not in fact clarify the status of a speech act with recourse to some
suppositions or other. Furthermore, argumentation processes—like emergency
operations as a means of solving problems—do not always work—for example,
precisely because maieutic dialogues do not by any means "have to lead to an
elimination of the problem after only a few steps". In addition it is not at all *certain* but rather false that each agreement we reach through maieutics about what
we presuppose in arguing (a question that, as mentioned, is entirely irrelevant to
the practice of dialogue) is an agreement *in truth*. The dialogue partners could be
mistaken.

These preliminary remarks should have already made it clear that the dialogue that Kuhlmann wants to use to refute Albert, Rohs and Ros will have a hard
time fulfilling its intended purpose. I quote Roh's version of this argument, since
Kuhlmann refers to it:

The question at issue is whether *a* is a condition of the possibility of meaningful argumentation. The sceptic doubts this, and the transcendental philosopher aims to prove it. If *a*
truly is a condition of the possibility of meaningful argumentation, then the sceptic, who is
arguing, will have to rely on *a*. If however *a* is not a condition of the possibility of meaningful argumentation, the sceptic will not need to rely on it. Now it is assumed to be up for
debate whether *a* is a condition of meaningful argumentation...So the argument cannot
use the premise that the sceptic relies on *a*; this would make the argument circular. One
could appeal to some evidence that *a* is a condition of meaningful argumentation...But it
would be circular if one were to try to provide additional support for this evidence through
a reflexive argument premised on the idea that the sceptic in arguing relies on *a*. For
whether the sceptic does this is just what is at issue in the discussion. This argument holds
valid regardless of which concrete proposition *a* stands for, such that no sentence about the
conditions of possibility of meaningful argumentation can be justified reflexively.[124]

Kuhlmann tries to refute this argument in having B, his proponent of transcendental pragmatics, accept the following challenge of sceptic A: "I dispute

the validity of the law of non-contradiction, this law does not hold" (=r). The dialogue that follows, during which significantly fewer arguments occur to Kuhlmann's sceptic than is the case with real sceptics, takes up more than two pages. I will try to sketch the essential points here. After some back and forth, B explains to the sceptic:

You say: "The law of non-contradiction doesn't hold." You are refusing to concede the validity of the very principle that would allow the person hearing this thesis to understand that in your opinion it *really* is not valid; that is, that you don't at the same time think or say that "the law does hold." Explain to me please what exactly it is that you mean here. Before I know that I can't respond appropriately or rationally to r.

The sceptic responds to this, and quite rightly:

But now you're acting dumb on purpose. In fact you understand my statement precisely, as shown by your initial reaction. One can respond sensibly to such a statement without it being entirely clear which presuppositions are being made, and if this is the case then your reflexive argument doesn't hold water.

To which B says:

You're mistaken there, at least as far as it concerns this rather important type of presupposition. If I began by treating r as a normal attempt to dispute something, this is due to the fact that I understood the intention behind the statement r, namely the intention to dispute something, and that I then, as is usual in normal communication, silently corrected the "error" implicit in r according to a variation of this understanding. And this charitable act is at the same time the foundation of our discussion now, in which I treat *every single utterance* from you in this way, since otherwise we wouldn't be having the discussion we seem to be having. If you continue to insist on your thesis and at the same time insist that you are not insisting, cannot insist etc., then I have to end this episode—we couldn't call it a conversation. However, this would mean (a) that you have not disputed anything such that I have to draw consequences from it, and (b) it's on you now, you have to tell me how I can respond to r appropriately. As long as you haven't answered this definitively, for which no possibility is in sight, I have won.[125]

This is where the feigned dialogue ends; at this point nothing further occurs to Kuhlmann's sceptic. So let us loan him a few more ideas here. A could answer:

I challenged you to *show* me that I'm wrong; you haven't shown me anything, but rather just threatened me—threatened not to recognize my assertion as an assertion and even to break off communication. And in this you seem to be very much in line with the true point of Kuhlmann's "strictly reflective dialogue", where according to Kuhlmann B tries "to lead A into a dilemma, namely that either his thesis [r] is wrong or that his utterance cannot count and function as that which it is supposed to be in A's view, since an essential precondition [non-r] for the validity of the utterance as an assertion is lacking".[126] But all you have shown so far is that *you* are not *willing* to recognize my utterance as an assertion as long as I don't recognize your favoured assertion non-r. This might say something about you personally but it says nothing about communicative theory. After all, others—logicians who study paraconsistent logical systems, for example, but not just these—have no difficulty recognizing my thesis r as an assertion and responding to it accordingly. This refutes your thesis.—Possibly now you'll say that these people respond to r as an assertion only because they "implicitly" make the silent "charitable act", this correction of the alleged "error" supposedly implicit in r. Of course these people would dispute this. How do you intend to prove to them that they are wrong? With a reflexive argument meant to show that in arguing with someone they have to assume that this person assumes non-r? This would land you back in Roh's circle, which you had hoped to escape—even worse, in an *unending regress of circles*. I doubt that this is a step forward (if the law of non-contradiction holds, then it isn't) or that it distinguishes reflective argumentation as a particularly desirable form of philosophical argumentation.—But even if no one *can* respond "appropriately" to r (and who defines this: you?), this implies the validity of non-r only if the additional premise q holds that an assertion that cannot be appropriately responded to is false. Naturally one would first have to justify this premise, which you unfortunately neglect to do and which would likely be very difficult for you.—You claim that it is only the law of non-contradiction that enables the person hearing my thesis r (such as yourself) to even understand that I mean the principle really doesn't hold and that I don't at the same time mean that it does hold. Now, in fact I do mean that the principle doesn't hold and that the contrary assertion is false. Thus I do *not* say that the principle doesn't hold *and* holds. The law of non-contradiction says: a statement p and its negation non-p cannot both be true. This is an all-sentence. The negation of this sentence means that there is at least *one* statement that is both true and false, but not that *all* statements are true and false. You might want to counter this with the principle of *ex falso quodlibet*, so that *everything* would follow from the negation of the law of non-contradiction, including that the law of non-contradiction holds. But I am afraid that this follows only in the classic propositional logic, not in the para-consistent logic that I prefer to follow. So you can be assured that I definitely do dispute the law of non-contradiction. And you should be capable of responding to this.—Incidentally, even if I were to argue for the radical thesis that every statement is both true and false, and if you were unable to respond to this "sensibly", this still isn't the question at issue. To defuse Roh's argument it is not enough to show that you cannot *respond* to my thesis (your incompetence cannot count as an argument); rather, you must *show* me, prove to me—and with the help of a *reflexive argument*—that r is false. But you can't do this for the reasons already given, even if the "maieutic deftness of the final justifier"[127] demanded by Kuhlmann did not fizzle out in your case with the threat of breaking off communication.

Thus Kuhlmann by no means succeeds in defusing the argument that strict reflection is circular, and he simply *posits* what it should demonstrate or justify. For it *is* without a doubt circular and biased. Not only is it incapable of *infallibly* justifying anything, but it is not a suitable procedure for justifying or showing anything at all. And thus Kuhlmann's reflexive argumentation, his "strict reflection", not only fails at the task of proving the law of non-contradiction (which incidentally I do recognize, but just not on the basis of "strict reflection") as an argumentative presupposition but of course fails all the more at the task of "identifying/demonstrating" [*aufweisen*] those other discourse norms that Apel and Kuhlmann—and Habermas—have to offer.

It is not difficult to demonstrate this in the "strictly reflective dialogue" with which Kuhlmann's transcendental philosopher responds to the following remarks by A:

Your argumentation for final justification of discourse ethics is predicated on the idea that asserting or even just meaning p has certain social implications that can be utilized for a foundation of ethics. I would claim that in my meaning p or my asserting p there are no social implications that pertain to other subjects, particularly not the concession of certain rights for these other people. In such a case I only mean that p is true, that things are as p states, and this does not involve any reference to other people and any particular rights of these people (=s).[128]

A person who asserts or means something does not have to refer to any argumentative community in asserting or meaning.[129] Thus he does not have to concede any sorts of rights to others with his assertions. Kuhlmann's dialogue is of course not in a position to show the opposite, not least because it limits the sceptical challenger to silly affirmative remarks like "yes, for Zeus" or "yes, for the dog",[130] which a real sceptic faced with B's arguments would have a hard time relating to. This is aggravated by the fact that the "dialogue" ends with a *monologue by the final justifier without the sceptic having agreed to the former's conclusion at all*—unlike what is usually understood as "maeuitics", here the sceptic's answer is clearly not a relevant concern. This is the case with all of Kuhlmann's dialogues. Thus even in dialogue with a *fictitious* sceptic—who could equally well be depicted differently with different fictitious affirmations—Kuhlmann reveals the transcendental–pragmatist's maeuitics to be not the classic expository kind aimed at the rational persuasion of the other party but rather the *"maeuitics" of monological decrees.*

What sort of proof does Kuhlmann's transcendental–pragmatic philosopher B believe he can rest his declaration of victory on? He has A, who as we mentioned is rather indisposed, confirm that he is interested in *certainty* and thus has to consider objections, even *wish* for objections, that point out aspects he had overlooked, so that he would take back his questionable claim "upon valid objections", "no matter who the objection comes from".[131]

But why should A confirm all this? After all he could answer:

First of all: I am *not* interested in certainty. Certainty is impossible. Why should I strive for something I can never reach? Justified knowledge is enough for me (where "justified" obviously should not be understood in terms of "final justification"). Secondly: I hold my claim s to be justified, just as I do my claim that I am not impotent. I do not wish for objections to the one or the other claim. It may be that *you* believe that there is nothing greater in life than arguing; I know better than this. Thus I don't have the slightest desire to waste my time continually dealing with some objections or other. Not even *you* seriously desire objections to every assertion that you make. Thirdly: even if I *wished* for objections to every assertion, this doesn't mean that I concede to someone the right to objections. An inquisitor can *deny* someone the *right* to objections to the "true belief", and at the same time *wish* for these objections to occur simply because he loves his work. Fourthly: I cannot guarantee that I will take back my claim if these unwelcome and undesired valid objections were to be produced—and not due to any obstinacy on my part. That I don't wish for objections does not mean that I wouldn't take back my claim anyway if I held an unwelcome objection to be valid. The reason is rather that it hasn't escaped me—unlike you—that *we do not always recognize valid objections as such.* If I interpret a certain chemical process as an example of an xy-reaction, it could be that someone produces valid objections to this that I don't recognize as such, since I lack sufficient knowledge of chemistry to be able to fully understand and assess the objection. Fifthly: if I have significant doubts about the objector's knowledge of chemistry and judge him to be a prattling know-all, I will stick to my interpretation of the process. If however I hold him to be a Nobel Prize-winner in chemistry, I will revise my opinion, even if I may not be able to *recognize* the objection as valid. And this means that it is by no means a matter of indifference "who the objection comes from". And this is entirely rational of me.—Furthermore it doesn't matter to me whether you change your opinion. I only wanted you to know what my standpoint is and what I think of it. I have reached this goal and thus I consider the conversation to be over. And if you contradict me one more time I'm going to thrash you.

In the face of these statements, B's response

So then you have admitted that with your conviction or statement, you have conceded everyone capable of contradicting you the right to do so[132]

does not seem cogent. Since a sceptic could very well respond to B's question with these statements, Kuhlmann's belief in the power of reflective arguments is a superstition.

Let us assume—counterfactually—that the sceptic has let himself be persuaded that he recognizes certain alleged rules of argumentation. But then he knows only that *he* recognizes the rules on the occasion of a certain reflection—it has not been shown that he *necessarily* recognizes them, let alone that *everyone* necessarily recognizes them.

Kuhlmann counters this objection—which we have already seen above in the form of McCarthy's objection to Apel[133]—with the following remarks; for the sake of simplicity I have interrupted the quotation at suitable points with commentary:

The imputation that our problem here concerns the generalization of a contingent and highly particular experience that I have with myself in the attempt to dispute the validity of the rules of argumentation is false, and thus it makes no sense to ask: I have had this experience myself, but does it hold for everyone else? Rather it works the other way around: it is only because this experience can be had by all rational subjects that it is a valid experience for me.[134]

First of all: *whether* this experience can be had by all rational subjects is a part of the question, and something that would need to be shown rather than assumed. Second: only I can have the experience of being myself; does this make the experience "invalid"? And how should we understand this talk of the "invalidity" of an *experience*? The expression "invalid experience" is likely just as empty as "implicit recognition".

Kuhlmann goes on:

For only when I do what I do correctly, which means here: correctly dispute the validity of rules of argumentation, only then do I get as a valid result that I cannot dispute the validity of these rules without self-contradiction.

What the word "then" tries to pass off as the justification of the thesis is only assumed by the thesis from the very beginning. For *whether* one gets the result that one *cannot* dispute the validity of the rules recognized in this concrete reflective situation is precisely part of the question at issue.

Acting correctly means: acting according to the rules that one must act in accordance with if one wants one's action to count as disputing (or as an assessment of the result) for oneself or any other competent subject.[135]

Why do the rules have to be necessary and general—particularly if, as we might interpret this "or", it is enough to dispute something *for oneself*? Then it suffices to use rules that are valid for oneself; whether or not they hold valid for others is irrelevant. Furthermore, even if one wants to dispute something such that the act of disputing counts for others as well, why should not that be possible with *other* rules besides those one is currently using?[136] However, Kuhlmann claims that it militates against this objection, for one thing that we have yet to find an alternative "equal or superior type of argumentation", and for another that, as he alleges, some x can count as a form of argumentation only if it shows sufficient commonalities with the paradigmatic case in terms of which "we have formed the very concept of 'argumentation'".[137] With this response Kuhlmann assumes that we identify an act as argumentation using rules that the act recognizes or follows. This assumption is unfounded. When someone flicks a light-switch, I recognize this act as the flicking of a switch without knowing whether the agent in doing so has recognized the ideal communicative community, his stepmother or anything else. I recognize an act in the agent's *behaviour*. Obviously, if I were to find out that the agent did not purposefully flick the light-switch, not just in the sense that he thought it was a heating-switch but rather in the sense that his hand twitched due to some neuro-muscular disturbance, then I no longer consider the flicking of the light-switch to be an *act*. In identifying acts of argumentation I proceed just the same. I consider the behaviour of the person and based on this attribute to him certain *intentions*, but which *rules* he follows in realizing his intentions and in manifesting that behaviour is absolutely irrelevant to the classification of his act. Even if we did all follow or recognize the same norms in arguing, we do not *have* to do this to argue. It basically holds true of each and every system of rules that there is an alternative system of rules that would also be capable of producing the same behaviour with the same objectives. Thus we might happen to use the same type of argumentation in arguing even while we all follow or assume *different* rules in doing so. Incidentally, Kuhlmann does not identify acts of argumentation any differently than I do. If he ascertained without a doubt that he himself, Albert, Keuth, Einstein and Putnam assume *entirely different* norms in their verbal behaviour that we normally call "argumentation", he would not in all seriousness say based on this alone that all of these people use *different* types of argumentation (and if he did, it would be worrying), never mind that only *he* himself, Kuhlmann, is truly arguing. Furthermore, we cannot rule out the possibility that we will one day find ways of acting (possibly in outer space?) that no longer meet our *paradigms* of argumentation, namely, "*our*" way of arguing (whose, anyway: the white male transcendental–pragmatic philosophy professor's?)—even though we would subsume them under our *concept* of argumentation (since concepts and paradigms are not the same). How should we be able to rule this out a priori—unless, that is, as Albert claims, due to a lack of imagination?[138]

It is no different with Apel's exclusion of the possibility that Habermas conceded at one point, namely, that of a *change in our* reason in the course of a change in our environment. Apel opposes "casting our argumentative practice as *contingent*", as it is

not sensibly conceivable…, that our *reason*—defined as the embodiment of the presuppositions of argumentation that are not disputable without *p.s.* [performative self-contradiction;
U.S.]—could ever change. For how are we supposed to make sense…of this assumption?
What would its *sense* consist in?…In my opinion the answer to this question has to be:
we can only understand the idea of a possible *change in our reason* as a *falsification* of our
presuppositions mentioned above. However, for this we would have to already presuppose
the reason defined by us, since without this assumption we would not be able to understand
what *falsification* means.[139]

If we nominally *define* our reason this way, then a change in our reason is not
sensibly conceivable, simply because such a change is excluded by definition. If we
define reason as chocolate cake, then it is out of the question that reason thus defined
could be an apple pie or the embodiment of the presuppositions of argumentation
that are not disputable without performative self-contradiction. And if we define
reason as that which is not disputable at all, under any circumstances, without performative self-contradiction, then of course this cannot change. Naturally there is
no reason why we should take up Apel's definition. In any case, if we did, then the
word "reason" thus defined would no longer refer to what we commonly understand
as reason. In other words, if we take Apel's definition to be a *real* definition (i.e. an
explication of an existing concept and not just a stipulative introduction of a new
one), it is wrong. To reduce reason to rules of *argumentation* is an under-determina-
tion of reason. If one wishes to conceive of reason as a system of rules (and it could
also be conceived as a capacity, an ability, a disposition, etc.), then it would be the
system of rules of rational behaviour *generally* (in the broadest sense of "behaviour",
including thinking and feeling). Ultimately we not only argue rationally but also sew
rationally or kill rationally or just behave rationally in general, whereby arguing is
only *one* kind of behaviour and not always the most rational kind. If Apel thinks differently, he would have to demonstrate his opinion with an analysis of language use
and not just by decreeing his own idiosyncratic "insights".

Thus, the question that needs to be settled if we are not to bias the results again
in the typically definitional and dogmatic manner of transcendental pragmatics,
is whether the purported argumentative presuppositions that *we ourselves* cannot
dispute without performative self-contradiction could never change. And when
Apel says here that we could imagine a change in reason only as a falsification
of the presuppositions, it should be pointed out that he himself has already conceded the falsehood of certain of these presuppositions, in characterizing their
rightness as *counter*factual and *fictitious*.[140] So these falsifications are not only
conceivable for Apel himself; in fact he has already falsified them. Furthermore,
why can "we", why above all can Apel, conceive of a *change* in reason only as a
falsification of presuppositions? If our reason is the embodiment of the presuppositions we make, then a change in reason would mean only a change in these
presuppositions and not their *falsification*. Only a falsification of reason demands
a falsification of the presuppositions. And, incidentally, one could also appease this
demand even if it were impossible (and Apel as mentioned already conceded that
it is not impossible) to falsify the presuppositions under their own (after all only

"implicit") supposition. For the falsification could occur from the standpoint of a changed, possibly improved rationality, or even the one and only true rationality, which is no longer reliant on these presuppositions. Apel does not provide a single argument as to why one should not be able—now—to imagine this sort of thing. Of course we can imagine it. I just did. Yet as mentioned we do not have to imagine any falsification of the presuppositions at all to imagine a *change* in reason. It suffices to conceive a change in the presuppositions. And why should this be impossible? Why should we not be able to conceive now under our current presuppositions that our presuppositions could *change* in the future—and, with them, reason itself? Apel does not give a single reason for this. I myself can readily imagine such a change. If Apel cannot, then he lacks imagination.

But back to Kuhlmann. He continues:

> The act of disputing is not an event that can be more or less forcibly subsumed under an external generality after the fact, rather it is from the outset and in itself conceived as a case of a binding rule for all argumentative subjects, as a general phenomenon from the outset; if not, it does not count as disputing.[141]

Again: *if* this is the case, was the question. In all this verbiage Kuhlmann has yet to give us any justification *that* it is so, proffering instead various kinds of circle and solemn avowal.

> If this is the case then the same result has to emerge for all argumentative subjects insofar as they act correctly, that is, orient themselves around the same rule. That a universally valid result will arise from correct action is an expectation that is analytically bound to the act of disputing (which relies on the distinction: according or contrary to the rule) and first gives it its sense.[142]

It is not the case, and thus Kuhlmann's conclusion would be false even if it were logically sound. The result that *I recognize* the rule *now* in this reflective situation might be universally valid (and that only means: true). However, the question is whether the *rule* is universally valid. And why should this be the case? Because Kuhlmann finds it to be "analytic"? It is not analytic. It could be that one has to accord with the rule R in arguing—accord with, that is, not intentionally *follow*: "In arguing, a creature with an X-brain has to recognize the rule x and a creature with a Y-brain, the rule y!" According to this rule R, an X-brain clearly has to recognize the rule x in arguing and a Y-brain y. Neither of these two brains has to recognize *R* in order to act in *accordance* with this universally valid argumentative norm. Thus an X-brain would be in error if it concluded from *its* recognition of the rule x that a Y-brain also had to recognize the rule x. So maybe transcendental pragmatic philosophers would also do better to avoid inferring from themselves to others.

> Thus in formulating the result of the argument of final justification as necessarily valid for everyone, we are not leaving the adequately understood scope of what is to be justified strictly reflexively.[143]

This claim is, as we saw, unfounded.

2.2.2.2.3. The Failure of the Criterion of Final Justification

Let us now recall the larger project and the question (a) mentioned above.[144] Norms or presuppositions of argumentation are to be demonstrated that constitute conditions of possibility of argumentation. We should be able to verify, using Apel's criterion, whether a certain norm or presupposition is one of these conditions. But how do we know, and with certainty, that this criterion is the *right* criterion? Should this not have to be justified somehow, and, moreover, infallibly?

We saw above that a final justification of this criterion (which is, after all, supposed to be the *sole* criterion of final justification) would be circular. Final justification of the criterion is simply absent. Furthermore, we have already seen above that there is no escape from either fallibility or the Munchhausen trilemma.[145] The "criterion of final justification" is false.

Furthermore, it is self-contradictory. Let us recall the exact description of this criterion:

If I cannot dispute something without self-contradiction and at the same time cannot justify it deductively without formal–logical *petitio principii*, then it counts as one of the transcendental–pragmatic presuppositions of argumentation that one has to have always already recognized if the language game of argumentation is to retain its *sense [Sinn]*. Thus one could also call this transcendental–pragmatic type of argument the *final justification from the conditions of sense/meaning [sinnkritische Form der Letztbegründung]*.[146]

For all of his alleged "demonstrating/identifying" of "argumentative presuppositions", Apel himself has *never carried out* this test! He always breaks off these tests triumphantly upon allegedly demonstrating a performative self-contradiction, apparently on the extremely hasty assumption, which he of course does not justify any further, that the second condition of his criterion must also be satisfied. It seems that he is absolutely certain—tellingly enough, *before* making adequate use of his criterion of final justification!—that the result he prefers will emerge.

Let us carry out this test, since Apel neglected to. Apel characterizes the norm "Act as if you were member of an ideal communicative community!"[147] as the "finally justified ideal principle of discourse ethics".[148] Let us look at the following derivation:

(1) If I cannot dispute something without current self-contradiction [*aktuellen Selbstwiderspruch*] and at the same time cannot justify it deductively without formal-logical *petitio principii*, then it counts as one of the transcendental–pragmatic presuppositions of argumentation that one has to have always already recognized if the language game of argumentation is to retain its sense. Thus one could also call this transcendental–pragmatic type of argument the final justification from the conditions of sense/meaning.

(2) I cannot dispute the ideal principle of discourse ethics without current self-contradiction and at the same time cannot justify it deductively without formal-logical *petitio principii*.

(3) Something that has final justification is valid.

(4) So the ideal principle of discourse ethics is valid.

According to Apel the premises (1), (2) and (3) will obviously, one must assume, be valid and the derivation deductively flawless. So where is the "formal–logical *petitio principii*"? Well, we cannot find any. But we can find something else: a *reductio ad absurdum*. It follows from the conjunction of (1), (2) and (3) that the ideal principle of discourse ethics has final justification. Yet *that* this follows from (1), (2) and (3) without formal-logical *petitio principii contradicts* the statement that the principle has final justification. So the conjunction of (1), (2) and (3) has to be false. Now, certain of Apel's remarks admittedly do contradict the validity of (3). I have pointed out several times already that for Apel certain presuppositions of argumentation (which as such have per se final justification according to Apel) are *counter*factual. But if they are counterfactual, that is, if they do not accord with the facts, then they are not valid—which Apel seems not to be entirely clear on, even when he recognizes the "realist correspondence theory of truth" as "'granted' as a basic intuition".[149] Yet if Apel drops (3) the programme of final justification loses its sense, since the point is to justify certain norms as *valid*. In fact Apel is probably of the opinion that (3) follows directly from the meaning of "final justification". So what we see here is a veritable contradiction for which the criterion of final justification bears sole responsibility—for of course it is irrelevant what principle or "presupposition of argumentation" one assigns to x and then inserts into the second premise. In summary: Apel's criterion of final justification is absurd and thus false.

Incidentally, it is difficult to proceed the way Alfred Berlich does, who, when he sees that the condition that rules out the formal-logical *petitio principii* can principally not be satisfied, simply "reads" this condition such "that it only says that the uncircumventable knowledge sought for cannot be justified without already supposing the validity of what is to be justified".[150] For if one does not read the expression "formal-logical *petitio principii*" as "formal-logical *petitio principii*" but as something *else*, such as what Berlich offers in the quotation above, then one has quite clearly read it wrongly. Furthermore, even *after* reading Berlich's critique Apel continues to insist on the condition of a formal-logical *petitio principii* and explains that "the indisputable *presuppositions* [have to] function as premises, if one wants to justify them with logical derivation".[151] As mentioned, he is mistaken here.

However, Apel *has* to cling to his decreed criterion of final justification if he is not to expose the entirety of transcendental pragmatics as nonsense in his own person. For if he were to admit that the criterion of final justification he has championed so far is false, that he was mistaken even concerning the criterion of final justification, then naturally the question arises whether he may not also be mistaken about some new modified criterion—particularly if the method of "presenting" [*Aufweis*] (the correctness of) this criterion is as circular as it was with the previous criterion. And we see this circularity at work if we simply replace (as proposed by Berlich) the condition of formal-logical *petitio principii* with the condition that something that has final justification cannot be justified without already *presupposing* it. For if we apply this principle to itself, that is, if we try to justify this principle with this principle, we end up in a formal-logical *petitio principii*: when

I grant the claim that I cannot dispute the new criterion of final justification without performative self-contradiction and cannot justify it without presupposing it, then the final justification of this new criterion of final justification follows only if it is true that those things have final justification that one cannot dispute without performative self-contradiction and cannot justify without assuming them. But whether this is true—whether the new criterion of final justification is correct—is precisely the question. As we see, this is a veritable circle—quite apart from the fact that the question of how we would *ascertain* this sort of thing rather than simply decreeing it leads us down the dead ends discussed above.

So if Apel were to concede that he is mistaken about the criterion of final justification, then we can see no reason why he might not be mistaken in the future as well. We can see no reason even if he does not concede this, for I have just *proven* with all logical coherence that Apel's criterion of final justification is self-contradictory and thus false. So Apel is mistaken. But then Apel should ask himself how he intends to know that whatever criteria he proposes are correct. He cannot provide any justifications, for they are circular; and one criterion of final justification circularly justified is just as good—just as poorly justified, that is—as any other purported criterion of final justification circularly justified. We do not necessarily have to trust the results of his reflections, since he has already been mistaken once while continually assuring us that that was entirely impossible. Clearly it was not. And thus, to put a finer point on it, Apel has to ask himself how he actually comes to think that a purported criterion of final justification that he proposes covers the presuppositions of *argumentation*. It might rather cover the conditions of possibility of, let us say, dogmatic pronouncements—perhaps even the sufficient conditions of dogmatic pronouncements. In fact, Apel's criterion explicitly requires that the presuppositions (of whatever they may be) that he puts forth can be justified only circularly (whether formally or methodically). Yet circular "justifications" are a paradigmatic example of dogmatic pronouncements, thus giving rise to my question. And how should we found a rational morality on the conditions of dogmatic pronouncements?

Perhaps, in order to evade these sorts of questions, Apel would simply insist—dogmatically—on the condition of the formal-logical *petitio principii*. This dogmatism can hardly be of any help given our proof of the absurdity of this condition, and all of the same questions continue to suggest themselves—as rhetorical questions, admittedly, since the answers are so readily apparent.

Furthermore, this "criterion of final justification" suffers from additional flaws that come to light when we "read" it as not requiring a formal *petitio principii*. For aside from the fact that it cannot deliver any *final* justification, it is also fails to deliver any final *justification*. Even Habermas raises this objection against Apel:

> Demonstrating the existence of performative contradictions helps to identify the rules necessary for any argumentation game to work; if one is to argue at all, there are no substitutes. The fact that there are *no alternatives* to these rules of argumentation is what is being proved; the rules themselves are not being *justified*.[152]

Of course, Habermas is not entirely clear on the grave consequences of this circumstance. Justifying something means justifying it as *valid*. In so far as the criterion of final justification cannot deliver any *justification* of these presuppositions of argumentation, it cannot say anything about their validity. And in fact they can be *counter*factual, thus wrong. Then the question is how Habermas intends to derive the *validity* of the principles U or D from argumentative presuppositions allegedly demonstrated by performative self-contradictions. This is clearly a faulty inference.

Furthermore, *presuppositions* of argumentation are not *rules* of argumentation. It is true that Apel hardly uses the expressions "rule of argumentation" or "rule of discourse"; he prefers to talk of presuppositions. But one would naturally like to know what *relevance* these presuppositions are supposed to have unless they *regulate* discourse and argumentation. Incidentally, Habermas speaks quite clearly of "*rules* of discourse". Following Alexy he lists the following, among others:

(3.1) Every subject with the competence to speak and act is allowed to take part in a discourse.

(3.2) a. Everyone is allowed to question any assertion whatever.
    b. Everyone is allowed to introduce any assertion whatever into the discourse.
    c. Everyone is allowed to express his attitudes, desires, and needs.

(3.3) No speaker may be prevented, by internal or external coercion [i.e. coercion inside or outside of the discourse], from exercising his rights as laid down in (3.1) and (3.2).[153]

These rules are by no means recognized or adhered to in discourses (I am speaking here of actual recognition, not "implicit" recognition). Naturally (3.1) is a rule about discourses, and thus it could be called a "rule of discourse", but only in the same sense that "eat chocolate pudding in discourse" is a rule of discourse. But the point is not to *invent* rules of discourse but rather to *find* them. This is the stated ambition of the proponents of discourse ethics; and to make good on this they would have to show that the discourse rules they "demonstrate" do in fact play a role in real discourses. Now Habermas himself admits that these rules "are not *constitutive* of discourses in the sense in which chess rules are constitutive of real chess games". And he explains:

Whereas chess rules *determine* the playing of actual chess games, discourse rules are merely the *form* in which we *present* the implicitly adopted and intuitively known pragmatic presuppositions of a special type of speech...[154]

A form of presentation is not a rule, and naturally the so-called rules of discourse are *not at all* constitutive of discourse. As Habermas himself acknowledges, they do not have to be followed for a discourse to occur. According to Habermas

discourse rules (3.1) to (3.3) state only that participants in argumentation must *assume* these conditions to be approximately realized, or realized in an approximation adequate enough for the purpose of argumentation, regardless of whether and to what extent these assumptions are *counterfactual* in a given case or not.[155]

First of all, these rules do not *state* that at all; they make no mention of assumptions (if they are *supposed* to state something else, then they should have been formulated differently). Second, it is not clear *why* one is supposed to *assume* this sort of thing; one clearly does not have to in order to be able to argue, and in fact one should avoid doing so at all costs so as not to end up in the contradictions that

Apel[156]—and evidently Habermas as well—unfortunately seem to find entirely normal. Third, these assumptions still do not in any way *regulate* discourses. Elsewhere Habermas has claimed that the "ideal speech situation" is "an operatively effective fiction",[157] and the same should then hold for the argumentative presuppositions allegedly constituting the ideal communicative situation. But "operative efficacy" is not regulation. A person's intellectual abilities are clearly also operatively effective in his argumentation, but abilities are abilities and not rules.

Furthermore, Habermas contradicts his thesis about the operative efficacy of these assumptions of the sufficient fulfilment of the "rules of discourse" when he says (with the intention, of course, of arguing *for* them):

> Discourses take place in particular social contexts and are subject to the limitations of time and space. Their participants are not Kant's intelligible characters but real human beings driven by other motives in addition to the one permitted motive of the search for truth. Topics and contributions have to be organized. The opening, adjournment, and resumption of discussions must be arranged. Because of all these factors, institutional measures are needed to sufficiently neutralize empirical limitations and avoidable internal and external interference so that the idealized conditions always already presupposed by participants in argumentation can at least be adequately approximated. The need to institutionalize discourses, trivial though it may be, does not contradict the partly counterfactual content of the presuppositions of discourse. On the contrary, attempts at institutionalization are subject in turn to normative conceptions and their goals [*normative Zielvorstellungen*], which spring *spontaneously* from our intuitive grasp of what argumentation is. This assertion can be verified empirically by studying the authorizations, exemptions, and procedural rules that have been used to institutionalize theoretical discourse in science or practical discourse in parliamentary activity. To avoid the fallacy of misplaced concreteness, one must carefully differentiate between rules of discourse and conventions serving the institutionalization of discourses, conventions that help to actualize the ideal content of the presuppositions of argumentation under empirical conditions.[158]

Now, we should call only those things rules of discourse that are rules of discourse. It is Habermas who fails to do this. But to get to the contradiction mentioned above: if, as Habermas says, "the idealized conditions" are always already *presupposed*, if "participants in argumentation must *assume* these conditions to be approximately realized, or realized in an approximation adequate enough for the purpose of argumentation"—then how does it occur to them, and to Habermas, that institutional measures are needed to generate these very conditions? Someone who thinks that "empirical limitations and avoidable internal and external interference" need to be "sufficiently neutralize[d]" first before the sufficient conditions of argumentation are satisfied clearly does not assume that they are already satisfied. And if he does assume this, perhaps in the obscure and certainly inoperative "implicit" fashion, then this person—as well as Habermas, for example—ends up in a *performative self-contradiction* with his explicit statement that sufficient conditions of argumentation have to first be established and thus are *not* yet satisfied (with catastrophic political consequences, incidentally, since one would no longer be able to criticize, for example, censorship and suppression of freedom of speech without performative self-contradiction[159]). It is clearly impossible to aspire to normative conceptions and their goals as long as one assumes that those goals have already been achieved. And in fact we do not aspire to the conditions of discourse that Habermas lists, and not because we consider them already achieved but because they are not particularly worth aspiring to. Let us take the rules (3.1) and (3.3). In practice they would mean abolishing prisons, since a prisoner in Berlin can hardly take part in a medical conference held in Boston. Furthermore, one would have to tolerate it when strangers wanted to take part in the discourse one was having with a date. And women's shelters would not be able to prohibit men—such as the men of the women taking shelter—from taking part in their discourses on domestic violence. (3.1) and (3.3) are unacceptable and false. The same holds for comparable reasons for all of the rules listed under (3.2). That these rules are *not* recognized—contrary to Habermas's complete misconstrual of the facts—"can be verified empirically by studying the authorizations, exemptions, and procedural rules that have been used to institutionalize theoretical discourse in science or practical discourse in parliamentary activity". For if the participation of all were one of the goals set by the "normative conceptions" and thus something to aspire to in our attempts at institutionalization, then we would try to allow as many people as possible to take part in discourses and to open them to everyone. In fact this does not happen. The assessment of competences Habermas mentions, for example, does not aim at admitting as many as possible into the dialogue but rather only the most competent possible—which excludes the less competent or incompetent. So clearly (3.1) is *not* a normative conception. It is also clear that the rules (3.2) and (3.3) can hardly function as normative conceptions if special authorizations are set up at the expense of others' non-authorization (to speak, for example) or exemptions (from certain issues or claims) or even just procedural rules. It is not just that all of these things merely fail to satisfy the rules (3.2) and (3.3), despite sincere effort—rather, they run entirely *contrary* to them. So the empirical method of justification for rules of discourse actually disproves the transcendental–pragmatic method used by Habermas. Whatever it is that the "presuppositions of argumentation" turn out to be, they are certainly not *rules of discourse*.

Furthermore, the "technical method of justification" also confirms this.[160] Discourse ethics mentions at least three different goals of discourses. If we take discourse to be a means of settling conflicts of action, it is evident that the rules (3.1) to (3.3) are not very suited to this. If we want to arbitrate between two warring parties, it is not necessarily advisable to invite the known war criminals to the negotiating table. In fact both parties might make it a precondition of the negotiations that certain people are not brought to the table. To generously admit these hated war criminals to the discourse anyway, citing the rules (3.1) to (3.3), would hardly be constructive. In addition it would be sound policy *not* to introduce certain "attitudes" and notions concerning the other party into the discourse—or the discourse might end rather abruptly. And a little lying and deceit, or any tactical influence such as dangling possible rewards or just flashing a nice smile and friendly glance, can be very helpful in resolving conflicts—and are often indispensable. Conflicts of action are only in the rarest of cases resolved by the "forceless force of the better argument".

If, however, we take discourse to be an activity for answering the question of which norms should be enforced or which norms are valid, as Apel and Habermas do, and the answer to this question as one that admits of truth (or of "rightness"), then deceptive manoeuvres and lies are ill-advised; but it would make good sense to evaluate people's competences and exclude certain insufficiently competent people from participating in the discourse. Occasionally we hear that the necessity of excluding certain people from the discourse or not listening to them in these circumstances ultimately comes down to a lack of time. If we had an unlimited amount of time, we could let *all* speakers state their piece. We could counter this by saying: if a discourse is an activity to answer a question, then this is because we *want* the answer. And we will not be prepared to wait an eternity for the answer; we cannot even accept waiting just 200 years for the answer, since then we will never get it. To argue with Kant: there is a contradiction in the will of a participant in discourse who wills an answer and yet is prepared to wait an eternity to get it. Perhaps one could object that one wants the right answer, the *truth*, and that the probability that one has not overlooked anything or made an error rises if one takes the arguments of *all* speakers into account. This may be correct but it is nonetheless irrelevant. A statement does not become any more true for being more *probable* and more firmly shored up epistemically and argumentatively. When we desire the truth, when we want to know something, then, I repeat, we cannot accept the terms of a discourse organized such that it will never deliver a result in our lifetime—that will *never* provide us with a result. But someone might say that this is due to certain "empirical limitations", such as our current expected lifespan. The *ideal* case would be a discourse that could in fact be continued for ever—perhaps by immortals. Yet here we might ask: why is a discourse "ideal" that—due to the fact that it allows every speaker, even the most incompetent, to contribute, no matter how useless—ultimately takes *longer* to arrive at the truth than a discourse that excludes certain speakers and speech acts and thus arrives at the result *more quickly*? If we *want* the truth, then better sooner than later. Of course, depending on the question we will place more or less value on the degree of justification—in one case we would prefer a well-justified answer, in another case perhaps a *particularly* well-justified answer. Depending on how much relative certainty we hope for regarding the correctness of the particular answer, we will sometimes accept a longer discourse. But of course we would also rather have the particularly well-justified answer sooner rather than later—which disqualifies the purportedly "ideal" discourse. Furthermore, the "empirical limitations" mentioned just happen to be those that affect us. And when it comes to the question of which rules *we* have to follow in discourse for it to fulfil its purpose, then we have to take these limitations into account. Otherwise we could also take omniscience as the relevant ideal. In that case we would no longer need any discourse but rather just solitary contemplation.

Thus no matter which of the three stated goals of discourses we consider, the instrumental justification of the "rules of discourse" of discourse ethics proves to be false.

Additionally, it is not even clear in what sense the entities relating to this "criterion of final justification" should be *presuppositions* of argumentation at all. For one thing, the first part of the criterion is completely unsuited to the identification of presuppositions of argumentation, if only because it fails to say anything. A "performative contradiction"—and this is what Apel means when he speaks of a "current self-contradiction" in his criterion of final justification—is defined by Apel as a contradiction between the propositional content of a speech act and the argumentative presuppositions made in executing this speech act. Thus the explanation "whatever one cannot dispute without self-contradiction is a presupposition of argumentation" reduces to the tautological statement "a presupposition of argumentation is a presupposition of argumentation", making it rather uninformative and thus unsuitable as a criterion.[161] And if we adopt Berlich's way of reading the second part of the criterion, it also fails to say anything—or else it is, as mentioned, absurd.

But let us assume for the sake of argument that the term "performative self-contradiction" could be introduced with recourse to the concept of "implicit recognition" non-circularly. This assumption changes nothing. The question is to what extent the rules listed by Habermas and Apel are *presuppositions* of argumentation, as the concept "argumentative presuppositions" obviously suggests. After all, in arguing one does not need to make use of them as premises—as we have seen—or as methods. The method of argumentation is simply argumentation (and that would mean adherence to the *constitutive* rules, should there be any)—and not some set of rules "implicitly recognized" in some dubious way. If in carrying out a proof with litmus paper I "implicitly recognize" that the Easter bunny exists, then the litmus paper is the method of proof and not the "implicit recognition" of the Easter bunny. Hence no *circle* necessarily has to arise in the attempt to justify the "presuppositions of argumentation", certainly not because of the exact wording of the criterion of final justification (although it might well arise from the *question begging* and dogmatism of the final justifiers). But such a circle would have to arise if we were actually dealing with necessary *preconditions* of argumentation. The fact that the purported presuppositions of argumentation cannot be disputed without performative self-contradiction, that is, that it is impossible to argue without "implicitly recognizing" them, is not enough to make them real preconditions of argumentation. For ultimately one cannot argue without it being true that $357 + 468 = 825$, or that the morning star is identical to the evening star and Cicero with Tullius—but it would clearly be incongruous to speak here of *preconditions* of argumentation. Here it could be objected that one does not have to implicitly recognize the three statements. But that is just the point: the proponents of discourse ethics have to explain *how* the necessity of "implicit recognition" of the purported presuppositions of argumentation actually makes them *presuppositions* of argumentation. But they still owe us this explanation; in fact, they cannot even explain what "implicit recognition" is at all. So what we see here is again a case of false labelling. The obscure entities supposedly demonstrated or identified by the purported criterion of final justification are—whatever else they may happen to be—in no way presuppositions of argumentation.

2.2.2.3. The Problem of the Status of the So-called Presuppositions of Argumentation and Rules of Discourse

But if the transcendental–pragmatic philosophers had really succeeded in demonstrating these necessary presuppositions of argument, what would this imply for a justification of morality? Apparently very little, since as we saw these rules are neither constitutive nor regulative rules of discourse; one does not have to follow them in conducting a discourse, nor do they have a regulative effect within the discourse. In other words, *they have no recognizable normative force.*

And in fact Apel and Habermas concede that many of these presuppositions of argumentation are *counter*factual, that is, false, that is, invalid. It apparently escaped the attention of both philosophers that this means the failure of their programme of moral justification; one could hardly be required to follow *invalid* norms.

Evidently this circumstance did not escape Wolfgang Kuhlmann, who responds to B. Stroud's objection against transcendental arguments, namely, that the necessity of an assumption does not imply its correctness.[162] Kuhlmann says:

> ...once one concedes, as Stroud did, that the doubt that the world is so-and-so presupposes that we think that the world is so-and-so—and this means nothing more or less than that our doubt is only meaningful when the presupposition mentioned is true—then subsequently one can no longer meaningfully (and from the position of a seemingly detached observer) claim: but maybe the world is entirely different. For if we claim the latter statement to be meaningful, then the statement *is* true that "the world is so-and-so," and this means that the world is so-and-so. And if one claims this presupposition to be false, rejects it, then it is presupposed that one has not meaningfully doubted that the world is so-and-so.[163]

We should begin by noting that argumentative presuppositions would not be conceptual necessities even if argumentation and thought were the same (which is out of the question). As Kuhlmann himself admits, one only has to "implicitly recognize" the argumentative presuppositions, but one can easily genuinely dispute them, so one can *think* them to be false.[164] This is just what I am thinking, which I would have a hard time doing if not doing it were necessary. So Kuhlmann's argumentative presuppositions are by no means conceptual necessities. Furthermore, the sentence "the doubt that the world is so-and-so presupposes that we think that the world is so-and-so" means not only that our doubt is not meaningful (whatever that might mean) if we fail to make the presupposition, but also that doubt is by its very nature *impossible* unless we make the presupposition. But the sentence "One has to *make* the presupposition in order to be able to doubt it" is quite different from the sentence "The presupposition has to be *true* for one to be able to doubt it." But even if the statement "the world is so-and-so" were meaningful only if the world really were so-and-so, the *claim* that this statement is meaningful does not imply the presence of the state of the world at issue; rather, this would follow from the possible *fact* that this statement really is meaningful. And maybe it is not "meaningful" in Kuhlmann's sense of "meaningful"; yet it still could be *true*. That this is a real possibility is precisely Stroud's objection, and Kuhlmann would have to *show* that this is not the case, instead of simply assuming it. Furthermore, doubting in the sense of fallibilistic reservation is different from disputing. If I *do not accept, do not think* that the world is so-and-so, then in terms of the Stroudian presupposition I have not yet thought at all, and so have not yet thought that the world is not so-and-so. Of course, I do think, for example, that there is no other life outside of the earth and its orbit but within our solar system—but at the same time I maintain fallibilistic reservations about this, that is, doubts, and thus I *also* think that I could be mistaken, that maybe there could be other life in our solar system. Similarly, even if I have to think that the world is so-and-so, I can still think that it *might not* be so-and-so. Under the Stroudian presupposition this thought would still be possible. And even if the possibility of the world being different could *not* be thought, it could still be *realized*, and so the thought that the world is so-and-so could be false. Once more Kuhlmann merely presupposes that what we cannot think is therefore impossible and what we have to think is necessary—without justifying it. And finally, again, necessary presuppositions, at least in the transcendental–pragmatic sense of "implicit recognition", are in any case not conceptual necessities, and thus the Stroudian presupposition clearly allows us to declare necessary *presuppositions* to be false. In summary: Kuhlmann's argumentation (quoted above) misses the point, since argumentative presuppositions, as understood by discourse ethics in the sense of what is "implicitly recognized", are *not* conceptual necessities; second, in every sense but that last—which is true but talks right past the Stroudian reservations—every single sentence is false; and third, it is a case of *question begging*.

Vittorio Hösle also tries to show that "conceptual necessities at the same time have to be ontological necessities",[165] whereby like Kuhlmann he mistakenly identifies the statements that allegedly have final justification—which the argumentative presuppositions supposedly do—with conceptual necessities. Yet the criterion of final justification that Hösle endorses does not provide this identification at all. And in fact I am easily able to think that the proposition that Hösle ascribes final justification to, "final justification is possible", is false. Indeed, that is just what I do think. So finally justified propositions are by no means conceptual necessities. Hösle might object here that I at least cannot conceive this without "pragmatic self-contradiction"[166] (which I would dispute), but even "pragmatically" self-contradictory thought is still thought, and Hösle would have to show that "pragmatically" self-contradictory thought is necessarily false. Let us examine his argument for the truth of "finally justified" propositions:

Finally justified knowledge may have nothing to do with reality. Yet this proposition too is also dialectically contradictory. For if there truly is knowledge with final justification, i.e. apodictic knowledge, then it is not possible to *legitimately*, i.e. with a claim to truth, reflect one's way out of it and relativise it—of course the proposition is *psychologically* possible, but if it is merely psychologically possible then we do not need to take it seriously here. When I start getting ready to raise myself to a meta-level and compare finally justified knowledge to a fictitious reality, then I am forgetting that the point of the proof of final justification is just to understand that finally justified knowledge is the condition of possibility for every assertion with a claim to validity, thus also of this comparison. I might compare the epistemic mode of an

ant with an objective world, but not my own, since unlike the knowledge of the ant I have
to always already presuppose my own epistemic mode for my comparison. It follows from
this that:

> ... Finally justified knowledge is at the same time knowledge of an objective reality.[167]

This argumentation, too, is rife with question begging. This applies first of all to
the very *expression* "finally justified knowledge", since knowledge is by definition
true knowledge, otherwise we speak of it as error. But since Hösle also speaks otherwise of finally justified *sentences* and adds that these are *not* analytic sentences,[168]
we can and must understand "finally justified knowledge" as "finally justified sentences". The use made here of the expressions "legitimately" and "psychologically"
is also questionable. Hösle explains "legitimate" reflection to be reflection "with
a claim to truth". Now thinking is a psychic act, and thus it is difficult to see how
thinking is not supposed to be psychological. And when I think that "justified
knowledge may have nothing to do with reality"—and I do in fact think this—then
I think it with a claim to truth. If Hösle wishes to dispute this, it would first of all
be entirely counter-intuitive, second something that requires justification rather
than simple proclamation and third it gives rise to the question of why Hösle even
goes into this sentence at all if it purportedly cannot be thought with a claim to
truth—and thus allegedly does not need to be taken seriously. Hösle apparently
takes it very seriously or else he would not go into it, and thus he clearly finds
himself here in a pragmatic self-contradiction, one actually deserving of the name.
If "merely psychologically" does not mean without claim to truth, then it should
probably mean: "falsely". And this would presuppose what needs to be proven in
the first place. This also holds for the peculiar argument that one could assume the
possibility that finally justified sentences are false only if one forgets "the point of
the proof of final justification". For the *point* of a proof is first of all the *goal* of the
proof. Now, the goal of Hösle's proof of final justification was by no means what
he declares it to be here, namely, "that finally justified knowledge is the condition of possibility for every assertion with a claim to validity", but rather simply
that there *is* final justification.[169] And the point of individual final justifications is
simply the demonstration of finally justified propositions. Of course, these finally
justifying philosophers connect their "final justifications" to the *further* goal of
showing "that finally justified knowledge is the condition of possibility for every
assertion with a claim to validity". That an argument of a purported proof has a
certain point, a certain goal, however, is not enough to make this point or this goal
valid. *All* arguments and proofs have certain goals, but not all of them are valid.
Moreover, demonstrating that a sentence has final justification means, according
to the criterion of final justification, only that it "a) cannot be disputed without
pragmatic self-contradiction and b) cannot be proven without its validity being
presupposed".[170] The condition that the sentence must be "the condition of possibility for every sentence with a claim to validity", never mind the condition that
it must be *true*, do not come up here or in any other of Hösle's definitions of
final justification (and Hösle does not exactly foster clarity by providing several
such definitions and not just different but synonymous *formulations* of the name
definition).[171] So if it is the *goal* of the criterion of final justification to show that

finally justified sentences also fulfil these last two conditions (and despite Hösle's assumption to the contrary, the second of them does not follow from the first), then he has fallen short of his goal, for the criterion of final justification does not allow an inference from the final justification of a sentence to the satisfaction of *these* two conditions. This would have to be shown with *further* arguments—and this, incidentally, is the *point* of the objection that sentences with final justification can still be false; evidently Hösle has not understood this point. He does not provide any further arguments—once more he merely presupposes what he would have to prove. And finally, if Hösle can compare the epistemic mode of an ant with the objective world, then naturally a fallibilist and defender of the Munchhausen trilemma can compare the epistemic mode of an objective idealist with the objective world. This is what I have done here, with the result that the "epistemic mode" of objective idealists may lead to a great many things but not to knowledge.

Let us assume—counterfactually—that the transcendental–pragmatic philosophers had succeeded in demonstrating the *validity* of argumentative presuppositions. What would this entail for the justification of morality? Evidently still not very much, since the argumentative presuppositions and rules of discourse are, as their names suggest, presuppositions of argumentation and rules of discourse (whereby we should make sure not to confuse the two, as the proponents of discourse ethics do). That is, *the scope of their validity is limited to argumentation and discourse*, and since we can also choose *not* to argue or discuss, these argumentative presuppositions and norms of discourse are *not uncircumventable*.

Even Habermas realizes this:

> It is by no means self-evident that rules that are unavoidable *within* discourses can also claim to be valid for regulating action *outside* of discourses.... In any case, a separate justification is required to explain why the normative content discovered in the pragmatic presuppositions of *argumentation* should have the power to *regulate action*.
> One cannot demonstrate a transfer of this kind as Apel and Peters try to do, namely by deriving basic ethical norms *directly* from the presuppositions of argumentation.[172]

Of course, what Habermas does not recognize are the disastrous consequences this circumstance has for his version of discourse ethics as well. Unlike Apel, he does not try to *directly* derive basic ethical norms from the presuppositions of argumentation, but he does try to justify the universalization principle U "through a transcendental–pragmatic derivation from presuppositions of argumentation",[173] with the aim of setting up U as the standard to measure the validity of *norms of action* even for situations *outside* of discourse. But if according to the principle U "every valid norm has to fulfil the following condition":

> All affected can accept the consequences and the side effects its general observance can be anticipated to have for the satisfaction of everyone's interests (and these consequences are preferred to those of known alternative possibilities for regulation),[174]

and if the principle U is derived from presuppositions of argumentation, the validity of which is limited to discourse, then based on the laws of logic this derivation can hardly extend the scope of U's validity. So the problem is not the directness of Apel's inference from the validity of discourse norms to their validity outside of discourse; rather the problem is that derivations—if they are correct— can make explicit what is contained in the premises but not alter the content of the premises, which means that something cannot suddenly be added in the course of the derivation that was not previously there, no matter how indirect or circuitous the derivation. In our case this means that the scope of validity cannot be suddenly extended. If the principle U is valid only in discourse, then it cannot be inferred from the circumstance that a norm of action satisfied the conditions of validity stated in U that this norm is valid outside of the discourse. Habermas's circuitous detour has the strategic advantage of veiling this problem somewhat, but not the philosophical advantage of solving it. So Habermas is also unable to demonstrate any transfer of validity from discourse to other situations.

Matthias Kettner likewise fails in this endeavour. His argumentation is:

If "rational" as an attribute of a person means that the person is able to give reasons for their actions and convictions when asked; and if "rational" also means that it is not a matter of indifference to this person if other people (would) evaluate the reasons given as irrational, i.e. criticize them, then *every* practice in which people understand themselves as rational agents connects back to the authoritative basis of communicative rationality, and continually and efficaciously if more or less indirectly.[175]

As our previous discussion showed, this first premise is false, at least as long as being able to *give reasons* means more than simply *having* reasons.[176] And of course the second premise is also false, since as long as someone acts with sufficiently good reasons—more precisely, as long as the action seems rational to the person after a sufficient consideration of the matter—then the action and the person as agent are rational even if the person is indifferent as to whether others (would) criticize the reasons given as irrational. If he acts with good reasons, then he acts with good reasons, and someone could clearly have good reasons to pay no heed to the criticism of others—for example, if he is justified in thinking that the others do not quite see the entire situation.

Even if both of Kettner's premises were correct, his conclusion would still be false. The "communicatively rational" is what is *discursively justifiable*. But someone could easily satisfy both conditions stated in the premises without this person's reasons being accepted in discourse. Thus, even these premises do not change the fact that not everything that is justifiable towards others, that is, in discourse, is for that reason necessarily rational; and conversely very much of what could be eminently rational for an agent acting alone is not discursively justifiable, that is, not justifiable towards others.[177] Thus contrary to Kettner's assurance on this point,[178] discourse ethics is after all an "ethics just for discourse" and embroils itself in a "veritable aporia".

Now, the transcendental–pragmatic philosophers dispute the circumventability of discourse—in this point Kettner is a heretic. However, Apel's defence of the uncircumventability of discourse is self-contradictory and thus fails.[179] It is not necessary to go into this issue here. Nevertheless, it might be illustrative to consider the pertinent remarks of other transcendental–pragmatic philosophers and to show, based on some additional arguments from Apel, that the circumventability of discourse of necessity goes hand in hand with the normative circumventability of *norms* of discourse—that is, with their insignificance for situations outside of discourse.

Audun Øfsti thinks very little of Habermas's arguments against the direct validity of discourse norms in situations of action:

These arguments strike me as weak, indeed, bordering on incomprehensible. Habermas argues as if there were no identity between the arguing subject (thus the participant in discourse) and the agent of action; as if the *subject to be rationally persuaded* had nothing to say to the *agent*. As if what we have to suppose and accept in a discussion can promptly be forgotten as soon as the demonstration or the argumentation is over. As if one were only a rational subject in that very moment that one is presenting arguments, and otherwise some animal for which the principle of non-contradiction, the categorical imperative etc. have absolutely no bearing!—Is this anything more than a simple conflation of the "object" or *scope of application* of a claim to validity with the context of its justification?[180]

Indeed, Øfsti does not comprehend Habermas's arguments. Habermas does not at all claim that what we have to suppose and accept in a discussion can be promptly forgotten. He does not by any means claim that norms of action that can be justified in discourse as *also* being valid outside of discourse lose their justified validity when we find ourselves outside of discourse—he claims the exact opposite. However, he also claims that the *norms of discourse* that we have to follow (or presuppose) *in discourse* might possibly *not* be valid outside of discourse. "You should not lie" is an example of these discursive norms. According to proponents of discourse ethics, we have to obey this *in* discourse. And we have to obey it categorically: lies are absolutely forbidden *in* discourse, since if one lies, even out of good motives, one is no longer conducting a discourse in the sense of discourse ethics, but rather acting strategically. But clearly we do not necessarily have to obey this outside of discourse. Thus within discourse we do not have to suppose that a norm that is valid within discourse also holds outside of discourse. And Apel himself explains this—in discourse. Thus he speaks of a "condoned necessary lie" in the famous Kantian dilemma.[181] But if a lie is condoned in this situation, then the prohibition on lying clearly has *no* validity in this situation, since if it were valid one could *not* be permitted to lie in this situation. Furthermore, he writes: "Whoever claims something (in argumentative discourse!) thereby commits himself to justifying it upon demand", and the exclamation point makes it clear that Apel holds the opinion in his philosophical discourse that the commitment to justification valid *within* discourse does not necessarily hold *outside* of discourse. And finally in the second part of his discourse ethics he declares *strategic* action to be possibly morally condoned *outside* of discourse,[182] although it is categorically forbidden *within* discourse.[183] In this context it should be easy to understand the concerns of Habermas and others.

What is more difficult to understand is the fact that, *despite* the considerations just discussed, Apel insists that the rules holding valid within discourse also hold valid outside of discourse. This amounts to a self-contradiction, and all the efforts of transcendental–pragmatic philosophers to eliminate this contradiction between the parts A and B of transcendental–pragmatic discourse ethics fail.[184] An example of Apel's insistence on this point can be found in his argument directed against Ilting:

> As was already emphasized previously, in *sincerely* arguing we have implicitly already recognized not only the *principle of universalisation* but also this: that principles valid in *discourse unencumbered by action* should also be *applied* to solve conflicts of interest in the world of everyday life in which communication is not unencumbered by action....
>
> This was recently disputed with the argument that in discourse unencumbered by action—meaning under the assumption of a special ethics only valid for this—one could come to the conclusion that the conflicts in the world of everyday life can in principle only be solved *strategically* in the sense of the thoroughly calculated self-interest. Yet this argument strikes me as demonstrably false: either it assumes that the subjects of argumentative discourse are entirely different from the subjects of real-world communications; or it assumes that argumentative discourse is a self-contained game without any function in life. Both assumptions contradict the result of self-reflection of whoever seriously engages in argument. As sincere participants in argument we *know* (in the sense of the indisputability upon pain of performative self-contradiction):
>
> 1. that in argumentative discourse, despite the reflective disencumbrance from the necessities of action in practical life, we are identical with the subjects of real-world interaction, and furthermore
>
> 2. that sincere argumentative discourse about practical (ethical) questions ("practical discourses") have precisely the function of producing a possible decision about the claims to validity under dispute in real-world conflicts. This clearly cannot be achieved through violence or through strategic communication such as negotiations...[185]

It is immediately clear that the circumstance mentioned in (2) provides an indication of why norms of action justified in discourse should also be followed outside of discourse, but does not in any way answer the question of why those rules of *discourse* or presuppositions of *argumentation* followed within discourse in justifying norms of action should also be valid outside of discourse. Here Apel bypasses the problem entirely. Incidentally, it is possible for me to take part in discourse with others and find a norm N justified, and then afterwards, outside of the discourse, come to reconsider the situation on my own and reject N—and this can be advanced against Øfsti and Habermas. Or, even if I continue to consider the norm justified, I can decline to follow it with good reasons, since the justification of a norm does not yet imply the justification of its observance.[186]

It remains unclear, however, why proponents of Ilting's argument should make the strange assumptions that Apel ascribes to them in the second paragraph of the above quotation. Since this is by no means obvious, Apel would have to justify his astonishing standpoint—which he neglects to do. However, the falsity of his standpoint can be readily demonstrated. It is important to note that Apel does not mean the two assumptions in the sense of presuppositions of argumentation, since it is precisely a part of his argument that one does not "performatively" make these assumptions, but rather assumes their negations (i.e. the points [1] and [2]). So here Apel can mean only "assumption" in the sense of a logical presupposition. If, as a proponent of Ilting's argument, I now declare that "*We* can decide in discourse to conduct *ourselves* only strategically in practical life", then this sentence already semantically presupposes—more than this, it *says*—that *we* in discourse are identical to *ourselves* in practical life, since otherwise we would be unable to use the terms "we" and "ourselves", and would be compelled to speak of "we" and "they"; and it *says* that decisions about our practical life can readily be made in discourse. In short, the objection is not refuted by Apel's assumptions (1) and (2) but rather, ironically, is based on them.

Apel's misreading of the problem becomes especially clear in this context if we consider that we could grant him his false statement that this alleged presupposition of argumentation is always already implicitly recognized in sincere argumentation; "that principles valid in discourse unencumbered by action should also be applied to solve conflicts of interest in the world of everyday life in which communication is not unencumbered by action". How does this help against the objection that argumentative presuppositions are valid only within discourse? We could, after all, apply this objection to this presupposition of argumentation itself and say: it is valid only within discourse that principles valid in discourse unencumbered by action should also be applied to solve conflicts of interest in the world of everyday life in which communication is not unencumbered by action. But there is, within discourse, no world of practical life in which communication is not unencumbered by action—as the principle itself even explicitly states; the nonsensical comes to its senses in this principle, one could say. So this principle would then have no validity, it would have absolutely no area of application. It would clearly be counterfactual, as we are used to hearing of argumentative presuppositions—that is, false. Thus it can hardly be seen as an argument against limiting the scope of validity of discourse norms to that of discourse itself. In other words, Apel wishes to use the alleged existence of this presupposition of argumentation as an argument against limiting the scope of validity of argumentative presuppositions to discourse, but this argument itself works only under the presupposition of that which it seeks to prove, namely, that the validity of argumentative presuppositions cannot be limited to discourse. So Apel's argumentation is circular and thus invalid, even within discourse itself.

Finally, Wolfgang Kuhlmann makes the following attempt to defend the uncircumventability of discourse and its norms:

The attempt to relativise the validity of the basic ethical norm to the field of discourse is less plausible if we consider *argumentation in the broader sense*, as we have to do here; that is, every type of serious consideration of which it could be said that the subject takes the possibility of errors or mistakes into account and does x rather than y because this person has reasons, reasons that at least in principle can be reconstructed (regardless of what quality), for thinking x to be right and y wrong (whatever "right" and "wrong" might mean here). If we understand the expression "argumentation" in this broader sense, than it becomes difficult to see what the relativizing effect of this objection is to consist in. The opponent becomes enmeshed in difficulties when it comes to naming a situation in which a subject of norms is not arguing in this sense. Should the opponent succeed in finding a clear counter-example, it will be of little use, since then we can answer that a normative subject that clearly is not arguing in this sense cannot be counted as a rationally accountable normative subject (at least not for the case in question).[187]

To begin with, while Kuhlmann's extension of the concept of "argumentation" might be "necessary" for what he wishes to demonstrate, it is not admissible. First of all, not every type of serious consideration is argumentation; second, not every argumentation is an argumentation with others; and third, not every argumentation with others is a discourse.[188] Thus it is difficult to see why one should recognize or assume such a rule as, for example, that all participants in a discourse have equal status, when one is not conducting a discourse at the moment. After all, one does not have to recognize the rules for boiling rhubarb while parachuting. Thus his argument already fails to hold water.

In addition, Kuhlmann's opponent does not become enmeshed in difficulties at all when it comes to naming a situation in which the subject of norms is not involved in "serious consideration". Let us picture someone who precisely plans the murder of his aunt for her inheritance—that is, he seriously considers it—but now, the time of planning past, he takes action: as he strangles her, he has but one thought—or maybe he even states it with a truth claim: "Now I'll kill you!" At this moment he is thinking, but not *considering* (again, two different matters that one should take care not to conflate), and in that moment, at least on the assumption that he is certain of his decision, the possibility of mistake or error has no bearing on his thought. This does not mean that he has ruled out the possibility; rather, at that moment, he simply is not thinking about it, he has his hands full. Yet it would be entirely inappropriate to deny this subject his accountability for the act. Of course we ascribe his crime to him as a crime, since he had planned it in detail and was not in any mental confusion in carrying it out. And aside from the fact that it makes no sense to imagine this murderous nephew recognizing the equal status of his aunt while he was considering and planning his murder—another situation in which Kuhlmann would have to have recourse to the meaningless notion of "implicit recognition", to a mystification—it is entirely absurd to imagine him recognizing the equal status of his aunt while he strangles her. On this point Kuhlmann seems to be contradicted also by his mentor Apel, who says:

…it is essential to note that whoever in practical life practises the standpoint of power through openly strategic speech acts, has not entered into a *discussion* of the legitimacy of his or her standpoint. For this very reason this person does not have to recognize the normative primacy of non-strategic communication, either implicitly or explicitly.[189]

With this concession—which holds not only for strategic *speech* acts but also for strategic acts such as murder, rape and torture—Apel concedes just what he disputes elsewhere, namely, that discourse is very much circumventable. (And incidentally, discourse and non-strategic communication, as we saw, clearly have no *primacy* over strategic speech acts; the latter are *not* parasitic on non-strategic communication.[190] But even if they were parasitic and non-strategic communication (such as perhaps in discourse) originary, this would change nothing about the *circumventability* of discourse and thus the limitation of the validity of argumentative presuppositions. This is shown by Apel's remark above: outside of discourse, at least in the case of the open practice of a "standpoint of power", one does not need to recognize argumentative presuppositions, such as the presupposition of the normative primacy of non-strategic communication. "Originary" and uncircumventable are not the same.)

Be that as it may, in any case the nephew in our situation does not need to consider anything. And when Private Meyer is given the order "Meyer, execute the Jew!", and he follows it blindly, as they say, he also does not need to engage in any consideration. Thus the norms of argumentation would also have no validity in these situations; and, measured by their standard alone, no moral considerations would speak against either the murder of the aunt or crimes of war committed in blind obedience. This strikes me as a very significant "relativizing effect".

The upshot of this is: the presentation/identification of presuppositions of argumentation—even if it were to succeed—could not contribute anything to a programme of moral justification. First of all, they are *invalid*, and second, even under the assumption of their validity, their own *scope of validity* and that of any moral principles that might be derivable from them would be *limited to discourse*. Thus the moral justification programme of discourse ethics already sets off on the wrong foot and falters.

2.3. THE UNTENABILITY OF THE PRINCIPLE U AND THE FAILURE OF ITS ALLEGED DERIVATION

Both Habermas and Apel believe in the validity of the principle U, which states:

Every valid norm must satisfy the condition that the consequences and side effects its *general* observance can be anticipated to have for the satisfaction of the interests of *each* could be freely accepted by *all* affected (and be preferred to those of known alternative possibilities for regulation).[191]

This principle is completely untenable and accordingly cannot be justified. Here I will begin by examining the failure of Habermas's attempted justification of U (and D). In light of Christoph Lumer's[192] logically detailed and crushing recent critique of Habermas's hopes for such a derivation, which can be seen as the last word on the subject, I will stick to the most basic points in my demonstration that the principle U is *unjustified*. In closing I will mount a *direct* attack on U with a *justification of the negation of U*—as well as the negation of the idea that participants in practical discourses have to account for this principle.

According to Apel, the universalization principle U can be demonstrated with the argument from performative contradiction, that is, with strict reflection. However, since Apel's strict reflection, as we saw in detail, consists in the circular "proof" of what was already dogmatically assumed, what we have here is not a means of demonstration but rather a ritual of dogmatic pronouncement.

Habermas, as we saw, makes use of this in his "demonstration" of argumentative presuppositions—without U. But he intends U itself to be won through a *derivation* from these argumentative presuppositions. He has never carried out this derivation; however, he expressed his faith that it *could* be derived (in which case, why does not he do it?) with the optimistic words:

> If every person entering a process of argumentation must, among other things, make presuppositions whose content can be expressed in rules (3.1) to (3.3) and if we understand what it means to discuss hypothetically whether norms of action ought to be adopted, then everyone who seriously tries to *discursively* redeem normative claims to validity intuitively accepts procedural conditions that amount to implicitly acknowledging (U). It follows from the aforementioned rules of discourse that a contested norm cannot meet with the consent of the participants in a practical discourse unless (U) holds, that is,
> Unless all affected can *freely* accept the consequences and the side effects that the *general* observance of a controversial norm can be expected to have for the satisfaction of the interests of *each individual*.
> But once it has been shown that (U) can be grounded upon the presuppositions of argumentation through a transcendental–pragmatic derivation, discourse ethics itself can be formulated in terms of the principle of discourse ethics, which stipulates,
> Only those norms can claim to be valid that meet (or could meet) with the approval of all affected in their capacity as participants in a practical discourse.[193]

I have already shown that this derivation would not be of very much use even if it worked, since according to Habermas's own conception it cannot be assumed that the argumentative presuppositions are valid outside of discourse.[194] If they do *not* hold valid outside of discourse—and in fact, they do not—and if we can *derive* U from them, as Habermas wishes, then logically U will also not hold outside of discourse. This would not recommend it as a moral principle.

Furthermore, what Habermas calls U in this quotation, namely, the condition *that* "all affected can *freely* accept the consequences and the side effects that the *general* observance of a controversial norm can be expected to have for the satisfaction of the interests of *each individual*", is not at all the same as U.[195] Rather, U declares that every *valid* norm has to *satisfy* this condition.[196] This is a *normative* statement, whereas the condition itself is purely *descriptive*—it states that something is such-and-such, not that it should be such-and-such. And there is no route from *is* to *should*: from Habermas's statement that a norm can meet with the approval of all participants in a practical discourse only if the norm satisfies this condition, it by no means follows that the norm is *valid* only in this case—that is, that U is also valid. Thus Habermas's attempt at a derivation fails of necessity.

Moreover, from the alleged fact that participants in a practical discourse recognize the rules of discourse (3.1) to (3.3), and from our knowledge of "what it means to discuss hypothetically whether norms of action ought to be adopted", we clearly cannot derive even the purely descriptive statement that the participants in discourse "implicitly recognize" U or that only those norms that satisfy the conditions for the validity of norms set by U meet with the approval of all participants.

Clearly somewhat stronger premises are needed, and in fact in the first published version of his attempt at a derivation Habermas did introduce the additional premise that "we attribute to justified norms the sense of regulating social matters in the common interest of those who might be affected."[197] However, this premise is nothing but another formulation of U itself, which makes the derivation circular. In other words, either we allow this premise—in which case we have a circular proof—or we leave it out, and then nothing follows, or in any case not U.

Ernst Tugendhat, too, among others,[198] pointed this out again in his "Lectures on Ethics" published in 1993.[199] Habermas complains about the accusation of circularity:

Tugendhat's criticism refers to a version of my argument which I revised already in the second [German] edition of *Moral Consciousness and Communicative Action*, that is, in 1984 (!); cf. Habermas, *Justification and Application*, p. 179, n. 17.[200]

So let us compare:

In the original edition of *Moralbewußtsein und kommunikatives Handeln* (Frankfurt, 1983), pp. 102 f., I employed an overly strong notion of normative justification. This error has been corrected in subsequent German editions and in the English edition...[201]

And another such footnote is offered:

The concept of the justification of norms must not be too strong, otherwise the conclusion that justified norms must have the assent of all affected will already be contained in the premise. I committed such a *petitio principii* in the [original] essay on "Discourse Ethics"...[202]

What should we make of this alleged correction? First of all, Tugendhat's objection was that Habermas's argumentation is mistaken one way or another; that, depending on whether it makes use of the premise in question, it is either circular or inconclusive. This error can hardly be "corrected" by leaping enthusiastically onto the other horn of the dilemma.

Moreover, the footnotes that Habermas cites are incorrect even if we apply them only to the problem of circularity. They are in fact mere lip service. It is true that in later editions of *Moral Consciousness and Communicative Action* Habermas no longer introduces U in the premises. But his claim to have *already* corrected the error of circularity in the second edition suggests that he no longer commits this error; which, however, he continues to do as before. Thus in this same text, *Remarks on Discourse Ethics*, on the same page as the footnote where he declares his having corrected the circularity error, in the next footnote he makes *affirmative* reference to William Rehg's "detailed proposal for carrying through this justification".[203] And, as we might expect, Rehg's derivation of U "succeeds" only because he rigs together for himself a curious definition of a norm as something meant to regulate "conflict situations in light of an interest-regulating value that has priority for all involved parties", so flying in the face of all ordinary language use and linguistic intuition.[204] It does, indeed, follow from this definition that all affected can freely accept the consequences that a norm can be expected to have for the satisfaction of the interests of each individual. If this were not the case, then the "interest-regulating value" could hardly have "priority for all". Thus if norms have to fulfil the condition U *by definition*, then the reason that these norms meet with consent has nothing at all to do with "rules of discourse" and "communicative communities" in the slightest—contrary to what Rehg would like to suggest with his derivation that superfluously comprises nine premises. The real reason is much simpler, namely, that in that case there are no other norms.

Rehg's definition of a norm is of course clearly false—so much so that it makes the discourse principle itself superfluous—and it, too, assumes what is to be proven.[205] At least here Rehg did not take any pains to veil the circularity. In a more recent publication, however—and Habermas also makes affirmative reference to this "derivation"[206]—he positions it differently and concedes:

In step (1) we already find something looking quite close to (D)...[207]

We could figure that, if one assumes D, it is a relatively simple matter to derive D, but astonishingly enough at the end of Rehg's derivation we find neither D *nor the explicit goal of the proof, U*, but rather—which Rehg evidently fails to notice— *something else entirely*. However, since his starting point of simply assuming D is rather brazen, I do not feel it necessary to go into the other defects of his "derivation" here.

Habermas's affirmative reference to Rehg's circular "justifications" of U can hardly be seen as a *correction* to the circularity error. Despite the lip service documented in diverse footnotes, Habermas has not derived any real consequences from the critique of Tugendhat and others.

Moreover, we can see this not only in Habermas's affirmation of Rehg's circular "justifications" but also in the most recent exposition from Habermas himself of the derivation of U and the justification of discourse ethics. Here Habermas explains

that (U) can be rendered plausible from the normative content of the presuppositions of argumentation *in connection with a* (weak, hence nonprejudicial) *concept of normative justification*,[208]

after only two pages previously he had spoken of

the conception of normative justification in general expressed in (D).[209]

In other words, here Habermas derives U from D,[210] whereas elsewhere he has tried to derive D from U. Evidently it does not matter so much to Habermas what is derived from what and how; Habermas's so-called justificatory programme is much more an *attempt* at a *rationalization* after the fact of preconceived moral and political *biases*. Thus Habermas here not only flies in the face of logic; he argues in direct *contradiction* to the explanation already cited above, which we characterized as mere lip service for this very reason:

The concept of the justification of norms must not be too strong, otherwise the conclusion that justified norms must have the assent of all affected will already be contained in the premise. I committed such a *petitio principii* in the [original] essay on "Discourse Ethics"...[211]

Yet the "concept of justification of norms"—which, together with "the normative content of the presuppositions of argumentation", he wants to derive U from—is, according to his most recent exposition, expressed in D, which says *exactly this*: that justified norms must be able to have the assent of all affected. Clearly Habermas did not make his unfortunate error only "in the [original] essay on 'Discourse Ethics'"; he continues to make this slip 13 years later in J. Habermas (1999*a*), pp. 42 ff. More precisely, in 1983 Habermas had in fact "only" introduced U into the premises; now he directly and nonchalantly slips D *itself* into the premises—rather than avoiding the circle, he draws it tighter—while parenthetically assuring us in all innocence that this procedure is "non-prejudicial". Now, it *is* prejudicial—"The concept of the justification of norms must not be too strong, otherwise the conclusion...will already be contained in the premise"—and thus Habermas's response to Tugendhat's objection is entirely off-point. There is no justification of discourse ethics.

This is not at all to be regretted, since the principles U and D are false anyway, and the participants in practical discourses will certainly not subscribe to them.

Why should they? According to a statement of Habermas, practical discourses concern the question of "whether norms of action ought to be adopted".[212] Now if this is the case, why should the participants in practical discourses make their consent to the norm dependent on the anticipated consequences that the *general observance* of a norm would have for the satisfaction of the interests of each individual? Would it not be more logical if they concerned themselves only with the effects of the *adoption* of the norm (whether its institutionalization or the mere affirmation or declaration of its validity)? Of course the answer is clearly: yes. So if participants in practical discourses concerning the adoption of norms recognize that the general observance of a norm would be in the interest of each individual, but not its *adoption* (and the adoption of a norm does not guarantee its general observance), they will of course *not* consent to this norm. And if, conversely, they recognize that the general observance of a norm is not in the interest of each individual, but its adoption is, they will consent to it.

According to another of Habermas's statements—and these diverse statements are not compatible with one another—the function of practical discourses is "to settle conflicts of action by consensual means".[213] This description of their function is incorrect, particularly because what Habermas considers consensus is only a consensus reached by purely argumentative means. When people conduct practical discourses, that is, discourses on moral questions, they do try to convince the listener (and for this purpose not all listeners have to be participants in the discourse), but not just with arguments; they also use emotion, rhetoric and all means of "achieving strategic influence", and the conflict resolution that discourse *might* be aimed at does not have to be consensual either (why not, for example, through majority decision?). In thus defining the function of practical discourse as the consensual resolution of conflicts, Habermas once more slips the conclusion that is to be justified into the premises.

But let us grant Habermas this point about the function of discourse. The question then arises as to what "assent" means in this case. As Habermas explains:

Repairing a disrupted consensus can mean one of two things: restoring intersubjective recognition of a validity claim after it has become controversial or assuring intersubjective recognition for a new validity claim that is a substitute for the old one.[214]

Evidently the assent concerns only the *assurance* or restoration of intersubjective recognition—that is, as it relates to the validity claim of a norm, the *adoption* of a norm.[215] So all of the same objections that I advanced in the preceding paragraph against the thesis that participants in practical discourses take U in account can be raised again here.

According to yet another of Habermas's statements, practical discourse is "a procedure for testing the validity of norms that are being proposed and hypothetically considered for adoption".[216] Do members of a discussion who are testing the validity of a norm really take the principle U into account? To find the answer we have only to look to reality, which is not hard to find in this case. The answer is that *some* members of a discussion, for example, proponents of discourse ethics, recognize U and account for it in their considerations, at least according to their claims; others, in contrast—the overwhelming majority—reject the principle U and measure the validity of norms according to divine will, or traditional moral principles, or a contractual principle, etc. Those devoted to the will of God, traditionalists, natural rights proponents, utilitarians, contractualists and others clearly do not consent to norms only when in their opinion the norms "satisfy the condition that the consequences and side effects its *general* observance can be anticipated to have for the satisfaction of the interests of *each* could be freely accepted by *all* affected (and be preferred to those of known alternative possibilities for regulation)".[217]

Moreover, we can see here that it is not only untrue that participants in practical discourses make their consent to a norm dependent on the consequences of its general observance, but it is also very much false to claim that a norm can meet with the consent of all participants of a practical discourse only when its general observance is in the interest of each individual. And this does not hold just for those practical discourses concerned with testing the validity of a norm, but also for those concerning the adoption of norms or the consensual settlement of conflicts of action. For even if we were to assume—counterfactually, as we have seen—that all participants in practical discourses were concerned with the consequences of the *general* observance of a norm, why should they be concerned with its consequences for *each individual*? Why should the participant A, who according to our assumption is concerned with the general observance of a norm, not consent to a norm N whose general observance would harm the interests of many others but would be in *his* overriding interest? Of course, the answer is: if the consequences of the general observance of a norm are in his overriding interest and are preferable to the consequences for his interests of the general observance of every other norm, and he is aware of this, then he will consent to this norm, even if it is in his opinion harmful to the interests of others. Each person consents to whatever is in his or her own interests, in his or her own opinion (whereby one's own interests are not necessarily egocentric, but will in point of fact never extend so far as to include an interest in protecting the interests of *each individual*).

We could get around this very evident fact only by speaking of "general consent" rather than just "consent". And, in fact, among participants of a practical discourse concerned, for example, with the adoption of a norm, only those norms will be able to meet with *general* consent whose adoption is consistent with the interests of *each* individual. However, it does not follow from this that each individual participant in the discourse makes allowance for the *recognition* of the principle U (or a modified version of the principle based on the question of the adoption of a norm). The individual participant in discourse would, as explained, already assent to a norm in *his* own interest; hence he would at most subscribe to the principle "let whatever is useful to me find consent", whereas no one would subscribe to the principle U. People *cannot* act differently. Moreover, it is of course clear anyway that "consent" cannot just be revised to mean "general consent" if we are here concerned with a programme of moral justification. Circles are to be avoided in such a programme, not just in word but in deed. If contrary to logic we were to attempt to derive a normative element—such as a moral criterion of validity— from descriptive elements, then why should we choose the descriptive premise that a norm finds *general consent* only when the condition of validity named in U holds, in order to then "conclude" the validity of U? Why not choose the premise that a norm can find consent only *among Lebanese Sunnites* when it is consistent with the interests of Lebanese Sunnites, for example, in order to then "conclude" the validity of "those norms are valid that Lebanese Sunnites could consent to"? We cannot find a reasoned answer to this from Habermas. If he were to surreptitiously change "consent" to "general consent", that is, decide in favour of the first premise, he would only have once more biased the result of his derivation and entangled himself in a circle. But as long as he sticks to simple "consent", then he lacks the premise he needs for his "derivation" even if it were the case that it is the consequences of the *general observance* of a norm that participants in practical discourses are to make their consent to the norm dependent on—which, as we saw, is not the case.

Thus Habermas's claim

that a contested norm cannot meet with the consent of the participants in a practical discourse unless (U) holds, that is,

Unless all affected can *freely* accept the consequences and the side effects that the *general* observance of a controversial norm can be expected to have for the satisfaction of the interests of *each individual*,[218]

founders on four points: in speaking of *the* participants, the *general observance*, the interests of *each individual* and the acceptance by *all*. His claim is wrong.

However, it is not only his claim that participants in a practical discourse take U into account that is unfounded; his claim about the rightness of U is likewise unfounded. So it is quite fortunate that participants do *not* account for U in their practical discourses.

Why is U wrong? Under the assumption that there are any valid norms—Apel and Habermas make this assumption, and here I will also take it as given—under the assumption that a norm such as "you should respect human rights" is valid, the principle U is wrong because it would imply the *invalidity* of all morally relevant norms, including the obligation to observe human rights. As I have already emphasized many times, even in an "ideal speech situation" we cannot realistically expect any agreement on morally relevant norms from a practical discourse between billions of people (and who knows how many intelligent forms of alien life, since moral norms apply to *all* rationally accountable creatures); the notion that we could all reach a consensus belies a quixotic naivety on a breath-taking scale.

Habermas has certain difficulties squarely facing this reality. He quite correctly formulates an objection by Steven Lukes:[219]

A consensus on generalizable interests can be expected, he claims, only if the theory postulates either homogenous societies or abstract discourse participants such as Rawls's parties in the original position and thereby assumes that flesh-and-blood actors are surreptitiously transformed into intelligible beings under the communicative presuppositions of rational discourse.[220]

Yet he then succeeds in ignoring this objection. He affirms that he "leaves the identity of the participants and sources of conflict originating in the lifeworld untouched",[221] only to then continue to take for granted, without any hint of justification or any further mention of Lukes's concerns, precisely what Lukes had disputed with rather convincing reasons: namely, that real-world participants in discourse made of flesh and blood would be able to arrive at a consensus. In responding to Lukes elsewhere Habermas likewise contents himself with a mere *repetition* of the doctrines of discourse ethics, instead of explaining *how* he imagines this consensus actually coming about. He says, rather,

...I do not understand why he regards this requirement [the conditions of validity stated in U] as too strong. He seems to assume that there is a zero-sum relationship between the individual differentiation of needs and the generalisability of collective interests. But there are enough counter-examples—from traffic rules to basic institutional norms—to make it intuitively clear that increasing scope for individual options does not decrease the chances for agreement concerning presumptively common interests....A unified society of abundance would be a necessary condition for the functioning of the universalisation principle only if we had to suppose that the alternative needs (wishes, inclinations, values, and so forth), which normative regulation is supposed to take into account, exclude *a priori* consensual regulation at a higher level of abstraction.[222]

It is rather curious that Habermas fails to understand why Lukes finds the requirement too strong, since the reasons that Lukes gives for his concern are not so very difficult to understand. Habermas himself recognizes "that disputes about basic moral principles ordinarily do not issue in agreement". And this fact speaks rather strongly *against* the possibility of consensus in practical questions—which, moreover, contrary to Habermas's suggestion, is confirmed precisely by the dissent prevailing in discussions of traffic regulations (such as speed limits) and basic constitutional norms (there are those who criticize the constitution of their state or even openly oppose it). Now, according to Habermas this objection "loses its force if we can name a principle that makes agreement in moral argumentation possible in principle".[223] But this principle is supposed to be U; and of course, for the objection to lose any of its force, it would have to be *shown* that the principle thus named does, in point of fact, make agreement possible in principle. One has hardly sapped the objection of its force merely by naming *any* principle whatsoever and *claiming* that it makes agreement in moral argumentation possible in principle. But this is exactly what Habermas does. He never demonstrates the mysterious consensus-enabling force of U, but rather only postulates it. This postulate can be directly countered with the same empirical facts already mentioned. Ultimately, according to Habermas, the participants in a practical discourse necessarily have to give their *assent* to the principle U. So if this principle did enable consensus, then a consensus would have to have been reached in practical discourses. But this has not happened. So the premise that U enables consensus is false.[224]

Here it might be objected that real, existing practical discourses do not come sufficiently close to the ideal practical discourse conceived as the standard, but that in the latter it would be possible to reach a consensus. According to Habermas, certain discourses, like parliamentary discourses in the USA or the Federal Republic of Germany, do apparently come close enough to this ideal to ground legitimacy.[225] But even if one did grant the validity of this objection, it would still be the case that Habermas bears the burden of proof;[226] and he has not taken any steps to acknowledge this burden. Instead he limits himself to the rather unsatisfying remark:

> The point in discourse-ethical universalisation consists…in this, that only through the communicative structure of a moral argumentation involving *all* those affected is the *exchange of roles* of each with every other forced upon us.[227]

First of all, an exchange of roles consists in my *putting myself in the other's position*. However, when for example a Jewish concentration camp inmate *tells* the camp guard, or a critic of the regime *tells* the dictator, about the terrors of the camp or of suppression and living in fear for one's life, the camp guard or the dictator are not yet thereby compelled to *put themselves in the other's position*, that is, to imagine how they themselves would have felt if they were suppressed, terrorized or treated like vermin. But even if they were to do this, if they did in fact imagine how they would feel in their victim's position, this would change nothing about their own interests, which, after all, are what U is meant to consider. The consequences and side effects of the general observance of the norm "camp guards should not be punished for any deeds committed in the service of National Socialism" is without a doubt freely acceptable to at least the overwhelming majority of camp guards, but not to the victims. And the victims' depreciative stance towards this norm will not go away if they put themselves in the position of their oppressors. Conversely, putting oneself in the position of the oppressed might under some circumstances lead to a bad conscience on the part of some oppressors—so much so that they would be ready to freely accept the consequences and side effects of the general observance of the norm demanded by the victims, namely, "crimes against humanity should be severely punished." But this is of course not true of *all* the oppressors. The depressing truth is that some of these oppressors would get a particular thrill from putting themselves in the role of their victims and even become nostalgic. This is how our real world is. The same holds for the exchange of roles between dictators and their victims. This exchange of roles will not change anything about the interests of the oppressed such that they could freely consent to the consequences and side effects that the general observance of the norm implemented by the dictator, namely, "Anyone who calls for overthrowing the government or conspires to overthrow the government in word or deed should be punished by death", has for the interests of each individual. And the exchange of roles will change just as little about the interests of the dictator such that he consents to the consequences and side effects of the general observance of the norm "governments should be democratically elected, or else they should abdicate power." Another such example is the exchange of roles between a rapist and his victim. This exchange of roles cannot possibly deliver what Habermas expects of it—a miracle, it would seem.

While Habermas proves unable to support his accrued burden of proof, it is comparatively easy to show the converse: why no consensus can emerge in a practical discourse—especially but not only in a discourse wherein the participants let themselves be guided by the "rule of argumentation" U. Let us take another example. Habermas writes:

Murder and deceit are not wrong merely because they are not good for those whom they victimize. As norms of action they are wrong *in general* because they do not express a *generalizable* interest.[228]

Now, of course murder *as a behavioural norm*, for example, as the norm "You should murder", will doubtless not find any general consent in a practical discourse between (at least) all people capable of speech. This also holds—contrary to Habermas's assumption—for the norm "You should *not* murder",[229] since murder does not encroach on any generalizable interest. After all, someone could have an interest in murdering his rich and hated aunt for her inheritance, and accordingly this person A would *not* be able to freely consent in a practical discourse to "the consequences and the side effects that the *general* observance of a controversial norm can be expected to have for the satisfaction of the interests of *each individual*", since the general observance of this norm would mean that he cannot murder his aunt and thus cannot prematurely acquire his inheritance in order to satisfy his other interests. Here one could respond that the general observance of the norm under dispute would also have the consequence that A is not murdered—which *is* in his interest. And this interest in not getting murdered himself can be expected to be stronger than his interest in murdering his aunt. Assuming that this is so (and this is not always necessarily the case; can we not desire someone else's death more than our own life?), what have we gained? Not very much, since while the general observance of the prohibition on murder would make it impossible to kill the aunt, a non-general observance of the prohibition on murder does not necessitate the murder of A himself but merely implies the *risk* of his murder. And he might be perfectly willing to accept this risk—which, moreover, could be very slight—as the price of the profit he expects from murdering his aunt. This nephew A is *ex hypothesi* an exemplification of certain actually existing people. So it remains true that the non-general observance of the prohibition on murder accords with his interests, whereas the general observance of the norm does *not* accord with his interests. Moreover, the prohibition on murder certainly does not satisfy the conditions stated in the more precise formulations of U, namely, that the consequences and side effects of the general observance of a norm "are preferred to those of known alternative possibilities for regulation"[230] by *all* affected. In light of his interests, A can hardly prefer the norm "You should not murder" over the norm "You should not murder A."

This example shows that a "relatively homogeneous society of surplus" is by no means a *sufficient* "condition for the functioning of the principle of generalization",[231] since even if a society of paradisiacal surplus were to put an end to avarice (which I strongly doubt), there would still be hate, jealousy, the hunger for power and sundry other needs or desires that can be satisfied only at the cost of others—one could think of the needs or desires of child-molesters, rapists and serial killers—and after all, every need or desire, every interest, may be given expression in practical discourse.[232] Furthermore, this shows that, contrary to Habermas's claim, there can be no "consensual regulation at a higher level of abstraction"[233] in such cases of directly conflicting interests as with the nephew and his aunt. There is no single norm that could satisfy the principle U. The general observance of any norm such as "You should not kill anyone", "You should not deprive anyone of freedom or opportunity", or "Act with an orientation to mutual understanding and allow everyone the communicative freedom to take positions on validity claims"[234] could certainly not by freely accepted by *everyone* in all their consequences and side effects—for example, not by the nephew A, for reasons that are quite evident. There is no "level of abstraction" at which we could hope to reach a consensus.

In summary, we can say that the principle U is in practical discourses neither assumed nor justified nor correct. It is contrived, unjustified and false.

2.4. THE FAILURE OF HABERMAS'S JUSTIFICATION OF CONSENSUS THEORY

In the previous section we saw how in recent writings Habermas and Rehg simply presuppose the principle D in order to derive from it the principle U. We also saw that this derivation disqualifies itself from the very outset, since participants in practical discourses to resolve conflicts of action or to settle questions of which norms are to be adopted or are valid *should not*, rationally, assume the principle D, never mind the principle U, and mercifully do not do so at all. Even if proponents of discourse ethics could at least justify D, this would not be enough to save discourse ethics, since, although Habermas describes D as the "principle of discourse ethics",[235] it is clear that U is actually the central and characteristic principle of discourse ethics—otherwise Habermas would not be interested in deriving U from D but rather could content himself with D.

Be that as it may, as long as there remains any plan to derive U from D, discourse ethics has to rely on the consensus and discourse theory of validity. Its proponents will not be able to content themselves with the positing of D, despite their apparent penchant for doing just that; or in any case this positing will not convince anyone. They will have to justify D. Yet we saw that the justification of D directly from the argument of performative self-contradiction fails; it is not any kind of justificatory procedure at all but rather dogmatic and circular.[236] The universal–pragmatic derivation from presuppositions of argumentation likewise fails.[237] If, however, as claimed by consensus theory, those statements—normative statements as well—on which a consensus would be reached in an (ideal) discourse are valid, then the principle D would follow directly from this (whereby the "practical discourse" that D refers to naturally has to be imagined as an ideal practical discourse, or else the consensus actually reached could be an illusory consensus[238]). Consensus theory would offer itself as the last possible saviour of discourse ethics. However, the converse also holds: *the falsity of consensus theory implies the falsity of discourse ethics.* For the latter has to assume that practical discourse, which allegedly is nothing other than an activity in which the presuppositions of argumentation are fulfilled, which in turn is supposed to coincide with the acceptance of U, leads to correct/valid norms. Otherwise U and D cannot supply the conditions of validity of norms.

Consensus theory *is* just this assumption; which gives rise to the question of its validity. Let us turn now to Habermas's attempt at a justification of the consensus and discourse theory of truth and correctness.

Discourse ethics relies on consensus theory. So it does not bode well that the "classical" consensus theory—that is the version of consensus theory that holds those propositions to be *necessarily* true that meet with (consensual) assent in an ideal discourse—is false; who would dispute this today? Even consensus under the ideal conditions specified by Habermas does not at all guarantee the truth of a proposition.[239]

One way out would be to accept the well-known critique of consensus and discourse theory, to scale down its claims somewhat and to argue that discourse ethics should not be understood as *equating* validity with successfully passing the review process of ideal discourse, but rather as merely saying that the *best evidence* or the *best justification* for the validity of a claim is that it has successfully passed the review process of ideal discourse.[240] So passing the review process is not a *guarantee* of validity.

Although this does take the wind out of the sails of certain arguments against consensus and discourse theory, it changes nothing—and this is the essential point—about the connection between discourse theory and discourse ethics. If it is *not* true that discourse is the best (if not infallible) test of the validity of a claim, then we have no reason to take the principles U or D as our ultimate and final standard in reviewing norms rather than any other principles. Discourse ethics is in that case still as unjustified as ever.

The question of the suitability of U and D ("why should it be the case that only valid norms find consent under the conditions of practical discourse?") remains, but takes a slightly different form: why should discourse be the best test of claims of validity? Why not private experiments or private evidence rather than discourse? Here Habermas would surely reply that evidence can always be critically questioned in discourse; yet discourse itself, or even consensus reached under ideal conditions, can always in turn be put into question by private evidence. And this is not another case of the chicken and the egg, since it is clear that if I want to test a claim I can usually do without discourse but never without evidence.

This is so, for one thing, because discourse is de facto neither a necessary nor a sufficient condition for validity[241]—we can normally validly recognize a red ball or a horse as such without it. However, Habermas dislikes these sorts of example

…because elementary statements like "This ball is red" are component parts of everyday communication; their truth is hardly ever disputed. We have to look for analytically fruitful examples in places where substantive controversies erupt and where claims to truth are systematically questioned.[242]

We have to look for analytically fruitful examples in places where they arise, and not only where our preconceptions are in no danger—at least if we are concerned with the truth and not mere propaganda. Since a statement does not have to be controversial to be true, the fact that there is normally *no* dispute over statements like "this ball is red" or "that is a horse" shows precisely that one can normally determine the truth of these statements reliably on one's own and without any discourse. If one were *unable* to do this, there would be occasion for dispute. But clearly one can.

Second, since even when we wish to discuss something we have no basis for argumentation without evidence; and third, the evidence that we are in fact taking part in a discourse cannot itself be subject to discursive review, since this would lead to a regress. At some point the spade has to hit solid earth—not in principle but in the concrete situation—and this happens at the level of evidence and not discourse. And finally we should note that this all presupposes an ideal discourse; but if we are free to construct idealizations, then a situation of ideal evidence is certainly not a worse situation for testing (being, *ex hypothesi*, ideal) than an ideal discourse. It is the ideality that makes each test so good and not evidence or discourse as such.[243] So then, why should it be to discourse above all that we give this special status?

Habermas's (mistaken) answer, it seems to me, consists in building a certain *internal* connection between truth claims or validity claims and ideal discourse or consensus. Discourse as a procedure to "redeem" validity claims is "not extrinsic to the *sense/meaning* [*Sinn*] of truth and rightness",[244] as Habermas himself says. And with a view to our current question this could mean: even if another procedure were ("extrinsically") equally well suited as a test, this test would not be commensurate to the *sense/meaning* of validity or the *sense/meaning* of "redeeming" or justifying validity claims. *This* is what would give discourse its distinguished status.

In what follows I will present a critical examination of the argumentation for this distinguished status, above all as depicted by Habermas in his essay "Wahrheitstheorien". Although there is already a sizeable number of good critiques of consensus and discourse theory, many of them do not primarily tackle the *argumentation* underlying consensus theory but rather confront the claims and implications of this theory with contradictory evidence (such as by showing that a statement that finds consensual agreement in ideal discourse can still be false); or else the critiques single out *particular* arguments introduced in support of consensus theory, without—in my opinion—delivering a sufficiently detailed reconstruction and critique of the course of argumentation *as a whole*.

However, just this sort of detailed point-by-point critique, using old arguments (which to some extent have already been swept under the carpet by discourse theorists) and also (as I hope) new arguments, can show that hardly a single step in Habermas's argumentation is valid. And this sort of criticism would then pertain to even the weakest claim of the discourse theory of truth and rightness—which is the aim of the present section. Perhaps the weakest claim was formulated in an interview by Habermas, responding rather modestly to critical questions:

The discourse theory of truth only claims to reconstruct an intuitive knowledge of the meaning of universal validity-claims which every competent speaker has at his or her disposal.[245]

Since this claim underlies all discourse theories inspired by Habermas, an argument showing that it is not justified would at the same time be a refutation of various other versions of discourse theory, even those that make similarly weak claims. This includes, besides the "classical" consensus theory, a non-consensual discourse theory that equates validity in practical questions with successfully passing the discursive test but not with ideal *consensus*.[246] It also includes those versions that do not subscribe to this equation but see consensus or successfully passing the test of discourse as the best evidence or justification for validity. It also affects those conceptions that cannot be called discourse ethics strictly speaking but nonetheless maintain the interpretation borrowed from discourse ethics of "universal validity claims".

Why, then, is the claim of discourse theory unjustified? Let us look at Habermas's argumentation. We could summarize it as follows:

Habermas claims that a proposition acquires its assertoric force through being embedded in a speech act. He concludes from this that truth is a validity claim that speakers make with certain speech acts, namely, assertions. And when someone makes a claim, he is committed to "redeeming" this claim, just as in the case of a promise. According to Habermas, these claims involve a reference to the procedure of *discursive* redemption, i.e. to redeeming them in argumentation in a discourse unencumbered by action and free of domination or hegemony [*herrschaftsfrei*]. But, according to Habermas, this procedure is not extrinsic to the *meaning* of truth. Rather, the meaning of truth *consists* precisely in this procedure, thus in the justified consensus that according to Habermas the procedure can lead to in principle under ideal conditions. Thus it is the ultimate and final standard for all questions of validity.

The very first step in this argumentation is already profoundly wrong.

A proposition takes its assertoric force from being embedded in a speech act; i.e. from the circumstance that someone can assert this proposition. Searle demonstrated how the very same propositional content can recur in diverse speech acts such as commands, questions, promises and assertions, but that only in constative speech acts (assertions) does the propositional content occur in the *form* of a proposition.[247]

If it is true that a proposition[248] acquires its assertive force only from the fact that someone *can* assert it, then it is not necessary for someone to *actually* assert it for it to have this force. Or, to put it differently: each and every proposition has assertoric force before it is asserted, since every proposition can be asserted. Thus practically speaking assertions have nothing to do with assertoric force, since it is unclear *what* the connection is actually supposed to consist in here.

Yet in the second sentence of this quotation Habermas claims that a proposition acquires its assertoric force only from its *actual* embeddedness in a speech act. Only *in* assertions can any propositional content arise in the form of a proposition. But this is not true. If a computer is programmed to print out sentences and their negations, these might include sentences that no one has ever asserted. We could also ask ourselves, upon reading these sentences, whether or not they are true. And one of two contradictory sentences will have to be true—even if it is *not* asserted. To move beyond this example of the computer, here is another example: "There are creatures living on Jupiter that have 9,876 fingers and 12 toes." I have not *asserted* this statement. I simply provided it as an example. Nonetheless, someone who understands the sentence very well, but perhaps wishes to demonstrate his knowledge or simply prefers true statements as examples, can judge this sentence and its propositional content—a propositional content, and a sentence, which were never asserted in a speech act, either by myself or by anyone else. Evidently propositional content can take the form of a proposition not only in assertions but also in other forms of proposition generally (which is of course why we call them "propositions"). It follows from this that a statement by no means has to be embedded in a speech act in order to have assertoric force.[249]

Furthermore, Habermas's assumption that propositional content has to have assertoric force to be capable of having a truth value is unfounded. Alongside propositions such as "it is raining" there are non-assertoric sentences or clauses such as questions, conditional clauses or consecutive clauses. Let us assume that someone asserts the implication: "if it rains, the street will get wet." The truth value of this asserted implication depends on the truth values of the propositions contained in the two clauses it connects. If these propositions have no truth value, then neither does the sentence. Yet the conditional and consecutive clauses in implications have no assertoric force themselves. And they do not get asserted through the assertion of the implication between them. If someone asserts that the street gets wet when it rains, this is not the same as the assertion that it is raining or that the street is getting wet. So if the capacity for sentences or propositional contents (i.e. "thoughts" in Frege's sense of the word) to have a truth value were dependent on their assertoric force or even on their being actually asserted, it would be impossible to assert implications with any truth value whatsoever. But this *is* possible. So the capacity of sentences and propositional contents to have truth value does not depend on their being asserted or having assertoric force.[250]

But even if a proposition did need to have assertoric force to be capable of having a truth value, and even if it could receive assertoric force only from being embedded in an assertion, Habermas's answer to the first question he poses in his essay would still be flawed, that is, his answer to the question "what is it exactly of which we can say that it is true or false"[251] (directly following the quotation above from p. 128):

We can answer our first question by saying: truth is a validity claim that we connect with propositions by asserting them.[252]

Or, at another place:

Truth is what we call the validity claim that we connect with constative speech acts.[253]

The question was: "What is it exactly of which we can say that it is true or false?", and the answer, according to Habermas, is: "Truth is a validity claim." Since the truth claim is the validity claim in question, it follows that what we call true or false is our claim that something we say is true or false. This explanation is not just externally in contradiction with Habermas's statement that only "propositions can be called 'true' or 'false'",[254] it repeats this contradiction internally and is thus self-contradictory (since what we say is not a claim but rather a proposition). Unless, that is, we are nonsensically operating with two different concepts of truth here, whereby the one relating to validity claims can hardly be brought into accord with our linguistic intuitions.

Adding to this immanent contradiction is the fact that truth is certainly *not* a validity claim. This becomes entirely clear when we look two sentences later at a claim that, astonishingly, Habermas intends as justification of his theory:

When I assert something, I make the claim that the statement that I assert is true.[255]

Quite right: when I assert something, I make the claim *to* truth, namely, the truth of the statement that I assert. But this certainly does not mean that truth *is* a claim. If I buy a bag of cement and demand that the cement be given to me, I make a claim to the cement—a cement-claim. I can also make purchase claims or pension claims. But it would be somewhat adventurous of me to conclude that a claim *is* a purchase or a pension or cement. A purchase is an economic act; cement, a construction material. Similarly, truth *is not* a validity claim; it is, rather, that *which is claimed* with this claim. Ultimately even Habermas recognized this. In a response to critics he conceded: "The truth *claim* made for 'p' is certainly not identical to the truth or the validity of 'p'...." Indeed. However, shortly after this concession Habermas tries to ward off criticism:

The point of the discourse theory of truth is that it aims to justify why the question of what it means that truth conditions for 'p' are satisfied can be *answered* with the explanation of what it means to use arguments to redeem or justify this claim that the truth conditions for 'p' are satisfied with arguments.[256]

But, as we saw, the discourse theory of truth aims to justify this with recourse to the premise that truth is a validity claim; and this premise is false. So contrary to

Habermas's claim (see the following quotation below as well) it is just as futile to try to explain the meaning of truth with reference to the pragmatics of speech acts as to explain the "meaning of cement" with reference to the pragmatics of speech acts (I come back to this point below).

Moreover, Habermas's "explanations" are hopelessly circular. First, the specific validity claim of assertions, namely, the truth claim, is introduced as the claim that what is asserted is true. So the concept of the truth claim gets explained using the concept of the truth claim.[257] We also read that truth is a validity claim, specifically: a truth claim, thus a claim to truth. Here the concept of truth is explained using the concept of truth. And finally an assertion is explained to us as that with which I raise a claim to truth for a proposition; and conversely the truth claim is explained as what I raise in asserting. Habermas could hardly have given us a less informative analysis.

Habermas does try to avoid this circularity by defining the speech act of asserting non-circularly through specific commitments to justification:

Constative speech acts contain the offer to have recourse if necessary to the *experiential source* from which the speaker draws the *certainty* that his statement is true.[258]

Yet this recourse is not at all specific to this speech act. When I *suggest* (this is also a speech act) going to the swimming-pool, I can have recourse to the weather report predicting oppressive heat (an experiential source), from which I draw the certainty that my suggestion is good. Of course, here one could try to construct a distinction between suggestion and assertion by assuming that suggestions require a reference to norms for their justification. But this is not the case. There is no norm here: "when the weather is oppressively hot, go to the swimming pool." Furthermore, assertions do not necessarily include any commitment to justification at all. Habermas introduces this to explain why the listener can *rationally* accept the "speech act offer".[259] But if, looking out of the window, I say to someone who has no direct view to the outside "it's raining", it is not at all clear to what extent any recourse to experiential sources could be an *additional* motivation for the listener to accept my assertion. The listener already knows which experiential source I am using, since he can see that I am looking outside. Of course he could assume that I am mistaken. But then it is unclear why the sentence "I can see that it's raining" would convince him of the contrary. And if he thinks that I am lying, then no additional justifications that *I* give him could be convincing. The rational justification for accepting these speech-act offers consists not in any supposed individual commitments to justification on the part of the speaker but rather in the existence of a *sanctioned institution* called assertion. In fact it is precisely the *point* of this sort of institution to make continuous recourse to justifications unnecessary. Speakers are sanctioned (when they are caught) for lies or for making assertions for which they have absolutely no evidence. This sanctioning guarantees these speech acts a certain reliability and *with this* the rationality of their acceptance. However, it does not follow from the fact that I should have some evidence for my assertions that I have to *provide* it. These two different things are conflated by Dieter Wunderlich, who writes: "Since it is clearly not possible for someone to assert something and at the same time deny having any evidence for it, this is analytically part of the concept of assertion as a speech-act."[260] I can agree with this, but I deny that the following sentence is meaningless, as Wunderlich thinks it is: "P, but I am neither willing nor able to prove that p (neither now nor at any point in the future)." I hereby assert that there was just a pigeon on my balcony (which flew away in the meantime). This *is* an assertion, but I am not able to justify it: how could I? I have no witnesses, nor do I have a time-travelling machine. And concerning my willingness, I am not committed to justifying this sentence to people who doubt my truthfulness or my ability to recognize a pigeon from three metres' distance. In this case, demanding of me: "Provide the evidence for this assertion!" is not an appeal to any obligation or commitment that I might have, and thus not the demand for the satisfaction of a justified claim, but rather silly at best and likely impertinent as well.

Two sentences later Habermas continues:

Assertions cannot themselves be either true or false; they are justified or unjustified. The performance of constative speech-acts demonstrates what we understand as the truth of propositions; thus the speech-acts themselves cannot be true. Truth is understood here as the sense/meaning [*Sinn*] of using propositions in assertions. The sense/meaning [*Sinn*] of truth can thus be explained with reference to the pragmatics of a certain class of speech-acts.[261]

Let us look at the last two sentences. Here Habermas uses the same German word, *Sinn*, for the "sense/meaning of using propositions" (*de[r] Sinn der Verwendung*) as he does for "the sense of truth" (*Der Sinn der Wahrheit*). The word has two possible meanings here, either *meaning* or else the *purpose* or *function* of something (the *Sinn* of an act is its purpose or function). In the fourth sentence "sense" can only be "meaning", since Habermas's goal here is an explication of the meaning of "truth".[262] The "sense of using" cannot be meant in this way (or else it becomes itself meaningless). So we have to read this as saying: truth is understood here as the purpose of using propositions in assertions. Now the stated purpose of using propositions in assertions is just this: to connect propositions with a truth claim by using them in this way (by asserting them). Thus it follows: the meaning of truth is the purpose of raising the truth claim for a proposition. This surprising result brings Habermas in contradiction with his original claim that truth is a validity claim (since claims and purposes are two mutually exclusive categories). Furthermore, this is hardly very informative, since—again—it is circular. And third, the proposition can serve this purpose without being true.

So we see that the equation of truth with a validity claim or with the "use of propositions in assertions" makes little sense. Truth is *neither* the connection of a truth claim with a proposition, *nor* the raising of this claim, *nor* the claim itself. Competent speakers call "truth" something entirely different, contrary to Habermas's claims.

Let us note that so far Habermas has been unable to justify even any initial plausibility for his thesis that the meaning of truth can be explained "with reference to the pragmatics of a certain class of speech acts". So far everything speaks against this kind of approach.

Nonetheless, Habermas continues his argumentation and tries to further specify the connection between truth and the pragmatics of speech acts with the following thesis:

A proposition is true when the validity claim of the speech acts with which we assert the proposition using sentences is justified.[263]

This statement is false. Let us take the Kantian dilemma: the Gestapo are at the door and ask Franz whether he is sheltering a certain unjustly persecuted person. Franz says "no." For this assertion—and lies are nothing other than assertions, that is, assertions of what is false with the aim of deceiving—Franz raises a validity claim, according to Habermas. Is Franz justified in raising it? Of course he is, as Habermas himself knows.[264] If he does not raise this claim, the innocent victim of persecution will be killed.

The problem here lies in Habermas's conflation of two things he had previously explicitly distinguished (and this conflation is once more necessary for his argumentation): on the one hand, the validity claim that the speaker makes for the speech act *itself*, that is, the claim that the speech act is justified and its performance appropriate; and, on the other, the validity claim that is made with the speech act in connection with the proposition. The latter is the validity claim that the statement is *true*. This claim cannot pertain directly to the speech act itself, since, as Habermas himself argues, assertions "cannot themselves be either true or false; they are justified or unjustified."[265] So while the validity claim made for the proposition, the truth claim, is unjustified or, to put it better, not fulfilled, the *raising* of this claim—and the speech act *is* this raising of the claim—is very much justified.

And now it is clear on the face of it that determining whether the validity claim of a *speech act* is justified necessarily involves a reference to the pragmatics of speech acts. But for determining whether the validity claim made for a *proposition* is justified or not—that is, the *truth claim*—the pragmatics of the speech act are of course irrelevant. As we saw in the Kantian dilemma, the validity claim of the speech act and the speech act itself can be justified without the truth claim raised for the proposition being justified or the proposition being true, and vice versa; and here the truth claim of course *had* to be raised or else the lie would not have been successful.

Thus Habermas has still proven unable to explain the exact nature of the connection between the "sense/meaning of truth" and the "pragmatics of a certain class of speech acts". Instead, time and again we have only uncovered reasons that militate *against* this connection.

In his next step Habermas tries to derive the reference of validity claims to argumentation and thus to discourse from the "pragmatics of speech acts":

...a validity claim can only be redeemed [*einlösen*] through arguments.[266]

This statement is likewise false. First of all, we do not speak of "redeeming" claims. We can back up a claim, satisfy it, live up to it, but not "redeem" it. However, it is quite acceptable to say in English that someone "redeems" his promise, and completely normal to say in German: "*Er löst sein Versprechen ein.*" And in fact Habermas draws this connection to promising in the rather inimitable sentence:

The truth of a proposition means the promise to reach a rational consensus on what has been said.[267]

Yet precisely the case of promising shows how inapplicable Habermas's equation of redeeming and justifying is. If a retailer promises to deliver cement to me tomorrow, he does not "redeem" this promise by entering into discourse wherein he provides arguments *that* he will deliver the cement; rather, he redeems his promise *by delivering* the cement.

And whereas I *cannot* redeem my promise to do something tomorrow today, but only after the fact, that is, after giving my promise, just the opposite holds for my claim that the proposition I assert is true. For I cannot redeem this claim after the fact (and certainly not in discourse). I can redeem it only now by *actually* speaking the truth in the very moment when I claim to be speaking the truth. The *justification* that I have spoken the truth is *not* the satisfaction of the claim; rather, my *saying* the truth is the satisfaction of this claim. So validity claims in this sense clearly do *not* refer to their "redemption" within a discourse.

I said, "validity claims in this sense". For there are two basic kinds of claims, with different implications. Habermas fails to differentiate between them. First of all, one can make claims that one can only fulfil oneself, such as when I claim to be speaking the truth. We have just discussed this case. But one can also make claims the fulfilment of which one demands *from others*: we see this kind of claim when I call for the (rational) *recognition* of my statement as true. ("With their illocutionary acts, speaker and hearer raise validity claims and demand they be recognized."[268]) Habermas seems to be thinking of this kind of claim when he compares validity claims with legal claims. Just as I can procure recognition of legal claims through certain legal procedures, I can also procure rational recognition of these validity claims through discursive procedures.[269]

However, several points should be noted here. First, it is wrong to say that I *demand* recognition of the proposition as true. This would imply a reduction of assertions to demands. More than this: the notion that the recognition of validity claims is *demanded* reduces *all* speech acts to demands. "I assert that *p*" would be reformulated as "I demand recognition of *p* as true"; "I ask whether *p*" would mean "I demand recognising *p* as in question and to be clarified"; "I command that *p*" would mean "I demand recognition of *p* as a command." If it were true that we demand recognition of validity claims—and thus if all these reformulations were accurate—then what makes an assertion an assertion or a question a question would shift from the performative side of the speech act (the two-word opener "I assert", "I ask", etc.) to the side of the *propositional content* (the content following the two-word opener). In other words, the distinction between assertion and question would no longer be a distinction between two different types of *speech acts*. The absurdity of this conclusion compels us to drop the premise, namely, that recognition is *demanded* for validity claims. But this implies no less than the non-existence of anything like a "discursively redeemable validity claim" as an inextricable component of assertions.

There is another reason why we cannot reasonably *demand* the rational recognition of the truth of a proposition. It clearly makes no sense to say: "I demand that you recognize p as rational." If the other party is not rational, then he *cannot* recognize p rationally. If he is rational and has no good reasons for this recognition, then he again *cannot* recognize p rationally. And if he is rational and has good reasons for this recognition, then he *will* recognize p—he cannot not do it—since he is compelled by the "forceless force of the better argument".[270] What would be the point of demanding something that the other party either cannot do or cannot fail to do? The demand for rational recognition makes no sense one way or the other.

If we cannot demand rational recognition (which already is no longer the recognition of a *claim*), we at least might be able to *bring it about* by providing rational reasons for this recognition. This cannot, of course, imply a reference to consensus. A consensus is neither a procedure (it is a state, rather) nor is it a reason.[271] A discourse, on the other hand, can be a procedure, and can be used to provide good reasons. But the very same arguments introduced above against the idea that discourse is the best or the final test of the validity of propositions can be used similarly here to refute the idea that discourse is necessary or generally sufficient to bring about rational recognition of the truth of a proposition. Of course, sometimes it is sufficient. But sometimes—and in most ordinary cases—the mere assertion of something suffices, too. If I say to a friend, "Yesterday I read a story by Borges alone in my apartment", this should be sufficient to bring him to the *rational* recognition of just this proposition. It is rational because he has no reason to doubt the truth of my statement. If he were to doubt it, then it is unclear how discourse would be able to change anything, since then he would be doubting my truthfulness, and according to Habermas claims to truthfulness cannot be discursively redeemed.[272]

Thus we have established that there is no intrinsic connection between discourse and the "redeeming" of validity claims or the rational recognition of propositions as true.

Following his statement that whether a state of affairs is the case gets decided by "the course of argumentation",[273] Habermas summarizes his considerations thus far:

True is what we call propositions that we can justify. The meaning of truth, which is implicit in the pragmatics of assertions, can only be sufficiently explained once we can say what "discursive redemption" of experienced-based validity claims means. And precisely this is the goal of the consensus theory of truth.[274]

Now truth and justification are clearly not the same. Yet Habermas claims that this concern, "that truth is not to be conflated with the methods of achieving true statements",[275] does not apply to the theory he is arguing for. And he remarks:

The claim that truth and rightness are discursively redeemable validity claims for utterances pertains to argumentative practice in general and by no means to certain methods for achieving true propositions or correct commands. Of course it is, so to speak, in the nature of validity claims that they are able to be redeemed; and what they are redeemable by is what constitutes their meaning. If I want to explain a certain legal title such as a property right, I can refer to the guarantees I have in the case that another party should dispute my right: as a legal title I can procure general recognition for my property with the help of certain legal procedures if need be. This is also the case with truth as a validity claim. The meaning of this class of claims refers to a distinguished mode of testing that they are to pass. Of course the "behaviour" of argumentatively bringing about a consensus wherein the discursive validity claim is redeemed is not external to the meaning of truth and correctness.[276]

Aside from the fact that there is no such thing as "discursively redeemable validity claims", there are considerable flaws in these averments of Habermas's.

First, the meaning of a property claim does *not* consist in the legal procedures with which I can procure recognition of it. One could procure recognition of a property claim through the same process as a claim to job protection, but this does not mean that the two things are the same; they do *not* have the same meaning.

Maybe one could respond here that these legal procedures constitute the meaning not of a specific legal claim but of legal claims *as such*, generally (although Habermas did choose a concrete example, namely, property rights). The description of the procedures could explain what a legal claim is generally without distinguishing between property claims and other claims; and a legal claim, the thesis might go, is defined by the procedures with which one procures its recognition. But this is unfounded. A legal claim is defined by *laws*. If I were to explain to someone what a legal claim is, I would say that it is a claim that is justified by appeal *to legal norms* and defined by them. A legal claim can *be* justified, even if I do not get justice in the *procedure* due to the available evidence. For this reason legal scholars distinguish between formal and material law. Since discourse is also neither necessary nor sufficient as a testing procedure, we can make an analogous distinction here. The meaning of validity claims is not to be found in discourse.

Second, a theory of truth cannot be concerned with the meaning of the claim but rather, as stated in the quotation itself, with the sense/meaning of truth (or the meaning of "truth"). (Unless, that is, one claims, as Habermas does: "Truth *is* a validity claim." Here we see again that this bizarre way of speaking is not a mere lapse but rather necessary for Habermas's argumentation, whether he is aware of this or not.[277]) And here we can see with particularly striking clarity that the meaning of truth cannot be explained in terms of the "redemption" (in the Habermasian sense) of the claim, if we take seriously this analogy of the legal claim that Habermas appeals to again and again.

Let us suppose a concrete case involving my property rights to the sack of cement that I bought; and let us suppose further that I really could explain the meaning of this property right to someone (which, for the above-mentioned reasons, is not so) by explaining which legal procedures I could make use of to ensure that I finally receive the cement. There could even be a special court for cement claims (a "distinguished mode", that is), just as there are labour courts and administrative courts. But specifically or generally, even if my legal explanations managed to reveal to my listener what a cement claim is, they have certainly not helped him to learn what cement is. Not even the judges have to know what cement is in order to carry out the procedure properly, and not even I as the claimant have to know this. Naturally this sort of knowledge *can* sometimes be necessary, but then these are exceptions or borderline cases; and in any case the definition of "cement", if the court has to look it up for the case, will *not* make any mention of legal (or discursive) procedures, but rather chemical facts and the function of cement in construction. To learn what cement is, we have to examine *cement itself*—and does not this make sense?—and not some legal or argumentative or discursive or any other kind of procedures for ruling on *claims* on cement.

Clearly this whole discussion of truth *claims* does not shed the faintest light on the question of what *truth* is.

Let us now look at Habermas's last step, that is, the transition from mere discourse theory to consensus theory. Taking up where he left off in the block quotation above, Habermas continues:

> ...the only agreement we can reach in discourse is a *justified consensus*....but the meaning of truth is not the circumstance that a consensus is somehow achieved, but rather: that anytime and everywhere, as long as we enter into a discourse, a consensus can be reached under conditions that show it to be a justified consensus.[278]

That a consensus can be reached anytime and everywhere under ideal conditions of discourse is of course another false statement.[279] This is completely clear for norms of action, that is, for practical questions. Habermas's standard response, namely, that a consensual agreement can be reached at a higher level of abstraction, is not convincing. Even if a consensual agreement on a "norm" of such unrivalled abstraction as "do the right thing" could be reached (which is itself not even certain), this "norm" would have absolutely no normative content, precisely because it says nothing by itself. It is the vacuity of its content that enables consent at all. In the very same moment that the norm begins to express something of any substance and thus becomes effectively normative, there will hardly be any more hope of consensus.

But even for *theoretical* questions a consensus cannot necessarily be reached by rational speakers, even under ideal conditions. This can be shown with Goodman's "queer" predicates.[280] The speaker A might conclude inductively from the fact that all emeralds examined so far are green that those emeralds examined after a future point in time t are also green, whereas the speaker B might conclude inductively from the fact that all emeralds examined so far are grue (either examined before t and green or not examined before t and blue) that all emeralds examined after t are blue. And there is no absolute criterion we can use to call B less rational than A. Rationality and justification are relative, not only with regard to situations (for the situation in ideal discourse is, after all, the same for each individual in terms of the data and arguments presented) but also with regard to individuals and their dispositions.[281] So it is not the case that a consensus can always be reached with all people (in so far as they are rational) under ideal conditions. So here, as well, consensus theory remains unjustified.

Recently Habermas suggested a revision of his previous theory of truth and rightness.

> The truth predicate refers to the language game of justification, that is, to the public redemption of validity claims. On the other hand, truth cannot be identified with justifiability or warranted assertability. The "cautionary" use of the truth predicate—regardless of how well

"p" is justified, it still may not be true—highlights the difference in meaning between "truth" as an inextricable [*unverlierbar*, literally "unlosable"] property of statements and "rational acceptability" as a context-dependent property of utterances. This difference can be understood within the horizon of possible justifications in terms of the distinction between "justified in our context" and "justified in every context". This difference can be cashed out in turn through a weak idealization of our processes of argumentation, understood as capable of being extended indefinitely over time. When we assert "p" and thereby claim truth for "p" we accept the obligation to defend "p" in argumentation—in full awareness of its fallibility—against all future objections.[282]

According to Habermas this allegedly "reactive concept of 'discursive redeemability', which is not oriented to ideal conditions [of complete justification] but to the refutation of potential objections" represents a correction of his "earlier conception of truth which was still influenced by Peirce."[283]

But just these kinds of attempted revision show that the discourse theory of validity cannot be fixed. First of all, we have already seen in detail that it is an unfounded and false claim that the truth predicate refers "to the language game of…the public redemption of validity claims"—and this is not revised by Habermas. Since truth, as Habermas aptly puts it, is an inextricable property of statements, the truth predicate logically refers only to a certain irreducible property of statements, namely, *truth itself*, and not to the language game of the "redemption" of truth *claims*. Habermas is also correct to say that, no matter how well justified a proposition *p* is, it could still be not true. But here as well he does not draw the logical conclusion. Since if a proposition could be flawlessly justified and *yet still* be false, then it could also be justified in *all* contexts and *yet still* be false. (In addition, a proposition that is justified in all contexts does not necessarily have to be very well justified in any one of these contexts.) So the difference between truth and rational acceptability can only be *mis*understood in the way Habermas wishes. And, incidentally, Habermas's proposed idealization is anything but weak. If we are to understand "justified in every context" as "justified in every *possible* context", then this *includes* even ideal speaking situations. We could of course also read "justified in every context" as "justified in every *real* context"; but this would be hard to reconcile with Habermas's intention of providing a concept of truth that is "purified of all connotations of correspondence",[284] since with the reference to *reality* more than mere *connotations* of correspondence theory are introduced into the alleged discourse theory of truth. Furthermore, as we well know, there are infinitely many true statements that cannot be justified in all real contexts, let alone all possible contexts. The propositions "$E = mc^2$", "there are meat-eating plants", "an American will be the first man on the moon", "on 21 June 1998 the German football team plays the Yugoslavian", etc., are difficult to justify in the situation in which Hannibal and his followers found themselves crossing the Alps. These propositions are not justifiable in all situations, but are nonetheless true. Habermas's claim that true propositions are justified in every context is false. Given this situation, it hardly makes a difference any more that Habermas fails to explain to us *when exactly* a proposition should in his opinion be justified, although this would be important information. So we can conclude that Habermas's latest explanations concerning the concept of truth are just as faulty as his previous ones.

We can summarize the problems afflicting Habermas's argumentation in the direction of a discourse theory of truth as follows:

First, a proposition can be true without anyone raising a truth claim for it with the help of a speech act. There is no connection between truth and the pragmatics of speech acts.

Second, even if a statement could be true only when we raise a truth claim for it with a speech act, this truth claim could still be unjustified, and thus the proposition could still be false, without the *speech act* itself being unjustified. Here as well there is no connection between truth and the pragmatics of speech acts.

Third, a truth claim cannot be redeemed through discourse and argumentation. Furthermore, discourse has no special distinction as a procedure for testing propositions. That is, even if there were a connection between truth and the pragmatics of speech acts, there would still be none between truth and discourse.

Fourth, even if truth claims could be redeemed only in discourse, this "redemption" would only guarantee the justification of the proposition and would not explain the *meaning* of truth claims or guarantee the *truth* of a statement.

Fifth, even if this procedure could ensure the truth of propositions and explicate the meaning of truth claims, it would say nothing about the "meaning of truth"; that is, it can as little explain what truth is or what "truth" means as it can explain what cement is or "cement" means.

Sixth, even if ideal discourse were able to reliably distinguish between justified and unjustified validity claims, this does not place it in an internal relation to the idea of consensus.

None of these "even-ifs" is satisfied. Habermas's argumentation fails. Not only the consensual discourse theory of validity, but also the non-consensual theory is unfounded and false. And with this we have also established that discourse ethics itself—and along with it a series of its assumptions which keep popping up in other contexts—is untenable.

2.5. THE UNSOLVED PROBLEM OF THE APPLICATION OF NORMS JUSTIFIED BY U OR D TO REAL SITUATIONS

According to Habermasian discourse ethics, as we know, a norm can be valid only if the condition U is satisfied, that is, if

all affected can *freely* accept the consequences and the side effects that the *general* observance of a controversial norm can be expected to have for the satisfaction of the interests of *each individual*.[285]

Now, it has been pointed out that the observance of certain norms, which allegedly would be in everyone's interest in case of their *general* observance (by which, as we recall, Habermas means its *universal* observance, that is, its observance by all and always), is nonetheless not a reasonable expectation or imperative according to our moral intuitions as long as they are *not* generally observed.[286] "You should not kill" is unreasonable if I can defend myself from an attempt on my own life only by killing my attacker. If it is possible to save an innocent person from execution only by lying to the persecutors (to be referred to as the Kant dilemma from here on), then it is not imperative to speak the truth. This should be enough to demonstrate the implausibility of U. The proponents of U, however, claim that the norms are very much justified by U and that the problem consists only in their *application*.

> Valid norms are valid only in a "prima facie" sense. Regardless of whether they rest on double negations, *all* rights and duties play the same role in discourses of application, namely, that of reasons. In cases of conflict between norms, it can be shown only on the basis of a maximally complete description of all relevant features of the given situation *which* of the competing norms is appropriate to a particular case. Norms that are overruled by this "single appropriate" norm do not lose their validity because they are not "pertinent." They remain valid even if they do not apply to the given case. This already entails that the deontological force of normative validity cannot be interpreted simply as an *unconditional* or absolute ought, as it is by an *ethics of conviction*.
>
> On the contrary, normative validity [*Sollgeltung*] has the intersubjective sense that a behavioural expectation is equally good "for all", not that it has desirable consequences for a particular addressee...[287]

These remarks do not refute the stated objection to Habermas's discourse ethic in the slightest; they are rife with inconsistencies, as I aim to show here.

It is first of all contradictory to claim on the one hand that norms are "valid *only* in a 'prima facie' sense", and then to claim just a few sentences later that norms "do not lose their validity because they are not 'pertinent'". If a norm is *only* prima facie valid, that is, at first glance but not upon closer examination (which follows in the discourse of application), then this means that they are actually *not at all* valid, but only *seem* valid upon cursory inspection.

This contradiction belies the difficulties involved in claiming that it could be allowable not to follow valid moral imperatives. The validity of an imperative consists precisely in its being true *that* we should follow it, as Habermas himself knows quite well:

> Normative validity is the existential mode of norms. They are expressed in ought-sentences: in the situations given one ought to (or: it is imperative to) perform the action x (or abstain from it).[288]

Although it is quite correct that a situation that the norm does not apply to does not limit the norm's validity, it is very much a limitation of its validity if the norm *ought* not to be applied in a situation that in fact the norm *does* apply to.

So it does not bring us any further to claim that all norms play the role of reasons in discourses of application. If two norms contradict each other, then they contradict each other, no matter whether they play the role of reasons in a discourse of application or the role of examples in a philosophical text of certain contradictions that can be found in certain programmes of moral justification. If one wishes to avoid arbitrariness in a discourse of application, one should avoid recourse to mutually contradictory norms, in light of the principle of *ex falso quodlibet.* Conversely, this also means: if the *correct* result of a certain chain of reflection—even one starting from the consideration, "on the one hand one ought not to betray innocent people, but on the other hand one ought not to lie either"—is that ultimately one should lie in that particular case, since otherwise it would mean the death of an innocent, then this implies the *invalidity* of the norm that one should not lie. The same holds, unwittingly, for Habermas's explanation:

An untruthful statement that saves the life of another is no less morally commanded than killing in cases of self-defense or refraining from offering assistance to avoid a greater evil are morally permissible.[289]

The norm that one ought not to lie unless it would save another's life is *different* from the norm: one ought not to lie. The one norm calls on us never to lie, the other one does not. And it would be incorrect to claim that the first norm is just a more "concrete" version of the second. "Almost all swans are white, just not the Australian ones" is not a more concrete version of the statement "swans are white", but rather a contradicting statement that *falsifies* it. And if it is imperative to follow the first norm, as Habermas says, then logically it cannot at the same time be (validly) imperative to follow the second. It is, then, rather inconvenient for discourse ethics if the latter norm is admitted as valid by the principle U.

Yet one could ask: in the case of a conflict of norms, does the imperative to follow the one rule exclude the imperative to follow the other? Could there not be a true dilemma, not just a prima facie dilemma? Now, as far as it concerns mere *factual validity*, this can very much be the case. If some code of law prohibits killing and also prohibits lying, and these two norms come into conflict in a concrete case, both norms are of course still *factually* commanded (they remain norms sanctioned by the code of law). But then this code of law is inconsistent. The same holds for a moral theory.

Of course, Habermas maintains a strict distinction between the factual validity of a norm in actual social contexts and its rightness or normative validity (determined using the principle U). But clearly the commands "do A" and "do not do A" cannot both at the same time be correct. In a case where observance of the one norm means an infringement of the other, they cannot both properly be commanded. Whereas these sorts of conflict between norms are possible in the area of factual validity, they are excluded in the area of normative validity subject to philosophical scrutiny. And thus either of these, a factual moral system or a philosophical theory that admits of such conflicts of norms, is inadequate.

Habermas cannot elude this problem by pointing out—quite correctly, as it happens—that a norm does not lose validity by being irrelevant in a certain given case. For the norms that according to Habermas are justified by U include the two prohibitions "You should not kill" and "You should not lie", which conflict with Habermas's postulated allowance of an "untruthful statement that saves the life of another"[290] or the killing of another in self-defence, and *are always pertinent.*

For the sake of contrast let us take a norm that is *not* always pertinent. A judge is subject to just such a norm when his office obliges him to give a murderer a certain sentence X (or a sentence between X and Y). If it turns out that the accused did not commit murder, then this is *not* a case in which to apply this norm. Applying a norm means performing the action demanded by it (when certain conditions are fulfilled) with the intention of following the norm (since without this intention it would be an action in contingent conformity to the norm). So this is not a case for applying the norm, since on the one hand the norm says "*if* this and that is the case, do X", and on the other hand these specified conditions are not given. This means that the norm specifies the cases for its application in the if-clause, as certain of Habermas's statements also suggest.[291] So if a norm ought not to be applied in a case that is not a case of its application, this does not affect its validity in the slightest.

Now the question arises of where Habermas could possibly detect any relevant if-component in a norm such as "do not kill." This component does not necessarily have to already be explicit. But one can make it explicit; for example, "in the office of judge you ought to give a murderer the sentence X" can be readily reformulated as "if a murderer is brought before you in your capacity as judge, you ought to give him or her the sentence X." The case is somewhat different with a norm such as "you ought not to kill" or "do not kill." We could say: if we read the norm as a command to forbear from doing something, and if we assume furthermore that one can forebear doing only things that one has the possibility of doing, then cases where no one is around to be killed could be cases where the norm is inapplicable; with this interpretation, we could come up with a formulation of the norm such as "if you can kill somebody, do not kill him." But here there is a decisive difference from the judge's norm: for the judge it is possible to perform the then-component even when the if-component is not satisfied (i.e. the judge could punish an innocent person, even knowingly), but with our reformulated prohibition on killing this is not possible (one can kill someone only when it is possible to kill someone). So the if-component is trivial and irrelevant to our problem; the prohibition on killing can still be seen as categorical in the only relevant sense of categorical, since the "restriction" of its application by the if-component is not one of prudence or any moral or ethical restriction but rather one of mere practical possibility, which is trivially given for all actions. In any case, contrary to Habermas's interpretation *all* cases in which killing is possible are cases of application for the prohibition on killing, and clearly this also holds for cases where someone *has* in fact killed in self-defence. Besides, it is an unnecessary complication to read the norm as a command to forebear doing something. It is more correct to interpret what it commands as simply *not* doing something. And simply not performing an action is different from forbearing to do it; an agent *cannot* kill (or *cannot* lie) in any situation.

Here finally someone might respond that the norms that Habermas proposes such as "You should not kill" and "You should not lie" are not meant the way they sound. Habermas concedes:

...prohibitions of the form "You should not kill" create the impression that such conduct is forbidden "unconditionally" in the sense of strict generality—that is, for everyone under all circumstances and for all time, in short, *categorically*.[292]

But he does not want them understood this way[293]—which makes it quite negligent of him to have not formulated them differently from the beginning so as to avoid this deceptive impression.

How are they intended? One interpretation—which, however, Habermas decisively rejects—could be that the norms in question are to be understood as principles of optimization. Thus Robert Alexy understands the constitutional commandments as imperatives for optimization and defines them as follows:

Accordingly principles are imperatives for optimization characterized precisely by their being able to be satisfied in various degrees and the appropriate measure of their fulfilment depending not only on the factual but also on the legal possibilities. The area of legal possibilities is determined by incompatible principles and rules.[294]

In contrast,

rules are norms that can only ever be fulfilled or not fulfilled....The law for passing on the freeway makes this particularly clear. One can either pass on the left or on the right.[295]

Unlike conflicts of principle, in conflicts of rules only one of the two can be valid in a particular situation.[296]

Günther blurs this distinction when he writes:

But the requirement to apply a norm relative to the factual and normative (legal) possibilities of a situation can be applied to *every* norm. It does not just depend on the norm itself whether we apply it with or without considering the particular circumstances of a situation.[297]

It is quite correct that it does not depend on the norm itself whether we apply it with consideration of the particular circumstances. But this insight of Günther's fails to address the problem. The problem is whether (and, as the case may be, how) the norm *should* be applied. And whether we *should* apply norms with or without considering the particular circumstances of a situation *does* depend on the norms themselves, that is, on the conditions of application specified in their if-components (if any). If we interpret the norms in question as rules in Alexy's sense of the term (and this is just what they are, since it is possible to not kill a person but impossible to not kill him "a little less"; likewise, it is not possible to not lie to someone "a little less"—the negation "not" does not leave any room for quantification here), then only one of the two can be valid.

With principles it is a different matter.

Conflicts of principle occur outside of the dimension of validity, in the dimension of relative weight, since only valid principles can come into conflict.[298]

Alexy mentions the example of the Lebach case in which a prison inmate brought a lawsuit over the reports about him in the press.[299] In this case the principle of the protection of privacy (which is in law *explicitly limited*, in that the principle does not state simply "you should protect privacy" but rather "you should protect privacy *within the bounds* of certain laws and principles") conflicts with the freedom of the press (likewise characterized as relative to certain other laws). In this concrete case the protection of privacy is subordinated to the freedom of the press. But this does not invalidate the first principle; on the contrary, this first principle does not stand in the way of a single report, but only of repeated reports that are no longer covered by the interest in current information. In other words, the two principles affect each other reciprocally; protection of privacy is limited by freedom of the press and vice versa. In the case of the prohibitions on lying and killing, we lack this sort of reciprocal effect whereby the correct action so to speak emerges as a result of the different forces. Rather, in these cases only *one* of the two norms is applied. For while a judge can very well say that he has protected the privacy of certain persons to an extent limited by law (which includes the countervailing principles as well), even if to a lesser extent than would have been practically possible, I cannot reasonably claim, I say it again, that, as I shot some-one to death, I did not really kill him, even if I did "not kill him a little less" than would have been practically possible; and I could not claim that I still have not really lied to someone, although I have "not lied to them a little less" than strictly possible. Admittedly one could read this "prohibition" on killing as an impera-tive for optimization in another sense, namely, "kill as little as possible." However, this reading can come up only in the context of our attempt to figure out how these imperatives *could* be meant in order to resolve Habermas's curious prob-lems of validity. As long as we take the statement *literally* it is quite clear that the moral command is a categorical one. "You should not kill" does not mean that one should refrain only from killing animals; it does not mean that one should kill as little as possible; nor does it mean that one should not kill by and large but may be permitted to do so in self-defence; it means, simply and clearly, *that one should not kill*, and between "not" and "absolutely not" there is only a rhetorical difference, not a semantic one.

Be that as it may, there is in any case, as we saw, a very profound difference between principles and rules: two principles that are recognized as applicable (in the semantic sense) to a single case in which they conflict can be weighed against each other, whereas two rules that are applicable (in the semantic sense) to the same case—they both "fit"—and conflict with each other cannot possibly both be valid. Whereas with principles it could make sense to speak of "coherence", this is not so in the case of contradictory rules such as the prohibition on killing and the prohibition on lying. If Günther does not want to see norms as principles of optimization, then he can no longer see two conflicting norms as both valid at the same time. Now principles of optimization are hardly conceivable without recourse to the idea of the good, and so from the very outset they are at odds with the deontological approach to justification taken by Habermas and Günther (or at least what they understand as a deontological approach). And in fact, as noted, Habermas and Günther do explicitly reject the interpretation of the norms justi-fied by U as principles of optimization.[300]

Another attempt to save matters with a reinterpretation could consist in read-ing "You should not kill" as an abbreviated form of a norm with if-components. A proponent of the Habermasian discourse ethics might argue that when we praise norms such as "You should not kill" and "You should not lie" in everyday life, or when we preach them from the pulpit, it is clear for everyone listening that these norms are meant in the sense of *guidelines* one should adhere to as far as *possible*, which however allow of *exceptions*. And these exceptions are just such cases as self-defence or the Kant dilemma, such that the norms in question do *not* in fact conflict with the right to self-defence and the obligation to lie when it saves an innocent life.

If we weaken the force of the imperatives "You should not lie" and "You should not kill" with this interpretation such that the situations of self-defence or the Kant dilemma no longer count as applications (and applications are, for norms without if-components, all situations, and otherwise are just those stated in the if-components), then the feared norm conflicts no longer arise. However, it should be emphasized that a norm such as "You should not kill" does not come with any qualifiers such as "as far as possible" or anything similar. In terms of its pure seman-tics, "You should not kill" does not mean that one should kill as little as possible or infrequently, but simply that one should *not* kill; one transgresses against this command in *every* case in which one kills. If the expression "You should not kill" is not used in this strict sense in everyday language, this still does not excuse philoso-phers who use this expression without further comment in their treatises on the problems of moral justification, since in my opinion we could expect them to for-mulate the norms they discuss *precisely* as they are meant—it is first and foremost the philosopher's responsibility, not the reader's, to avoid misunderstandings.

The fact that Habermas speaks of the imperative to say an untruth to save an innocent life and the moral permissibility of killing in self-defence as examples of *norm conflicts* speaks against this interpretation, according to which the norms "You should not kill" and "You should not lie" are ones that are from the very outset restricted in their scope of application by implicit if-components. The nec-essary lie and the permission to act in self-defence could not conflict with the prohibitions on lying and killing if the conditions of application attached to these norms failed to include these two emergency situations. But of course it could be that Habermas simply fails to notice this (deonto)logical connection. After all, he suggests an interpretation of "You should not kill" as something like "if this norm is generally observed, then you too should not kill" when he writes:

The validity of moral commands is subject to the condition that they are *universally* adhered to as the basis for a general practice.[301]

If this does in fact hold for the imperatives "justified" by U, then U is evidently not very valuable as a principle of validity. Since in reality no important moral imperative is universally adhered to, according to this statement there would be no valid moral imperatives.

A different strategy to lend relevant if-components to norms such as "You should not kill" and "You should not lie" can be seen in Habermas's explanation "that the deontological force of normative validity cannot be interpreted simply as an *unconditional* or absolute ought, as it is by an *ethics of conviction*."[302] If the *deontological force* itself is conditional, then naturally even those norms that are categorically formulated such as "You should not lie" are in fact to be understood from the very beginning as "If the condition x holds, then you should not lie." Of course, if the deontological force is conditioned, then not lying is imperative in a certain case C only on the condition that x holds—and the imperative to speak an untruth to save the life of an innocent is also subject to the *same* condition; since the word "should" will of course not have any different meaning in the sentence "You should not lie" from its meaning in the sentence "You should lie to save the life of an innocent." But in a situation such as the Kant dilemma, if the condition x is fulfilled, then it is fulfilled—and not only for the imperative to speak an untruth, but *also* for the imperative not to lie. And in this situation that would mean that it is imperative simultaneously to tell the truth *and* an untruth. So we do in fact have a norm conflict here, once again in the form of a flagrant *contradiction*. Only *one* of the two norms can be valid. We face the exact same problem as before.

Moreover, one would like to know *what* general proviso applies to deontological force. To judge from Habermas's statements, it is apparently that of *appropriateness*. Thus "You should not lie" would mean from the outset "If it is appropriate, you should not lie." However, this sounds a lot like a sheer tautology (after all, should not one always do what is appropriate?) and thus has no particular informational content. One would have to know *when* it is appropriate not to lie, what appropriateness means in the case of *each single norm*. Here Habermas refers to Günther's proposed criterion of coherence and appropriateness,[303] which reads:

A norm Nx is appropriately applicable in Sx [a situation; U.S.] if it is compatible with all other norms Nl applicable in Sx that belong to a form of life Lx and can be justified in discourse.[304]

But this whole train of thought started from the idea that two valid norms could conflict, that is, the imperative to speak an untruth to save an innocent life and the prohibition on lying. Both of these norms are very much applicable in certain situations, but are *incompatible with each other*. If in a certain situation I can save the life of an innocent person only by lying to the persecutors, then the prohibition on lying is in this case incompatible with the imperative to lie out of necessity; and the converse holds as well. So according to Günther's criterion of coherence *neither* of these two norms would be appropriately applicable in this situation. Yet Habermas wanted to reach the conclusion that the prohibition on killing is very much applicable but not the prohibition on lying.

In view of the exact wording of the criterion, one might be tempted to argue that the prohibition on lying is not "applicable" here according to the criterion and thus cannot conflict with the prohibition on killing. But what does "applicable" mean according to the criterion? Since the prohibition is very much applicable in the sense that it is possible to not lie in this situation, and the question is precisely whether one *may* or *should* lie, "applicable" in the sense of the applicability criterion could again mean only "appropriately applicable" in the sense that the norm *should* or *may* be applied. But if "appropriately applicable" and "applicable" mean the same, then we find ourselves caught in a circle; for now, to determine whether the prohibition on killing is appropriately applicable, we have to decide whether the prohibition on lying is appropriately applicable. If it is, then it conflicts with the prohibition on killing and renders this latter norm inapplicable. Yet to determine whether the prohibition on lying is appropriately applicable, we would have to know whether the prohibition on killing is appropriately applicable; for if it is, it conflicts with this former norm and is thus itself no longer applicable. But the very point of this procedure was to determine *whether or not* the prohibition on killing was applicable in the first place. We have to know this in the first place to even get the procedure off the ground. So the procedure does not work.

Furthermore, the idea of prefixing this condition of appropriateness to every norm as an if-component—aside from the fact that this condition is circular and thus unfit for use—also leads to circularity on the part of the justificatory criterion U itself. If, as Habermas claims, the norm "You should not kill" is compatible with the permission to kill in self-defence, since situations of self-defence supposedly do *not* count among the conditions of appropriateness and thus of applicability, then the norm "You should not kill" according to Habermas no longer *means* that you should not (i.e. never) kill, but rather only that one should not kill under conditions in which killing is inappropriate. So it is *this* norm that would have to be justified in justificatory discourse. Now according to Habermas the participants in justificatory discourse have to judge whether the consequences and side effects the general observance of the norm can be expected to have for the interests of each individual can be freely accepted by all. And for this they have to know whether it is appropriate, for example, to kill a couple of hostages in order to demonstrate resolve and extort money. If this is appropriate, then killing hostages is clearly *compatible* with the general observance of the norm that one should not kill when it is inappropriate, since one does *not* infringe against the norm in killing hostages to extort money and thus this is not a case of non-observance. But how should our discourse participants determine what is appropriate and what not? By using Günther's criterion of appropriateness, which reads, to repeat:

A norm Nx is appropriately applicable in Sx if it is compatible with all other norms Nl applicable in Sx that belong to a form of life Lx and can be justified in discourse.[305]

Now our discourse participants find themselves in a justificatory discourse in which they seek to determine to what extent a norm is justified. To assess this, they have to know when it is appropriate to carry out the then-component of this norm. But to know this, they have to know, among other things, which norms are justified. This question has to be answered in a justificatory discourse. But to answer the question of which norms are valid—which norms conform to U—they have to know, for each of these norms, under what conditions it is appropriately applicable. To know this, they have to know, for each of the norms, under which conditions it is compatible with all other justified norms. To know this, they have to already know all of the other norms that can be justified in a justificatory discourse. So they have to already *know* if the norm is valid in order to *assess* its validity in the first place. This places the discourse participants in an intractable circle. Thus Günther's and Habermas's applicability criterion is not only circular in itself but also renders the criterion of justification itself circular.

This shows us, moreover, that Günther's and Habermas's strict distinction between discourses of justification and discourses of application is erroneous. Habermas[306] quotes Günther in support of this distinction:

In justification only the norm itself, independently of its application in a particular situation, is relevant. The issue is whether it is in the interest of all that everyone should follow the rule....In application, by contrast, the particular situation is relevant, regardless of whether general observance is also in the interest of all (as determined by the prior discursive examination).[307]

As we have seen, in a justification discourse we do have to account for when the observance of the norms under assessment would be appropriate—and for this purpose we have to consider not just a particular situation but many different particular situations.

Naturally the converse holds as well: to determine whether one should follow a norm in a particular case, one has to also ask whether the norm is justified. The validity of a norm can hardly be irrelevant to the question of its appropriate application. Habermas's as well as Günther's remarks on this issue occasionally seem to suggest that they expect participants in application discourses to simply presuppose the validity of the norms they are testing for applicability. But why should they do this? This presupposition might be a more or less reasonable demand in jurisprudence, but it makes no sense in the moral discourses of application. However, Habermas seems to have an additional argument for this distinction. As he explains,

...the principle of universalization, as a rule of argumentation, must retain a rational, and thus operational, meaning for finite subjects who make judgments in particular contexts. Hence it can demand at most that in justifying norms, those consequences and side effects be taken into account that general adherence to a norm can be *anticipated* to have for the interests of each on the basis of the information and reasons available to them at a particular time.

Clearly, only situations actually used by participants, on the basis of their state of knowledge, for purposes of paradigmatically explicating a matter in need of regulation can be taken into account in the conditional components [*Wenn-Komponente*] of a valid norm....The question of whether norms determined to be valid with reference to anticipated typical situations cited as exemplars are also *appropriate* for similar situations actually occurring in the future in the light of the relevant features of *these* situations is left unanswered by justificatory discourses. This question can be answered only in a further discursive step, specifically, from the *changed* perspective of a discourse of application.[308]

It is quite correct that a previous concrete justificatory discourse B^1 cannot necessarily anticipate every situation that might arise for a future discourse of application A. However, in B^1 it is also not necessarily possible to anticipate every situation that might be relevant for a future *justificatory* discourse B^2. A and B^2 may in fact be identical. Habermas's correct insight that one cannot necessarily anticipate everything allows only for a distinction between various concrete discourses such as between B^1 and A or between B^1 and B^2, and not between discourses of justification and of application as such, since justificatory discourses *are* discourses of application and vice versa. Thus the current epistemic limitations of justificatory discourses (which are always discourses of application as well) do not need to be rectified by future discourses purely of application; rather, in the future we can have a new justificatory discourse (which is always a discourse of application as well).

Moreover, Günther himself calls this possibility the "simplest answer", but obviously he prefers the more complicated answers, summarily rejecting the simplest one in favour of pure discourses of application.[309] Any good reasons he may have for this he withholds from the astonished reader. However, 250 pages later in a different context he says something that could be read as an argument for his answer, namely:

Since this justification only relates to the decision to select a norm [that is appropriate for a situation; U.S.] and not to the universal reciprocity of a norm, it has a significance independent of validity.[310]

This is surprising to hear. After all, one wants to select the *right* norm—and a norm is the right one only when it is valid, as Günther well knows[311]—and not the wrong one. And rightness certainly relates to validity. It is *imperative* to follow the appropriate norm. As Alexy writes:

The result of every correct consideration of the basic law allows us to formulate a corresponding norm of the basic law in the form of a rule under which the particular case can be subsumed.[312]

We can generalize from this: the result of every consideration of norms allows us to formulate a corresponding, more specific norm under which the particular case can be subsumed. And this corresponding norm has to be valid if the selection was decided on appropriately; according to discourse ethics, that is, it has to be justifiable by U.

Moreover, contrary to Habermas's claim it is anything but "clear" why the if-components of *valid* norms should be made dependent on the limited perspective of certain concrete discourses, discourses in which one could after all arrive at *false* results. The *ideal* practical discourse is an exception to this. Unlike in one of our real practical discourses, *every* individual capable of speech must take part in this discourse. After all, the principle D of discourse ethics states:

Only those norms can claim to be valid that meet (or could meet) with the approval of all affected in their capacity as participants in a practical discourse.[313]

But not all affected take part in each concrete and real justificatory discourse. This is the reason why not every situation of application can be accounted for in a justificatory discourse. But things are completely different in an ideal practical discourse, in which all affected do participate. How should even a single situation of application remain unaccounted for in such a discourse? After all there are individuals in each situation of application affected by the application of the norm. If these individuals take part in the justificatory discourse, they do not need to strain themselves to anticipate anything in order to account for the concrete situation; they can use their direct knowledge of the situation. This does not mean that all consequences and side effects of the general application of a norm can be anticipated in an ideal justificatory discourse, that is, in a justificatory discourse in which no affected individual is excluded and which thus represents the ultimate forum of review according to discourse ethics. It does mean, however, that all *situations of application* can be anticipated. Thus the ideal justificatory discourse—that is, the true and authoritative justificatory discourse—has no need to be amended or supplemented by a discourse of application. Rather, it already includes this discourse.

So we can say in summary that the second attempt to save these norms such as "You should not kill" or "You should not lie" by reinterpreting them fails (the first attempt being their reinterpretation as imperatives of optimization). Both of the possible if-components more or less clearly proposed by Habermas would "solve" the problem of conflict and contradiction (in so far as we can speak of this as a solution at all under these circumstances). But the addition of the if-component "if what is demanded in the then-component is universally adhered to" leads to the practical irrelevance of norms, and the addition of the if-component "if it is appropriate to do what is demanded in the then-component" leads to disastrous circularities.

In closing, let us return to the beginning and recall that the immediate occasion for our discussion of the conditions of application and questions of appropriateness was Habermas's claim of the compatibility of the norms "You should not kill" and "You should not lie" with the validity of the permission to kill in self-defence and the imperative to speak an untruth to save the life of an innocent.[314] Let us now assume—counterfactually—that Habermas and Günther had succeeded in finding a solution to the problem of compatibility with the help of a criterion of coherence. Would this in any way answer to our *original* objection, as I formulated it above: "The observance of certain norms, which allegedly are in everyone's interest in case of their *universal* observance, is nonetheless not a reasonable expectation or imperative according to our moral intuitions as long as they are *not* universally observed"? Even if we were to assume that the first two norms could be interpreted using Günther's criterion of appropriateness to make them compatible with the latter two norms and thus with our moral intuitions, and in addition that all of these norms satisfied the criterion of validity U, the question still arises: how is it supposed to be possible for *all* norms justified by U to be compatible with our moral intuitions and *all* of our moral intuitions with U? One could respond that we do not need to reach this sort of congruence, that one should after all be allowed to use a philosophically justified moral principle as a corrective to our ingrained moral intuitions. This is quite right, but conversely one should be allowed to test an allegedly philosophically justified moral principle against our moral intuitions. After all, Habermas aspires to a "reconstruction" of these intuitions, so it would be rather awkward if the product of his supposed reconstruction, U, were to contradict them. And in fact Habermas's statements on the compatibility of the prohibitions on lying and killing and the exceptions made for self-defence or the necessary lie are clearly nothing but an attempt to square U itself with our intuitions. Now, many will agree in light of their moral intuitions that a criterion of validity is rather useless if it is not satisfied by the following norm: "If someone is attacking small children at risk of their lives, and you are directly in a position to stop him without endangering your health or that of anyone else, then stop him!" This norm *cannot* be universally observed, since it is impossible to attack small children *and* stop oneself. (A situation, incidentally, in which the conditions of application of this norm are not satisfied is a situation only of universal non-infringement of the norm, not of universal observance.) This holds for *all* allowances for necessary defence. Since there is no universal observance of these norms, there are also no consequences and side effects of its universal observance; and something that does not exist and could not exist could also not be accepted, either freely or otherwise, as U demands. So all allowances for necessary defence are automatically false. And thus U itself is false.

In order to have a better overview, let us summarize the results:

According to Habermas, norms justified by U are norms justified in view of the consequences and side effects of their *universal* observance, such as "You should not kill" or "You should not lie." One objection against this is that the observance of such norms is not always imperative in real situations—which would falsify U as a principle of normative validity. Habermas tries to answer this objection by pointing out that norms that are not "pertinent" in a concrete situation, that is, a situation where their conditions of application are not satisfied, do not for that reason lose their validity.

Now the norms "You should not kill" and "You should not lie" are *categorical*, that is, they have no if-components and thus are pertinent in every situation or at least in every situation in which any permissions for necessary killing or lying are also pertinent. So if it is imperative to lie in certain situations, as Habermas himself says, then this imperative is a contradiction of the prohibition on lying. This is so even if both are taken up as reasons in a discourse of application, since, contrary to Habermas's wishful thinking, contradictory reasons are as unable to be both valid as are contradictory norms that are not reasons. Therefore, U is falsified.

As a defence against this argument it was then claimed that the norms in question are not meant to be understood categorically. It would then have to be clear how they are meant, what they do in fact mean. For example, does the norm "You should not kill" allow only the exception of the killing of contract killers by the targets of their attack, or does it also allow the killing of their targets by the attacking contract killers? These purported norms can hardly function for us as norms if they do not supply us with these details; they are not norms at all.

One possible way of interpreting these norms would be as imperatives of optimization. However, this interpretation runs counter to Habermas's and Günther's deontological approach or at least to their understanding of a deontological approach, and is explicitly repudiated by both.

Another possible reinterpretation would be to affix if-components to these norms.

One such possible if-component in Habermas's case could be the universal observance of a norm as a condition of application. Since this condition is not satisfied in reality according to Habermas, this would lead to the complete practical irrelevance of the norms purportedly justified by U.

Another possible if-component we find with Günther and Habermas would be the appropriateness of following the norm's then-component, seen as a condition of its application. This makes it necessary to clarify what "appropriate" means. The coherence criterion mentioned by Günther is much too general an answer to provide any normative content; second, it is circular in itself, and third, it leads to a circle between the criterion of appropriateness and the criterion of justification, which makes this latter criterion circular as well.

Even if this criterion of appropriateness were able to harmonize certain norms allegedly justified by U (i.e. in light of the consequences and side-effects of their *general* observance) with certain other imperatives that we intuitively hold to be correct and apply to *real* situations, nonetheless a number of our essential moral intuitions and the norms based on them remain *logically impossible* to square with U. U is and remains wrong.

Let us now summarize the results of Chapter 2.

Habermas's and Apel's preliminary considerations are not able to lend any plausibility to their project of deriving or even directly adopting a universally valid justifying principle of moral norms from the rules or presuppositions of communication. Rather, a critical review of these considerations shows the basic approach of the project to be unjustified. Accordingly, it also fails in execution. The "method" used by Apel and Habermas to identify the presuppositions of argumentation is circular and dogmatic. It not only fails to deliver a final justification—it fails to deliver any justification. Conversely, we have shown that the "discourse rules" and "presuppositions of argumentation" postulated by Habermas and Apel are neither discourse rules nor presuppositions of argumentation; nor are they moral norms. The principles U and D cannot be derived from them. The attempted derivations that we have been given so far introduce that which is to be proven into the premises and are thus circular. Moreover, U and D are completely unacceptable and counter-intuitive anyway as principles of moral justification and as formulations of the conditions of validity of norms. No norm can fulfil their stated conditions. However, those norms which Apel and Habermas allege they can justify under ideal conditions of discourse are under real conditions unacceptable and unreasonable. The attempts of discourse ethics to solve this problem of application lead to insurmountable contradictions and fall apart.

3

The Failure of Discourse Ethics and the Theory of Communicative Action in Their Attempted Empirical Demonstration and Application to Politics, Law and Society

In Section 2.5 we tackled the problem of how the norms allegedly justified with U or D in terms of *ideal* situations could be applied to *real* situations. Habermas's and Günther's explication on this point remained rather abstract. Only the transcendental-pragmatists have undertaken—somewhat delicate—attempts to arrive at any concrete orientation of action. Yet this has never evolved into anything more than an attempt, and the transcendental-pragmatists have not presented any further concrete possibilities of application for the theory of communicative action or communicative rationality or for discourse ethics—except, perhaps, for a small Apelian venture, following Habermas's footsteps, into the discussion of Kohlberg's developmental psychology.[1]

Habermas, however, proposes further areas of application for his theory of communicative action and for discourse ethics.[2] Habermas does not make all of these proposals concrete by outlining a theoretical approach, never mind an actual theory. Nevertheless, for the sake of completeness I will at least make some mention of those proposals that are not further specified. The others will be subject to more thorough investigation as appropriate.

3.1. PSYCHOLOGY

Habermas is primarily interested in two areas of psychology: developmental psychology, specifically the two related but not identical sub-fields of moral development and the development of the self, and the analysis of the forms and consequences of "communication pathologies".

3.1.1. The Development of the Self

Habermas's thoughts on the development of self[3] are essentially an eclectic mix of cognitive developmental psychology, symbolic interactionism and analytical ego psychology.[4] They are of interest to us here only in so far as they relate to the so-called theory of communicative action and the alleged insights of universal-pragmatics. These relations are more than modest.

One relation to the theory of communicative action consists solely in Habermas's thesis that the reproduction of the "lifeworld" and hence also the "formation of personal identities"[5] can be achieved only through the medium of communicative action. However, Habermas neglects to explain exactly *how* the process of socialization and the formation of personal identities are to be achieved through communicative action. Thus we cannot acknowledge any particular contribution to developmental psychology in this thesis of Habermas's, particularly as it lacks justification and is incorrect.[6]

Only in one place does Habermas make a connection to universal-pragmatic insights—under the heading "Universal-pragmatic Pointers to the System of Self-Demarcations".[7] Here he writes:

My introduction of the system of demarcations of the self conceived as subjectivity against the objectivity of external nature, the normativity of society and the intersubjectivity of language is initially an intuitive proposal. For it to attain any systematic value we would have to be able to demonstrate corresponding structures in the medium through which the subject realizes its demarcations. For this I use universal-pragmatics.[8]

He does so by claiming, in line with universal-pragmatics, that with every speech act one necessarily raises four validity claims, namely, truth, rightness, sincerity and understandability. These claims would thus correspond to the "system of demarcations".[9]

What can we say about this? *First*, a subject develops identity not only by means of its demarcations but also at least as much by means of the precise opposite, namely, *identifications*, as the concept "identity" would suggest. A theoretical approach to the development of self that does not sufficiently account for this is misguided from the outset. *Second*, it is not difficult to see that Habermas assumes, in the above quotation, that language is the medium in which the subject realizes these demarcations. However, this assumption is ad hoc, since prior to this Habermas had written:

The self forms itself through the interaction of an incrementally "internalized", internally reflected nature with an environment that presents itself as differentiated for the adult self. The environment presents itself in at least three regions: external nature, language, and society.[10]

So initially it is not language but this interaction with the environment that is the medium we seek. Of course, one might claim that this interaction is itself linguistically mediated. In fact, however, it takes a while before a child begins to speak and understand language, whereas it begins to interact with its environment from the very first moment. Thus language is not necessary for this sort of interaction. Moreover, even when the child finally does speak, it does not interact with its environment solely by means of the medium of language but rather also by means of non-linguistic actions (i.e. actions that are not speech acts) and non-linguistic auditory, visual, olfactory, gustatory and tactile impressions. Thus if Habermas's proposal is to "attain any systematic value"—on the assumption this could be achieved by demonstrating "corresponding structures in the medium through which the subject realizes its demarcations"—Habermas would have to examine several other media besides just language. *Third*, it is not even clear why this assumption should hold in the first place. The correspondence is supposed to pertain to three or four dimensions of differentiation. What would such a correspondence prove? If the medium by means of which I demarcate myself, as it were, against the rain, namely, an umbrella, is not in itself rainy in any way, but rather umbrella-esque, this does not prove that the umbrella cannot serve to demarcate me against the rain. And the fact that nothing in non-linguistic actions and visual perceptions can be shown to correspond to the four areas of language, society and inner and outer nature does not prevent non-linguistic actions and visual perceptions from counting among those media that serve the interaction with the environment. So the presupposition that Habermas wishes to use to bring universal-pragmatics into play is made from thin air. In psychology the only way to have an "initially...intuitive" hypothesis attain "any systematic value"—on the assumption, at least, that the hypothesis is meant to explain anything *beyond* mere intuition—is to *empirically confirm* it. Its mere combination with a philosophical construction such as universal pragmatics is certainly not enough to accomplish this. *Fourth*, Habermas fails to justify the assumption that, if any validity claims are relevant for the demarcations of the self, they have to be *universal*. Why not non-universal claims as well? If this were the case, then the distinctions between dimensions of self-demarcation would have to be finer than those proposed by Habermas and thus would not correspond to universal-pragmatics. *Fifth*, it is not even true that the four validity claims mentioned by Habermas are universal.[11]

We can thus conclude that universal-pragmatics is incapable, both fundamentally and due to some by no means inessential details (the fourth and fifth points above), of providing any "pointers" to the stated "system of self-demarcations"—which moreover possesses only limited validity. Thus universal-pragmatics does not offer a contribution to the analysis of the development of self, and conversely the analysis of the development of self is not in a position to offer any support for universal-pragmatics.

3.1.2. Moral Development

Habermas has not contributed anything to the psychology of moral development, nor does he claim to. However, he does claim that Kohlberg's developmental psychology validates his own "discourse theory of ethics", albeit "indirectly".[12] In fact this relation of validation cannot possibly obtain; there is no bridge from *is* to *ought*. Habermas himself has to concede this, ultimately, and thus elsewhere he quotes Kohlberg approvingly:

Science, then, can test whether a philosopher's conception of morality phenomenologically fits the psychological facts. Science cannot go on to justify that conception of morality as what morality ought to be.[13]

Discourse ethics purports to explicate and conceptualize certain universal moral intuitions.[14] It is these phenomenological findings about the universality of certain moral intuitions, namely, those allegedly expressed through U and D, that would have to accord with psychological facts. However, the research of developmental psychologists shows that the great majority of people do not find themselves at the post-conventional level of moral development, let alone at the post-conventional level expressed by U and D. While Habermas conceives the moral standpoint expressed in U and D as the end state of moral development, that is, as its *highest stage*,[15] the overwhelming majority never makes it past the fourth stage. Habermas himself is aware of this, and thus at one point speaks merely of the "intuition potential that becomes accessible to everyone with the transition to the *post-conventional* level of autonomous morality".[16] Just prior to this, however, on the very same page of the German original, he has explained that the concern is with "which moral theory is best able to reconstruct the *universal* core of our moral intuitions, that is, to reconstruct a 'moral point of view' that claims *universal* validity".[17] Those intuitions that are accessible to us only at the post-conventional level, however, can hardly be said to form the universal core of our moral intuitions—unless, that is, quite non-universalistically, we read "us" from the outset as those individuals who find themselves at the post-conventional level. In short, the phenomenological findings of discourse ethics are by no means confirmed by developmental psychology, but rather falsified by them.

Moreover, developmental psychology would still not confirm the phenomenological findings of discourse ethics even if these were more modest and claimed to explicate only *post-conventional* intuitions. For as Habermas himself writes:

> The debate among moral philosophers cannot be settled with the *psychological* assertion that Kantians have better, structurally privileged access to their moral intuitions than do rule utilitarians or social-contract theorists in the Hobbesian tradition...The debate among cognitivist moral philosophers, however, is concerned with the question with how and by what conceptual means the *same* intuition potential that becomes accessible to *everyone* with the transition to the *post-conventional* level of autonomous morality can most adequately be explained. It is a question of a better explication of an intuitive knowing, which, at the postconventional level, has already taken on a reflective character and to that extent is from the beginning already oriented to rational reconstructions. This contest can be settled only on the field of philosophical argumentation, not on that of developmental psychology.[18]

3.1.3. Communicative Pathologies

In his paper "Reflections on Communicative Pathology" Habermas writes:

> Freud introduces the ego function of unconscious repression as a mechanism of linguistic pathogenesis. The repression of conflicts that are not consciously resolved, that is, not on a basis of consensual action, leaves traces that take the form of communicative disturbances. Intrapsychic disturbances of the communication between parts of the personality system are analogous to disturbances in family communication. Of course the analysis of such

deviations presupposes knowledge [*Kenntnis*] of the kind of communication that can be characterized as "normal". But when can a communication be considered undisturbed, not systematically distorted, or "normal"?

And he adds:

First, we have to explain the sense in which we mean to talk about the normalcy conditions of communication.[19]

Why do we have to first explain this? If we are speaking of communicative *pathologies*, then it seems rather obvious that we need a *clinical* notion of normalcy. Yet Habermas writes that the "*clinical notion* of normalcy stems from the field of somatic illnesses", and remarks: "Transferring this notion of normalcy to the realm of psychic or communicative disturbances is difficult…."[20] Well, difficult or not, in any "Reflections on Communicative Pathology" every *non*-clinical notion of normalcy obviously takes us off-topic. In fact this is exactly what happens to Habermas:

Thus we return to where we began our reflections, having found that we cannot avail ourselves of the available statistical, clinical, or cultural notions of normalcy that are at our disposal. Rather we have to make explicit the normative content inherent in the notion of linguistic communication itself. The expression "undistorted communication" does not add anything to mutual linguistic understanding [*Verständigung*], for "mutual understanding" signifies the telos inherent in linguistic communication. I would like to establish the conditions of normalcy of linguistic communication by way of a conceptual analysis of the meaning of "mutual understanding" because I assume that every speech act has an unavoidable, as it were, transcendentally necessitating basis of validity. I want to develop the thesis that every communicative actor has to commit to fulfilling universal claims to validity….

Of course, if complete agreement [*Einverständnis*], which encompasses all four components [the four Habermasian validity claims], were the normal state of linguistic communication, then it would not be necessary to analyze the process of reaching mutual understanding under the dynamic aspect of *bringing about* agreement….Mutual understanding is a process that seeks to overcome a lack of understanding and misunderstanding, insincerity toward oneself and others, and disagreement. And it does so on the common basis of validity claims that aim at reciprocal recognition.[21]

An *explication* of the conditions of normalcy for linguistic communication— and the only possible explications are clear ones, such as take the form "communication is normal if and only if…"—is nowhere to be found in Habermas's work, either here or elsewhere. However, the passage quoted here does allow us to conclude that communication is normal for Habermas if and only if it *aims* at the fulfilment of the validity claims mentioned. A basic response to this might be: even if the expression "undistorted communication" added nothing to that of mutual understanding, the fact that a certain instance of communication does not aim at the fulfilment of purportedly universal validity claims, and thus according to Habermas does not pursue the telos inherent in linguistic communication, would nonetheless imply solely that it is being used *for other purposes*. This does not imply that such communication is somehow abnormal, never mind abnormal in a *clinical* sense, that is, pathological. For example, the telos inherent in a series of boxing strikes is to win against an opponent in hand-to-hand combat. If a boxer uses these series to warm up rather than to defeat an opponent, he is not using them according to their inherent telos, but this does not necessarily mean that he is using them in an "abnormal", let alone a pathological, manner. The use of horseshoes for playing the game of horseshoes rather than for their inherent telos of protecting horses' hooves is likewise neither abnormal nor pathological. And to take one more example: the telos inherent in sexual intercourse is clearly pro-creation (or, as modern biologists might put it, the recombination of genes). Yet contraception and sexual intercourse for mere pleasure are not only not patho-logical but quite normal. Thus Habermas's conceptual analysis of the meaning of "mutual understanding" is irrelevant for an identification of the conditions of normalcy for linguistic understanding as well as for an identification of commu-nicative pathologies, as shown by a conceptual analysis of terms such as "inherent telos", "normal" and "pathological".

A second and no less fundamental problem goes hand in hand with the first problem. In the passage quoted above explicating the conditions of normalcy of linguistic communication through a conceptual analysis of "mutual understand-ing", Habermas argues that every *communicative* actor has to commit to fulfilling universal claims to validity. He also claims in the same passage that communication is a *process of mutual understanding* per se; but this is incorrect, since as Habermas himself knows "even a disturbed communication is a communication."[22] But then a conceptual analysis of "mutual understanding" could produce the conditions of normalcy only for communication *oriented towards mutual understanding* at best (and as we just saw, it does not even achieve this).

Here the parasitism argument would be quite convenient if it could show understanding-oriented communication to be normal relative to strategic com-munication. Aside from the fact that this argument is false and cannot even show the latter to be *parasitic* on the former,[23] we should note that the parasitic is not to be equated with the *abnormal*. Wooden tables, for example, are parasitic on trees, but it does not follow that wooden tables are an abnormal form for wood to appear in, let alone a pathological one. And one can exhale only if one has inhaled at some point; thus exhalation is parasitic on inhalation, but it is not an abnormal or pathological component of breathing for that reason. Furthermore, using a hypodermic needle for subcutaneous injection or removal of a substance is parasitic on its use to penetrate skin; yet it hardly follows from this that the use of a hypodermic needle to penetrate skin is normal, or, conversely, that its use to inject or remove a substance is abnormal or pathological. Moreover, according to Habermas himself not all types of strategic communication are "systematically distorted", that is, abnormal.[24] But since they are, according to him, nonetheless parasitic, he cannot claim here that parasitism amounts to abnormality without contradicting himself.

So the fact remains: by analysing "mutual understanding" (*Verständigung*) one could only in the best case identify the conditions of normality, and hence of abnormality, of *understanding-oriented* communication—and in fact even this is impossible. Thus Habermas's way of trying to clarify the normalcy conditions is *at cross purposes* with the characterization of pathological or, in his jargon, "systematically distorted" communication that he finally provides (after introducing several examples of such systematically distorted communication and contrasting examples that often afford very little contrast):

The comparison of these examples shows that communication can be systematically distorted only if the internal organization of speech is disrupted. This happens if the validity basis of linguistic communication is curtailed *surreptitiously*; that is, without leading to a break in communication or to the transition to openly declared and permissible strategic action. The validity basis of speech is curtailed surreptitiously if at least one of the three universal validity claims to intelligibility (of the expression), sincerity (of the intention expressed by the speaker), and normative rightness (of the expression relative to a normative background) is violated and communication nonetheless continues on the presumption of *communicative* (not strategic) action oriented toward reaching mutual understanding.[25]

It follows, namely, from this characterization of "systematically distorted communication" that it involves *strategic* communication and not understanding-oriented communication. In systematically distorted communication, as Habermas tells us, we are only *presumed* to be operating on the basis of action oriented towards reaching understanding; there is only the "*appearance* of consensual action".[26] This is confirmed by Habermas's examples of "systematically distorted communication". He gives the example of a woman who, "for the sake of [the] strategic goal" of saving her marriage, "keeps up the appearance of reciprocating the affection of her husband whom she has long detested".[27] Deceiving someone is Habermas's classic example of strategic action. Thus, and for the reasons previously mentioned (communication is not necessarily oriented towards reaching understanding and non-understanding-oriented communication is not abnormal, never mind pathological), it is entirely unclear how this allegedly "systematically distorted communication" is supposed to involve any breach of the conditions of normalcy for linguistic communication. Deception in strategic action is entirely normal.

So how does it occur to Habermas to see this as some sort of breach? It is not that he simply and blithely uses the conditions of normalcy for communication oriented towards reaching understanding as the standard of normalcy for other forms of communication, since he explicitly does not include declared and legitimate strategic action in his definition of systematically distorted communication. Incidentally, this too brings his definition into contradiction with his approach of explicating the conditions of normalcy of linguistic communication through a conceptual analysis of "mutual understanding", since strategic action, even when it is declared and legitimate, is not oriented towards *reaching understanding*. The conditions of normalcy for declared and legitimate strategic action would thus have to be explicated in some other way. But to return to our question—the answer is: Habermas is evidently of the mistaken opinion that, as long as one maintains at least the *appearance* of "consensual action", one has to fulfil the same (or at least some of the same) presuppositions of argumentation as in truly consensual action. Habermas says about his example of the woman who deceives her man about her feelings:

The speaker knows that she is acting strategically, but conceals it from the other in order to maintain the foundations of consensual action in appearance. This gives rise to two levels of communication. At the level of manifest behavior, the communicative presuppositions of consensual action are met. At the level of latent behavior, one of the participants is acting strategically and intentionally violates the presupposition of sincerity.[28]

Now, it is completely normal for a strategic actor not to be sincere. This is so normal, in fact, that it remains rather unclear how the speaker here could encroach upon any purported presuppositions of sincerity. What does Habermas mean by this? He writes:

> In discussing the "transcendental" place value of the validity basis, one might think that it is impossible to diverge from the universal demands that ground validity, that the internal organization of speech is inviolable. If that were the case, we would not even need to explicate the normative foundation of speech since the normal conditions of communication from which a speaker could not diverge would be of no interest for analyzing distorted patterns of communication.[29]

But is what "one might think" in fact a misunderstanding? After all, Habermas writes that "[i]t is not possible to want to communicate *and* to express oneself unintelligibly or misleadingly: herein lies the necessitating moment that is reminiscent of a transcendental necessity."[30] And: "Again, transcendental necessitation is evident in the fact that one cannot want both to make oneself understood and to express one's intention insincerely."[31] Clearly a breach of the presuppositions of argumentation is quite impossible in the use of language *oriented towards reaching understanding*. Of course we have to distinguish these presuppositions of argumentation in a strict sense, that is, preconditions of *argumentation itself*, from the presuppositions that participants in argumentation have to *make* or *assume* in arguing. Habermas is also aware of this distinction, though he typically ignores it:

> If one wanted to make a serious comparison between argumentation and chess playing, one would find that the closest equivalents to the rules of chess are the rules for the construction and exchange of arguments. These rules must be followed in *actual fact* if error-free argumentation is to take place in real life. By contrast, discourse rules (3.1) to (3.3) state only that participants in argumentation must assume these conditions to be approximately realized, or realized in an approximation adequate enough for the purpose of argumentation, regardless of whether and to what extent these assumptions are counterfactual in a given case or not.[32]

Thus, in contrast to the rules for forming and exchanging arguments, conditions (3.1) to (3.3) are not *themselves* presuppositions of argumentation; that is to say, these conditions do not have to be fulfilled. Rather, *presupposing* their fulfilment is a precondition of argumentation. Thus, speakers are not "transcendentally necessitated" to *fulfil* these conditions, but rather only to *assume* or *presuppose* them.

In light of these considerations it is clear that the woman deceiving her husband cannot possibly be encroaching upon any transcendentally necessitating presuppositions of argumentation. The circumstance that the basis of consensual action is preserved in appearance does not change this to the slightest degree, despite what Habermas seems to think. The fact is that one cannot preserve the appearance of consensual action *and* forgo raising a claim to sincerity at the same time. This being the case, Habermas errs when he writes that the woman "is acting strategically by suspending the sincerity claim".[33] What she "suspends" is not the *claim* to sincerity—she has to maintain this claim if she does not want to undo the appearance of consensual action—but rather *sincerity*. The suspension of sincerity does infringe the presuppositions of consensual action[34]—just as, according to Habermas, the adoption of an orientation towards reaching understanding in communicative action has to infringe the rules of strategic action—but this is irrelevant and is not a breach of transcendental "necessitations", since the woman in this case is not operating on the basis of consensual action. Of course, with her suspension of sincerity she infringes a presupposition made, *ex hypothesi*, by the *other*, namely, her husband's presupposition that she is acting sincerely. But the (fulfilment of the) presupposition made by her husband is not a presupposition for maintaining the appearance of consensual action; it is only a presupposition of maintaining the appearance of consensual action *that* her husband makes this presupposition. Thus, in her non-fulfilment of her husband's erroneous supposition she also does not infringe any transcendental presuppositions of argumentation.

The result of this analysis of Habermas's example for "systematically distorted communication" can be generalized, and thus confirms what we have already seen: Habermas's characterization of "systematically distorted communication" shows it to be a certain form of *strategic* communication. And strategic communication is subject not to the transcendental presuppositions and conditions of normalcy of communication oriented towards reaching understanding, but rather to those of strategic communication. It necessarily fulfils *these* transcendental presuppositions and does not necessarily infringe any of *these* conditions of normalcy, which, we should recall, are not the same as transcendental presuppositions. However, since the concept of distortion includes the concept of a deviation from the normal state, Habermas's characterization of the types of strategic action encompassed under "strategically distorted communication" *as* "strategically distorted communication" is ill-conceived. Thus our examination of the second fundamental problem with Habermas's approach takes us on a different path to the same result as our examination of the first problem: Habermas's conceptual analysis of "mutual understanding" is irrelevant both for the identification of the conditions of normalcy for linguistic communication and for the identification of communicative pathologies.

Habermas apparently wants to justify his use of the term "distortion" in yet another way. Thus he explains, prior to the characterization of "systematically distorted communication" quoted above:

I use the term "distortion" to stress the insight that the internal organization of speech expresses universal and unavoidable presuppositions of linguistic communication. The transcendental necessity implied by this feature of ineluctability or of a lack of alternatives does not imply inviolability. Rather, it means that the violation of the internal organization of speech gives rise to pathological mutations of the patterns of communication. In other words, the pathogenesis can be traced back to problems that exert pressure on the external organization of speech.[35]

Is a violation of the inner organization of speech not already a mutation of the patterns of communication? Here, in contrast with the arguably decisive Habermasian definition of "systematically distorted communication" examined above, it sounds as if the violation of the inner organization of speech were at least itself not yet a pathological mutation, but instead the *cause* of the pathological mutation. However, the conceptual analysis of "mutual understanding" was clearly supposed to provide us with the conditions of normalcy of linguistic communication *in the form of* the internal organization of speech; it purportedly "expresses universal and unavoidable presuppositions of linguistic communication" and "*consists in* the universal pragmatic regulation of sequences of speech acts, and this regulation does not require any backing by social norms owing to its transcendentally necessitating nature".[36] We might therefore ask from where we are supposed to derive those conditions of normalcy (or, to put it better, conditions of health) that serve as the measure, not of the violation of the internal organization of speech, but rather of the *pathological mutation of patterns of communication* caused by this mutation. Without actually clarifying what exactly patterns of communication are supposed to be, if not the internal organization of speech, Habermas evidently finds the necessary standard of measure in the "*universal presuppositions of communicative action*".[37] It might seem that we had already located these presuppositions previously in connection with his "conceptual analysis of the meaning of 'mutual understanding'", which made reference to the "communicative actor";[38] but here he evidently draws on the fact that at least two people are necessary for communication and thus for patterns of communication, and he mentions the presuppositions "that the participants mutually consider each other to be *accountable*" and "that they mutually consider one another *ready and willing to reach mutual understanding*".[39] Why precisely the presuppositions of *communicative* action are to provide the suitable standard of measure, even though systematically distorted communication belongs to *strategic* action and even though Habermas himself knows that "[t]his general communicative presupposition of a mutually attributed willingness to reach mutual understanding does not hold for strategic ... action"[40] (at least not for every form of strategic action), is also left unexplained. Here his parasitism argument cannot help him either, since it is not only false but also, as we have already seen, irrelevant to the problem in question.

Oddly enough, Habermas never even mentions these two presuppositions or the deviations from them in any of his examples of "systematically distorted communication", and, more oddly still, they are even *fulfilled* in several of his examples.[41] How does Wittgenstein put it? "...a wheel that can be turned though nothing else moves with it, is not part of the mechanism."[42] And it is not hard to see which wheel here is not part of the mechanism: Habermas furtively uses just the *clinical* measure of normalcy. He does not identify "pathological mutations of the patterns of communication" by means of a deviation from the standard of allegedly universal presuppositions of communicative action, which, as mentioned, play no role at all in his examples of "systematically distorted communication" anyway, but rather he identifies them from the very outset by reference to the fact that they are the *expression and the cause of mental disturbances.*

That they are conceived as both the expression *and* the cause can, for instance, be seen in the following passage, for example:

> However, conflicts of identity, on the one hand, and the distorted communicative structures within which such conflicts smolder, on the other, are part of a circular process. The conflicts, as it were, cause the systematic distortion, yet can be traced back to deficiencies of ego organization (in the parents' generation), which in turn were produced in deviant formative processes, that is, in families with distorted communicative structures.[43]

Thus, the "pathological effects" that allegedly follow from the violation of validity claims, that is, of the internal organization of speech,[44] relate not just to a pathological mutation of the patterns of communication, but rather, more importantly, to a pathological mutation of the psyche of the *communicants*. But then the "transcendental necessity" of the "presuppositions of linguistic communication", which according to Habermas "means that the violation of the internal organization of speech gives rise to pathological mutations of the patterns of communication",[45] means above all that the violation of the internal organization of speech triggers pathological mutations in the psyche of the communicants. And just as Apel has recourse to this thesis in the course of his argumentation for the "uncircumventability" of the argumentative situation,[46] Habermas, as we all know, needs the thesis in the course of his argumentation for the uncircumventability of communicative action.[47] We will return to this thesis shortly; for the moment we should recall that the examples Habermas uses to exemplify "transcendental necessitations" are very much examples of inviolability: "It is *not possible* to want to communicate *and* to express oneself unintelligibly or misleadingly: herein lies the necessitating moment that is reminiscent of a transcendental necessity."[48] So here we are dealing with two entirely *different* "necessitations", and using the same term for two entirely different things is both the cause and the expression of confusion. It is, in any case, an outrageous misuse of language to label the imperative not to violate the internal organization of speech—an imperative obtaining under the *condition* that one wants to avoid pathological psychic mutations, that is, a *hypothetical* imperative—a "transcendental necessity". Moreover, the alleged transcendental necessities can hardly be discovered by reflection on purported performative self-contradictions; quite the contrary, psychological field research is needed. But then it is false when Habermas argues that in reconstructing the "internal organization of speech", which is also constituted by such "transcendental necessities" among other things, "we cannot avail ourselves of the...clinical [notion]...of normalcy."[49] Rather, this notion is a *presupposition* of the reconstruction. In other words, either we can avail ourselves of the clinical notion of normalcy without any problem—in which case we no longer need Habermas's "conceptual analysis of the meaning of 'mutual understanding'"—or we cannot—in which case this conceptual analysis does not provide us with all of the "transcendental necessities" of linguistic communication that allegedly constitute the standard of normalcy. In the former case Habermas's "conceptual analysis" is superfluous, in the latter it is insufficient. In fact it is the former case that holds.

Let us now cast a brief glance at Habermas's uncircumventability thesis, which he formulates in a prominent position as follows:

[Individuals] do not have the option of a long-term absence from contexts of action oriented toward reaching an understanding. That would mean regressing to the monadic isolation of strategic action, or schizophrenia and suicide. In the long run such absence if [*sic!*] self-destructive.[50]

Since, however, there are no monads—as Habermas himself would have to concede if he wants to distance himself from the "philosophy of subjectivity"—there also cannot be any "monadic isolation". Of course there is isolation, but this is hardly destructive per se. Moreover, Habermas does not provide any arguments for the thesis that the absence from contexts of action oriented towards reaching understanding isolates, and indeed there are no arguments for it. On the contrary, one can win the greatest affection by giving gifts and rewards, that is, through exercising empirical influence in Habermas's sense. Without this kind of influence, on the other hand, that is, without occasionally doing good things for others and thus without an occasional recourse to strategic behaviour, one would probably end up isolating oneself very quickly.

We still have to deal with the thesis of schizophrenia and suicide. More precisely, we are left with the schizophrenia thesis alone, since *rational* suicide is of no use for Habermas's thesis of uncircumventability. Is the thesis that the absence from contexts of communicative action leads to schizophrenia or at least to psychic disturbances confirmed by Habermas's consideration of communication pathology? Quite the contrary, it contradicts the thesis. Habermas explicitly *excludes* declared and legitimate strategic action from "systematically distorted", pathogenic communication. Thus, leaving contexts of communicative action and entering into contexts of declared and legitimate strategic action—and declarations can also be made with speech acts not oriented towards reaching understanding—should not yield any pathogenic effects (according to Habermas's own arguments), let alone lead to suicide.

Moreover, we should recall that communicative action, strictly speaking, does not exist. *Thus we are all "always already" absent long term from contexts of communicative action (in a strict sense)*, or rather: we have never been in their presence. Thus, if Habermas's schizophrenia thesis were correct and the strict definition of communicative action is to be taken as the decisive one—and it is—we would all already have long been schizophrenic, including Habermas.

And finally, Habermas cannot even provide any evidence for the thesis that every "systematically distorted communication" has pathogenic effects in the long term. The studies he refers to suggest at most that certain narrowly defined forms of communication can in certain circumstances lead to mental disturbances—as anyone who reads them will easily see. By no means do they show that *all* kinds of illegitimate and non-declared strategic communication lead to mental disturbances in the long term. They do not claim anything of the sort, not even with other words. Conversely, they do suggest that certain forms of *communicative action* have a pathogenic potential. Laing, who is extensively quoted in Habermas's "Reflections on Communicative Pathology", writes in another passage:

The characteristic family pattern that has emerged from the studies of the families of schizophrenics does not so much involve a child who is subject to outright neglect or even to obvious trauma, but a child who has been subjected to subtle but persistent disconfirmation, usually unwittingly. For many years lack of genuine confirmation takes the form of actively confirming a false self, so that the person whose false self is confirmed and real self disconfirmed is placed in a false position.... The schizogenic potential of the situation seems to reside largely in the fact that it is not recognized by anyone...[51]

The non-validation of the real self and the validation of the false self hardly correspond to Habermas's description of strategic action, as something guided by "following rules of rational choice" and by "egocentric calculations of utility",[52] as they occur *unintentionally* here, thus *without reservation*. However, nothing about the description of the schizogenic situation contradicts Habermas's definition of *communicative action*. So, evidently, certain forms of communicative action also bear a certain schizogenic potential.

Thus we can conclude that Habermas's universal pragmatics and the theory of communicative action do not contribute anything to the analysis of communicative pathologies.

3.2. EVOLUTION

3.2.1. Hominization

Habermas writes:

Anthropogenesis should also be capable of throwing light on whether the universalistic claims of formal pragmatics can be taken seriously. We would have to be able to find the formal-pragmatically described structures of action oriented to success and to understanding in the emergent properties that appear in the course of hominization and that characterize the form of life of socioculturally sociated individuals.[53]

Whatever this is supposed to mean exactly, there is hardly anything to suggest that Habermas's rather thin remarks on hominization can provide any contribution to its analysis or any confirmation of formal pragmatics.

He argues:

We can speak of the reproduction of *human* life, with homo sapiens, only when the economy of the hunt is supplemented by a familial social structure. This process lasted several million years; it represented an important replacement of the animal status system, which among the anthropoid apes was already based on symbolically mediated interaction..., by a system of social norms that presupposed *language*.[54]

Aside from the fact that the assertion of the first sentence seems rather arbitrary, Habermas also does not explain why this system, namely, the system of social roles, is necessarily based on language. Rather, he limits himself to explaining that motive formation through social roles depends on three particular conditions, namely, that the participants can exchange the perspective of the participant for that of the observer, that they possess a temporal horizon that extends beyond the immediately actual consequences of action, and that the social roles have to be connected with mechanisms of sanction, which "consist...in the ambivalently cathected interpretations of established norms". And he adds: "For a number of reasons these three conditions could not be met before language was fully developed."[55] He neglects to mention what these reasons are.

And even if we assumed, with Habermas, that language is a *presupposition* of hominization, this would still not yet lead us to infer to the particular significance of communicative action as follows:

> The structures of role behavior mark a new stage of development in relation to the structures of social labor; rules of communicative action, that is, intersubjectively valid and ritually secured norms of action, cannot be reduced to rules of instrumental or strategic action.
>
> ...Production and socialization, social labor and care for the young are equally important for the reproduction of the species; thus the familial social structure, which controls both—the integration of external as well as of internal nature—is fundamental.[56]

This way of contrasting the structures of role behaviour and the structures of social labour would be plausible only if we could remove intersubjectively recognized and non-instrumental rules of interaction from the realm of production, as Habermas perhaps attempted a few pages previously.[57] However, this is not possible; intersubjectively recognized and non-instrumental rules of interaction are part and parcel of the labour process.[58] Moreover, *The Theory of Communicative Action* mentions only *one* rule of communicative action, namely, the rule that the participants "pursue their individual goals under the condition that they can harmonize their plans of action on the basis of common situation definitions."[59] If we do not set our notion of "harmonization" so high that communicative action can no longer exist at all, then labour can also—or *especially*—arise in the form of communicative action. Furthermore, we have already seen that communicative action can quite definitely be traced back to strategic action.[60] And finally, the fact that socialization might be just as important for the reproduction of the species as material production does not in any way speak in favour of communicative action; for the latter's contribution to socialization is either quite small (in the case of the broader concept of communicative action) or nil (in the case of the narrower concept of communicative action).[61]

Habermas's remarks on hominization provide neither a contribution to an analysis of the subject nor a confirmation of formal pragmatics.

3.2.2. Socio-cultural Evolution

According to Habermas, historical materialism is in need of "reconstruction".

> In the present connection, *reconstruction* signifies taking a theory apart and putting it back together again in a new form in order to attain more fully the goal it has set for itself. This is the normal way (in my opinion normal for Marxists too) of dealing with a theory

that needs revision in many respects but whose potential for stimulation has still not been exhausted.[62]

It becomes clear what Habermas considers in need of revision when he argues against Marx that:

Rationality structures are embodied not only in amplifications of purposive-rational action—that is, in technologies, strategies, organizations, and qualifications—but also in mediations of communicative action—in the mechanisms for regulating conflict, in world views, and in identity formations. I would even defend the thesis that the development of these normative structures is the pacemaker of social evolution, for new principles of social organization mean new forms of social integration; and the latter, in turn, first make it possible to implement available productive forces or to generate new ones, as well as making possible a heightening of social complexity.[63]

The development of these normative structures follows, according to Habermas, "developmental logics in Piaget's sense".[64] The following extensive quotation offers a concise summary of his position, which, while it does certainly contain elements of historical materialism, hardly "reconstructs" it:

Our discussion has led to the following, provisional results:
a. The system problems that cannot be solved without evolutionary innovations arise in the basic domain of a society.
b. Each new mode of production means a new form of social integration, which crystallizes around a new institutional core.
c. An endogenous learning mechanism provides for the accumulation of a cognitive potential that can be used for solving crisis-inducing system problems.
d. This knowledge, however, can be implemented to develop the forces of production only when the evolutionary step to a new institutional framework and a new form of social integration has been taken.

It remains an open question, *how* this step is taken. The *descriptive* answer of historical materialism is: through social conflict…But only an analytic answer can explain *why* a society takes an evolutionary step and how we are to understand that social struggles under certain conditions lead to a new level of social development. I would like to propose the following answer: the species learns not only in the dimension of technically useful knowledge decisive for the development of productive forces but also in the dimension of moral-practical consciousness decisive for structures of interaction. The rules of communicative action do develop in reaction to changes in the domain of instrumental and strategic action; but in doing so they follow *their own logic*.[65]

First of all, it is clear that the development of "normative structures" allegedly expressing themselves in the "mediations of communicative action" can hardly be "the pacemaker of social evolution" if, as Habermas notes, the rules of communicative action develop *in reaction* to changes in the area of instrumental and strategic action. The learning mechanism, for example, that leads to a mythological picture of the world in the Neolithic age, according to Klaus Eder (whose research Habermas uses at length to support his notions on social evolution)—that is, the learning mechanism that, as Habermas puts it, "provides for the accumulation of a cognitive potential that can be used for solving crisis-inducing system problems",

in this example by making the transition to a *state* order—is not so very "endogenous". These "neolithic inventions", and thus the escalations of the *productive
forces*,

extend the domination of external nature: the contingency in interactions with nature is
reduced, while at the same time nature's own peculiar laws have become a greater phenomenon requiring explanation. The simultaneous reliability and arbitrariness of the divine
figures determines the cognitive structuring of the world: nature, as a realm of objects that
can be influenced, can also enact punishment if humans fail to subordinate themselves to
its laws.

And this transition can be "characterized as the transition from an animistic
world-view to a mythological one".[66] Thus it is, instead, the escalation of productive forces that presents itself as the "pacemaker of social evolution."

In fact there is no one clear "pacemaker of social evolution". Social changes—to
avoid the term "evolution"—are the effects of historical contingencies. Habermas,
who claims that he wishes to avoid overextending the evolutionary approach into
a philosophy of history[67] and to "provide an alternative to the philosophy of history…, which is no longer tenable",[68] overextends the evolutionary approach and
produces an untenable philosophy of history by transferring Piaget's concept of
evolution to history. The question arises: *why* should this transfer be admissible?
Habermas provides little more in the way of reasons than a passing reference to
"homologous structures of consciousness in the histories of the individual and
the species".[69] There may well be such a homology between *structures* (or there
may not be), yet what requires justification is a homology in the *developmental
logic*. Why should we expect to find *this* sort of homology? Klaus Eder answers this
question as follows:

The cultural variations that this process of the conventionalization of law builds on are
dependent on structural changes in the mental structures shared by members of the society. The processes of constructing reality can be conceived analogously to the ontogenetic
processes of the development of thought and action: the learning processes that a child is
able to move through due to its competence are just as systematically pre-structured and
irreversible as socio-cultural learning processes. The reason for this can be found in the
fact that the deep structure that antecedently guides both learning processes is the *same*.
The structures that guide the construction of reality on the part of children are identical to
the structures that guide this construction of reality in socio-cultural evolution. For this reason the *formal* characteristics of development such as irreversibility, hierarchical arrange-
ment of stages, and invariance in the progression of stages are also the same.[70]

Eder falls victim to a profound error here. The structures that guide the construction of reality on the part of the child change from one stage to another—
this is the whole point of the Piagetian theory of development—such that the
construction of reality of a child up to two years of age are guided by structures
of the so-called sensorimotor stage, for example, and those of a child between
two and seven years of age by the structures of the so-called preoperational stage.
Eder's idea that the structures guiding a child's construction of reality are identical
to those guiding the construction of reality in socio-cultural evolution implies

that there are stages of *socio-cultural* evolution in which the societal construction of reality is guided by those structures that characterize the sensorimotor or the preoperational stage of a child's development. However, this implication is false, if only because children up to seven years of age can hardly be participating in decisive ways in the social construction of reality. Thus we can infer from this result that Eder's hypothesis is false.

It is adults who undertake the social construction of reality, and the overwhelming majority of them in all societies find themselves at the Piagetian *concrete operational* stage,[71] or between the Kohlbergian stages 3 and 4, whereby in so-called primitive societies a mixed form of stages 2 and 3 is most frequently found, and in our liberal-democratic societies most are at a mixed form of stages 3 and 4.[72] Thus, while there have clearly been significant changes in societal structures between the Stone Age and the modern day, we have progressed only *one* Kohlberg stage at most. And even this difference can only be seen as an increase in moral competence given a certain ethnocentric partisan bias. Thus Carolyn Edwards has argued, very convincingly in my opinion: "...different modes of moral decision-making are appropriate for the tribal versus national frames of reference. In terms of Kohlberg's stage system of moral judgment, stage 3 is the type of thinking most suitable for a face-to-face community, while stage 4 is more suitable for the national state."[73] In other words, in a tribal society, it is *inappropriate* to judge at the fourth level and thus it is a sign of *greater* competence to judge at the third rather than at the fourth level. The organization of the state does not follow the fourth stage; instead, this stage is an *adaptation*—in certain individuals—to the new circumstances. Thus it should be clear that, despite what Eder and Habermas would like to believe, not even the significant "cultural variations" that led from neolithic society to modernity "are dependent on structural changes in the mental structures shared by members of the society". *Thus there is no historical developmental logic comparable to the ontogenetic developmental logic.*

It is also quite doubtful whether, as Habermas insistently claims, "societies learn evolutionarily in 'institutionally embodying' the rationality structures that are *already distinctly formed* [*bereits ausgeprägt*] in the received cultural tradition, that is, in using them for the reorganization of systems of action".[74] We have, after all, seen problem-solving behaviour among primates as well, who do not necessarily have to resort to their "received cultural tradition" to find a solution for a problem facing them (such as reaching for a banana that the experimenter has made more inaccessible through certain new obstacles). So why should much more intelligent people—societies—not be capable of solving systematic problems by using their *intelligence*, by *inventing* new institutions and the "rationality structures" embodied therein, rather than being dependent on recycling whatever "rationality structures" are already available in the culture? I have not found an answer to this question anywhere in Habermas's work—and not in Eder's either.

With this in mind, it might be worthwhile to take a critical look at Habermas's "(very tentative) attempt to distinguish *levels of social integration*".[75] Thus he explains that the mythological world views still immediately enmeshed with the system of action of neolithic societies were accompanied by "conventional patterns of resolving moral conflicts of action", whereas the "legal regulation of conflict" was undertaken "from preconventional points of view (assessment of action consequences, compensation for resultant damages, restorations of status quo ante)". Early civilizations [*frühe Hochkulturen*], in contrast—evidently due to their institutionalization of the "rationality structures" of mythical world views—finally developed "conflict regulation from the point of view of a conventional morality tied to the figure of the ruler who administers or represents justice (evaluation according to action intentions, transition from retaliation to punishment, from joint liability to individual liability)".[76] Habermas provides no evidence of any sort for his opinion that the mythical world views of neolithic societies were accompanied by conventional patterns of conflict resolution, nor does Eder. Eder's explications tend to suggest rather that these conventional patterns of conflict resolution can be seen in some myths (by no means in *the* myths) of certain "neolithic" or tribal societies that had already reached a certain level of complexity—and that these patterns can then in turn be seen as reactions to previous increases in complexity. But of course a myth can anticipate future increases in complexity. Since, for this reason too, the societal structures described in a myth do not have to be identical to the structures of the society that produces this myth, the discrepancy between any possible conventional patterns of conflict resolution in myths and the—alleged—preconventional patterns in reality does not have to be interpreted as a deficiency of any kind. Thus it is implausible to conceptualize the transition from neolithic society to the society of the early civilizations [*frühe Hochkulturen*] as a learning step "in the dimension of moral-practical consciousness".[77]

We find a similar relation between modernity and the more developed civilizations [*entwickelte Hochkulturen*]. Habermas sees these civilizations as equipped with "postconventional legal and moral representations", which then, among other things, allow "postconventionally structured domains of action" in modernity, that is, the "differentiation of a universalistically regulated domain of strategic action (capitalist enterprise, bourgeois civil law), approaches to a political will-formation grounded in principles (formal democracy)".[78] It is entirely unclear what is supposed to be post-conventional about a universalistically regulated domain of strategic action such as capitalist enterprise. It is not even clear what a concept that designates a stage of development in moral consciousness is supposed to mean if applied to capitalist enterprise. And the formation of will in "formal democracy" certainly does not occur at a post-conventional level. Habermas does not so much demonstrate the existence of diverse patterns of species-wide development "homologous" to patterns of individual development as project the latter onto the former.

Finally, it has to be asked where the connection is actually supposed to be found between Habermas's philosophy of history and "formal-pragmatic insights" or a "theory of communicative action". In the passage summarizing his position, which I quoted extensively above, he does write that "the rules of communicative action" develop according to "their own logic".[79] Yet even if we ignore the fact that the rules of communicative action do not *develop*, but rather simply follow from

Habermas's definition of communicative action, and were the same in the neolithic era as they are today, *their* logic can hardly be very relevant to the "endogenous growth of knowledge".[80] For this growth, which after all according to Habermas is expressed primarily in changes in *world views*, occurs not through communicative *action* but rather through thinking and the exchange of ideas. But Habermas has as little use for the particular logics of *these* processes as he does for the purported logic of communicative action. Instead, as we have seen, he has recourse above all to the developmental logic of the ontogenesis of moral consciousness. Thus, despite what he claims, no ostensible logic or developmental logic of communicative action plays any role in his abortive analysis of "socio-cultural development".

With one exception: when it comes to the "normative implications"[81] of his developmental theory, that is, when it comes to *normatively* distinguishing [*auszeichnen*] the stages of socio-cultural development that are allegedly "higher" (according to the logic of development) from the lower stages (i.e. if it comes to the claim that they are *preferable* from a moral point of view), the homologies with ontogenesis could not possibly be of any use to him anyway. It is an instance of the naturalistic fallacy to infer from the (ostensible) fact that a certain stage of the ontogenetic development of moral consciousness is the highest *according to the logic of this development* the *normative* conclusion that this stage is worth striving for and comprises what morality ought to be. In just the same way, it is an instance of the naturalistic fallacy to infer from the (ostensible) fact that a certain stage of socio-cultural development is the highest the normative conclusion that it is of higher *value* and worth striving for.[82] Thus Habermas does well to try another way of normatively distinguishing those stages of social integration that are allegedly higher in terms of developmental logic. However, this attempt takes him to another dead end:

For a living being that maintains itself in the structures of ordinary language communication, the validity basis of speech has the binding force of universal and unavoidable—in this sense "transcendental"—presuppositions. The *theoretician* does not have the same possibility of choice in relation to the validity claims immanent in speech as he does in relation to the basic biological value of health. Otherwise he would have to deny the very presuppositions without which the theory of evolution would be meaningless. If we are not free then to reject or to accept the validity claims bound up with the cognitive potential of the human species, it is senseless to want to "decide" for or against reason, for or against the expansion of the potential of reasoned action. For these reasons I do not regard the choice of the historical-materialist criterion of progress as arbitrary. The development of productive forces, in conjunction with the maturity of the forms of social integration, means progress of ability in both dimensions: progress in objectivating knowledge and in moral-practical insight.[83]

We have already seen that the presuppositions of argumentation are in fact circumventable.[84] The validity claims are also not universal. But even if raising truth claims (which corresponds to the dimension of "objectifying cognition") were unavoidable, why should it be "senseless" to decide against the development of productive forces? What if, for example, their continued development kills us all? And that the forms of social integration that are allegedly more mature according to the logic of development are also *right*, that is, the *normatively better* forms of social integration, is something that Habermas simply *assumes* here. However, he would have to show it.

Thus we can conclude that Habermas's thoughts on "socio-cultural evolution" are an example of an untenable philosophy of history that neither provides confirmation of the "theory of communicative action" or "formal pragmatics" nor, conversely, finds any support in them.

3.3. CRITICAL SOCIAL THEORY?

3.3.1. Habermas's Theory of Order

Habermas's theory of communicative action is among other things a theory about how the coordination of actions, and ultimately social order, is possible.

I have treated communicative and strategic action as two variants of linguistically mediated interaction. It holds only for *communicative action* that the structural constraints of an intersubjectively shared language impel the actors—in the sense of a weak transcendental necessity—to step out of the egocentricity of a purposive rational orientation towards their own respective success and to surrender themselves to the public criteria of communicative rationality. The trans-subjective structures of language thus suggest a basis for answering, from the point of view of action theory, the classical question of how social order is possible. The atomistic concept of *strategic* action does not provide us with any equivalent answer. If it nonetheless is to serve as the basic concept in a sociological theory of action, then it has to be explained how contexts of interaction that emerge solely from the reciprocal exertion of influence upon one another of success-oriented actors can establish themselves as stable orders.[85]

We have already gone into the assumptions behind this argumentation in great depth above; they are all false. Nonetheless, here I would like to take a closer look at Habermas's attempt to solve the problem of order.

As regards theoretical questions of order, Habermas writes:

A theory of action that is to answer these questions must be capable of stating the conditions in which alter can "link up" his actions to those of ego.[86]

Thus he intends

to explicate the conditions that have to be satisfied by a communicatively achieved agreement that is to fulfil functions of coordinating action.

His explication reads:

With his "yes" the speaker accepts a speech-act offer and grounds an agreement; this agreement concerns the *content of the utterance*, on the one hand, and, on the other hand, certain *guarantees immanent to speech acts* and certain *obligations relevant to the sequel of interaction*. The action potential typical of a speech act finds expression in the claim that the speaker raises for what he says—in an explicit speech act by means of a performative verb. In acknowledging this claim, the hearer accepts an offer made with the speech act. This illocutionary success is relevant to the interaction inasmuch as it establishes between speaker and hearer an interpersonal relation that is effective for coordination, that orders scopes of action and sequences of interaction, and that opens up to the hearer possible points of connection by way of general alternatives for action.[87]

Before we move on, I would like to note that of course threatening someone with a weapon, that is, strategic action not oriented towards reaching understanding, can also, clearly, be effective for coordination. And if an explanation of social order based solely on the concept of strategic action has to explain "how contexts of interaction that emerge solely from the reciprocal exertion of influence upon one another of success-oriented actors can establish themselves as stable orders", then the same should also hold in reverse—as we do not wish to apply a double standard here—that is, an explanation of social order based solely on the concept of communicative action has to explain how contexts of interaction that emerge solely from communicatively produced agreement can establish themselves as stable orders. This question becomes all the more pressing when Habermas writes:

That social order is supposed to produce and reproduce itself by way of processes of consensus formation might seem at first glance to be a trivial notion. The improbability of this idea becomes clear, however, as soon as one reminds oneself that every communicatively achieved agreement depends on the taking up of "yes"/"no" positions with regard to criticizable validity claims. In the case of communicative action, the double contingency that has to be absorbed by all interaction formation takes the particularly precarious shape of an ever-present risk of disagreement that is built into the communicative mechanism itself, whereby every disagreement has a high cost.... Rational motivation, which rests on the fact that the hearer can say "no," constitutes a maelstrom of problematization that makes linguistic consensus formation appear more like a disruptive mechanism.[88]

So Habermas decides to seek shelter under the concept of a "lifeworld". He appropriates "the material content" of Husserl's investigations

by assuming that communicative action, too, is embedded in a lifeworld that provides risk-absorbing coverage in the form of a massive background consensus.[89]

Habermas claims that this concept of the lifeworld is a "complementary concept" to that of communicative action. Obviously, however, we are dealing instead with a case of false labelling here, as the concept of the lifeworld (on the supposition that it explains *anything* at all) takes over the explanatory duties that the concept of communicative action was actually supposed to fulfil and yet, despite bold declarations made on its behalf, cannot fulfil.

Moreover, if we so generously allow the concept of communicative action to seek aid and support wherever they can be found, why should someone who wants to explain social order with recourse to the concept of strategic action not, *likewise*, appropriate the material content of Husserl's investigations

by assuming that strategic action, too, is embedded in a lifeworld that provides risk-absorbing coverage in the form of a massive background consensus?

As we have quite thoroughly explained, strategic action can very much orient itself in the light of a background consensus, and it can also adopt the pursuit of certain consensual norms as a goal to be accounted for in weighing goals, means and side effects. If the background consensus is so constituted that it absorbs the risk that contexts of interaction would fail to establish themselves, then it absorbs this risk and it *establishes* these contexts of interaction. So it is not entirely clear how communicative action, in seeking support from the concept of the lifeworld, is supposed to gain any ground against the concept of strategic action on the issue of explanatory value when strategic action also makes direct use of this means of support.

Evidently Habermas thinks that the concept of communicative action can explain the emergence of this background consensus *itself* and thus is the more fundamental explanatory concept. After all, he claims again and again that "it is certainly true" that the lifeworld reproduces itself "only via communicative action".[90]

But rather than solving the problem in any way, this merely shifts it onto another level. Habermas's entire argumentation runs in a circle: first he wants to explain social order through communicative action. Then he himself points out the "improbability of this idea", given that "rational motivation, which rests on the fact that the hearer can say 'no'", and which is constitutive of communicative processes, also presents us with "a maelstrom of problematization that makes linguistic consensus formation appear more like a disruptive mechanism". Therefore communicative action is, he says, dependent on a lifeworld "that provides risk-absorbing coverage in the form of a massive background consensus". The lifeworld, in turn, and with it this "massive background consensus" is to be reproduced through communicative action. However, we can see the improbability of this idea if we note that the "rational motivation" constitutive of communicative processes, which "rests on the fact that the hearer can say 'no'", brings with it a "maelstrom of problematization that makes linguistic consensus formation appear more like a disruptive mechanism". Thus we have arrived at that question that motivated the introduction of the concept of the lifeworld in the first place: how can communicative processes lead to consensus and social order of their own power?

Habermas does not give us any reasonable answer to this; apparently he believes that he can summarily define the sociological problem of order out of existence with suitable analytic distinctions at the level of speech act theory. Let us take a closer look at this.

The "illocutionary success is relevant to the interaction", Habermas tells us, "inasmuch as it establishes between speaker and hearer an interpersonal relation that is effective for coordination." But how does one achieve this illocutionary success? And above all, how do we achieve it without once more allowing strategic action to creep back in as the ultimately decisive coordinating factor? Habermas writes:

We are now in a position to say that a speaker can *rationally motivate* a hearer to accept his speech act offer because—on the basis of an internal connection among validity, validity claim, and redemption of a validity claim—he can assume the *warranty* [*Gewähr*] for providing, if necessary, convincing reasons that would stand up to a hearer's criticism of the validity claim. Thus a speaker owes the binding (or bonding: *bindende*) force of his illocutionary act not to the validity of what is said, but to *the coordinating effect of the warranty that he offers*: namely, to redeem, if necessary, the validity claim raised with his speech act. In all cases in which the illocutionary role expresses not a power claim but a validity claim, the place of the empirically motivating force of sanctions (contingently linked with speech acts) is taken by the rationally motivating force of accepting a speaker's guarantee for securing claims to validity.[91]

Assuming the warranty towards another that one can justify, with reasons, the "validity claims" one raises, is just as much an instance of strategic action as the use of force—at least if we understand the term "strategic action" as Weber did, and Habermas takes the concept from Weber. And the (possibly) rationally motivating force of arguments is just as much an *empirical* phenomenon (if we could not *experience* it, how would we know of it?) as, conversely, the motivation produced by a demand with menaces ("your money or your life") to hand one's wallet over to a mugger is *rational*. Habermas's contrasts are inappropriate to the matter at hand and purely rhetorical. Moreover, the warranty that one is saying the *truth* is entirely sufficient—the speaker does not need to take on the warranty for being able to *justify* his statement. How could I justify my statement that I had a nightmare last night or that I spent the night alone reading a Lovecraft story if I have no witnesses and no other means of documentation? I cannot justify it. The hearer either believes me or does not.

But even if we turn a blind eye to Habermas's idiosyncratic choice of words for a moment, we have to raise the objection here that illocutionary acts do not produce "binding effects" on their own, but rather only "under the assumption of certain social and institutional constellations as well as psychic dispositions"—and then it would have to be explained where these come from. Habermas responds to this objection from J. Weiß[92] as follows:

It is precisely this that I maintain; however, the pragmatic concept of language allows for another, non-empiricist description of the same thing.[93]

In at least one passage Habermas had not maintained "precisely this", in my opinion, but rather explicitly denied it.[94] However, let us look past this and turn to his thesis that the development of these necessary binding effects of communicative acts can be described non-empirically: nowhere does Habermas justify this thesis; he merely repeats it, continually. Thus he writes:

This second aspect, from which society appears as the sum of enabling conditions [instead of society under the first aspect as a limitation of the room to manoeuvre; U.S.], cannot be subjected to empirical analysis.[95]

Why is that? Habermas mentions "the cooperation of cultural tradition, social integration and the socialization of individuals" as enabling conditions—are these not empirical phenomena? And the objects of the "formal-pragmatic" (hence allegedly non-empiricist) "description of the lifeworld's resources", namely, "background knowledge, forms of solidarity and skills"[96]—are they not empirical phenomena? Habermas himself says that the sociological (which means here:

empirical) view describes "the *same* phenomena"[97] as the formal-pragmatic analysis. But if they are the *same* phenomena, then they have the *same* properties. Thus, if the sociologically described phenomena x, y and z are empirical phenomena, then they are still empirical phenomena when we describe them formal-pragmatically. Just as a dog does not metamorphose into something else if we call it a "bow-wow", a societal phenomenon is not transformed into something non-empirical if we mark it with formal-pragmatic labels. Of course, "empirical" is different from "empiricist". An "empiricist" description, one would assume, describes them *as* empirical phenomena. It might also be possible to give them a non-empiricist description, that is, to describe them as non-empirical phenomena. But if they *are* empirical, then such a non-empiricist description is *false*. However, it is of course not even clear what should be non-empiricist about concepts such as "background knowledge, forms of solidarity and skills" or concepts such as "speech act", "binding force" or "rational motivation".

Just as Habermas fails to provide a non-empiricist description of the emergence of the presuppositions of communicative action, he also fails to provide any plausibility for his rather peculiar thesis that the "symbolic reproduction" of society occurs *only* through communicative action. This thesis, too, he only repeats continually instead of justifying it.[98] Of course, this lack of justification should hardly be surprising, since the thesis is false.[99] Habermas himself rejects it in responding to critical objections and explicitly corrects his earlier opinion, but then continues to cling to this very same opinion a few pages later—and still does so today.[100] The motivation for this irrational and dogmatic insistence most likely stems from the fact that to concede that the lifeworld does *not* reproduce itself *solely* through the "medium of communicative action", but rather, if at all, only to a very small extent, would amount to the concession that the concept of communicative action has absolutely no explanatory value for the theory of social order.

It is not hard to see why the thesis in question is false. Habermas defines communicative action as action "in which *all* participants harmonize their individual plans of action with one another and thus pursue their illocutionary aims *without reservation*".[101] "Without reservation" means playing with an open hand, that is, sincerely and without any "ulterior motives". Moreover, all exercise of "strategic influence" (such as by threatening punishments or promising rewards) is ruled out.[102] Now, the reproduction of the lifeworld consists, according to Habermas, in cultural production, social integration and socialization. These can hardly be distinguished from one another as neatly as Habermas seems to suggest in his scheme.[103] Be that as it may, one might tend to think that children's upbringing and education would play a significant role in all three processes. Does this upbringing happen communicatively (in the Habermasian sense of the word)? Hardly. Reward and punishment, in whatever form, are essential elements in raising children, along with so-called observational learning, the assumption of roles, and identification with role models. All these are basically unconscious processes, and in any case do not rely on the vehicle of communicative action. When a child learns to behave in a certain way through observation, it is not because the child came to a "communicative agreement" with someone about its behaviour. In fact, children tend to appropriate the examples of conduct that they observe—which are thus non-linguistic—rather than the contents of eloquent moral lectures; and of course even moral lectures themselves aim not at *rational* agreement but rather at *agreement* plain and simple. Their pathos makes them examples of rhetorical and "emotional" influence, and only in the rarest cases are they examples of a "communication oriented towards reaching understanding" in the Habermasian sense. "Communicative action" plays an entirely subordinate role, if any, in children's upbringing.

Furthermore, media such as newspapers and television are involved in the three processes of reproduction that Habermas identifies. Is the tabloid editor really supposed to have *sincerely* announced the world's downfall? Are we really supposed to picture him as entirely without reservations in reporting on immigrants seeking asylum and imagine that he had nothing in his thoughts but "rational agreement"—and not, for example, the number of papers sold? And the tabloid certainly reaches quite a few more readers than the "serious" newspapers, and thus makes a greater contribution to "cultural reproduction", to "integration" (though not the integration of all, naturally) and socialization. But even editors and journalists in more serious media (along with professors, incidentally) cannot avoid having ulterior motives, such as career considerations, against the background of the empirical influence of factions and interest groups. And where these agendas play a role, it is by definition no longer communicative action.

There are additional sites of "symbolic reproduction", such as pubs, parliamentary debates, seminars, churches, schools and the very life that one observes and takes part in (observational learning is not limited to children). In so far as conversations are conducted in these places and in such situations, arguments will frequently play a role as well. However, as soon as not just purely theoretical questions but practical ones are concerned—questions that bring values, attitudes and emotions into play—agreement will not be reached exclusively through arguments, as Habermas demands of all agreement reached communicatively[104]—but rather, as Stevenson quite rightly notes,[105] through all sorts of *non*-argumentative means of influence, such as the way arguments are presented, affection or dislike for the one presenting the argument, unconscious group dynamics, etc. There is not, in point of fact, any agreement in practical questions where such factors do not play a role. This means, however, that in point of fact there is *no rationally motivated agreement (in the Habermasian sense) in practical questions.*

And, finally, one might think that whether a person grows up in a slum or a luxurious villa has a significant impact on that person's socialization; and whether or not a society suffers from massive unemployment and extreme inequality in the distribution of wealth and oppressive debts could be expected to have certain repercussions for its processes of integration and cultural reproduction. Material conditions might also affect the processes of "symbolic reproduction" one way or another. However, as Habermas rightly notes, "[m]aterial production takes place through the medium of the purposive activity with which sociated individuals intervene in the world",[106] and as we know Habermas makes a distinction between the purposive activity of "teleological action" and communicative action. Social purposive action is still *strategic* action.

Thus Habermas's thesis that the "symbolic reproduction" of society occurs through communicative action is unfounded;[107] and thus the concept of communicative action has absolutely no explanatory value for the theory of social order.

This is also confirmed if we look at the matter from another angle and ask ourselves *how* exactly the communicative coordination of action is supposed to function. As far as I can tell, this question has never been raised, probably because it is considered a "trivial notion", to use Habermas's phrasing, "that social order is supposed to produce and reproduce itself by way of processes of consensus formation". For although we have seen that the *presuppositions* of the processes of forming consensus are anything but trivial, it does seem trivial that actions can be coordinated by means of an agreement *if* an agreement is reached. However, this overlooks what *Habermas* means by "agreement". For according to him a consensus is measured

against truth, rightness, and sincerity, that is, against the "fit" or "misfit" between the speech act, on the one hand, and the three worlds to which the actor takes up relations with his utterance, on the other.[108]

Thus consensus is a consensus about the truth, sincerity and rightness of a *speech act*. This is a very peculiar concept of consensus—and very telling of Habermasian theory's lack of thoroughness in both its conception and its execution, a theory rich in stipulation and speculation but poor in careful analysis.[109] For of course the son can believe his father's announcement that he will give the son a sound spanking to be quite sincere, quite well-founded in its existential presuppositions and quite *legitimate* based on the traditional notions of the authority of parents that he was raised with, without for that reason being in *agreement* with *what* the father announces.[110]

Interestingly, however, Habermas writes:

Reaching an understanding functions as a mechanism for coordinating actions only through the participants in interaction coming to an agreement concerning the claimed *validity* of their utterances, that is, through intersubjectively recognizing the *validity claims* they reciprocally raise.[111]

Yet it is plain to see that reaching an understanding *cannot* function as a mechanism for coordinating actions in this way; the consensus established in this manner regarding the "validity" of a speech act is not sufficient. Let us assume that someone invites me to a party. My accepting this invitation would in fact, and trivially so, have an action-coordinating force (although I could of course still decline to go, but then I would have to explain myself). However, very little follows from my recognition of the sincerity and rightness as well as the truth of the existential presuppositions of the invitation, that is, from the fact that a consensus in the Habermasian sense of the term has been reached, since *this* consensus does not yet amount to an acceptance of the invitation. And, conversely, one could also accept the invitation without having reached consensus in the Habermasian sense of the term. The same holds of other speech acts that are essential for the coordination of actions, such as requests, demands and commands. For example,

I could easily agree that B is entitled to *request* that I give him information about a certain person, but this does not yet mean that B is also entitled to *receive* this information or that I am obliged to provide it. I could have good reasons to refuse the request without therefore having to view his speech act as inappropriate. Of course, the mutual recognition of the validity of a speech act by both speaker and hearer may very well produce the "illocutionary force of an acceptable speech act", which according to Habermas "*consists in the fact that it can move a hearer to rely on the speech-act-typical obligations of the speaker*". Habermas lists a number of obligations, namely, that the speaker must "regard a question as settled when a satisfactory answer is given; drop an assertion when it proves to be false; follow her own advice when she finds herself in the same situation as the hearer; place emphasis on a request [*einer Aufforderung Nachdruck verschaffen*—this actually implies the use of threats] when it is not complied with;…and so on"[112] (the latter two obligations are, incidentally, Habermasian fictions, apart from the fact that a request that comes with an implicit *threat* cannot be called "illocutionary" according to Habermasian terminology). Yet they clearly are not sufficient to solve the problem of social order. For if I consider an invitation to be "valid", I may well expect that the host will grant me entrance to the party, but this does not yet amount to any actual *coordination* of our actions. The inviter does not know if I will in fact come, and the *harmonization* of our plans of action required in communicative action[113] has not yet been achieved. And since it is not so much the acceptance of invitations that occupies the centre of the problem of order but rather the observance of norms, the falsity of the following statement by Habermas apologist Klaus Günther is quite fatal for any attempt to solve the problem of social order in terms of a theory of communicative action:

In the special case of action norms, these illocutionary obligations become especially relevant, because the propositional content of the speech act refers directly to human action, so that the acceptance of a regulative speech act entails the illocutionary obligation to do what is required in order to satisfy the valid norm.[114]

This statement is false because the acceptance of a speech act is not identical with the acceptance of the propositional content of the speech act. The acceptance of a speech act consists, after all, according to Habermas, in the recognition of the three validity claims of the speech act,[115] thus in the recognition of its "validity". Now, norms, as we well know, according to Habermas, cannot attain to truth, but rather only to rightness. Thus the truth claim of a statement such as "You should not have sexual intercourse before marriage" has to refer to the statement's *existential presuppositions* and not to the norm it expresses. But the *claim to rightness* of a speech act also refers not to the speech act's propositional content but rather to the speech act itself, that is, to whether the speaker is entitled to its *performance*.[116] Now I myself, as someone who recognizes the right to free speech, am very much of the opinion that someone is *entitled* to express that particular normative statement, and I likewise recognize the existential presuppositions of the normative statement (those addressed by the statement exist, as does sexual intercourse), and I could also recognize the sincerity of such a statement. However, why all of this is supposed to *oblige* me—whether "illocutionarily" or otherwise—to *follow* said norm is a mystery to me. A norm is not made valid merely by virtue of the fact that the *speech act* that serves as the vehicle of its assertion is "valid". In short, *an agreement in Habermas's sense of the word does not achieve anything for the coordination of action.* For that we need an agreement *about the matter at hand* (which, incidentally, tends to be empirically motivated), an agreement to *take up* an invitation, to *act in accordance* with the request. However, for this sort of agreement about the matter itself it is clearly neither necessary nor sufficient to "reach an understanding" in Habermas's sense of the term. Moreover, this also means, as already explained, *that there is no communicative action in the strict sense of the term,* namely, if we define it as action that is coordinated by the "illocutionary binding forces" of speech acts.[117]

But let us assume for a moment—counterfactually—that it is possible to reach an agreement on the matter at hand, an agreement that actually serves to coordinate action, by means of an agreement about the "validity" of a statement pronouncing a norm. This still would not solve the problem of order, since *which* norm is agreed to is not exactly incidental to the solution of the problem. If, for example, the utterance declaring the norm "it is imperative for all to wage war against all" is recognized by everyone as valid and this has an effect in the coordination of action, then this would achieve order in a *certain* sense, namely, in the sense that the war of all against all would be the product of *consensus.* But since Hobbes we have tended, quite rightly, to see the problem of order as the problem of why there is *not* a war of all against all. However, this requires us to explain why *certain* norms, such as "You should not kill", tend to find more recognition than other norms, such as "Let us all bash each other's skulls in." Habermas not only fails to offer us an answer to this question from the perspective of his speech act theory; he does not even pose the question. Evidently speech act theory is not a particularly suitable means of solving the problems of social order.

Bearing in mind some of the results from the previous chapters that are relevant to this problem, we can summarize the misery of Habermas's treatment of the problem of social order as follows:

First, despite Habermas's assurances, communicative action is nothing but a particular form of strategic action. Thus, if Habermas could prove that it were possible to explain the emergence and persistence of social order with recourse to the concept of communicative action, this would merely prove that it can be explained with recourse to the concept of strategic action.

Second, even if, for the sake of argument, we take "strategic action" to refer only to strategic action that is not also communicative action, there is still no discernible reason why, as Habermas claims, it should hold "only for *communicative action* that the structural constraints of an intersubjectively shared language impel the actors...to step out of the egocentricity of a purposive rational orientation towards their own respective success and to surrender themselves to the public criteria of communicative rationality". If these "structural constraints" are to be found in the "intersubjectively shared language" itself, then *every* use of this intersubjectively shared language—not just the communicative use of language but the strategic use as well—must of necessity place the actors under these structural constraints. The converse holds as well: if these structural constraints are *not* present in the strategic use of language, then they are also not to be found in the intersubjectively shared language per se; and then, contrary to Habermas's argument, the "trans-subjective structures of language" do not offer a basis for answering "the classical question of how social order is possible". The whole idea of wanting to solve the problems of social order first and foremost if not exclusively with considerations of linguistic philosophy is entirely implausible.

Third, if an explanation of social order based solely on strategic action has to show "how contexts of interaction that emerge solely from the reciprocal exertion of influence upon one another of success-oriented actors can establish themselves as stable orders", as Habermas calls for, then *conversely* an explanation of social order based solely on the concept of communicative action must *for its part* explain how contexts of interaction that emerge solely from communicatively generated agreement can establish themselves as stable orders. This is particularly so since Habermas himself concedes that the "maelstrom of problematization…makes linguistic consensus formation appear more like a disruptive mechanism". Habermas's explanation is that communicative action is embedded in a lifeworld that "provides risk-absorbing coverage in the form of a massive background consensus". Aside from the fact that here the concept of the lifeworld, despite Habermas's assurances to the contrary, takes over the explanatory work for the theory of order that the concept of communicative action was actually supposed to fulfil, strategic action is embedded in just the same lifeworld as communicative action and can thus draw upon the same "risk-absorbing coverage" as communicative action in explaining how contexts of interaction establish themselves as stable orders. A concept of communicative action based on the concept of the lifeworld has absolutely no explanatory advantages over the concept of strategic action in solving the problem of social order.

Fourth, Habermas believes that the concept of communicative action can also explain the emergence of this background consensus itself and thus is in fact the fundamental explanatory concept and cannot be summarily replaced with the concept of the lifeworld. He claims that the lifeworld reproduces itself "certainly only by means of communicative action". Yet this argumentation moves in circles. First Habermas wants to explain societal order by means of communicative action; but then, faced with the "disruptive" "maelstrom of problematization" inherent in the linguistic processes of understanding that mediate communicative action, he points to the "improbability of this idea" and explains that communicative action is reliant on a lifeworld that "provides risk-absorbing coverage in the form of a massive background consensus". The lifeworld, in turn, and thus that "massive background consensus" that is at issue, are to be reproduced through communicative action alone. But how is the "maelstrom of problematization", the "disruptive mechanism" of linguistic processes of reaching understanding, supposed to provide for the production of consensus? Thus the circle begins anew, and a solution eludes us.

Fifth, Habermas's claim that this recourse to the lifeworld that communicative action depends on can be (correctly) described in "non-empiricist" concepts is unfounded. Phenomena such as "background knowledge, forms of solidarity and skills" or "speech acts", "binding forces" and "rational motivation" not only can be empirically described—they *are* in fact empirical phenomena, which follows from Habermas's own description of them. Moreover, Habermas's claim that the lifeworld can reproduce itself only by means of communicative action is likewise false. In fact, communicative action plays hardly any role at all in this. The lifeworld reproduces itself almost exclusively *strategically*, even if we take "strategic action" to refer only to non-communicative strategic action. Thus the concept of communicative action, unlike that of strategic action, has absolutely no explanatory value for social order.

Sixth, even if we assume for the moment that communicative action could in fact reproduce the lifeworld and also, with the support of the lifeworld, lead to consensus in the Habermasian sense, this would still not have resolved anything for the theoretical problem of social order. Consensus is, for Habermas, a consensus about the truth, rightness and sincerity of a speech act. However, to *coordinate action* it is necessary to reach an agreement about the *matter itself*, and in particular an agreement about what is to be done—and this sort of agreement is not at all the same as an agreement about the validity of a *speech act* stating what is to be done. This confusion is quite symptomatic of Habermas's tendency to replace reflection with stipulation and social theory with philosophy of language. In any case, Habermas's thesis that "[r]eaching an understanding functions as a mechanism for coordinating actions only through the participants in interaction coming to an agreement concerning the claimed *validity* of their utterances, that is, through intersubjectively recognizing the *validity claims* they reciprocally raise" is false. Reaching an understanding, in the Habermasian sense, does not function as a mechanism for coordinating actions.

And finally, even if a consensus, in the Habermasian sense of the term, about the validity of an utterance pronouncing a norm did lead to an action-coordinating agreement about the *matter itself*, this agreement could consist in a war of all against all. The question of why this does *not* happen, *how* it is possible to avoid a war of all against all, cannot even be adequately raised, let alone answered, from the constricted perspective of Habermas's speech act theory. His abstraction from the concrete interests of success-oriented actors in favour of his appeal to "trans-subjective structures of language" inevitably leads him right past the theoretical problem of social order.

In short, Habermas's attempt to answer the question of how social order is possible with recourse to the concept of communicative action fails.

3.3.2. The Colonization Thesis

With his "theory of communicative action" Habermas aims to clarify "the normative foundations of a critical theory of society".[118] However, to show that one has in fact produced these foundations of a critical theory of society, rather than the foundations of a relatively uncritical affirmation of the status quo or the foundations of nothing at all, it is not sufficient to present these purported foundations themselves; one has to present at least a rough sketch of the critical theory of society that fits them.

Now, the second volume of the "Theory of Communicative Action" does in fact bear the promising title "A Critique of Functionalist Reason." There Habermas explains that we have to distinguish

mechanisms of coordination that harmonize the *action orientations* of participants from mechanisms that stabilize nonintended interconnections of actions by way of functionally intermeshing *action consequences*. In one case, the integration of an action system is established by a normatively secured or communicatively achieved consensus, in the other case, by a nonnormative regulation of individual decisions that extends beyond the actors' consciousness. This distinction between a *social integration* of society, which takes effect in action orientations, and a *systemic integration*, which reaches through and beyond action orientations, calls for a corresponding differentiation in the concept of society itself.[119]

Habermas initially introduces this differentiation between *system* and *lifeworld* as an analytic distinction resulting from the adoption of different perspectives; however, Habermas then reifies the distinction in claiming that system and lifeworld have become *uncoupled* from one another. And yet:

It is not the uncoupling of media-steered subsystems and of their organizational forms from the lifeworld that leads to the one-sided rationalization or reification of everyday communicative practice, but only the penetration of forms of economic and administrative rationality into areas of action that resist being converted over to the media of money and power because they are specialized in cultural transmission, social integration, and child rearing, and remain dependent on mutual understanding as a mechanism for coordinating action.[120]

And this conversion of areas of the lifeworld into systematic integration, which supposedly is accompanied by "pathologies", is what Habermas calls the "colonization of the lifeworld".[121]

The critical component of the Habermasian theory of communicative action is exhausted in just this colonization thesis. However, no other thesis of his has met with such universal rejection as this one; even critics well-disposed towards Habermas can make nothing or very little of it. And in political discourse, at least today, it plays practically no role at all. Nonetheless, Habermas continues to uphold it. Thus in the following we will have to once more rehash its descriptive and normative deficits.

We are already familiar with Habermas's formal-pragmatic concept of the lifeworld. He contrasts this with the concept of the system. As remarked, this distinction is initially an analytic one. However, "[t]he communication-theoretic concept of the lifeworld developed from the participant's perspective", Habermas writes, "is not directly serviceable for theoretical purposes; it is not suited for demarcating an object domain of social science", that is, a "region within the objective world...."[122] And so Habermas develops a sociological concept of the lifeworld[123] and opposes this lifeworld to a system likewise reified into a region within the objective world. He then distinguishes between the two of them as follows:

The social is not absorbed as such by organized action systems; rather, it is split up into spheres of action constituted as the lifeworld and spheres neutralized against the lifeworld. The former are communicatively structured, the latter formally organized....they stand *opposite* one another as socially and systemically integrated spheres of action. In formally organized domains, the mechanism of mutual understanding in language, which is essential for social integration, is partially rescinded and relieved by steering media. Naturally, these media have to be anchored in the lifeworld by means of formal law. Thus, as we shall see, the types of legal regulation of social relations are good indicators of the boundaries between system and lifeworld.

...The law no longer starts from previously existing structures of communication; it generates forms of commerce and chains of command suited to media of communication. In the process, traditionally customary contexts of action oriented to mutual understanding get shoved out into the environments of systems. Using this criterion, we can locate the boundaries between system and lifeworld, in a rough and ready way, such that the subsystems of the economy and the bureaucratic state administration are on one side, while on the other side we find private spheres of life (connected with family, neighborhood, voluntary associations) as well as public spheres (for both private persons and citizens).[124]

And now lifeworld and system are supposed to be uncoupled from one another, so much so that the "subsystem" of the capitalist economy is allegedly a "block of more or less norm-free sociality".[125]

Understandably, no one wanted to buy this thesis. And so Habermas responded to critics by trying to relativize "what is meant by this proposition" as follows:

It describes the fact that, with the advent of the capitalist economic system and a state apparatus in which power linked to an office or person has been assimilated to the structure of a steering medium, action domains have differentiated out that are primarily systemically integrated. These are now integrated only indirectly through the agency of consensus mechanisms, namely to the extent that the legal institutionalization of steering media must be *coupled* to the normative contexts of the lifeworld. In this context, the expression "norm-free sociality" led to misunderstandings. It is obvious that commercial enterprises and government offices, indeed economic and political contexts as a whole make use of communicative action that is embedded in a normative framework. Leaving aside the fact that the functional contexts of media-steered subsystems cannot simply be marked off topologically from one another and made to match certain institutional complexes, my thesis amounts merely to the assertion that the integration of these action systems is *in the final instance* not based on the potential for social integration of communicative action and the lifeworldly background thereof—and ["although" would be more in line with the German text] these systems make use of both.[126]

This attempted "relativization" is inconsistent. It is *precisely* when "economic and political contexts as a whole make use of communicative action" that these contexts are integrated *directly* through "the agency of consensus mechanisms". Elsewhere Habermas writes:

Where reputation or moral authority enters in, action coordination has to be brought about by means of resources familiar from consensus formation in language. Media of this kind cannot uncouple interaction from the lifeworld context of shared cultural knowledge, valid norms, and accountable motivations ...[127]

Habermas should know that the opinions of experts play a decisive role in coordinating action in production processes and economic processes generally as well as in administration. The resource that the experts make use of to coordinate action is the trust in valid knowledge, that is, a resource of linguistic consensus formation.[128] Thus, evidently, the economic and administrative systems are not uncoupled from the lifeworld.

Moreover, *precisely* because "the legal institutionalization of steering media must be *coupled* to the normative contexts of the lifeworld", and according to Habermas it must,[129] the "integration of these action systems" depends *in the final instance* on the lifeworld's potential for social integration. Thus he says about law:

Law used as a steering medium is relieved of the problem of justification; it is connected with the body of law whose substance requires legitimation only through formally correct procedure. By contrast, legal institutions belong to the societal components of the lifeworld.[130]

So if the formally correct procedures were not legitimized by the *lifeworld*, then the steering medium would also not be *legitimized* by the formally correct procedures and its steering function would be severely compromised or even nullified. There is no "uncoupling".

Thus it follows from Habermas's own premises together with certain quite evident facts that the alleged lifeworld pervades and sustains this entire ostensible system. Conversely, the ostensible system pervades the entire alleged lifeworld. In this point as well Habermas was obliged to do a little relativizing:

...the talk of the uncoupling of system and lifeworld unfortunately also conjures up images of the lifeworld being stripped of mechanisms of system integration. In this regard I am guilty of a reifying use of language: the lifeworld is "uncoupled" solely from media-steered subsystems, and of course not from the mechanisms of system integration as a whole.[131]

And:

Although social integration occurs via communicative action, action domains of the lifeworld which are primarily integrated socially are...neither free of power nor free of strategic action.[132]

This "of course" is completely inappropriate if we recall that Habermas drew the boundaries between system and lifeworld with the explanation that the two spheres "stand *opposite* one another as socially and systemically integrated spheres of action".[133] Whatever is integrated by mechanisms of system integration would, by this criterion, not be a part of the lifeworld. Moreover, the areas that Habermas typically refers to as "lifeworld" (such as the family) are not socially integrated, that is, through action oriented towards reaching understanding, which Habermas himself acknowledges a mere four pages after the relativizations quoted here, in a passage more closely attuned to reality:

As the lifeworld, however, by no means offers an innocent image of "power-free spheres of communication," the presuppositions for orientation toward reaching understanding are met without reservations, i.e. without deception and self-deception, only if the improbable conditions of non-repressive forms of life prevail. Otherwise, social integration proceeds via norms of domination which sublimate violence, on the one hand, and consensus formation in language which fulfils the conditions for latent strategic action, on the other.[134]

To be sure, the key concepts are a little mixed up here. Given how Habermas defines "consensus", the consensus formation in language cannot possibly fulfil "the conditions for latent strategic action". And social integration, *in Habermas's sense*, also cannot accomplish this. Systematic integration, on the other hand, is very much capable of this. And it also works the other way around; for in latent strategic action, the actors will certainly not harmonize their action orientations with each other (nor will they in manifest strategic action, if we read "harmoniza-tion" as "reaching understanding" in the Habermasian sense). Rather, latent stra-tegic actors try to *deceive* their opponents as to their action orientation. Thus what we see here is an integration that pervades the various action orientations. It is first and foremost just the actions themselves that are coordinated, but an integration of the *consequences* of the actions can easily follow. In fact, it *has* to follow—as Habermas himself sees:

Survival imperatives require a functional integration of the lifeworld, which reaches right through the symbolic structures of the lifeworld and therefore cannot be grasped without further ado from the perspective of participants.[135]

In this context Habermas speaks of the "*lifeworld as a system*". To be sure, he says this regarding the *material* reproduction of the lifeworld. Yet, first, this qualifi-cation is irrelevant, since the question is not whether the *symbolic structures* of the lifeworld are functionally integrated, but rather whether the *lifeworld* itself is—and he answers this here in the affirmative. Second, this qualification is also erroneous, since the symbolic reproduction of the lifeworld is also systematically integrated,[136] even apart from the very evident fact that the symbolic reproduction naturally *depends on the material reproduction*, meaning that the systematic inte-gration of the material reproduction is already, based on this fact alone, necessarily always a systematic integration of the symbolic reproduction. Thus, according to Habermas it is only in the exceptional case of non-repressive forms of life that social integration does not occur through latent strategic action—"social integra-tion" not in Habermas's sense, since this is by definition impossible, but in its ordinary sense. But then in real terms social integration *always* occurs via latent strategic action, and given that the reproduction of alleged lifeworlds, such as fam-ily and neighbourhood, is always systematically integrated, this leaves us with two possibilities. Either we *define* private areas of life and public realms as the lifeworld; in which case *the lifeworld*, no less than the system, *is systematically integrated*. Or else we define lifeworlds according to Habermas's criterion, namely, that they are integrated normatively and through mechanisms of consensus, and thus definitely not systematically; in which case *there is no area of society that is the lifeworld*. Then, of course, the system would indeed be uncoupled from the lifeworld, but this is certainly not how Habermas intended his thesis to be understood.

So the theory of the uncoupled lifeworld and system is false, which entails the falsehood of the colonization thesis.

Aside from the fact that the colonization theory is false, it is also not particularly critical, as many authors have pointed out. As Ingebord Maus succinctly puts it:

Habermas's region-specific distinction between system and lifeworld has a purely defensive character. It focuses exclusively on the threat to the lifeworld presented by the direct encroachment from systematic mechanisms from the state and the economy, and is resigned to leaving those areas that are "already" defined as systematically independent...to their own devices.[137]

Habermas is not just to be criticized here for wanting to leave the system largely to its own devices; that he wants to leave the lifeworld to itself is to be criticized no less:

The demands of the student movement, that formal rules and institutions, which up till then had been taken for granted, should be questioned, cannot be simply transferred, in my view, to the lifeworld context in general.[138]

And similarly:

A theory developed in this way [i.e. the theory of communicative action] can no longer start by examining concrete ideals immanent in traditional forms of life. It must orient itself to the range of learning processes that is opened up at a given time by a historically attained level of learning. It must refrain from critically evaluating and normatively ordering totalities, forms of life and cultures, and life-contexts and epochs *as a whole*.[139]

When Habermas's theory, which is untenable anyway, implies such constraints on social criticism, this hardly speaks against the critical evaluation and normative ordering of totalities, but rather against the theory.

We should note, however, that while this uncritical self-limitation on the part of Habermas's critique, particularly with a view to the "lifeworld", tries to pass itself off as a theoretical consequence of any theory "developed in this way", it in fact probably owes more to a pre-theoretical predilection for the status quo, or, we might say, to the philosopher's internal censor. It is true that anyone desiring to teach a society something would be wise to take into account which learning processes are possible in the first place. But it is not the learning capacities of societies that define the limits for *change*. The German society of 1949 was quite differently structured from that in 1944 thanks to the changes *imposed on it* by the Allies, but it is rather doubtful that the Germans were already more enlightened in 1949 than in 1944 or were already committed in 1949 to the new democratic structures. Moreover, even if a thoroughly fascist and racist society were incapable of learning, it fortunately does not follow from this that we may not or cannot *assess the society as a whole critically and normatively*.

And nothing of the sort follows from Habermas's concept (or concepts) of the lifeworld. The formal–pragmatic lifeworld seems to be so defined that it includes only whatever knowledge (whether true or alleged) is not being criticized or discussed *at that particular moment*.[140] But this definition does not stand in the way of a critique of *other* lifeworlds. And as it concerns sociological lifeworlds, one is quite able to criticize *one's own* as well without any difficulties. For even if we conceive the sociological lifeworld as the area of society that is reproduced or integrated through communicative action, this means only that we cannot criticize the formal–pragmatic lifeworld presupposed in every communicative act, that is, in every act of *reproduction*, in this very same act, not that we cannot criticize *that which is reproduced* in this act, the sociological lifeworld. Production and product are not the same, after all. And even if we define not just the formal–pragmatic lifeworld but also (as Habermas seems to do elsewhere[141]) the sociological lifeworld as that knowledge (or that sphere of society) that is not explicitly treated or criticized at that moment, this means only that it is impossible to criticize *everything* about the totality or form of life or culture or epoch in which one lives—since one cannot criticize the lifeworld component of it. It does not, however, mean that one cannot criticize the totality or form of life or culture or epoch in which one lives *as a whole*.

The adoption of *system theory*, on the other hand, does indeed constrain the possibilities for critique. That fact that Habermas *does* adopt it so willingly is a sign that he does not criticize functionalist rationality so much as fall prey to its temptations.[142] Thus he is unable to make his turn to system theory at all plausible. He names a series of reasons why system theory relies on the concept of the lifeworld,[143] but he provides only one reason why system theory is at all necessary:

> The problem of unintended action consequences can, of course, also be treated from the perspective of the lifeworld. In more complex cases, this analytical strategy soon comes up against limitations if it is meant to clarify how aggregated action consequences reciprocally stabilize one another in functional contexts and thus engender integrative effects. Such investigations must be based on a more appropriate model; and of those on offer today, that of system-environment seems to afford the greatest explanatory potential.[144]

Yet we fail to find any actual explanation using systems theory of how exactly the aggregated consequences of action reciprocally stabilize one another, either from Habermas or from any other author—unless, that is, we take a smokescreen of technical-sounding metaphors to be an explanation. This should hardly be surprising, after all, since it is not conceivable how anyone should be able to explain societal processes, such as processes of integration, without recourse to the attitudes, motives and dispositions of actors, thus taking us to the level of action theory. As Alfred Bohnen notes:

> One of the lessons that we can take from the tradition of economic thought is just this: if there are anything like systematic properties of social formations, then the theoretical foundation for their *explanation* are the principles of human action and not the laws of "social psychology". In other words there is no need for any particular system theory sui generis.[145]

Nonetheless, Habermas makes this unnecessary transition to a system theory, and, as mentioned, this has consequences. Thus like Luhmann Habermas thinks:

> On the other hand, the internal dynamics of the capitalist economic system can be preserved only insofar as the accumulation process is uncoupled from orientations to use value [*Gebrauchswertorientierungen*]. The propelling mechanism of the economic system has to be kept as free as possible from lifeworld restrictions as well as from the demands for legitimation directed to the administrative system.[146]

And so Habermas does not hesitate to explain that a "a substantive justification is not only not possible, but is also, from the viewpoint of the lifeworld, meaningless" for "[m]ost areas of economic, commercial, business and administration law". Thus most of these areas—for which law functions *as the medium* according to Habermas—are "relieved of the problem of justification".[147] However, the economic distribution of goods that he had earlier still assigned to the realm of norms and communicative action based on the distinction between work and interaction[148] is in fact systemic to a large extent, that is, steered by market mechanisms and the medium of power,[149] as we see in the case of tariff negotiations. Thus from this and Habermas's system-theoretical premises it would follow that questions of normative assessment do not apply to the distribution of the goods produced. So it is perfectly consistent, if regrettable, that our "critical theorist" in fact entirely abstains from raising such questions—questions of *justice*, after all.

It is all the more regrettable since, contrary to Habermas's decree, one can in fact normatively assess most of the areas of economic, trade, business and administrative law as well as economic distribution. A negative assessment would in turn allow for normative implications regarding the inadequacy of that "body of law whose substance", according to Habermas, also "requires legitimations" (law as institution)—and that generates "law as a medium" and the resulting distribution through "formally correct procedure" in the first place.[150]

Moreover, the antipathy towards a *colonization* of the system by the lifeworld is theoretically consistent, but the antipathy towards a *replacement* of systemic areas by areas of the lifeworld is not. This seems to be clear to Habermas as well, and yet he remarks:

However, I believe for empirical reasons that there is no longer much prospect of the democratic reshaping from within of a differentiated economic system solely by means of worker self-management, in other words by switching its steering from money and organizational power *completely* over to participation.[151]

In a rather strange contrast to his lengthy praise of the lifeworld, nowhere does Habermas seriously discuss even a *partial* switch of the economic area over to participation at any length, let alone endorse it. Yet even aside from this, the rather defensive position he takes here (which he also sees as such[152]) is anything but convincing. For while there may very well be empirical reasons why switching to participation would homogenize a differentiated economic system and lead to a decline in material reproduction, if the lifeworld is as great as Habermas thinks, then its expansion could easily be worth such a decline. Yet Habermas does not even take this into consideration.

He also neglects a further possibility, which is very much open despite his indebtedness to system theory, namely, that of *replacing one system by another* or a *radical reorganization of the system*. Such a reorganization seems a rather obvious suggestion in light of the acute global and national inequalities of distribution and the catastrophic ecological costs of the current system (or systems).[153] But not for Habermas. As mentioned, this is owing not to any theoretical consistency but rather to a basic personal decision and a wilful blindness to certain realities:

Let us give our Marxist heart something of a shock [*Geben wir doch unserem marxistischen Herzen einen Stoß*]: capitalism has been very successful, at least in the area of material reproduction, and it still is. Of course from the beginning it has practised predatory exploitation on an enormous scale of traditional forms of life.[154]

Capitalism certainly has not practised exploitation only using traditional forms of life. Of course, Habermas knows this as well,[155] but he does the best he can to avoid letting this knowledge affect his assessment of the previous history of capitalism, as we can see. And to arrive at the opinion that capitalism has been entirely successful in the area of material reproduction requires a couple of shocks to the head and not just to the heart—namely, it requires remaining so short-sighted as to not see anything beyond the Western industrialized nations.[156] We also have capitalism in the third, fourth and fifth worlds—less successful in material reproduction, but all the more successful for that in marginalization.

Rolf Johannes illustrates how little Habermas's colonization theory has to do with a critical theory of society, as follows:

Where Marx denounced the distress and misery of the global reserve army of industrial labour as a consequence of the capitalist realm of necessity, Habermas, with his concept of the lifeworld, makes the slums into a realm of freedom, while those imprisoned in this realm slowly waste away, under the watchful eyes of the guards of the capitalist world market. In view of the misery in the nations of the so-called third world, our unemployed here at home are still quite happy to see the lifeworldly existence imposed on them "colonized" a little by a subsystem of state administration. If their lifeworld were not "colonized" by unemployment compensation, as in the undeveloped nations, they would not be able to interact with televisions, supermarket cashiers and pin-ball machines.[157]

However, Habermas does not let it bother him that so many authors find his colonization theory conspicuously uncritical for an allegedly critical theory of society. Instead he claims:

The normative criticism which McCarthy, Honneth and Joas make of what they presume are the conclusions to be drawn from my diagnosis of contemporary society proceeds from a counter-model based in praxis philosophy. The latter cannot exist, whether one likes it or not, without adhering to the untenable premise that it must be possible to conceive of the autonomous self-steering of a complex society as self-consciousness on a large scale. This figure of thought does not, however, do justice to the pluralist traits of a decentred society.[158]

Not one of the three authors mentioned assumes this premise,[159] and in fact no one who is exercising a normative critique of Habermas's model is in the least dependent on this premise, whether Habermas likes it or not. Habermas's claim to the contrary is spun from thin air, and he provides no justification for it in the text passage that he refers to in this context.[160] Neither revolution nor non-revolutionary changes aiming beyond the mere protection of the lifeworld assume that a society is self-consciousness on a large scale. This is rather obvious if we consider that there have been radical changes in diverse societies on the initiative of individuals without this premise being fulfilled, in the form of both reforms and revolutions. History can be made, as proven by history itself. Moreover, even if it were not possible to make any real improvement in societal conditions beyond Habermas's questionable and rather non-specific programme to protect the life-world, this would still not be a reason to abstain from critique.[161] Not everything that is necessary is necessarily good. One might expect this to be clear to an alleged critical theorist of society.

3.3.3. The "Discourse Theory of Law and Democracy"

Habermas's book *Between Facts and Norms* aims at providing "contributions to a discourse theory of law and of the democratic constitutional state", as the sub-title suggests,[162] as well as a contribution to their legitimation.

In the following I will begin by presenting the course of Habermas's argumentation in order to then examine it step by step to determine whether it lives up to its claim of contributing to the understanding and legitimation of the democratic constitutional state.

Habermas acknowledges the modern notion that legitimacy can be achieved only through self-legislation.

Members of a legal community must be able to assume that in a free process of political opinion- and will-formation they themselves would also authorize the rules to which they are subject as addressees.[163]

In order to then "decipher, in discourse-theoretic terms, the motif of self-legislation"[164] he turns to his discourse principle D, which reads:

Just those action norms are valid to which all possibly affected persons could agree as participants in rational discourses.[165]

He then has this principle branch out into a moral principle and a democratic principle according to its application, i.e. according to the type of norms at issue.[166] The democratic principle states

that only those statutes may claim legitimacy that can meet with the assent (*Zustimmung*) of all citizens in a discursive process of legislation that in turn has been legally constituted.[167]

Moreover, this democratic principle, Habermas maintains, "must also *steer the production of the legal medium itself*".[168] Thus, seemingly in accordance with radical democracy, Habermas concludes:

Consequently, the sought-for internal relation between popular sovereignty and human rights consists in the fact that the system of rights states precisely the conditions under which the forms of communication necessary for the genesis of politically autonomous law can be legally institutionalized.[169]

This formulation might be thought to be misleading.[170] After all, Habermas says that the conditions of communication are institutionalized "*through* a system of rights",[171] which would lead one to conclude that the system of (human) rights *is*, legally speaking, the institutionalization of these conditions of communication. Elsewhere, however, it becomes clear that "the sought-for internal relation" is only *one* sort of "internal relation" for Habermas,[172] namely, the one relation that is relevant for basic *political* rights above all, whereas certain other human rights, namely, the "classical human rights [*klassischen Freiheitsrechte*, that is, rights to liberty]", are in fact, in his opinion, a *precondition* for the legal institutionalization of "the forms of communication necessary for the genesis of legitimate law".[173]

Of course, in our legislative processes not everything—in fact, *nothing*—meets with the assent of all citizens in a discursive process of legislation. Habermas tries to give this fact a discourse- and consensus-theoretical reinterpretation; thus he concedes that compromises can also be legitimate, while emphasizing that these already presuppose the discourse principle.

...for the procedural conditions under which actual compromises enjoy the presumption of fairness must be justified in moral discourses. Moreover, bargaining first becomes permissible and necessary when only particular—and no generalizable—interests are involved, something that again can be tested only in moral discourses.[174]

The principle of *majority rule* in courts, parliaments or self-managing bodies, however—another example of a lack of unanimous assent—is for Habermas more than just a procedure for forming compromises. It is not merely justified by D; rather, D is inscribed into this principle as its own self-understanding and as something like its regulative principle:

Majority rule retains an internal relation to the search for truth inasmuch as the decision reached by the majority only represents a caesura in an ongoing discussion; the decision records, so to speak, the interim result of a discursive opinion-forming process. To be sure, in that case the majority decision must be premised on a competent discussion of the disputed issues, that is, a discussion conducted according to the communicative presuppositions of a corresponding discourse.[175]

If the premise is correct, this justifies the "*presumption* that fallible decisions are right"[176] that are arrived at in this manner; or, to use a formulation favoured by Habermas, that the decisions enjoy "the presumption of being reasonable".[177] In the light of this, Habermas then interprets the idea of self-legislation as follows:

...the discourse theory of democracy corresponds to the image of a decentered society, albeit a society in which the political public sphere has been differentiated as an arena for the perception, identification, and treatment of problems affecting the whole of society. Once one gives up the philosophy of the subject, one needs neither to concentrate sovereignty concretely in the people nor to banish it in anonymous constitutional structures and powers. The "self" of the self-organizing legal community disappears in the subjectless forms of communication that regulate the flow of discursive opinion- and will-formation in such a way that their fallible results enjoy the presumption of being reasonable. This is not to denounce the intuition connected with the idea of popular sovereignty but to interpret it intersubjectively.[178]

Habermas does see that the premise of competent discursive decision-making is problematic:

The sociological enlightenment seems to recommend a disillusioning, if not downright cynical, view of the political process. It primarily focuses our attention on places where normatively "illegitimate" power forces its way into the constitutionally regulated circulation of power[179]

such as the pressure of interest groups exercised beyond the hearing of public discourse. Habermas contrasts this with a "reconstructive sociology of democracy"[180] that, unlike the sociological enlightenment, focuses on those mechanisms that allegedly *run counter* to this imposition of illegitimate power. Thus he says of the constitutional state:

Within the framework of the constitutional state, the civic practice of self-legislation assumes an institutionally differentiated form. The idea of the rule of law sets in motion a spiralling self-application of law, which is supposed to bring the internally unavoidable supposition of political autonomy to bear against the facticity of legally uncontrolled social power that penetrates law *from the outside*. The development of the constitutional state can be understood as an open sequence of experience-guided precautionary measures against the overpowering of the legal system by illegitimate power relations that contradict its normative self-understanding.[181]

And this bringing-to-bear of suppositions, according to Habermas, functions well enough to safeguard legitimacy, that is, democracy, such that we can work towards a "more extensive democratization"[182] rather than, say, democratization itself.

A series of objections can be raised against Habermas's argumentation.

1. The principle D is at the foundation of Habermas's argument. However, as a legitimizing foundation it is unacceptable. Habermas has never justified this principle, for one thing; moreover, only under entirely unrealistic presuppositions does it not lead to absurd, disastrous consequences. In any case it is untenable. We can recall that:

(a) According to Habermas it can be derived from the so-called presuppositions of argumentation or rules of discourse

that a contested norm cannot meet with the consent of the participants in a practical discourse unless (U) holds, that is,

Unless all affected can *freely* accept the consequences and the side effects that the *general* observance of a controversial norm can be expected to have for the satisfaction of the interests of *each individual*.[183]

And we can allegedly derive D from this, which, incidentally, would be a transition from is to ought. To this day Habermas has yet to carry out either of these two derivations, as we have seen, and other authors that he turns to for help in this regard have failed at the job. There is no derivation of U or D.[184] Thus Habermas, who believes that we shoulder a justificatory duty with every assertion, has still not lived up to his own responsibility concerning an allegedly possible non-circular derivation of U or D. A mere proclamation of the principle, however, is not suited to serve as the philosophical basis of legitimation for a secular state.

(b) Even if we were to assume the correctness of D, it would only follow that there is, quite simply, *no legitimation at all*, and thus no legitimate norms or laws. For there cannot possibly be consensus on practical and moral questions in a discourse with all of humanity or even just with all (the millions of) one's fellow citizens of a state. Habermas has nothing to say to this objection. His persistent clinging to D and to the possibility of consensus is thus irrational and dogmatic.[185]

(c) Even if we assumed the practical feasibility of consensus, Habermas as a fallibilist would have to concede that he does not know with absolute *certainty* whether this or that norm can find consensus in practical discourse. Thus the following statement should present Habermas with a problem:

If it *were* the case (and we can never know for certain) that even just *one* of the affected (e.g. a child molester, a rapist, a dictator) could not consent as a participant in rational discourses to the norms "you should not molest children", "you should not rape", "you should respect human rights", *then these norms, it is true, could not claim any validity*. And then nothing could be said against child molestation, rape, or violations of human rights, at least not from a moral standpoint.

If Habermas contests this statement, he contests the correctness of his own theory. If he agrees to the statement, however, he places his own theory in a rather unfavourable light.

The principle of discourse D is absurd, and its absurdity carries over to every legitimation project that is naïve or dogmatic enough to choose to found itself upon D.

2. Even if we were to assume for now that D were correct, the Habermasian principle of democracy that emerges from this would still, contrary to its claim, have nothing to do with either autonomy or democracy.[186] According to the democratic principle, those laws are legitimate that the members of the legal community *could* consent to under certain specific conditions. Let us assume that under the ideal conditions of a practical discourse I could consent to a certain norm N. But if I do *not*, in reality, consent to this norm, and it is nonetheless imposed on me by the state under the threat of force, then of course we cannot say that I am acting autonomously in complying with the norm (no matter how Kant might have seen this, by the way). Whoever acts under a compulsion that is not self-imposed is not acting autonomously.

The same holds for democracy. It is a *necessary* condition for democracy understood as self-legislation that the people obey laws they *have given* themselves, not laws that they merely *would have given* themselves under certain conditions, no matter what conditions we may dream up.

3. Habermas's splitting up of the discourse principle is full of confusions, and contradicts his other statements on the moral principle and the discourse principle. In *Between Facts and Norms* Habermas writes:

With moral questions, humanity or a presupposed republic of world citizens constitutes the reference system for justifying regulations that lie in the equal interest of all. In principle, the decisive reasons must be acceptable to each and everyone. With ethical-political questions, the form of life of the political community that is "in each case our own" constitutes the reference system for justifying decisions that are supposed to express an authentic,

collective self-understanding. In principle, the decisive reasons must be acceptable to all members sharing "our" traditions and strong evaluations.[187]
This leads Habermas to his "democratic principle", according to which

only those statutes may claim legitimacy that can meet with the assent (*Zustimmung*) of all citizens in a discursive process of legislation that in turn has been legally constituted.[188]

This raises a whole series of questions that, if I am correct, have thus far never been asked. Habermas has declared again and again with the greatest emphasis— although, of course, without any rational justification for it—that "a contested norm cannot meet with the consent of the participants in a practical discourse", and hence in any process (such as a legislative process) concerned to determine "whether norms of action ought to be adopted", "unless (U) holds".[189] And in a text published four years after *Between Facts and Norms*, he once more says quite clearly:

A norm is valid IF AND ONLY IF the foreseeable consequences and side effects of its general observance for the interests and value-orientations of *each individual* could be *jointly* accepted by *all* concerned without coercion.[190]

If the "only" in Habermas's democratic principle is meant in the sense of the bi-conditional "if and only if", as the "only" in Habermas's various formulations of U always has been—and this is how we have to read it if "with ethical-political questions, the form of life of the political community that is 'in each case our own' constitutes the reference system for *justifying* decisions"[191] rather than merely constituting the reference system for their *rejection*—then the democratic principle contradicts the principle U. For even if a norm finds the consent of all citizens in a discursive process of legislation, this is still a far cry from it finding the consent of all *concerned* as participants in a practical discourse. Yet Habermas wants to rule out this kind of contradiction, since for him "[v]alid legal norms...harmonize with moral norms".[192] But then the democratic principle no longer states the conditions of legitimacy for legal norms, but instead merely a sufficient condition of their illegitimacy.
On the other hand, one of the central motifs in *Between Facts and Norms* is that Habermas by no means wishes to *conflate* valid legal norms with moral norms.

Valid legal norms indeed harmonize with moral norms, but they are "legitimate" in the sense that they additionally express an authentic self-understanding of the legal community, the fair consideration of the values and interests distributed in it, and the purposive-rational choice of strategies and means in the pursuit of policies.[193]

Yet this criterion also contradicts the principle U, which, as Habermas ceaselessly assures us, is implicitly recognized by the participants in practical discourses concerned with the adoption of norms—and this is, after all, what legislative discourses among citizens are concerned with—and which states, as we have just had occasion to recall, that norms are valid *if and only if* they satisfy the conditions of validity named in U. They do not have to fulfil any *further* conditions, such as that of expressing an "authentic self-understanding" of a certain segment of the discourse participants. Thus, if the principle U is correct, then valid legal norms do coincide with moral norms. Habermas has to make a decision in favour of either his ideas on the legitimacy of legal norms or his adherence to U—he cannot favour both.

On the other hand, it is also not clear *to what extent* a "fair consideration of the values and interests…and the purposive-rational choice of strategies and means" is supposed to take us beyond the conditions of validity stated in U. His formulation of U in *The Inclusion of the Other*, after all, to quote it again, reads:

A norm is valid IF AND ONLY IF the foreseeable consequences and side effects of its general observance for the interests and value-orientations of *each individual* could be *jointly* accepted by *all* concerned without coercion.[194]

Even if he had not included mention of value orientations here, a person's *interests* alone include those of maintaining or honouring certain values—interests can relate to anything. And how do matters stand with the purposively rational choice of strategies and means? The enactment of a legal norm that is *not* purposively rational for one or more of the discourse participants, that is, of a legal norm that after a deliberative weighing of the goals, means and side effects is *not* in the interest of one or more discourse participants, is thus clearly not in everyone's interest (as far as it can be anticipated) and so does not fulfil the conditions of validity stated in U. In other words, Habermas suggests that there are conditions of legitimacy for legal norms that extend beyond their morality, but de facto he fails to name any.

But let us assume for now, in contradiction to U, that legitimate legal norms have to do more than just fulfil the condition U. This, however, would mean that legal norms are in fact more exacting than moral norms. This would lead to the following problem:

To introduce such a discourse principle already presupposes that practical questions can be judged impartially and decided rationally. This is not a trivial supposition; its justification is incumbent on a theory of argumentation, which I will sketch provisionally in the next chapter. This investigation leads one to distinguish various types of discourse (and their corresponding sorts of reasons) according to the logic of the question at issue; it also leads to a distinction between discourse and procedurally regulated bargaining. Specifically, one must show for each type which rules would allow pragmatic, ethical, and moral questions to be answered.[195]

But in fact neither in his treatise "On the Pragmatic, the Ethical, and the Moral Employments of Practical Reason"[196] that he refers to here, nor in the "next chapter", does he explain which rules would allow ethical questions to be answered. Based on his "theory construction"—one of Habermas's favourite expressions— he would have to name a "rule of argumentation" for ethical discourses analogous to U, and then propose a programme of justification for it. And then he would have to actually carry out this programme. Habermas in fact neglects to mention either any justification or programme of justification or the required rule itself. On the other hand, as we will see in greater detail below, he upholds the "premise of a single right answer" for ethical and political discourses as well, that is, he assumes that the said "non-trivial assumption" is a given fact. In light of the deficits in his theory construction and in light of the justificatory deficits, this assumption is dogmatic.

Things do not look any better for the relation between the democratic principle and the discourse principle D than they do for that between the democratic principle and U. If the "only" in the democratic principle is meant in the sense of the bi-conditional "if and only if", then it *contradicts* D. If, however, "only" is just to be read as signifying a necessary condition, then it is in fact nothing more than a component part of the validity conditions of D. But in this case there would be no reason whatsoever why the democratic principle should establish "a procedure of legitimate lawmaking" and steer "*the production of the legal medium*"[197] as Habermas requires—and as he quite obviously requires in line with the "if and only if" reading. Thus, if this "only" is to be read literally the democratic principle cannot establish any procedure of legitimate lawmaking, since it does not name any sufficient conditions but only necessary conditions that could, of course, also be fulfilled by illegitimate legislative procedures. And for this reason we can hardly entrust the job of steering the production of the legal medium to the democratic principle, since it could easily steer us off a cliff. The possibility that there is no sufficient institutional accounting for the legitimacy conditions of *morality* in the production of the legal medium presents us with just such a cliff. And it is precisely off this cliff that Habermas steers. For in his explanations of how "the discourse principle is to be implemented as the democratic principle with the help of equal communicative and participatory rights",[198] this same philosopher who warns *others* that "[t]heory-formation must avoid the 'territorial trap'",[199] lists fundamental rights only of the *members of the legal community* and *citizens*[200]—in a perfect fit with his formulation of the democratic principle, which mentions only citizens. But this means that *the discourse principle cannot be implemented as the Habermasian democratic principle*. The *discourse principle*, after all, requires a consideration of *all affected*. However, those affected by the decisions of members of the German legal community about political asylum or laws governing weapons exports or restricting agricultural imports include not just the members of the German legal community themselves but those non-German people whose life prospects might look significantly more bleak thanks to these decisions. Thus, as long as one wishes to implement the discourse principle with the aid of equal rights to communication and participation, these legal rights cannot be reserved solely for "all members sharing 'our' traditions and strong evaluations"[201]—instead they have to extend to *all* of the affected. Yet Habermas does not allow for this possibility. Clearly, then, he does not owe his democratic principle to the "interpenetration of the discourse principle and the legal form",[202] but rather—and this might be the true meaning of the term *constitutional patriotism*—to the interpenetrations of the legal form and nationalism.

Thus we can conclude that in splitting up the discourse principle, in distinguishing between legitimate legal and moral norms and in imagining that the democratic principle owes its existence to the interpenetration of the legal form and the discourse principle, Habermas entangles himself in a whole series of contradictions that lead him only into further contradictions, no matter how we try to resolve them. It is not as if his arguments were merely premature or insufficiently developed; they are simply and irredeemably inconsistent. Habermas's *Between Facts and Norms* does not "decipher, in discourse-theoretic terms, the motif of self-legislation"; on the contrary, the ideas presented in it *contradict* the discourse principle. Moreover, the contradictions and confusions discussed here suggest in rather strong terms that Habermas did not, in point of fact, try to make the discourse principle fruitful for questions of legal, political and democratic theory through painstaking thought. Rather, it is hard not to feel that he did just the opposite: he uncritically accepted the status quo in order to then merely drape the legitimating mantle of the discourse principle over them. However, it does not fit.

4. Habermas claims to have demonstrated an internal connection between the sovereignty of the people and human rights. Above we distinguished between the two different sorts of connection that Habermas has in mind. One "consists in this: human rights institutionalize the communicative conditions for a reasonable political will-formation". However, Habermas himself concedes:

To be sure, this claim is immediately plausible only for political rights, that is, the rights of communication and participation; it is not so obvious for the classical human rights that guarantee the citizen's private autonomy.

Yet he answers to this objection as follows:

At the same time, we must not forget that the medium through which citizens exercise their political autonomy is not a matter of choice. Citizens participate in legislation only as *legal* subjects; it is no longer in their power to decide which language they will make use of. Hence the legal code as such must already be available before the communicative presuppositions of a discursive will-formation can be institutionalized in the form of civil rights. To establish this legal code, however, it is necessary to create the status of legal persons who as bearers of individual rights belong to a voluntary association of citizens and can, when necessary, effectively claim their rights.[203]

The point and the relevance of these remarks are not entirely clear. Certainly the "brick code" (the *concept* "brick", for example) has to be available to me in order for me to enter into a discussion about bricks—but I do not need bricks. Likewise, the legal *code*, the *language* of law, is not the *law* itself. One can *speak* the language of legal rights and even participate in legislative processes without *having* legal rights, which are the issue here. And more generally, one takes part in legislation first and foremost as a legislator; it is not necessary to be a legal subject. If Habermas wants to actually claim that the *existence* of legal human rights is a *presupposition* of legislation, then he would have to explain how he plans to escape the rather obvious infinite regress at work here—since legal rights are created in an act of legislation. It seems rather evident that he will not be able to answer this question.

It takes a more concrete and slightly more plausible turn when Habermas, four sentences after the passage just quoted, makes the following remark:

The internal relation between democracy and the rule of law consists in this: on the one hand, citizens can make appropriate use of their public autonomy only if, on the basis of their equally protected private autonomy, they are sufficiently independent; on the other hand, they can realize equality in the enjoyment of their private autonomy only if they make appropriate use of their political autonomy as citizens.[204]

Yet this is hardly a conclusion from his remarks about the "legal code". Instead private autonomy appears here once again as the mere institutionalization of the above-mentioned conditions of communication, and not as a *presupposition* of this institutionalization. Thus we can once more trot out the old objection: the classical rights of freedom are not necessary for the exercise of public autonomy. Certainly it implies the collapse of public autonomy when the citizens of a state are threatened with torture and imprisonment—that is, with a massive restriction of their private autonomy—should they cast a certain vote. However, this only proves that it is necessary to prevent *this sort* of instrumentalization of the restriction of private autonomy, namely, its instrumentalization for the purpose of restricting or even destroying public autonomy. Yet this prevention would occur, again, within the framework of the right to *public* autonomy. The prohibitions, however, on torture, imprisonment, invasions of private life, forced labour, dispossession, etc., that are inscribed in the Universal Declaration of Human Rights go beyond this. Thus human rights encompass *more* than the mere institutionalization of the "forms of communication necessary for the genesis of legitimate law" and the preconditions of this instrumentalization.

This unsolvable problem is compounded by the fact that Habermas seems to entirely disregard his own democratic principle here, which pertains to *counterfactual* consent. It is to this counterfactual consent that human rights must have an internal relation in Habermas's construction, one would think. Do they?

If we assume—as Habermas does—that many millions, even billions of people can reach a consensus on moral and practical questions, why should they not be able to reach a consensus to abolish freedom of speech? And if discursive majority decisions enjoy the presumption of being reasonable, this should also hold for discursive majority decisions to abolish discursivity. This by no means compromises the legitimacy of laws, even in the future, *after* abolishing discursivity, since Habermas's democratic principle does not require members of the legal community to actually, *in point of fact*, assent in discourse to the laws—it requires only that they *would* assent *if* they were to have such a discourse. Thus Habermas's democratic principle does not require the institutionalization of human rights.

Besides, the Habermasian assumption is false. *No one* would ever consent to a law in an ideal discourse or in the corresponding "legally constituted" discourse, no matter which law, including the law to abolish human rights—at least not when we are talking about millions of people. This, however, does not solve the problem of reconciling human rights and popular sovereignty. Instead we find that the democratic principle rules out there being even *one* legitimate law. Thus, our constitutional principles and human rights would also be illegitimate.

5. There is a third aspect in which Habermas's theory is incompatible with human rights. It is not just that D and the democratic principle rule out the legitimacy of human rights and that, even if these were legitimate, their abolition could enjoy the presumption of reasonableness due to the Habermasian interpretation of majority rule; as well, Habermas's theory implies the unreasonableness of *criticizing* violations of human rights.

According to Habermas, in arguing we have to suppose certain conditions to be "*sufficiently fulfilled*"; and if we do not, then supposedly we involve ourselves in "performative self-contradictions". The conditions we necessarily presuppose include it not being the case that "certain individuals are not allowed to participate, issues or contributions are suppressed, agreement or disagreement is manipulated by insinuations or by threat of sanctions, and the like."[205] This means, as Habermas himself emphasizes, that these conditions are largely identical to human rights. However, it would then follow that whoever *disputes* that human rights are sufficiently fulfilled, that freedom of speech is sufficiently respected, that yes/no positions are not suppressed or enforced too much by threat of sanction, *becomes entangled in performative self-contradictions.* In other words, it would, for instance, be impossible to criticize a terror regime for being a terror regime without performative self-contradiction—which for Habermas, as we know, means that it would be impossible to *rationally* criticize it as a terror regime. This is a very peculiar consequence for a "critical theory of society".[206]

6. Habermas's reinterpretation of majority rule in terms of the consensus theory is not just "[a]t first glance...not very plausible", as he says.[207]

Habermas explains that competent decisions made discursively by a majority "enjoy the presumption of being reasonable".[208] Yet he also writes that this does not mean "that the minority would have to accept the content of the outcome as rational and therefore would have to change their beliefs".[209] But Habermas cannot have it both ways. For if the minority does *not* have to accept the content of the outcome as rational or even as presumably rational, then it can reject it as *irrational*—and, incidentally, it in fact does just this most of the time, and often rightly so—and then the discursive decision of the majority does *not* enjoy the presumption of being reasonable *for the minority*. But then this decision cannot in and of itself, so to speak, enjoy the presumption of reasonableness, that is, the presumption cannot be intersubjectively or absolutely justified. For if it could, then any contrary conviction or even just any contrary supposition on the part of the minority would be *unjustified*, thus *irrational*—contrary to Habermas's intentions.

Thus the following claim, which is decisive for his "proceduralist conception of law", is *false*:

Majority rule owes its legitimating force to what Rawls calls an "imperfect" but "pure" procedural rationality. It is imperfect because the democratic process is established so as to *justify the presumption* of a rational outcome without being able to *guarantee* the outcome *is* right. On the other hand, it is also a case of procedural justice, because in the democratic process no criteria of rightness *independent* of the procedure are available; the correctness of decisions depends solely on the fact that the procedure has actually been carried out.[210]

If there were no other criteria of rightness *independent* of the majority decision produced by a "democratic process", then a *rational* rejection of a majority decision would be entirely impossible, and a sustained opposition would be *irrational* per se—which, incidentally, would also mean ultimately that the minority faction should rationally adopt the programme of the victors. It should be quite clear how incorrect the "proceduralist paradigm" of discourse theory is. In fact, in his debate with Peters[211] Habermas admits that "substantive reasons are what convince us that an outcome is right", and yet he argues that "the soundness of these reasons can be *demonstrated* only in real processes of argumentation, namely in defense against every objection that is actually raised."[212] I have already shown at great length that one can also arrive at justified convictions without discourse.[213] Moreover, here the issue depends on how we interpret the word "demonstrate." If Habermas means to argue that the soundness of arguments is demonstrated by their "confirmation" in a *majority decision*, then we are again faced with the same, entirely counter-intuitive result that one cannot rationally hold a democratically produced majority decision to be irrational or false. If, however, Habermas does *not* mean that the soundness of arguments can be demonstrated only by the majority decision, then this only confirms the finding that the democratically applied majority rule is *not* a "pure" procedure.

Moreover, Habermas's cognitivist interpretation of the rationality of laws is to be rejected. Parties assent to a law because they hold it to be rational *for them* to assent to the law—purposively rational, that is. They do not have to feel that it is rational for other parties with different interests. And even if they did feel this way, they could (and normally will) understand this rationality in the sense of the *purposive rationality of the assent* to the law, not in the sense of its *cognitive rightness*.

In a response to McCarthy, who also argues against Habermas's premise of "a single right answer"[214]—although without mentioning purposive rationality as an alternative—Habermas writes that "two things must be explained: (i) why the premise of a single right answer is at all necessary; and (ii) how one can, when necessary, reconcile this premise with the overwhelming evidence of persistent dissensus."[215] Despite this announcement, we find nothing in Habermas's response that would clarify this second question, except his remark that "we have to work as if with a bad bill of exchange for the future" [*wie mit einem ungedeckten Wechsel auf die Zukunft*].[216] Well, the bill is indeed bad, and in light of the "overwhelming evidence of persistent dissensus" and the fact that even Habermas considers the presumption that ethical and political discourses could be impartially judged and rationally decided to be "not a trivial supposition" and thus to be something that needs to be clarified in a "theory of argumentation"[217] (although as could be expected he still owes us this clarification[218]),the expectation that the bill will be redeemable in the future is about as rational as the hope of some of our contemporaries to see their bill for our salvation redeemed by the intervention of aliens (and anyway, how is a *future* consensus in practical questions imagined to be at all binding in the *present*?). Moreover, one might very well ask why we should accept a *bad* bill in a *justificatory* discourse of political philosophy.[219] It almost seems as if Habermas, who otherwise cannot castigate decisionist ethics enough, recommends to us an irrational act of faith here.

Apparently with this act of faith he hopes to escape the existential fear of the illegitimacy of allegedly democratically legitimated societies. For he answers the question "why the premise of a single right answer is at all necessary" by saying that "given McCarthy's premises, he cannot explain how democratic legitimacy is even possible."[220] This would show only the *necessity* of the premises at issue if it were necessary to explain how democratic legitimacy is at all possible. But why is this "necessary"? And *for whom*?

Yet another question arises, namely, *why* this explanation that is allegedly so necessary is impossible under McCarthy's premises. If we consult the Habermasian text, it would seem that in Habermas's opinion the explanation is impossible under McCarthy's premises because it is supposedly possible only under the Habermasian premise of the single right answer.[221] But as this is just what McCarthy disputes, Habermas's response turns out to be dogmatic and circular.

Moreover, the principle "what must not be, cannot be" is quite dubious. That is, even if the premise of the single right answer were "necessary" for any-thing—and certainly *something* can be found for which it is necessary, just as the possibilities of time travel and telepathic communication with parrots are neces-sary for *something*—this does not allow us to infer its *correctness*. Its *correctness* follows only if we make the further assumption that democratic legitimacy *is*, in fact, possible. And Habermas seeks to justify this premise with recourse to the premise of the single right answer—thus once more running headlong into a circle.

As matters stand, then, Habermas's cognitivist reinterpretation of majority rule in accordance with his discourse and consensus theory is untenable. It entirely ignores the political processes in modern pluralistic democracies and the self-understanding of the actors involved. Contrary to his claim[222] Habermas fails to reconstruct the democratic process; he *projects* his prefabricated and unacceptable constructs on it.

7. Habermas's reinterpretation of majority rule in terms of consensus theory is not just untenable as a theory of democracy; if taken seriously it would *actually undermine* democracy itself.

Habermas argues that competent discursive majority decisions "enjoy the pre-sumption of being reasonable".[223] However, he also emphasizes that "the outnum-bered minority give their consent to the empowerment of the majority only with the proviso that they themselves retain the opportunity in the future of winning over the majority with better arguments."[224] But how is this supposed to work? If the majority shares Habermas's opinion that majority decisions made compe-tently in this way enjoy the presumption of reasonableness per se, that is, that the majority decision is a criterion of reasonableness that at the same time *replaces* the criterial function of the individual reasons and arguments (and this is necessary if the majority rule is to be an example of *pure* rational procedure, as Habermas intends),[225] why should the majority then have to take the individual reasons into consideration again in the future after they have *already* been presented?[226] This would be superfluous and a waste of time. Thus from the outset minority opinions would no longer have any chance of being seriously heard. The prospect of "winning over the majority" is an illusion in this context. Every criticism would have one chance and one chance only; afterwards it would tail off unheard.

Now here one might respond that a community that thinks in this way would no longer be making decisions competently, as the theory more or less demands. In other words, this sort of community would no longer be an instance of the theory in application, and thus the example could not be used against the theory. Yet this ignores the *pragmatic* level of the critique, namely, the point that the theory itself turns against the community. If a community were to actually accept Habermas's theory, then this community would necessarily cease to function in the terms of this theory (if it ever had), for the reasons just mentioned. Not only does this theory have rather dubious political consequences, since its recognition negates its practice, but it is also pragmatically self-contradictory.

It is not just the idea of the pure procedural rationality of the majority principle that is destructive; the cognitivist interpretation of the majority principle is destructive, too. After all, the rationality of laws is for Habermas the same as their intersubjective rightness. This means, however, that if the majority is entitled to the presumption of reasonableness of a law, then they are also entitled to assume that this law not only expresses the interests of the *majority* but is also *right* plain and simple, and that its general observance is *also* in the interests of the *minority*. Why then should the majority still try to provide some way for the minority to offset the majority's preponderance of influence? This question points not to any self-contradiction on the part of the theory, but only to the fact that Habermas's purportedly "critical" theory ideologically transfigures the interests of the majority into interests that the majority are conveniently entitled to assume are *general* interests—even if we were to let go the idea of the pure procedural justice (and thus the "deciphering in discourse-theoretical terms" along with it). Thus, according to Habermas the will of the majority is rationally entitled to see itself as the general will, and, to put it in unmistakeably clear terms, from here it is a slippery slope to the opinion that the will of the *Führer* can see itself as the general will. This should not be taken to mean that both opinions are equally bad, but that *both* contradict what one would normally expect from a pluralistic democracy, that is, a certain *allowance* for the interests of minorities in many majority decisions, a certain *readiness to compromise*.[227] Due to his cognitivist prejudices, however, Habermas sets up a *contrast* between compromises and majority decisions in democratic processes.[228] Yet many majority decisions represent *intermediary forms* between direct realizations of the "uncompromised" majority will and negotiated compromises. It is not at all as Habermas imagines, that the minority "[f]or the time being…can live with the majority opinion as binding on their conduct insofar as the democratic process gives them the possibility of continuing or recommencing the interrupted discussion and shifting the majority by offering (putatively) better arguments".[229] Rather, they can live with it only when they do not feel entirely disregarded by the majority decision and when its effects still seem acceptable to them in consideration of all the circumstances, including the prospect of belonging to the majority in other decisions (and expecting then the acceptance of the minority). This condition is clearly not fulfilled merely by virtue of the fact that the minority might be able to overturn the decision someday through attaining a majority. And a majority that adopts Habermasian cognitivism cannot be expected to make any headway towards fulfilling this condition.

8. Moreover, *the very idea of self-legislation* entirely ignores the reality and the normative content of modern pluralistic democracies, even of democracies per se. This becomes particularly clear when we look at the ultimate results of the "deciphering in discourse-theoretical terms" of this idea. Let us review the idea of self-legislation:

Members of a legal community must be permitted to assume [*müssen unterstellen dürfen*] that in a free process of political opinion- and will-formation they themselves would also authorize the rules to which they are subject as addressees.[230]

And the "deciphering in discourse-theoretical terms" reads:

The "self" of the self-organizing legal community disappears in the subjectless forms of communication that regulate the flow of discursive opinion- and will-formation in such a way that their fallible results enjoy the presumption of being reasonable. This is not to denounce the intuition connected with the idea of popular sovereignty but to interpret it intersubjectively.[231]

This is untenable. One could just as easily say that a "democracy of the *Führer*" does not denounce the idea of self-legislation so much as interpret it fascistically. Both of these decipherings, the Habermasian and the Schmittian, are unfounded. The necessity expressed in the words "must be permitted to assume" is certainly not meant as a moral or a legal necessity. Even under a dictatorship it is not legally forbidden for the addressees of laws to believe that they would have authorized those laws themselves in a free process of political opinion- and will-formation. In fact it is quite welcome; this is what propaganda ministers of dictatorial states dream of. And this necessity cannot be meant in a moral sense, for quite a few reasons, including the fact that Habermas finds the "subordination of thought to the imperatives of morality" to be "paradoxical".[232] So here "must be permitted to assume" can only mean "must *rationally* be able to assume." Yet the members of a minority that have *not* freely assented to a law, since they find it to be an outright bad law, cannot possibly at the same time assume that they would have authorized the law themselves in a free process of political opinion- and will-formation. It is impossible to seriously think—except, perhaps, schizophrenically: "I have not assented to this law, since it is bad and foolish and not in my interest in the slightest. But if I had taken part in a free process of political opinion- and will-formation, I would have assented to this law, although it is bad and foolish and not in my interest." This way of thinking is clearly *not* rational, and thus majorities overruled by the *Führer* on a point of legislation, and minorities overruled by a majority, do not have to "be permitted to assume" and *cannot* rationally assume that they would have authorized the law themselves. They *know* that they *have* in fact not authorized it—and they assume that they would not have authorized it. The *self* of the members of the legal community is the self of these members, and not the self of the *Führer* or the self of subjectless forms of communication. Habermas's "deciphering" denounces the idea of self-legislation.

The fact that minorities overruled by majorities cannot see themselves as the authors of the laws passed against their will does not, of course, imply that there cannot be any democratic legitimacy. Rather it means that, if we feel that we have to explain democratic legitimacy, we have to explain it differently. There are well-known attempts to do just that. However, the idea of self-legislation, the idea that the addressees of a law have to be able to see themselves as its authors, is in any case a *construct* and is useless and unnecessary for pluralistic mass democracies (and not just for these). In resorting to this thoroughly ideological fiction of the eighteenth century, Habermas necessarily fails to do justice to the democratic process either descriptively or normatively.

9. Another of Habermas's suppositions that flies in the face of reality and would have disastrous consequences is his idea that "the internally unavoidable supposition of political autonomy" is brought "to bear against the facticity of legally uncontrolled social power that penetrates law *from the outside*", thus generating "precautionary measures against the overpowering of the legal system by illegitimate power relations that contradict its normative self-understanding".[233]

The claim that the *supposition* of political autonomy above all is to accomplish all this turns everything on its head. To *suppose* that no one sells bad used cars, that people offering commodities futures on the telephone speak only the truth, that the legal system is autonomous, and that the members of parliament are all on our side would not be quite rational and would lead to a couple of nasty surprises. The precautions Habermas speaks of arise, if at all, not from the *supposition* of the autonomy of the legal system but rather from *doubting* that autonomy. Moreover, for just this reason a *realistic and empirical* sociology should be able to do much more to shore up democracy and the autonomy of the legal system than Habermas's "reconstructive" sociology.

10. How, then, do matters stand with the effectiveness of these precautions?

Habermas mentions the public sphere as an ultimately decisive bastion of legitimacy. However, it is not at all clear how the public sphere should be able to so stem the tide of the invasive illegitimate power that a discursive decision can be made that is at least sufficiently competent. After all, as Habermas correctly notes: "No doubt...[the] assumption of an unsubverted [*nicht-vermachteten*, that is, unsubverted by illegitimate power effects] political public sphere is unrealistic."[234] Yet according to Habermas's own model the mere fact of a subversion of the communicative situation already violates the requirements of a competent discourse. Moreover, public spheres are not infrequently taken over by precisely the illegitimate power that they are supposed to repel. So we cannot expect any help from this quarter.

To be sure, I do believe, along with Habermas, that the vision of an "unsub-verted" public sphere [*nicht-vermachtete*, that is, not influenced by power—since this is impossible, I would prefer: educated, informed, open-minded, interested, and eagerly debating] "is not utopian in a bad sense."[235] But our concern here is with the legitimacy of the present society and not that of some future society.

Habermas does admit that "one will be rather cautious in estimating the chances of civil society having an influence on the political system. To be sure, this estimate pertains only to a *public sphere at rest*. In periods of mobilization, the ... balance of power between civil society and the political system ... shifts."[236] Thus Habermas points to civil disobedience and defends it as the "highest rung in the escalation of sub-institutional protest movements".[237] On the assumption for now that civil dis-obedience or other forms of "public unrest", such as demonstrations, actually can succeed in bringing about the competent discursive character of the majority deci-sions made thereafter, what about the other decisions? We do not find ourselves in a state of perpetual civil disobedience or even sufficient public unrest; thus all other decisions—including singularly important ones such as amendments to the constitution—would still be unable to enjoy the "presumption of being reason-able" and the claim to legitimacy.

It is a doubtful sort of democracy that can be legitimate only when we refuse to obey it.

11. To make matters worse, we also have to cast doubt on our assumption that civil disobedience can ensure a competent discursive character to the deci-sions made in response. In fact, when civil disobedience has any effectiveness it seems to succeed not so much by repelling illegitimate power and thus allow-ing the "forceless force of the better argument" to come to fruition so much as by making the earlier power-political decision too costly—whether in terms of money or election strategy. In revising their earlier decision, the decision-mak-ers try to generate a cheaper or more voter-friendly social peace. Thus here they yield to the pressure from the streets where in other cases they yield to pressure from lobbies. In terms of discourse theory, both forms of pressure are equally illegitimate.

Here one might object that I am drawing a certain sketch of civil disobedience that does not fit Habermas's definition.[238] According to Habermas civil disobedi-ence consists of "acts of nonviolent, symbolic rule violation [which] are meant as expressions of protest against binding decisions that, their legality notwithstand-ing, the actors consider illegitimate in the light of valid constitutional principles".[239] The actors proceed, according to Habermas, by appealing "to officeholders and par-liamentary representatives to reopen formally concluded political deliberations so that their decisions may *possibly* be revised in view of the continuing public criti-cism".[240] At the same time they also "appeal 'to the sense of justice of the majority of the community'" and try "to pursuade [sic!] public opinion...that a particular law or policy is illegitimate and a change is warranted..."[241] (as Habermas quotes Cohen and Arato approvingly).

In fact, however, the social phenomenon that we normally refer to as "civil diso-bedience" does not have to draw upon the constitution. It often simply draws on moral convictions, in light of which, moreover, the constitution itself might in some cases come under criticism as well. Furthermore, the principal agents of the civil disobedience distinguish themselves through their resolve more than any-thing else: they are *definite* about wanting a change, rather than merely putting the idea up for discussion so that it "may possibly" be accepted. Accordingly, when it cannot be avoided they insist upon their rights by *confronting* the majority's occasionally unreliable sense of justice and do not content themselves with merely "convincing" or "rationally motivating" others to respect their rights, but instead are ready to necessitate and force others to respect them—as non-violently as possible, of course.

That civil disobedience takes on this form is due to the actors' idea that certain rights take priority over discursive processes, as well as the notion—depending on the substance of the conflict—that, even if discourse is recognized as a decision-making procedure, there are nonetheless different degrees of being affected, according to which certain voices have to be weighted differently. Since there is no room in Habermas's discourse theory for either of these two ideas, and yet because for strategic reasons he wishes to retain the legitimacy of civil disobedi-ence, he is reduced to that romantic characterization of civil disobedience that we have just criticized. As a description of that social phenomenon that we are accustomed to call "civil disobedience" and that itself represents a power that is illegitimate in terms of discourse theory, it is false. However, if we take it as a *definition* of civil disobedience, it has the disadvantage of not capturing anything that really exists. And something that does not exist cannot really be a bastion of anything.

12. Nevertheless, and although the legitimacy of our constitutional principles has never been demonstrated in an ideal discourse (since there never has been such a discourse), Habermas simply *assumes* the legitimacy of our constitution and of the laws generated according to the procedures it prescribes. However, in doing so he steps right into a rather uncomfortable contradiction, as Mark Gould has noted:

> Habermas has recreated the positivist positions he criticizes in Luhmann and Hart....
>
> Habermas...presum[es] that procedures are only valid if they can withstand the prob-lematization of discussion within the ideal speech situation. However, in discussing actually existing legal systems (at least in Germany and the United States), he reduces the procedural legitimation derivative from moral discourse to the procedural legitimation derivative from secondary rules within the legal order. Thus the legitimacy of these constitutive rules is dependent on the fact that they may be redeemed at some time in the future. This does not differ in any essential (empirical) respect from Luhmann's contention that in situations where a law may be altered, its preservation may be taken as indicative of its legitimacy.[242]

Our allegedly "critical theorist" is revealed to be a closet positivist.

We can conclude, then, that Habermas's discourse theory is not capable of an appropriate theoretical conception of the democratic state, nor can it offer any legitimation of the democratic state. Moreover, a discourse-theoretical self-conception would only be dysfunctional for the democratic state—and would mean its abolition.

3.3.4. Habermas's Theory of Modernity

Thomas Mirbach claims:

> The "theory of communicative action" is a theory of modernity: both a diagnosis of the present and an emphatic [*nachdrückliche*] renewal of a robust [*emphatischen*] conception of modernity.[243]

Well, it is not *just* a theory of modernity—it is *among other things* a theory of modernity. Or, to put it better, it is supposed to be *useful* for such a theory. Does it succeed in this?

Habermas's conception of modernity is "robust" among other things because, though he occasionally *speaks* of the "dialectic of rationalisation"[244] and the "highly ambivalent content of cultural and social modernity",[245] in fact he does *not* assume any basic "dialectic" or ambivalence:

> Firstly: I believe that Western "logocentrism" stems not from an excess of reason but from a scarcity of reason. The privileging of entities in ontology, of consciousness in epistemology, of the proposition and propositional truth in semantics are three examples of this cognitivist constriction of the concept of rationality from periods far removed from one another....
>
> Secondly: the cognitive-instrumental compression of the modern concept of rationality into this one-sided mould reflects the objective one-sidedness of the lifeworld in its modernised capitalist form. Thus overcoming "logocentrism" cannot be just a concern of philosophical thought and of the theoretical activity of the social sciences. Both can of course help make the submerged dimensions accessible again, through the explorative power of reason itself.... When the paradigm of consciousness is supplanted by that of communicative understanding, then patient analyses can bring to light the potential of uncurtailed reason embedded in our everyday communicative acts.[246]

I share the opinion that Western "logocentrism" stems from a scarcity of reason and not from its excess. It stems from a scarcity of *purposive rationality*. This purposive rationality, moreover, unlike Western logocentrism (which, incidentally, Habermas's philosophy is itself an example of) can easily be reconciled with nature. However, it is not for that reason the key to paradise—and this should not be considered a reproach against it: the idea that a completely rational world would necessarily be a world of the true, the good and the beautiful is rather simple-minded.

For Habermas, who as we have seen has considerable difficulty distinguishing between instrumental rationality and purposive rationality, this purposive rationality is of course an evil stemming from the "curtailed" concept of rationality, as we have also seen. If, however, we were to carry out the "paradigm shift" favoured by Habermas, then we could allegedly expect the following:

The rationalization of society would then no longer mean a diffusion of purposive-rational action and a transformation of domains of communicative action into subsystems of purposive-rational action. The point of reference becomes instead the potential for rationality found in the validity basis of speech.[247]

And with the help of this point of reference Habermas intends to offer us "conditions for a *non-selective pattern of rationalization*", quite correctly referring to this idea as "rather risky" [*halsbrecherisch*: neck breaking].[248]

It is a headlong model if for no other reason than that the point of reference is of no use. I have already shown in great detail that Habermas's analyses of the meaning of the word "rational" show far more negligence than patience and that his definitions of rationality are thoroughly false in consequence.[249] It is *purposive rationality* that is the uncurtailed and complete rationality of action, whereas "communicative rationality" is at most a specific application of instrumental rationality that bursts like a soap bubble as soon as we try to expand it beyond its proper sphere to encompass general rationality of action or rationality per se.[250] Habermas's theory of rationality lacks all foundation.

Habermas's diagnosis of the era of modernity for its part is exhausted in the uncoupling and colonization thesis:

Such perceptions as allow one to infer the existence of subsystem-specific boundary-making first appear in modern societies. The philosophical discourse of modernity that I have analysed elsewhere is proof of how, in eighteenth-century Europe, the uncoupling of system and lifeworld within modern lifeworlds was interpreted as "diremption"—as the splitting-up and objectification of the customary traditional forms of life.

…The institutionalization of wage labour and of the individual household of private employees, the institutionalization of the fiscal state and the client relation that obtains between citizen and public bureaucracies are *experienced* as *incursions* into the traditional forms of labour and life.[251]

There is, first of all, no uncoupling of system and lifeworld, as we have seen; the uncoupling thesis and the colonization thesis are false.[252] Besides, it has to be noted that people will naturally experience *any* radical change in their forms of labour and life as incursions into the *traditional* versions of those forms of labour and life. In this regard the experiences of modernity are no different from those of the Neolithic revolution. And finally, it is probably safe to assume that the experience of a "diremption" of the customary traditional forms of life pre-dates the institutionalization of wage labour in modernity. The institutionalization of slavery in pre-modern times had already been experienced as a "diremption"—in particular by the slaves. Of course, they were generally not in the fortunate situation of being able to publish philosophical discourses for Habermas to analyse—otherwise Habermas would have been able to find evidence for the falsehood of his historical diagnosis.

Let us return to the "robust" quality of Habermas's conception of modernity. As we have seen, this conception owes its robustness partly to the fact that Habermas does not assume any ambivalence inherent in the "project of modernity"; he sees it as still waiting for, and worthy of, completion.[253] It also owes its "robustness" to

the related emphasis Habermas lays on "the universalistic achievements of modernity".[254] To be sure, these universalistic claims of modernity are repudiated from
various sides as presumptuousness, as an ideology that tries to cover up its own
actual particularism. Since Habermas doubtlessly believes—mistakenly, though—
that the essence of the "normative content of modernity" is captured and spelled
out in discourse ethics,[255] we can read Habermas's attempt to justify discourse
ethics as an attempted rebuttal of these criticisms as well.

As long as the moral principle is not justified—and justifying it involves more than simply
pointing to Kant's "fact of pure reason"—the ethnocentric fallacy looms large.[256]

However, as we have seen, Habermas's and Apel's attempts to justify the moral
principle of discourse ethics fail.[257]

Yet in the context of this problem Habermas does not actually make explicit
reference to his "programme of moral justification" so much as he defends modernity's claim to universality with the following quite curious argumentation:

[The criticism levelled against the idea of human rights by the critique of reason] fails to
notice the peculiar self-referential character of the discourses of enlightenment [*Diskurse
der Aufklärung*]. The discourse of human rights is also set up to provide *every* choice with a
hearing. Consequently, this discourse itself sets the standards [*schießt die Standards vor*] in
whose light the latent violations of its own claims can be discovered and corrected.[258]

Elsewhere he writes:

It is not the claim to complete inclusion that distinguishes modern discourses from other
kinds. The message of the world religions that emerged in the ancient empires was already
addressed "to all," and was meant to accommodate all converts into the discourse of the
faithful. What differentiates modern discourse, be it in science, morality, or law, is something
else. These discourses are directed by principle, and submit themselves to self-reflective
standards, in whose light factual violations of the injunction to complete inclusion can
at once be discovered and criticized…[The] mere fact that universalistic discourses are
frequently misused as a medium for concealing social, political, epistemic and cultural violence is by itself no basis for renouncing the promise that is bound up with this discursive
practice—all the less so since this practice provides both the criteria and the means for
ensuring that the promise is kept.[259]

These explanations ignore the problem rather than solving it or even grasping
it: if the discourse of enlightenment *and thus also its claims and the standards it
sets* fall under the suspicion of partisan bias, then everyone who holds this suspicion only feels it confirmed, with good reason, when they hear this starry-eyed
and thoughtless assurance that the latent violations of the discourse of modernity
against its own claims can be discovered and criticized in light of its own standards. *That* these standards and claims are universally valid and not just the expression of a particularism that *presents* itself as universalism is precisely what these
critics doubt.

Moreover, there is nothing "peculiar" about the self-referential character of the
discourse of modernity. *Every* complex system of thought, ideology, religion and
philosophy sets standards in light of which things are to be evaluated according

to that system—including the claims of the system itself. However, in each case it turns out that, despite the critical potential that is certainly to be found in these standards, they tend to shed a rather flattering light on the accomplishments of the "discourses" that so generously set them.

Furthermore, it is an untenable—if not downright ludicrous—assumption that principles, that is, meta-norms used for the assessment and justification of norms,[260] are an invention of modernity. Habermas used to be aware of this, too, in *Towards a Reconstruction of Historical Materialism*, where he drew a different distinction between the "ancient empires" and modernity. In ancient empires "the highest principles, to which all argumentation recurs, are themselves removed from argumentation and immunized against possible objections." In "the onto-logical tradition of thought", for example, this is achieved "through the concept of the absolute (or of complete self-sufficiency)". In modernity, in contrast, "religious faith and the theoretical attitude [become] reflexive", such that "[t]he advance of the modern sciences and the development of moral-practical will-formation [are] no longer prejudiced by an order that—although grounded [*begründet* = justi-fied]—[is] posited absolutely".[261]

Modernity, however, fails to adhere to its Habermasian description; thus one of the central documents of modernity, the US Declaration of Independence, states:

We hold these truths to be self-evident, that all men are created equal, that they are endowed by their creator with certain unalienable rights, that among these are life, liberty, and the pursuit of happiness. That to secure these rights, governments are instituted among men, deriving their just powers from the consent of the governed, that whenever any form of government becomes destructive of these ends, it is the right of the people to alter or to abolish it...[262]

This rather clearly has recourse to the concept of "complete self-sufficiency", this time in the form of *self-evidence*, just like in the ancient empires, and posits certain goals and the order serving them as *absolute*. And these human rights posited by modernity, which then determine the framework and the *limits* of parliamentary legislation in modern constitutions, *do* in fact serve to *prejudice* the moral and practical formation of will.

In fact, in responding to criticism Habermas has had to concede this prejudicial, dogmatic moment:

...the *performative meaning* of this [constitution-making] practice...already contains as a doctrinal [*dogmatischer*] core the...idea of the self-legislation of voluntarily associated citizens who are both free and equal. This idea is not "formal" in the sense of being "value free." However, it can be fully developed in the course of constitution-making processes that are not based on the previous choice of substantive values, but rather on democratic pro-cedures. Hence, there is a justified *presumption* that the deontological idea of self-legislation or autonomy is neutral with respect to worldviews, provided that the different interpreta-tions of the self and the world are not fundamentalist but are compatible with the condi-tions of postmetaphysical thinking...[263]

Aside from the fact that one does not have to be a metaphysician to reject human rights: a decision-making practice that is only neutral with respect to world views "provided" that interpretations of the self and the world that do not suit it are absent is certainly *not* neutral with respect to world views.

What, then, are "the criteria and the means" supposed to be that modernity supplies us with "for ensuring that the promise" to complete inclusion "is kept"? After all, the "ensurer" of this guarantee (i.e. the constitution-making processes as interpreted by discourse theory) is *designed* for the *exclusion* of certain interests.

Here one might fall back on that modern criterion par excellence, namely, *argumentative critique*. However, modernity did not invent this criterion; it had already existed. Modernity simply promoted it to an unusual extent. What is more, even if we ignore the fact that the "partiality of reason"[264] is still partiality, reason and argumentation are still not sufficient to guarantee rational agreement between rational people in normative questions—which are the questions at issue here. They cannot provide us with any objective or universally intersubjective criterion of normative validity.[265] Modernity's conspicuous tendency to interpret the norms that it propagates, such as human rights, as the expression of modern rationality, and to interpret their rejection as an eruption of unreason, can easily and with good reason be seen as the universalistic presumption of what is in fact particular.[266]

Only an enlightenment enlightened about itself would be a true enlightenment. The "enlightenment" or modernity that Habermas presents us with is one that considers itself illuminated more than it is. Thus Habermas's theory of communicative action fails as a theory and a diagnosis of the era and fails as a defence of modernity as well.

Conclusion

The claim to deliver a *justification* of an ethics or moral system or a critical theory of society can be made good only with a suitable *methodology*. The methods used by the proponents of discourse ethics are *not* suitable. Those alleged conceptual explications and analyses of ordinary language with which Habermas intends to clarify the meaning of "rational" and set the course for a distinction between purposive rationality and communicative rationality neither explicate nor analyse, as we have seen; instead they merely posit things that cannot withstand scrutiny. In general, as Anthony Giddens has noted, we see in "Habermas's writing something of a puritanical formalism. Often where one would like to see *evidence* presented to support a view that is proposed, a table is offered instead—as if the way to overcome potential objections is to pulverise them into conceptual fragments."[1] Apel's and Kuhlmann's method of "strict reflection" also turns out to be prejudicial by being circular and dogmatic; its "results" are also merely posited, not demonstrated.

However, we should acknowledge that Apel and Kuhlmann, and transcendental-pragmatists generally, have spent a long time responding to their critics (although there does not seem to be very much left of this attitude), even if that has always involved falling back on the same dogmatic postulates again and again. As one would expect from their philosophy, they did not resort to a blank refusal to enter into discussion. Habermas, on the other hand, despite his reputation among those who lack an overview of the debate, has shown a conspicuous tendency either to simply ignore fundamental and pointed criticism of his philosophy or to dismiss it sweepingly. Thus he continues to fall back on the transcendental-pragmatic figure of "argumentation" again and again, without even mentioning the sharp critique voiced from many quarters against the "'talk' of performative self-contradiction".[2] Furthermore, he feels "misunderstood" by Bar-Hillel's (1973) indignant critique of the universal-pragmatic approach, such that in his opinion "there is no point in replying to its particulars";[3] he single-handedly declares a significant paper by Albert (1971) to be a "remaining echo" of "a discussion [that] can be regarded as over";[4] Bolte's (1989) volume of papers by philosophers who emphatically use Marx and the Older Critical Theory against the younger one, which they see as "Uncritical Theory", as well as Keuth's (1993) thorough and rigorous critique of Critical Theory (particularly its younger form), were for a long time not even mentioned in a footnote by Habermas (in the meantime the latter has finally been mentioned in a footnote[5]); he deals with a comprehensive, extraordinarily perspicacious and detailed article of Gould's (1996) with an astonishing brevity, including an assertion, not backed up by any explanation, that Gould "confuses practically everything";[6] and he confesses to not even finishing Goodrich (1996), since Goodrich supposedly suspects him of "antisemitism" and "whoever denounces someone wants to speak about him, not with him."[7] This comes from someone who suspected Rudi Dutschke and his followers of "left-wing fascism"[8] and defames the postmodernists quite sweepingly as Young Conservatives [Jungkonservative].[9] While Habermas did very quickly take back his accusation of left-wing fascism, he did not deal with the theses of the 1968 movement in any sufficient depth. Rather than speaking *with* them, he spoke about them and limited himself, moreover, to drawing up psychological theories about them.[10] And as far the accusation of Young Conservatism is concerned, Lyotard responded to Habermas;[11] yet in his book *The Philosophical Discourse of Modernity*, where a discussion of Lyotard would have suggested itself, Habermas (who did not respond to Goodrich) mentioned Lyotard only in a subordinate clause[12]—almost ostentatiously, it seems. It is Habermas who lacks readiness for open discussion and for an engagement with all arguments, in particular with those arguments situated in the context of a radical critique instead of a sympathetic one. Moreover, Habermas hopes to see his theories confirmed by their possible empirical usefulness for certain select paradigms of empirical research, and yet "there are very real methodological and substantive problems confronting [these paradigms], and these Habermas has largely ignored."[13] And finally it does not exactly inspire trust when someone who already expects us to buy the logically questionable project of "a history of theory with a systematic intent"[14] concedes at the same time: "I think I make the foreign tongues my own in a rather brutal manner, from a hermeneutic point of view. Even when I quote a good deal and take over other terminologies I am clearly aware that my use of them often has little to do with the authors' original meaning."[15] What systematic value, what justificatory force, one might wonder, is a brutally distorted history of theory supposed to have?

This methodological inadequacy has the impact on the transcendental-pragmatic and universal-pragmatic project that is to be expected. As we have seen, hardly a single step in the argumentation on the long road from the analysis of speech acts to a "discourse theory of law and democracy" is valid. Accordingly neither Apel nor Habermas succeeds in showing discursive or communicative rationality to be "uncurtailed" in relation to purposive rationality. They likewise fail to show that their presumed norms of discourse are in fact norms of discourse and have substantial moral content. No derivation of the principles U and D from the discourse norms Habermas has postulated exists. Habermas likewise fails to demonstrate the empirical usefulness of his theories or to use them cogently to work out a theory of society, let alone a critical theory of society. In short, Apel and Habermas do not succeed in founding a "macro-ethics of humanity" or a "critical theory of society". The Younger Critical Theory is a failure.

Habermas's Relativist and Decisionist Turn

Jürgen Habermas likes to see himself as the defender of universalism against relativism or contextualism and of moral cognitivism against decisionism. Recently, however, hobbling behind the trend somewhat but still finding a way to "link" to it—we are speaking now of a pragmatism oriented towards Dewey and James rather than Peirce—he has taken the rather interesting turn described in this title—not so much in his self-understanding but rather unwittingly through the logical implications of his new position (which is philosophically more significant).

The following brief critique of Habermas's linguistic and pragmatic [*sprachpragmatisch*] realism is not just undertaken for its own sake; it should also serve as a foil against which the advantages of the less fashionable but correct realistic correspondence theory of truth can once more be cast in their proper light. Pointing out the decisionist implications of Habermas's arguments is a matter of fairness, since after someone spends decades criticizing decisionism it is only fair to put it on record when he himself, despite lip service to the contrary, becomes a party to it, whether he will or not.

Habermas sees two problems connected with the linguistic and pragmatic turn that he himself is known to espouse and with the "detranscendentalization" that it entails. After this turn, he writes,

the classical form of realism that relies on the representational model of cognition and on the correspondence between propositions and facts is no longer viable.[1]

Moreover, "[d]etranscendentalization alters the very concept of the transcendental",[2] and

transcendental rules…mutate into expressions of cultural forms of life and have a beginning in time. As a consequence, we may no longer without qualification claim "universality" and "necessity," that is, objectivity for empirical cognition…[3]

As an avowed universalist, Habermas would like to get around this problem, and moreover to do so on the basis of a pragmatist concept of reality and thus a pragmatist concept of truth. Let us take a closer look at this.

From a pragmatist perspective, reality is not something to be copied; we take note of it performatively—as the totality of resistances that are processed and are to be anticipated—and it makes itself known to us solely in the constraints to which our problem-solving activities and learning processes are subject.

The representational model of knowledge…misses the cognitive-operational significance of "overcoming" problems and of the "success" of learning processes.[4]

Is this accurate? Hardly. Typically it is precisely the proponents of the representational model of knowledge who place the greatest emphasis on our learning through a "cognitive–operational" interaction with the world, for example, in the form of experiments, arguing that only in this way do we learn what the accurate descriptions of the world are, after which these accurate descriptions (such as in the form of true propositions or convictions) are in turn of great use to us in overcoming problems. It is Habermas who misses the point, that is, the point of the representational models of knowledge. And how can Habermas claim on the one hand that reality is not something to be copied, while on the other hand he concedes: "To be sure, everything that is the case and can be represented in true propositions is true"? Moreover, even if it were true, as he thinks, that we do not assume a view of the world, based on its resistance to us, as the totality of facts (which of course Habermas himself does as soon as he concedes that everything is real that is the case) but rather "as a totality of objects"[5]—why should we not be able to describe parts of this totality of objects with propositions? Habermas gives us no answer to this.

He does, however, offer another specious assurance of the falsity of the correspondence theory:

Certainly, within the linguistic paradigm, the truth of a proposition can no longer be conceived as correspondence with something in the world, for otherwise we would have to be able to "get outside of language" while using language.[6]

This justification sounds very deep and poetic, but, to paraphrase Nietzsche, it is not even shallow, just flat. I do not have to get out of my hand while using my hand in order to grasp something else with my hand, such as a cup of coffee. I also do not have to get out of language while using language in order to grasp something else with language—such as a cup of coffee, a neutron star, a nuclear explosion or the social behaviour of chickens.

Moreover, Habermas goes on to cite Michael Williams in his defence:

We need only ask whether or not the "direct" grasping of facts on which such comparison [between linguistic expression and facts] depends is supposed to be a cognitive state with propositional content. If it isn't, it can have no impact on verification. But if it is, all we have been given is another kind of belief.[7]

My wish that the sun shine is a propositionally structured cognitive state, but not a belief: rather, it is a wish. My perception that it is raining is also not a belief, but rather a perception. This is shown by the fact that I could believe that it is raining without perceiving it, and conversely (since I might distrust my senses) I could perceive that it is raining without believing it. Thus it is that I can also compare my beliefs or any linguistic expressions with perceived facts as well. But then, one might object, is the propositionally structured perception, as propositionally structured, still outside of language? We can begin by answering, with William P. Alston, that there is "such a phenomenon as the *presentation* or *givenness* of something to one's awareness", which brings with it a visual differentiation of objects but by no means has to entail any conceptualization or propositional structure[8] (it should be added that I do not share Williams' rather curious premise that cognitive states without propositional content are irrelevant to verification, for how could we suppose sensory perceptions to be irrelevant to verification?). More important, however, is the simple fact that propositional structure or propositional content does not by itself constitute language. A brick building structured according to architectural principles is still a brick building and not, say, an architectural principle. And thus when we check whether the building accords with a certain architectural principle, we are not comparing an architectural principle with architectural principles or concepts, but we are comparing a principle with a building. The building is just as non-principle or non-conceptual as the principle or the concepts are non-building. Or, to put it more concisely: a ball with a name written on it is still a ball and not a name. Accordingly a propositionally structured or linguistically interpreted or conceptualized perception is still a perception and not language. For this reason, as mentioned, we can quite easily and fortunately compare our merely linguistic propositions with the extra-linguistic facts accessible to us through propositionally structured perception. To quote Alston again:

Why can't the whole perceptual package—sensory consciousness structured by conceptual-propositional-judgmental activity—be a way of cognizing external facts?[9]

Habermas, like the other linguisticists, does not have even a rudimentary sketch of a plausible response to this; thus linguisticism is and remains unjustified. (We might also be tempted to ask, merely in passing: on the assumption that Williams was right in the statement quoted by Habermas, where does Habermas get the idea that this does not apply to *the pragmatist conception as well*? In Habermas's pragmatist conception, which he explicitly labels a realist conception, is the resistance offered by reality not conceived as something outside of language, something that true propositions have to accord with or at least measure up to? But what is this supposed to mean, if the extra-linguistic is supposed to be entirely inaccessible as such? As a good pragmatist, Habermas might say that the truth of sentences shows itself in the successful cognitive–operational interaction with the extra-linguistic reality. But if the truth can show itself in this successful interaction, why could it not show itself in successful, that is, correct, perception and description?)

After this rather hurried defence of the realistic correspondence theory of truth, let us turn directly to our critique of the Habermasian conception of reality and truth. We should first note that often the resistances that "are to be anticipated" are absent or, conversely, resistances make themselves felt that were not to be anticipated. Thus I assume that, for Habermas, reality makes itself known to us in the *actual* "constraints" (whether past, present or future) "to which our problem-solving activities and learning processes are subject". But to whom does "our" refer? "Universal-pragmatists", "Germans", "people", "animals", "living creatures"? It is quite obvious that the resistances I encounter in the course of my life are not the same as those Habermas encounters—which would mean that we apparently inhabit different realities. And since we cannot uncouple the concept of truth from the concept of reality any more than we can uncouple the system from the "lifeworld", a relativism of truth follows from the relativism about reality that emerges here. (We can also see this in Habermas's talk of overcoming problems and the success of learning processes: since we do not all have the same problems or pursue the same goals, it could be that, given my particular problem, my confidence in a certain assertion leads to shipwreck for me, whereas for another person with a quite different problem confidence in the very same assertion brings nothing but smooth sailing.)

On the other hand, we would also run into a rather severe problem if Habermas meant this "our" to refer to all creatures sensible of resistance, and conceived reality as the totality of all resistances that these creatures encounter, such that the one and only reality, hence my reality as well, included those resistances that other fellow creatures besides myself encounter. If my reality includes resistances that I never experience, why should reality not also include resistances that no one experiences simply because there is not and never was or will be anyone in the right place at the right time? Clearly there is no reason to exclude that which no one ever notices. But then Habermas's consensus theory of truth has to be false. Yet he has by no means abandoned this theory, rather only attenuated it in one respect. He still continues to claim that

a proposition is true if it withstands all attempts to refute it under the demanding conditions of rational discourse.

Then he attenuates this by saying:

However, this does not mean that it is also true *for this reason*. A truth claim raised for 'p' says that the truth conditions for 'p' are satisfied.[10]

Yet, as we have already suggested, this qualification is incompatible with the claim preceding it. Even if Habermas were right that "we can only *establish* whether these conditions are satisfied by way of discursive vindication of the truth claim"[11]—and of course he is not at all right about this[12]—the question arises: if the conditions of truth are found in a reality that for Habermas is characterized precisely by its *resistance*, why should they suddenly be so obliging, complaisant, tame and docile as to keep within the domain of what can be ascertained through discourse? Pre-established harmony in "postmetaphysical thinking"?

Furthermore, the question arises as to what is actually supposed to be so "pragmatic" or "pragmatist" about this attenuated or realist version of the consensus theory. Reference to the fact that the theory takes the significance of overcoming problems and successful learning processes into consideration is not sufficient, since, as mentioned, the representational model does this as well (as do a slew of other theories of truth). And in point of fact, when Habermas characterizes his "pragmatic conception of truth" in greater detail, he tells a very different story—he outlines a kind of doubt-removal theory,[13] according to which "[t]he practices of the lifeworld are supported by a consciousness of certainty that in the course of action leaves no room for doubts about truth."[14] These "certainties of action", however, could become "shaken" by contrary experiences, which leads to the "transition to discourse". And Habermas then attributes to this discourse the exceedingly important role of the "retransformation of rationally acceptable assertions into performative certainties".[15] If this astonishing "reconstruction" of the "lifeworld" as a realm of pure naivety were right, then people who indulge in such practices as parachuting, diving or driving would hardly use a reserve parachute, the buddy system or a seat belt, and people with an important appointment would hardly set three alarms next to their bed or get up an hour or two earlier in case the car fails to start or the train is delayed, and finally the flourishing of the insurance industry would be entirely inexplicable. Yet Habermas, the philosopher, believes: "We don't walk onto any bridge whose stability we doubt."[16] Sometimes we do, the director Steven Spielberg objects, quite rightly: when, for example, we are being chased by a gang of sabre-wielding followers of the goddess Kali, whose ability and intention to kill us we have no doubt of, and the only way out is a rather questionable-looking bridge (cf. Indiana Jones, part II). And we do not just make risk–utility calculations in extreme situations—as the other examples show, they are part of how we negotiate our way in the world daily and an essential component of *pragmatics*, that is, the art of acting correctly.[17] Moreover, a thinker who loves to criticize theories that displease him for allegedly not being faithful to the actors' "self-understanding"[18] should expect to face questions about whether the description of lifeworld-actors as dogmatic simpletons uncritically abandoning themselves to all kinds of "certainties of action", without taking the fallibility of actions and convictions into account, does a better job of capturing their "self-understanding". Be that as it may, even if we overlook the flaws in the Habermasian doubt-removal theory just described, it is still a complete mystery how praise for the supposed re-dogmatizing achievements of discourse is supposed to make such a discourse theory "pragmatist". In short, it has all nothing whatsoever to do with pragmatism.

Let us now let the matter rest and turn to a second problem of relativism, namely, the problem confronting a transcendental philosophy that would like to continue to be transcendental yet without losing its connection to de-transcendentalization (clearly a lot could be said about this kind of schizophrenia, but we will spare ourselves that here). I have already quoted Habermas's assessment of this problem. What does his solution look like? It consists of "a single metatheoretical assumption". According to this assumption, the structures that form the transcendental conditions of possibility for the learning processes of our species themselves turn out to be the result of less complex, natural learning processes—*and thereby themselves acquire a cognitive content.*[19]

The learning analogy, which we apply to developments that are governed by mutation, selection and stabilization, portrays the endowment of the human mind as an intelligent solution to problems that itself developed under the constraints of reality. This perspective pulls the rug out from under the very idea that worldviews are species-relative.[20]

   Aside from the fact that a species-relative worldview is the least of Habermas's relativist problems (since his position, with its emphasis on the transcendental function of the "lifeworld", is obviously also threatened by cultural relativism, subcultural relativism and familial relativism), in light of the Habermasian conclusion, the question arises: why? The development that the functional design of shock absorbers has undergone in interaction with a resistant reality—for example, in the form of bad streets and rough terrain—qualifies them "as an intelligent solution to problems that itself developed under the constraints of reality". Yet, first of all, the cognitive content expressed in the design of shock absorbers is not found in the things themselves, but in the theories of the engineers. Accordingly, it would be more consistent to attribute the cognitive content of natural learning processes to the quasi-subject of these learning processes, that is, natural history, rather than to its products. Second, the developments in the design of shock absorbers are relative to the particular vehicle. A civilian car meant for city traffic has a different kind of shock absorber from that of a military off-road vehicle, and with good reason. The former are quite sensitive to small irregularities that the latter do not even register. The same holds for the brains of various species—which, from a pragmatist viewpoint, are the shock absorbers of reality. Since we cannot assume that the problems faced by the ancestors of humans in the course of evolution were exactly the same as those faced by the ancestors of water rats, chimpanzees, dolphins or the microscopic inhabitants of XLYEKRZFWZQRZ City on the planet &%$*", Habermas's "transcendental-pragmatist interpretation of evolution" (or whatever one might wish to call it) makes the notion of a species-relative world view unavoidable. Thus Habermas tries to refute relativism with an argument that in fact implies it.

Let us now turn to the topic of decisionism. Habermas makes a series of concessions (without, incidentally, even mentioning Hans Albert):

That a cognitive conception of morality is possible means only that we can know how we ought legitimately to govern our lives together if we are determined to take the sharply delimited questions of justice that—like questions of truth—are subject to a binary code out of the broad spectrum of conceptions of the Good about which it is no longer feasible to reach a consensus.[21]

Given the premise that "rightness" reduces to "rational acceptability", the binary decision, which must be unequivocal, somewhat acquires the character of a posit.[22]

Yet he still claims:

Nonetheless, talk about "decision" and "positing" points in the wrong direction. The skeptical move of opting out of the language game of *warranted* moral expectations, verdicts, and self-reproaches exists only in philosophical reflection, but not in practice: it would destroy the self-understanding of the subject acting communicatively. . . . as soon as [sociated individuals] seek to privilege a universally binding system of rules without the backing of a worldview, the only way open to them is that of a discursively produced agreement. The continuation of communicative action by discursive means is part of the communicative form of life, and this is the only form of life available to us.[23]

Since I have already dealt with the Habermasian (and/or Apelian) positions involved in this argumentation quite thoroughly, I will allow myself to be brief here. *First*, the "if" in the first quotation and the "as soon as" in the third hardly leave any room for cognitivist categorical moral principles. Instead, we are now obviously dealing with hypothetical imperatives. Even if, as Habermas claims, we cannot help but make the decision described in the "if"- and "as soon as"-clauses, this still in no way makes the consequent clause into a categorical imperative; at most it allows for a hypothetical imperative with a necessarily true conditional sentence.[24] *Second*, this hypothetical imperative is false anyway. Habermas himself concedes that even discourse ethics is "dependent upon a form of life that *meets it halfway*";[25] accordingly it is a central motif, the very premise actually, of *Between Facts and Norms* that a sanctioned enforcement of the binding system of norms is *not* superfluous. Moreover, even the very assumption that communicative action refers to discourse as the source of legitimation and arbitration in whatever conflicts may arise is erroneous.[26] *Third*, on the narrow definition of communicative action, which Habermas himself intends to be decisive, it can be shown that there is no communicative action.[27] Accordingly there are also no subjects of communicative action. Accordingly it is also not particularly tragic when the "self-understanding" of these non-existent subjects gets subverted. *Fourth*, even if we interpret communicative action in a broader sense,[28] it still by no means plays the part in the "symbolic reproduction of the lifeworld" that Habermas always ascribes to it whenever he finds it necessary for the justification of his moral conception (even though elsewhere he has acknowledged it to be illusory). Thus it should be no problem at all to leave this communicative action, and one does not have any need to fear certain pathological consequences for one's own psyche, as Habermas claims.[29] *Fifth*, even if we could drop out of the communicative form of life only at the cost of madness, this would not overcome us from one second to the next. Thus until it begins to set in, we "dropouts" would be healthy and competent speakers for whom, due to our decision, discourse ethics would have no validity. *In summary*, Habermas's conciliatory remarks change nothing about the actual implications of his current moral theory—which is decisionist.

Notes

INTRODUCTION

1. Habermas (1982), p. 233.
2. Habermas (1987a), pp. 396f.
3. Apel (1980), p. 226.
4. Ibid.
5. For the precise formulation of U and D see p. 51.
6. Herbert Keuth's (1993) critique of Apel and Habermas is detailed and precise, but it does not look closely into the theory of communicative action, and is not yet able to consider Habermas's "discourse theory of law and the democratic state" as presented in *Between Facts and Norms*. Keuth does present a very comprehensive discussion of discourse ethics. However, even in this area the current study does not rival Keuth's treatment so much as supplement it—aside from a certain unavoidable amount of overlap.

CHAPTER 1

1. Habermas (2003c), p. 309.
2. Habermas (1984), pp. 17f.
3. Habermas (1985d), p. 176, translation modified (the connotations of *unverkürzt* are better captured by translation as "uncurtailed", which is in fact used by some of Habermas's translators; in addition, *Vernunft* means reason, not rationality). Compare the original, Habermas (1989a), p. 605.
4. Ilting (1982), esp. pp. 622f.
5. Weber (1964), p. 18. The translation in Weber (1978), p. 26, is misleading.
6. But see Steinhoff (2000).
7. Habermas (1984), p. 10.
8. Compare Schnädelbach (1982), pp. 166ff.
9. Habermas (1984), p. 8. Translation slightly modified, see Habermas (1988), pp. 25f.
10. Habermas (1984), p. 9, translation corrected, see Habermas (1988), p. 26.
11. Habermas (1989a), pp. 128f.; and (2003a), p. 86.
12. Habermas (1984), p. 9, my emphasis.
13. Habermas (2003c), p. 313.
14. Ibid. p. 315.
15. Habermas (1984), pp. 8f., translation slightly modified, see id. (1988), p. 26.
16. Habermas (2003c), p. 315.
17. "What grounding [*Begründung* = justification] means, can be explained only in connection with the conditions for discursively redeeming validity claims." Habermas (1984), p. 39.
18. Ibid. p. 9.
19. Ibid. p. 307.
20. Ibid. pp. 9f., translation slightly modified, see Habermas (1988), p. 27.
21. Habermas (2003c), pp. 313f.
22. See for example Chisholm (1977), p. 14; also BonJour (1985), p. 8.
23. Habermas (1984), p. 21.
24. Habermas (1999b), p. 90.

25. Habermas (2003*c*), p. 315.
26. Ibid. pp. 315f.
27. Habermas (1984), p. 22.
28. Habermas (1984), p. 9, translation slightly modified, see Habermas (1988), p. 26.
29. Habermas (1984), p. 101.
30. Habermas (2003*c*), p. 217.
31. Habermas (1984), p. 294.
32. Habermas (2003*c*), p 234. I will return to this problem in Section 3.3.1.
33. Habermas (2003*c*), p. 234.
34. Habermas (1992*a*), p. 131. In the English translation in Habermas (2003*c*), p. 300, this clear concession is somewhat attenuated.
35. Habermas (1987*a*), p. 127. See also ibid. p. 126.
36. Habermas (2003*c*), pp. 299f.
37. See ibid. p. 221; idem (1985*d*), pp. 163f. and 169f.; (1996*e*), pp. 18f.; (2003*c*), pp. 326f.
38. See Sections 1.3.3 and 3.3.1, esp. 206–8.
39. Habermas (1984), p. 85.
40. Ibid. pp. 285f.
41. Ibid. pp. 101f.
42. Ibid. pp. 285f.
43. Habermas (1982), p. 234.
44. Ibid. p. 264, my emphasis.
45. Baurmann (1985).
46. Habermas (1991*c*), p. 241.
47. Habermas (1984), p. 286.
48. Ibid. p. 419, n. 23.
49. Dorschel (1990), p. 221.
50. Ibid. pp. 250f.
51. Ibid. pp. 251f.
52. Baurmann (1985), pp. 190ff. Compare also Johnson (1991), pp. 188ff.
53. Habermas (1984), p. 87.
54. Habermas (1979), p. 196, translation modified (the English translation puts "subjectively" between "oriented" and "each". There is, however, no *subjektiv* in the German original; see Habermas 1989*a*, p. 461).
55. Habermas (1984), p. 327.
56. Ibid. p. 296.
57. Habermas (2003*c*), p. 88.
58. Weber (1964), p. 17. The translation in Weber (1978), p. 24, renders "*zweckrational*" as "instrumentally rational". That is wrong and completely misleading.
59. Skjei (1985).
60. Habermas (1985*a*), p. 108.
61. Habermas (1984), pp. 285f.
62. See Section 3.3.1.
63. Habermas (1988), p. 394. (The translation omits this sentence, see Habermas 1984, p. 293.) In view of such statements it is quite irritating when Habermas responds to Lenoble's objection that even in an ideal speech situation there would be "no assurance of the success of any communicative act" (Lenoble 1996, p. 956) by writing: "Lenoble does not seem to realize that intentionalist provisos are pointless after a rigorously executed linguistic turn. Regardless of what the hearer thinks in doing so, his affirmative response to an assertion or command creates a social fact open

to public verification. In the course of further interaction it will also become publicly evident whether or not the addressee violates the obligations he has taken on with his "yes" (i.e., to take into consideration the fact that has been accepted as true; to carry out the commanded action, whatever his motives)." Habermas (1996d), p. 1522. If the illocutionary success of a speech act depends on the hearer recognizing its validity, which means: sincerely recognizing it as valid, "because he is confident that ego has the requisite knowledge and is sufficiently autonomous to guarantee the redemption of the validity claims he raises in communication" (Habermas 1987a, pp. 181f.); if a communicatively achieved agreement "rests on common convictions" (Habermas 1984, p. 287); if it "cannot be imposed by one side" (Habermas 1982, p. 264), then agreement, the illocutionary success of a speech act, has not been achieved if the hearer, unlike the speaker, is convinced of the falsity of the assertion and merely pretends to agree. How then can it possibly be irrelevant what the hearer thinks with his "yes"? When Habermas distinguishes between true consensus and false "consensus" precisely in terms of the absence or presence of intentionalist provisos, this distinction can hardly be "pointless"; it is indispensable. Thus the speaker cannot know with assurance whether his speech act was effective, "the course of further interaction" will not provide the speaker with infallible telepathic abilities and thus will not provide him with any assurance. Admittedly, one could note the mitigating circumstance to Habermas's credit that Lenoble misleadingly spoke of "undecidability", whereas the real issue is only—but still—with "fallibility". However, this does not change anything about Habermas's remarkably off-point accusation of the "pointlessness".
64. Habermas (1984), p. 294.
65. Ibid. pp. 293–5.
66. Habermas (1985a), p. 108.
67. Accordingly, Dietmar Köveker's justification of this claim, following Habermas, that Skjei misrecognizes the "structural properties of illocutionary acts" is also anything but convincing. It is interesting how Köveker justifies this: "Of course (purposive) intentions enter into speech acts. However, the linguistically structured coordination potential of these speech acts to 'connect' the actions of various agents to each other first provides the foundation for precisely that normative viewpoint under which all merely private action orientations can be criticized relative to consensually mediated action orientations." Köveker (1992), p. 306, n. 13. In fact it is hard to see how this explanation is even relevant to our problem. For as long as the speech acts with this alleged coordination potential are not defined in terms of this coordination potential or any structural properties, but rather in terms of intentions, then we are dealing with an intentionalist semantics (or pragmatics); particularly when, as we have seen and as Habermas himself underscores, certain perlocutionary acts have the same structure and the same coordination potential as illocutionary acts and thus these illocutionary acts cannot be defined in terms of their structures and potential.
68. Habermas (1985a), p. 108.
69. Habermas (2003c), p. 224, translation slightly modified (the original translation uses "shift" for "*Schaltung*", see idem (1992a), p. 72.
70. Habermas (2003c), pp. 332f.
71. Habermas (1979), p. 196, translation modified (see note 54).
72. Habermas (1984), p. 327.
73. Ibid. p. 295.
74. Habermas (1991c), p. 241.

75. Habermas (1984), p. 327.
76. Habermas (2003c), p. 220.
77. Habermas (1988), pp. 391, 392, 394, 398. The English translation, however, does not consistently translate the German word "*Erfolg*" as "success"; it sometimes translates it incorrectly as "result". See Habermas (1984), pp. 291, 293, 296.
78. Habermas (2003c), p. 217.
79. Ibid. pp. 217f.
80. Ibid. p. 218, German text in square brackets added.
81. Ibid. p. 226, text in brackets added. Compare also Habermas (1984), pp. 290ff. Later in Section 1.3.3 we will see that Habermas's definition of illocutionary acts has very strange consequences and is hence erroneous.
82. Habermas (2003c), p. 218.
83. Ibid.
84. Davidson (1980), p. 3.
85. See ibid. pp. 3–19; compare also Williams (1981), pp. 101–13.
86. Habermas (2003c), p. 226, my emphasis, explanation in square brackets added.
87. Ibid.
88. Habermas (1984), p. 293.
89. Habermas (1989a), p. 161, my emphasis.
90. Williams (1973), pp. 136–51.
91. Ibid.
92. Habermas (2003c), p. 218.
93. Ibid. pp. 218f.
94. Habermas (1984), p. 293.
95. Ibid. p. 84.
96. Ibid.
97. Apel (1984), pp. 75f.
98. Habermas (1984), p. 85.
99. Habermas (1985d), p. 154.
100. Habermas (1984), pp. 97ff., rejects Arthur C. Danto's idea that intentional bodily movements are basic actions. His explanations of this rejection are entirely implausible, and in any case he is once more arguing against the current of our ordinary use of language. Compare Tugendhat (1985).
101. Habermas (2003c), pp. 319f.
102. Habermas (1984), p. 39, text in square brackets added.
103. Compare Habermas (2003c), pp. 315–17.
104. Habermas (1984), pp. 17f.
105. Ibid. p. 11.
106. Ibid. p. 408, n. 4.
107. Ibid. p. 15, translation corrected (the German original speaks here of "*Kommunikation*", not of *kommunikatives Handeln*), see Habermas (1988), p. 34. Even if the original spoke of communicative action, this would, of course, not make a difference to my point.
108. Habermas (2001a), p. 20.
109. Habermas (2003c), pp. 315f.
110. Habermas (1984), p. 41.
111. Ibid. p. 287.
112. Stevenson (1965).
113. Habermas (2001a), p. 33.

114. Ibid. p. 32. See also idem (1999*b*), p. 93. "General" means *universal* here.
115. Ibid.
116. Habermas (1999*b*), p. 103.
117. Wellmer (1986), pp. 69–81.
118. Lumer (1990), pp. 248ff.
119. Alexy (1978), p. 55.
120. Ibid. p. 54.
121. Habermas (1999*b*), p. 92, the explanation in brackets is mine.
122. Habermas (2001*a*), p. 20.
123. Ibid.
124. Ibid. p. 33, text in brackets added.
125. Habermas initially "took" the presupposition of this primacy "to be trivial", until an objection of Thomas McCarthy's brought him to see that it was in need of a "careful justification". Habermas (2003*c*), p. 102, n. 92 (added in 1983). McCarthy states his objection in Oelmüller (1978*a*), pp. 134ff.
126. Habermas (1985*d*), p. 169. Compare also Habermas (1984), pp. 287f.
127. How astonishing it is is reflected in the variety of criticism it has attracted. See for example Culler (1985); Wood (1985); Tugendhat (1985); Cooke (1994), pp. 19ff.
128. Wood (1985), p. 160, underestimates this problem.
129. Habermas (1984), p. 287.
130. Habermas (2003*c*), pp. 315f.
131. Habermas (1985*d*), p. 169.
132. Habermas (2003*c*), pp. 301f.
133. Ibid. p. 330.
134. Ibid. p. 226.
135. Ibid. p. 304.
136. See Habermas (2003*c*), p. 339.
137. Habermas (1991*c*), p. 291, n. 58, translation slightly modified, see Habermas (1986*a*), p. 401, n. 58.
138. Maeve Cooke (1994), pp. 26f., suggests this strategy to make the theory more plausible, but does not seem particularly convinced of it herself.
139. Habermas himself explicitly rejects this thesis in Habermas (1991*c*), on p. 254, only to endorse it once more on p. 259. I owe this point to Gebauer (1993), p. 91. On p. 86 of his excellent book, Gebauer traces Habermas's ambivalence back to a certain antagonism between Habermas the sociologist and Habermas the justificatory logician. Evidently here the justificatory "logician" triumphed over the sociologist, since Habermas continues to hold this empirically false thesis even today. We will return to this below in the Sections 3.3.1 and 3.3.2.
140. See Section 1.3.2.2.2.1, pp. 58f.
141. Habermas (1984), p. 331, translation slightly modified (I substituted "normally" for "often" in line with the German original, see idem 1988I, p. 444).
142. Habermas (2003*c*), p. 302, translation slightly modified (I reintroduced the italics), see idem (1992*a*), p. 133.
143. Habermas (1985*d*), p. 169.
144. Habermas (1984), p. 287; compare also Habermas (2003*c*), p. 227.
145. Habermas (2003*c*), p. 338.
146. Ibid. pp. 340f. Translation slightly modified, see Habermas (1996*a*), p. 91.
147. See p. 57.
148. Habermas (1984), p. 408, n. 4.

149. Rolf Zimmermann justified this contention with the example of an imperative sentence. See Zimmermann (1985), p. 373. Habermas (1991c, p. 238) takes up a similar example of Tugendhat's (1985), p. 184, albeit in a somewhat different context, to explain that Tugendhat's analysis of imperative sentences is "contra-intuitive" and that he, Habermas, would like to "stick by" his own analysis. As the following arguments will make clear, he sticks by the wrong one.
150. Habermas (1984), pp. 86f.
151. Ibid. p. 95.
152. Ibid. p. 84.
153. Ibid. p. 87.
154. Ibid. p. 101.
155. Compare Zimmermann (1985), pp. 357ff.
156. See the quote pertaining to n. 97.
157. Habermas (1985c), pp. 208f.
158. Habermas (1984), p. 99. Compare also ibid. pp. 310ff.
159. Habermas (1988), p. 410, my translation. The translation in Habermas (1984), p. 305, might be somewhat misleading.
160. Habermas (2003c), p. 323. Incidentally, the bracketed "in the strict sense" is not to be found in the original text. See Habermas (1996a), p. 78.
161. Habermas (1984), p. 101.
162. Compare Kettner (1994); see also above, Section 1.2.1.1.
163. Habermas (2003c), p. 331.
164. Ibid. pp. 331f.
165. Vgl. Dorschel (1988), p. 6. In English, however, one can indeed say: "That is a valid question." Yet this is—contrary to the claims a *universal* pragmatics would have to make—not possible with most other speech acts. The German equivalent *Das ist eine gültige Frage* is nonsense. To use, as Habermas does, the term *"gültig"* in connection with *"Sprechakte"* is an abuse of the German language.
166. Habermas (1984), p. 8.
167. Ibid. pp. 9 and 86–96. Compare also Habermas (2003c), p. 220.
168. Habermas (2001a), p. 20.
169. Habermas (1984), p. 95.
170. Ibid. pp. 98f.
171. Ibid. p. 99.
172. Ibid. p. 286.
173. Ibid. p. 10.
174. Habermas (2003c), p. 309.
175. On the terminology, see the introduction of Chapter 1.
176. Habermas (1984), p. 99.
177. Ibid. pp. 99f. Compare also ibid. pp. 307f.
178. Ibid. pp. 286f., the bracket is in the text.
179. Ibid. p. 293, "and the understanding-oriented attitude" missing from the original translation, compare the German original, Habermas (1988), p. 394.
180. See Section 1.2.2.1, esp. pp. 31–5.
181. Habermas (1984), p. 295.
182. See Section 1.2.2.2, pp. 35f.
183. See Section 1.2.2.1, pp. 21f.
184. Habermas (1984), p. 99.
185. Köveker (1992), p. 296.

186. Habermas (2003*c*), p. 226, my emphasis.
187. See Apel (1992*b*), pp. 5ff.

CHAPTER 2

1. Habermas (1999*b*), p. 92.
2. Ibid. p. 67.
3. Ibid. p. 103.
4. See Section 1.3.2.1.
5. Habermas (1999*b*), pp. 43–115.
6. Ibid. p. 44.
7. Ibid. p. 63.
8. Ibid. p. 62, the explanations in brackets are mine.
9. Ibid.
10. Haferkamp (1985), p. 201.
11. Keuth (1993), pp. 270f.
12. Habermas (1999*b*), pp. 56f.
13. Ibid. p. 45.
14. Ibid.
15. Ibid. p. 48.
16. See Section 1.2.2.2, the quote pertaining to n. 97.
17. Habermas (1999*b*), p. 45, translation corrected, see Habermas (1991*a*), p. 55. ("*Berühmt*" means "famous", not merely "well-known".)
18. Habermas (1999*b*), p. 49, translation modified; the original does not say *gute Gründe* (good reasons) but simply *Gründe*, see Habermas (1991*a*), p. 59.
19. Ibid. pp. 51 and 57.
20. Ibid. p. 49.
21. Ibid. p. 44.
22. See the introduction to Section 1.3.2.2 as well as Section 1.3.2.2.1.
23. Habermas (1999*b*), p. 44.
24. See Sections 1.2.1 and 1.3.2.1.
25. Habermas (1999*b*), p. 62, my emphasis.
26. Ibid. p. 54, translation completed, see id. (1991*a*), p. 64.
27. Habermas (1999*b*), p. 56.
28. Ibid.
29. Ibid. p. 59f.
30. Ibid. p. 60.
31. Keuth (1993), p. 279f., even claims that with these remarks Habermas unintentionally abandons the consensus theory and hence discourse ethics as well.
32. See also below, Section 2.4, pp. 157ff. The German word for proposition is *Aussage*, and an *Aussage sagt aus*—it says or states something.
33. Habermas (1999*b*), p. 61.
34. Ibid. p. 93.
35. See on this below, Section 2.3.
36. Habermas (1999*b*), pp. 62f.
37. Habermas (1989*a*), p. 167.
38. Keuth (1993), p. 293.
39. Goodman (1955).
40. Compare Keuth (1993), p. 293.

41. Compare Lumer (1997), p. 43.
42. Keuth (1993), p. 306, nurtures the suspicion that the whole of discourse ethics is nothing but a definitional fiat. This suspicion indeed strongly suggests itself.
43. Habermas (1999*b*), p. 63.
44. Ibid. p. 65.
45. See ibid. pp. 67, 92, 103.
46. Alexy (1978), pp. 29f.
47. Ibid. p. 29.
48. Alexy (1978), p. 33.
49. Apel (1976), pp. 57ff.
50. Ibid. p. 61.
51. Ibid. p. 64.
52. Albert and Apel (1984), p. 116.
53. For instance ibid. pp. 87ff.
54. Ibid. p. 90.
55. Ibid. p. 117.
56. This sort of thing is quite vividly described by Simak (1992), p. 124.
57. Apel (1976), p. 72.
58. Ibid. pp. 72f.
59. Albert and Apel (1984), p. 89.
60. Gethmann and Hegselmann (1977), pp. 346 ff.
61. Albert (1982), p. 61.
62. Albert and Apel (1984), p. 108.
63. Apel (1987), p. 187.
64. Gethmann and Hegselmann (1977), p. 347.
65. See Apel (1980), p. 277. On the shortcomings of this concept, see Section 2.2.2.2.1, pp. 103ff.
66. Although the manner in which proponents of discourse ethics appeal to implicit recognition does. See Section 2.2.2.2.
67. Albert and Apel (1984), p. 89 and p. 112, n. 3; Apel (1987), p. 194.
68. Kuhlmann (1985*a*), p. 23.
69. Ibid. pp. 75f.
70. Ibid. p. 80.
71. Keuth (1988), p. 390, speaks of a "transcendental-philosophical belief in revelation".
72. Kuhlmann (1985*a*), p. 84.
73. Ibid. p. 92.
74. Keuth (1983), p. 332.
75. Kuhlmann (1985*a*), pp. 94f.; Apel (1987), p. 188.
76. Habermas (1999*b*), pp. 91f.
77. Kuhlmann (1985*a*), p. 184.
78. Albert (1982), p. 91.
79. Kuhlmann (1985*a*), pp. 102f.
80. Ibid. pp. 221f.
81. See ibid. pp. 152ff. and pp. 215–20. See on this also below, Section 2.2.2.3.
82. Kuhlmann (1985*a*), p. 222.
83. Ibid. p. 223.
84. Ibid. p. 207.
85. Compare Lukes (1982). Although the impossibility of such a consensus seems quite plainly evident to me, nonetheless below in Chapter 2.3, particularly pp. 149ff., I will go

into Habermas's quite vague notions about the feasibility of this consensus in greater detail and demonstrate their fallaciousness. Kuhlmann and Apel, incidentally, seem not to have any worries about the question of *how* this consensus is to arise.

86. Kuhlmann (1985*b*), p. 366.
87. Kuhlmann (1985*a*), p. 224.
88. Ibid. p. 225.
89. Ibid. p. 224.
90. Ibid. p. 183.
91. Kuhlmann (1993).
92. Apel (1987), p. 189.
93. See Kuhlmann (1985*a*), pp. 111ff.
94. Compare Berlich (1982), p. 261; Keuth (1993), pp. 241f.
95. Apel (1987), p. 196.
96. Ibid. p. 190.
97. Albert and Apel (1984), p. 118.
98. Ibid. p. 119.
99. Apel (1994), p. 94.
100. Apel (1996), p. 197.
101. Oelmüller (1978*a*), pp. 225–8.
102. Ibid. pp. 9f. The "renowned transcendental philosopher" is Thomas McCarthy; his objections are to be found ibid. pp. 134ff., 196 and 205f.
103. Apel (1995), p. 43.
104. Apel (1994), p. 94.
105. See Section 2.2.2.2.1, pp. 104ff. See also Steinhoff (2006), Section 2.3, pp. 81ff.
106. Apel (1992*a*), p. 111; idem (1987), p. 195.
107. Apel (1994), p. 94.
108. Apel (1987), p. 183.
109. Apel (1980), pp. 274ff.; idem (1993*a*), p. 54.
110. Ibid.
111. Apel (1996), p. 208.
112. Albert remarks about Apel that on the point of argumentative presuppositions he clearly "is to be put on par with the Pope". See Albert and Apel (1984), p. 109.
113. Apel (1995), p. 30, note.
114. Albert (1982), p. 79.
115. Keuth (1993), pp. 241f.; Rohs (1987), pp. 369f., Ros (1990), pp. 245f.
116. Schönrich (1994), p. 159.
117. See Keuth (1993), pp. 260f.
118. Apel (1980), pp. 274f.
119. Ros (1990), p. 245.
120. Kuhlmann (1993), pp. 229f.
121. Ibid. p. 233.
122. The readers can satisfy themselves on this point by reading Kuhlmann's dialogue.
123. Kuhlmann (1993), p. 230.
124. Rohs (1987), pp. 369f.
125. Kuhlmann (1993), pp. 235f.
126. Ibid. p. 229.
127. Ibid. p. 231.
128. Ibid. p. 236.
129. See Steinhoff (2006), Section 3.2, esp. pp. 159ff.

130. Kuhlmann (1993), p. 237.
131. Ibid.
132. Ibid.
133. See Section 2.2.2.2.2, pp. 111ff.
134. Kuhlmann (1985*a*), p. 116.
135. Ibid.
136. Compare Albert (1982), pp. 83f.; also Keuth (1983), pp. 334f. and (1993), pp. 242f.
137. Kuhlmann (1985*a*), p. 234.
138. Albert (1982), p. 84.
139. Apel (1994), p. 91.
140. See Apel (1980), pp. 280f.; (1984), p. 47. On this compare also Steinhoff (2006), Section 2.3, pp. 81ff.
141. Kuhlmann (1985*a*), p. 116.
142. Ibid. pp. 116f.
143. Ibid. p. 117.
144. See Section 2.2.2.1, p. 98.
145. See Sections 2.2.2.1, 2.2.2.2; compare also Steinhoff (2006), Section 3.3.2.3.3.
146. Apel (1976), pp. 72f.
147. Apel (1992*a*), p. 10.
148. Ibid. p. 13.
149. Apel (1987), p. 148.
150. Berlich (1982), p. 98.
151. Apel (1987), p. 186; compare also idem (1995), p. 30, note 1, as well as p. 31.
152. Habermas (1999*b*), p. 95.
153. Ibid. p. 89, text in square brackets added.
154. Ibid. p. 91, the third emphasis is mine, as well as Habermas's in the original. See idem (1991*a*), p. 101.
155. Habermas (1999*b*), pp. 91f., italics added in line with the German original, see Habermas (1991*a*), p. 102.
156. See on these contradictions Steinhoff (2006), Section 2.3, pp. 81ff.
157. Habermas (1989*a*), p. 180.
158. Habermas (1999*b*), p. 92, text in brackets added. Compare also Apel (1984), p. 61.
159. See Section 3.3.3, pp. 228, point 5.
160. On these various methods of justification see Section 2.2.1.
161. Compare Berlich (1982), p. 261; and Keuth (1993), pp. 241f.
162. Stroud (1968), p. 246.
163. Kuhlmann (1985*a*), pp. 153f.
164. See Section 2.2.2.2.1, pp. 104ff.
165. Hösle (1997), p. 187.
166. Ibid. p. 163.
167. Ibid. pp. 187f.
168. Ibid. p. 160.
169. See ibid. pp. 152–9.
170. Ibid. p. 163.
171. Compare ibid. p. 153.
172. Habermas (1999*b*), pp. 85f. As is well known, Ilting (1982) had already seen this before Habermas.
173. Habermas (1999*b*), p. 93; translation modified in line with the German original, see idem (1991*a*), p. 103.

174. Habermas (1999*b*), p. 65.
175. Kettner (1993), p. 327.
176. See Section 1.3.2.1.
177. See ibid.
178. See Kettner (1993), p. 326.
179. See Steinhoff (2006), Section 2.3.
180. Øfsti (1993), p. 302.
181. Apel (1990*a*), p. 116.
182. Apel (1992*a*), pp. 146f.; (1993*a*), p. 36.
183. As the transcendental–pragmatist Mathias Kettner concisely explains: "In the sector of practice that is discourse, *strategically rational* action is excluded; the procedural unified focus of discourse ethics demands essentially and exclusively *consensually rational* action." Kettner (1993), p. 344.
184. See Steinhoff (2006) Section 3.6.2.
185. Apel (1992*a*), pp. 142ff.
186. See Sections 1.3.2.1–1.3.2.2.
187. Kuhlmann (1985*a*), pp. 228f.
188. See Steinhoff (2006), Section 3.2.
189. Apel (1992*b*), p. 12.
190. See Section 1.3.2.2.2.1.
191. Habermas (2001*a*), p. 32. See also (1999*b*), p. 93.
192. Lumer (1997).
193. Habermas (1999*b*), pp. 92f.
194. See Section 2.2.2.3, p. 137.
195. Compare Lumer (1997), p. 46.
196. Ibid. p. 75f.; see also Habermas (2001*a*), p. 32.
197. Habermas (1983), p. 103.
198. Wellmer (1986), p. 102; Lumer (1997).
199. Tugendhat (1994), pp. 169f.
200. Habermas (1999*a*), p. 275, n. 67.
201. Habermas (2001*a*), p. 179, n. 17.
202. Habermas (1999*b*), p. 212, n. 7.
203. Habermas (2001*a*), p. 179, n. 18.
204. Rehg (1991), p. 40.
205. Compare Lumer (1997), p. 52.
206. Habermas (1996*e*), p. 531, n. 38.
207. Rehg (1994), p. 67.
208. Habermas (1999*a*), p. 45, translation completed, see Habermas (1996*b*), p. 63.
209. Habermas (1999*a*), p. 43. Here Habermas no longer mentions Rehg, instead referring to Konrad Ott's article "Wie begründet man ein Diskussionsprinzip der Moral". Ott (1996), pp. 12–50. There are many errors in Ott's article. Not only is the author unable to distinguish between (epistemic) justification and validity—for him "justified norms are valid" is a "trivial analytical sentence" (ibid. p. 41)!; evidently he is also unable to distinguish between a justification and a mere assertion: though he *claims* that D and U are "pragmatically implied" by certain presuppositions of argumentation along with other premises (ibid. pp. 42f.)—which, by the way, would still be of very little use—he does not even *attempt* to *demonstrate* this. So it is amusing at best when he declares discourse ethics to be "justified now" at the end of his article (ibid. p. 48).

210. This reversal in the direction of derivation can also be seen in Habermas (1996*e*), pp. 108f. Compare on this Lumer (1997), pp. 52f.
211. Habermas (1999*b*), p. 212, n. 7.
212. Habermas (1999*b*), p. 92.
213. Ibid. p. 67.
214. Ibid.
215. Of course the resolution of a conflict of action does not need to have anything to do with the adoption of a norm.
216. Habermas (1999*b*), p. 103.
217. Habermas (2001*a*), p. 32.
218. Habermas (1999*b*), p. 93.
219. Lukes (1982).
220. Habermas (2001*a*), p. 57.
221. Ibid. p. 58.
222. Habermas (1982), pp. 257f.
223. Habermas (1999*b*), p. 56.
224. See on this above, Section 2.1, esp. pp. 87ff.
225. See Section 3.3.3.
226. Compare McCarthy (1996), p. 1094.
227. Habermas (1982), p. 257.
228. Habermas (2001*a*), p. 62.
229. Ibid. pp. 63ff. Habermas introduces the norm "You should not kill" as an example of a valid norm. This implies the norm "You should not murder"—which I interpret here in the sense of "You should not kill from base motives."
230. Habermas (1999*b*), p. 65; also (2001*a*), p. 32.
231. Habermas is correct that *homogeneity* is not a precondition for the functioning of the principle of universalization—but the *compatibility* of the interests affected by a general observance of controversial norms is. This is absent from our real world—and "sources of conflict originating in the lifeworld" are after all to be left "untouched" (ibid. p. 58).
232. Habermas (1999*b*), p. 89.
233. Habermas (1982), p. 258.
234. Habermas (2001*a*), pp. 65f.
235. Habermas (1999*b*), p. 93.
236. See Sections 2.2.2.1 and 2.2.2.2.
237. See Section 2.3, esp. pp. 143–7.
238. See Habermas (1989*a*), pp. 176f.
239. Habermas himself concedes this. See Habermas (1992*c*), pp. 160f.
240. Logi Gunnarsson (1994) interprets Habermas this way. Although several of Habermas's statements suggest this reading, most others do not, in my opinion, such as the central statement that consensus theory provides a *definition* of truth. Admittedly Habermas himself is rather unclear about the status of his theory.
241. Compare Skirbekk (1982), esp. pp. 64–9; as well as Ilting (1976).
242. Habermas (1999*b*), p. 70.
243. On this last point compare Rescher (1993), pp. 54–9.
244. Habermas (1989*a*), p. 160, my emphasis.
245. Habermas (1992*c*), p. 160.
246. Compare for instance Alexy (1989); Benhabib (1992); Cooke (1993).
247. Habermas (1989*a*), p. 128.

248. "Proposition" is used here to translate Habermas's German term *"Aussage"*, which Habermas uses in the sense of the philosophical term "proposition", that is, not in the sense of "sentence" or "statement" (if the latter is meant to refer to a speech act). Thus, when I speak of a proposition "p", I am not referring to the linguistic sign between the quotation marks but to the expressed proposition, that is, to that *what* is said or expressed. I also use proposition or propositional content as interchangeable.

249. Cf. the somewhat differently positioned critique by Dieter Freundlieb (1975), pp. 83–7. According to Freundlieb the truth capacity of a proposition arises in a predicative act, which, however, like propositions, is not dependent on assertions. I hold any further such "act" unnecessary. See also the paragraph following this note.

250. Compare Geach (1985).

251. Habermas (1989*a*), p. 127.

252. Ibid. pp. 128f.

253. Ibid. p. 135.

254. Ibid. p. 128.

255. Ibid. p. 129.

256. Ibid. p. 554.

257. Compare Höffe (1976), p. 316, n. 7.

258. Habermas (2003*c*), p. 86, translation slightly modified, see Habermas (1989*a*), p. 434.

259. Habermas (2003*c*), pp. 85f.

260. Wunderlich (1982), p. 452.

261. Habermas (1989*a*), p. 129. The German word *Sinn* is practically untranslatable. Depending on context it can mean sense, meaning or purpose.

262. It is incautious of Habermas not to put the term "truth" in quotation marks in such a suggestively Heideggerian formulation as "the sense of truth", since it could give the impression that we are meant to look for the sense of some *entity* named truth. In fact Habermas does not share these sorts of problematic metaphysical and essentialist aspiration for the concept of truth. Accordingly formulations such as "truth is…" are not to be read in any way as ontological commitments. The question is when statements are true.

263. Habermas (1989*a*), p. 135.

264. Habermas (2001*a*), p. 63.

265. Habermas (1989*a*), p. 129.

266. Ibid. p. 135. The claim to sincerity is exempted from this.

267. Ibid. p. 137.

268. Habermas (2003*c*), p. 85.

269. Habermas (1989*a*), pp. 159f.

270. Ibid. p. 161.

271. Compare Wellmer (1986), pp. 72f.

272. Habermas (1989*a*), p. 139.

273. Ibid. p. 135.

274. Ibid. p. 136.

275. Ibid. p. 159.

276. Ibid. pp. 159f.

277. This is the suspicion of Thomas McCarthy (1989), p. 344. (1978), p. 303.

278. Habermas (1989*a*), p. 160.

279. Compare Lukes (1982); see also above, Section 2.3, esp. pp. 150ff.

280. See Goodman (1955).

281. Compare Steinhoff (1994).

282. Habermas (1999*a*), p. 37, translation slightly modified (I substituted "inextricable" for "irreducible"), see the German original, Habermas (1996*b*), pp. 53f.
283. Habermas (1999*a*), p. 274, n. 56, the brackets are part of the translation, translation completed, see Habermas (1996*b*), p. 44, n. 55. Compare also Habermas (1996*d*), pp. 1508 and 1518f.
284. Habermas (1999*a*), p. 38.
285. Habermas (1999*b*), p. 93.
286. Wellmer (1986), pp. 65f.
287. Habermas (2001*a*), pp. 63f.
288. Habermas (1989*a*), p. 146.
289. Habermas (2001*a*), p. 63.
290. Ibid.
291. Ibid. p. 13. The original (1991*b*, p. 114) talks of the *Wenn-Komponente* (If-component), which the translation renders "conditional components".
292. Habermas (2001*a*), p. 63.
293. Ibid.
294. Alexy (1985), pp. 75f.
295. Ibid. p. 76.
296. Ibid. p. 77.
297. Günther (1988), p. 272.
298. Alexy (1985), p. 79.
299. Ibid. pp. 84f.
300. Habermas (1996*e*), pp. 253ff.; Günther (1988), p. 268ff.
301. Habermas (2001*a*), p. 34.
302. Ibid. p. 64.
303. Ibid. p. 38.
304. Günther (1988), pp. 304f. Here Günther mentions two criteria of coherence or appropriateness, the first of which he does not consider practicable. The criterion quoted here is the allegedly useful second criterion.
305. Ibid.
306. Habermas (2001*a*), p. 37.
307. Ibid.; for the original, see Günther (1988), p. 55.
308. Habermas (2001*a*), pp. 36f., text in brackets added.
309. See Günther (1988), pp. 53ff.
310. Ibid. p. 307.
311. See ibid. p. 304.
312. Alexy (1985), p. 87.
313. Habermas (1999*b*), p. 93.
314. Habermas (2001*a*), pp. 63f.

CHAPTER 3

1. Apel (1992*a*), pp. 306–70. Here he proposes a seventh stage of moral development in order to resolve the typical application problems of conviction-based ethics that he encounters at the sixth stage. This proposal is more than bold if we consider that sufficient empirical evidence is already lacking for the existence of the sixth stage and that these problems of application for conviction-based ethics would not even arise if we were to content ourselves with stage 5, which is empirically based and in my opinion logically and morally superior.

2. See Habermas (1984), p. 139 and (1987a), pp. 383–403.
3. See all Habermas (2003b), pp. 69–94; (1987a), pp. 96–106; (1989a), pp. 187–270; (1992b), pp. 149–204; Döbert, Habermas and Nunner-Winkler (1980), pp. 9–30.
4. According to Belgrad (1992), Habermas's "outline" is "comprehensively developed" (p. 14), although oddly enough he finds that Habermas "did not develop any explicit theory of ego-identity" (p. 26). To my mind these two statements are contradictory. Be that as it may, Belgrad also considers Habermas's conception as very much amenable to critique.
5. Habermas (1987a), p. 137.
6. See Sections 3.3.1, pp. 204ff. and 3.3.2, esp. pp. 210–14.
7. Habermas (1989a), pp. 200ff.
8. Ibid. p. 200.
9. Ibid. pp. 205ff.
10. Ibid. p. 193; see also ibid. p. 197.
11. See Section 1.3.2.2.2.3, pp. 66ff.
12. Habermas (1999b), pp. 116f.
13. Ibid. p. 39. Habermas quotes Kohlberg (1971), pp. 222f.
14. See Habermas (1999b), pp. 195–203 and (1989c), pp. 33f.
15. See Habermas (1989c); as well as (1999b), pp. 116–94.
16. Habermas (1989c), p. 34, emphasis changed.
17. Ibid. p. 33, my emphasis.
18. Ibid. pp. 33f.
19. Habermas (2003a), p. 131, the bracketed text is part of the original translation.
20. Ibid. p. 132.
21. Ibid. pp. 136f., the English text in brackets is mine.
22. Ibid. p. 147, translation modified (the German original says "*gestört*", which means "disturbed", not "flawed"). See Habermas (1989a), p. 245.
23. See Section 1.3.2.2.2.1.
24. See Habermas (2003a), pp. 150 and 154.
25. Ibid. pp. 154f.
26. Ibid. p. 155, my emphasis.
27. Ibid. pp. 151f. my emphasis.
28. Ibid. p. 152. The first sentence of this quotation is omitted in the English text; see the German original, Habermas (1989a), pp. 249f.
29. Habermas (2003a), p. 146.
30. Ibid. p. 149.
31. Ibid. p. 151.
32. Habermas (1999b), p. 91f.
33. Habermas (2003a), p. 152.
34. However, it is noteworthy that it does not necessarily infringe the presuppositions that Habermas himself names in the text under discussion here (ibid. pp. 147f.). These two presuppositions, namely, that the participants *mutually consider* each other to be accountable and that they mutually *consider* each other to be ready and willing to reach mutual understanding, are in fact fulfilled in our example here. Only the presuppositions of the participants are unfulfilled, i.e. what they presuppose or consider to be the case is not the case.
35. Ibid. p. 147.
36. Ibid. p. 145.
37. Ibid. p. 147.

38. Ibid. pp. 136f.
39. Ibid. pp. 147f.
40. Ibid. p. 148.
41. As in the case of the woman who deceives her husband.
42. Wittgenstein (1953), § 271.
43. Habermas (2003a), pp. 169f.
44. Ibid. pp. 154f.
45. Ibid. p. 147.
46. Apel (1984), p. 58.
47. Habermas (1999b), pp. 99ff. See also above, Section 1.3.2.2.2.1, p. 59.
48. Habermas (2003a), p. 149, the emphasis on "not possible" is mine.
49. Ibid. p. 136.
50. Habermas (1999b), p. 102.
51. Laing (1998), pp. 83f.
52. See Habermas (1984), pp. 285 and 101.
53. Ibid. p. 139.
54. Habermas (2003b), p. 136.
55. Ibid. p. 137.
56. Ibid. pp. 137f.
57. See ibid. p. 132.
58. See Section 3.3.2, esp. pp. 212f.
59. Habermas (1984), p. 286.
60. See Section 1.2.2.1.
61. See also below, Sections 3.3.1, pp. 204ff. and 3.3.2, esp. pp. 210–14.
62. Habermas (2003b), p. 95.
63. Ibid. p. 120. Compare also Habermas (1987a), p. 173.
64. Habermas (2003b), p. 121.
65. Ibid. pp. 147f.
66. Eder (1976), p. 51.
67. Habermas (1995), p. 44. The English translation of this article omits the last paragraph
    of the original. See Habermas (2003b), p. 225, n. 44.
68. Habermas (1987a), p. 397.
69. Habermas (2003b), p. 99.
70. Eder (1976), p. 71.
71. Compare Lefrancois (1986), pp. 139f., as well as the studies named there.
72. Compare Snarey (1994), p. 286.
73. Edwards (1975), p. 525.
74. Habermas (1995), p. 260, my emphasis.
75. Habermas (2003b), p. 157.
76. Ibid.
77. Ibid. p. 148.
78. Ibid. pp. 157f.
79. Ibid. p. 148, emphasis removed.
80. Ibid. p. 147.
81. Ibid. p. 175.
82. Here we should also note that Habermas's statement that "every theory of development"
    has "normative implications" (ibid.) is to be emphatically rejected. Distinguishing a
    stage of development within developmental logic has nothing to do with *normatively*
    distinguishing this stage.

83. Ibid. p. 177.
84. See Sections 2.2.2.2.1–2.2.2.2.2 and 2.2.2.3, as well as Steinhoff (2006), Section 2.3.
85. Habermas (2003c), pp. 233f.
86. Habermas (1985d), p. 151.
87. Habermas (1984), p. 296.
88. Habermas (2003c), p. 236.
89. Ibid. p. 237.
90. Ibid. p. 248. Cf. also Habermas (1987a), pp. 2, 138, 142f., 204, 231, 267; as well as (1982), p. 237.
91. Habermas (1984), p. 302. On Habermas's distinction between "empirical" and "rational motivation" see idem (1987a), p. 181. For a critique of this see Dorschel (1990), pp. 232ff.
92. Weiß (1983), p. 113.
93. Habermas (1991c), p. 244.
94. Habermas (1987a), pp. 68f.
95. Habermas (1991c), p. 245.
96. Ibid.
97. Ibid. p. 249.
98. Habermas claims (1999b, p. 102) that he has shown the correctness of this thesis "elsewhere". However, if we turn to the passage Habermas mentions (1987a, pp. 140ff.), we do not find any kind of *justification* of the thesis, but rather just one more mention of the thesis itself following several arguments that do not even aim at a justification of it, but rather treat other questions.
99. Even a critic as well-disposed towards Habermas's project as Thomas McCarthy—who is in fact a proponent of it in many points—does not give this thesis the slightest credit. See McCarthy (1989), pp. 602–4.
100. See Habermas (1991c), pp. 254 and 259. Compare above, Ch. 1, n. 139.
101. Habermas (1984), p. 294.
102. Ibid. p. 287.
103. Habermas (1987a), p. 144.
104. Habermas (1984), p. 287.
105. Stevenson (1965).
106. Habermas (1987a), p. 138, emphasis removed.
107. See also below, Section 3.3.2, esp. pp. 210–14.
108. Habermas (1984), p. 100.
109. The critiques from Giddens (1982), esp. p. 331; Holzer (1988), pp. 997ff.; Keuth (1993), esp. pp. 324–44 and Tugendhat (1985), pp. 181f., among others, also take this general direction.
110. See Section 1.3.3, pp. 73f.
111. Habermas (1984), p. 99.
112. Habermas (2003c), p. 85, the text in brackets is mine. Incidentally, the "she" in these examples—and in many others—is not to be found in the German original.
113. Habermas (1984), pp. 285f.
114. Günther (1996), p. 1041. Günther's entire attempt to clarify how so-called "communicative" force functions fails with this decisive error.
115. Habermas (1984), pp. 305ff.
116. Ibid.
117. See Section 1.2.2, pp. 21f.
118. Habermas (1987a), pp. 396f.

119. Habermas (1987*a*), p. 117.
120. Ibid. p. 330.
121. Ibid. p. 331.
122. Ibid. p. 135.
123. Ibid. pp. 135ff.
124. Ibid. pp. 309f.
125. Ibid. p. 171.
126. Habermas (1991*c*), pp. 256f., the text in brackets is mine.
127. Habermas (1987*a*), p. 183.
128. See ibid. pp. 181ff.
129. See ibid. p. 154.
130. Ibid. p. 365.
131. Habermas (1991*c*), p. 257, translation corrected, see idem (1986*a*), p. 387.
132. Habermas (1991*c*), pp. 257f.
133. Habermas (1987*a*), p. 309.
134. Habermas (1991*c*), p. 254. This quotation also shows that strategic action occurring in the "lifeworld" cannot in turn have recourse to "an already existing lifeworld constituted through communicative action"—let alone have to have this recourse, as Habermas says elsewhere (2003*c*, p. 248), thus repudiating the insight just quoted. *When* and *where*, after all, should this lifeworld before the lifeworld be "already" constituted— prenatally in heaven?
135. Habermas (1987*a*), p. 232.
136. See Honneth (1985), pp. 321ff.
137. Maus (1987), p. 160.
138. Habermas (1992*c*), p. 111.
139. Habermas (1987*a*), p. 383.
140. See ibid. pp. 119–35; Habermas (2003*c*), pp. 239ff.; and it is given a particularly emphatic formulation, although not so clearly related to the formal–pragmatic concept of the lifeworld, in Habermas (1992*c*), pp. 109f.
141. Ibid.
142. Compare McCarthy (1989), pp. 580–604.
143. Habermas (1991*c*), pp. 251f.
144. Ibid. pp. 253f.
145. Compare Bohnen (1984), p. 200, my emphasis.
146. Habermas (1987*a*), p. 345, text in brackets added.
147. Ibid. p. 365.
148. Habermas (2003*b*), p. 132.
149. However, Habermas has quite unrealistic notions about power; among other things he believes that it relies on legitimation and thus is dependent on linguistic processes of consensus-formation. See Habermas (1987*a*), pp. 270–2. This is untenable, since one can clearly have the "disposition over means of enforcement that can be used to threaten sanctions or to apply direct force" (ibid. p. 268) that he holds necessary for power without this disposition being legitimate or considered legitimate.
150. Ibid. p. 365.
151. Habermas (1991*c*), p. 261.
152. Ibid.
153. Not necessarily in the sense of *abolishing* capitalism, but in the sense of a possible quite radical restructuring of it.
154. Habermas (1985*b*), p. 194.

155. See for instance Habermas (1987*a*), pp. 394f. and (1999*b*), p. 211.
156. Compare Johannes (1989).
157. Ibid. p. 58.
158. Habermas (1991*c*), p. 261.
159. See McCarthy (1989), p. 580–604; Honneth (1985), pp. 307–35; Joas (1986).
160. Habermas (1987*b*), pp. 357ff.
161. Compare Türcke (1989).
162. The German subtitle reads "Beiträge zu einer Diskurstheorie des Rechts and des demo-kratischen Rechtsstaats", which the English subtitle renders "Contributions to a Dis-course Theory of Law and Democracy". The German *Rechtsstaat* is usually translated as "constitutional state". In any case, *Rechtsstaat* means a state under the rule of law.
163. Habermas (1996*e*), p. 38.
164. Ibid. p. 104.
165. Ibid. p. 107.
166. Ibid.
167. Ibid. p. 110.
168. Ibid. p. 111.
169. Ibid. p. 104, translation slightly modified (the translation renders "*politisch autonom*" simply as "legitimate"), see the German original, Habermas (1994), p. 134.
170. I did just this in Steinhoff (1996*b*), p. 450.
171. Habermas (1996*e*), p. 110, my emphasis. Compare also Habermas (1999*a*), p. 259.
172. In this regard Habermas's formulation is in fact misleading in its one-sidedness.
173. See Habermas (2001*b*), pp. 117f., the text in brackets is mine.
174. Habermas (1996*e*), p. 167.
175. Ibid. p. 179.
176. Ibid. p. 180. There is no emphasis in the original, see Habermas (1994), p. 221.
177. Habermas (1996*e*), p. 301; see also Habermas (1994), p. 368.
178. Habermas (1996*e*), p. 301.
179. Ibid. p. 329.
180. Ibid. p. 287.
181. Ibid. p. 39.
182. Ibid. pp, 443f.
183. Habermas (1999*b*), p. 93.
184. See Section 2.3.
185. See ibid.
186. Compare O'Neill (1993); as well as Ingram (1993), p. 299. Ingram's critique refers to "some…earlier writings" of Habermas. However, I cannot concur with his claim that Habermas avoids the error in "more recent formulations". However, he prob-ably would not have claimed this after reading Habermas's *Between Facts and Norms*, which first appeared in English in 1996.
187. Habermas (1996*e*), p. 108.
188. Ibid. p. 110.
189. Habermas (1999*b*), pp. 92f.
190. Habermas (1999*a*), p. 42, translation corrected, see Habermas (1996*b*), p. 60, the capi-talization is mine.
191. Habermas (1996*e*), p. 108, my emphasis.
192. Ibid. p. 156.
193. Ibid. On Habermas's insistence on a distinction between moral norms and legal norms see also ibid. pp. 459f.

194. Habermas (1999*a*), p. 42, translation corrected, see Habermas (1996*b*), p. 60, the capitalization is mine.
195. Habermas (1996*e*), p. 109.
196. Habermas (2001*a*), pp. 1–17.
197. Habermas (1996*e*), p. 111.
198. Ibid. p. 128.
199. Habermas (2001*b*), p. 70.
200. Habermas (1996*e*), pp. 120ff.
201. Ibid. p. 108.
202. Ibid. p. 121.
203. Habermas (2001*b*), p. 117. Compare Habermas (1996*e*), pp. 126f.
204. Habermas (2001*b*), p. 118.
205. Habermas (2001*a*), p. 56.
206. Habermas (1996*e*), p. 82, translation corrected, see Habermas (1994), p. 109.
207. Habermas (1986*b*), p. 248.
208. Habermas (1996*e*), p. 301.
209. Habermas (1996*d*), p. 1494, translation slightly modified, see Habermas (1996*b*), p. 327.
210. Habermas (1996*d*), p. 1494f.
211. Peters (1991), pp. 253ff. and 258ff.
212. Habermas (1996*d*), p. 1508.
213. See Section 1.3.2.1.
214. McCarthy (1996).
215. Habermas (1996*d*), p. 1491.
216. Habermas (1996*b*), p. 336, my translation. The English translation in Habermas (1996*d*), p. 1502, does not accurately capture the sense of the German expression. What is meant is that the future owes us the "redemption" of the premise of the single right answer. The problem Habermas ignores, however, is that the future might have no inclination to pay—and perhaps for very good reasons.
217. Habermas (1996*e*), p. 109.
218. See point 3.
219. In fact Habermas's entire programme of moral justification is a bad check.
220. Habermas (1996*d*), p. 1492.
221. Ibid. pp. 1491ff.
222. See Habermas (1996*e*), pp. 21 and 287.
223. Ibid. p. 301.
224. Ibid. p. 179.
225. See point 6.
226. Habermas is also aware that the *repetition* of arguments plays a significant role. This, incidentally, speaks against a cognitivist interpretation of democratic processes, since repetition is a *rhetoric* means—as Habermas says: "…the dissenting opinion attached to the justification of a Supreme Court ruling, for example, is meant to *record* arguments that in similar cases might convince the majority of a future panel of judges." Habermas (1996*e*), p. 179, my emphasis.
227. For a critique of Habermas's cognitivist misinterpretations of the democratic process see Bernstein (1996), McCarthy (1996) and Rehg (1996). However, at least McCarthy's and Rehg's criticism is aimed more at cognitivist *constrictions* that are to be countered by emphasizing the concept of solidarity. My argument here is rather that Habermasian cognitivism, if it came to be societally accepted, would *undermine* the tolerance, moderation and solidarity in dealing with minorities that we more or less see, or at

least hope to see, in modern pluralistic democracies. A complementary relation is *not* possible.

228. Habermas (1996*e*), pp. 179f.
229. Habermas (1996*d*), p. 1494.
230. Habermas (1996*e*), p. 38, translation modified, see idem (1994), p. 57.
231. Habermas (1996*e*), p. 301.
232. Habermas (2001*a*), p. 85.
233. Habermas (1996*e*), p. 39.
234. Ibid. p. 488, text in brackets is mine.
235. Ibid. text in brackets is mine.
236. Ibid. p. 379.
237. Ibid. p. 382.
238. Compare ibid. pp. 382–4.
239. Ibid. pp. 382f.
240. Ibid. p. 383, my emphasis.
241. Ibid.
242. Gould (1996), pp. 1283f.
243. Mirbach (1984), p. 5. (The German *emphatisch* and the English "emphatic" do not have quite the same meaning.)
244. For instance Habermas (1992*c*), pp. 104ff.
245. Habermas (1987*b*), p. 338.
246. Habermas (1985*b*), pp. 136f.
247. Habermas (1984), p. 339.
248. Ibid. p. 240 See also McCarthy's critique (1989), pp. 566–79, where one can find several of Habermas's logocentric prejudices.
249. See Section 1.2.1.
250. See Ch. 1.
251. Habermas (1991*c*), pp. 255f.
252. See Section 3.3.2.
253. Paradigmatic for this is Habermas (1981), pp. 444–64.
254. Habermas (2001*b*), p. 146.
255. Although Habermas does not mention discourse ethics by name, nonetheless the explanations in Habermas (1987*b*), pp. 336–67, among others imply it.
256. Habermas (1999*b*), p. 197.
257. See Ch. 1.
258. Habermas (2001*b*), p. 120, translation modified, the brackets are mine. For the original, see Habermas (1998), p. 180. The English version translates "*Diskurse der Aufklärung*" as "discourse of modernity". That is somewhat misleading. It should also be noted that the German word *Aufklärung* does not simply mean a certain historical era, as does the English term "Enlightenment". It also means the process of enlightening people. I tried to capture this by using "enlightenment" (all lower case). Honneth (1994) presents a similar argument for discourse ethics and against Lyotard, see particularly p. 201.
259. Habermas (2001*b*), p. 148.
260. Habermas (1999*b*), pp. 161 and 166.
261. Habermas (2003*b*), p. 105, the text in brackets is mine.
262. Morison (1965), p. 157.
263. Habermas (1996*d*), p. 1505, the text in brackets is mine.
264. Habermas (1973), p. 194.

265. See Sections 2.1 and 2.3.

266. Incidentally, Habermas responds to the argument "against the individualistic character of human rights" (Habermas 2001*b*, p. 123), based on Confucianism, for example, with an instrumental argument rather than a normative one—which entirely misses the real problem. He claims (in unwitting agreement with the chorus of neo-liberal propaganda) that we cannot have capitalist modernization "without taking advantage of the achievements of an individualistic legal order" (ibid. p. 124)—that is, without those legal human rights. To use a formulation that Habermas employs to criticize others, we can say that this view "only betrays a lack of historical experience" (ibid. p. 120).

CONCLUSION

1. Giddens (1982), p. 335.
2. Forget (1991).
3. Habermas (2003*c*), p. 94, n. 6.
4. Habermas (1984), p. 109.
5. The present work, however (the German original was first published in 2001), did not have that much "luck".
6. Habermas (1996*d*), p. 1547.
7. Habermas (1996*d*), p. 1478, n. 7. Habermas declares here that Goodrich accuses him "of defending reason against the irrationalists, the conservatives, the postmodernists, the heretics, the nomads and the outsiders, the Jews". Translation corrected, see Habermas (1996*c*), p. 1560, n. 7. For this reason he feels accused of anti-Semitism. But why? Is it not possible to defend reason against everyone, including Jews, without being an anti-Semite? Be that as it may, Goodrich accuses him of racism about as much as he accuses him of conspiracy to burn heretics. I find Habermas's agitation inappropriate but also telling. What Goodrich sees in Habermas's conception of reason are certain totalitarian tendencies, namely, "a totalising desire to see an end to nonrational communication" (Goodrich 1996, p. 1458). Many postmodernists maintain this suspicion of Habermas's conception, and it is hardly a refutation of them to summarily break off the reception of adversarial arguments.
8. He said this on 9 June 1967 in Hanover following the funeral of Benno Ohnesorg. See Habermas (1981), p. 214.
9. Ibid., pp. 463f.
10. Compare Heide Berndt (1989).
11. Lyotard (1982).
12. Habermas (1987*b*), p. xix.
13. McCarthy (1978), p. 353.
14. Habermas (1984), p. 140.
15. Habermas (1992*c*), p. 128.

APPENDIX

1. Habermas (2003*d*), p. 10.
2. Ibid. p. 17.
3. Ibid. p. 18.
4. Ibid. p. 27.
5. Ibid. p. 27.

6. Habermas (2003*c*), p. 357.
7. Williams (1996), p. 232, as quoted by Habermas (2003*c*), p. 378, n. 26. The text in brackets is mine.
8. Alston (1996), p. 90.
9. Ibid. p. 94.
10. Habermas (2003*c*), p. 367. Compare also idem (2003*d*), p. 251.
11. Habermas (2003*c*), p. 368.
12. See pp. 51–2 and 154–67.
13. Habermas (2003*d*), pp. 36ff. and 252ff., as well as (2003*c*), pp. 369ff.
14. Habermas (2003*d*), p. 39.
15. Ibid. p. 253.
16. Ibid. p. 39.
17. Elsewhere I have invoked the relation between risk–utility calculations and the distinction between truth and justification to criticize Rorty's claim that his distinction makes no difference in practice. See Steinhoff (1997).
18. Habermas (2003*d*), pp. 24 and 241.
19. Ibid. p. 27, translation corrected, see Habermas (1999*c*), pp. 37f. The translation mistakenly renders what is in fact meant as the learning processes of our species (*Lernprozesse unserer Art*) as "our kinds of learning processes".
20. Habermas (2003*d*), p. 29, translation slightly modified; in line with the original I substituted "an intelligent" for "the intelligent".
21. Ibid. p. 272.
22. Ibid. p. 273.
23. Ibid. pp. 274f.
24. See Steinhoff (2006), pp. 67–70.
25. Habermas (1999*b*), p. 207.
26. See pp. 46–50.
27. See pp. 21–2, 72–7 and 206–8.
28. See pp. 21–2.
29. See pp. 184–93 and 200–19.

Bibliography

Hans Albert (1971), *Plädoyer für kritischen Rationalismus*, Piper, München.

—— (1975), *Transzendentale Träumereien. Karl-Otto Apels Sprachspiele und sein herme-neutischer Gott*, Hoffmann und Campe, Hamburg.

—— (1982), *Die Wissenschaft und die Fehlbarkeit der Vernunft*, Mohr, Tübingen.

—— (1987), "Die angebliche Paradoxie des konsequenten Fallibilismus und die Ansprüche der Transzendentalpragmatik", *Zeitschrift für philosophische Forschung* 41, pp. 421–8.

—— (1989), "Hösles Sprung in den objektiven Idealismus. Über die Verwirrungen eines ganz gewöhnlichen Genies", *Zeitschrift für allgemeine Wissenschaftstheorie* 20, pp. 124–31.

Hans Albert, Karl-Otto Apel (1984), "Ist eine philosophische Letztbegründung moralischer Normen möglich?", in: Karl-Otto Apel, Dietrich Böhler, Gerd Kadelbach (eds.), *Funk-Kolleg Praktische Philosophie/Ethik: Dialoge, Bd. 2*, Fischer Taschenbuch Verlag, Frankfurt/Main, pp. 82–122.

Robert Alexy (1978), "Eine Theorie des praktischen Diskurses", in: Oelmüller (1978*b*), pp. 22–58.

—— (1985), *Theorie der Grundrechte*, Nomos, Baden-Baden.

—— (1989), "Probleme der Diskurstheorie", *Zeitschrift für philosophische Forschung* 43, pp. 81–93.

William P. Alston (1996), *A Realist Conception of Truth*, Cornell University Press, Ithaca and London.

Karl-Otto Apel (1976), "Das Problem der philosophischen Letztbegründung im Lichte einer transzendentalen Sprachpragmatik", in: Bernulf Kanitscheider (ed.), *Sprache und Erkenntnis. Festschrift für Gerhard Frey zum 60. Geburtstag*, Innsbrucker Gesellschaft zur Pflege der Geisteswissenschaften, Innsbruck, pp. 55–82.

—— (1980), *Towards a Transformation of Philosophy*, transl. by Glyn Adey and David Frisby, Routledge & Kegan Paul, London, Boston and Henley.

—— (1984), "Läßt sich ethische Vernunft von strategischer Zweckrationalität unterschei-den?" in: Willem van Reijen, Karl-Otto Apel, *Rationales Handeln und Gesellschaftstheorie*, Germinal, Bochum pp. 23–79.

—— (1986), "Grenzen der Diskursethik? Versuch einer Zwischenbilanz", *Zeitschrift für philosophische Forschung* 40, pp. 3–31.

—— (1987), "Fallibilismus, Konsenstheorie der Wahrheit und Letztbegründung", in: Forum für Philosophie Bad Homburg (ed.), pp. 116–211.

—— (1990*a*) "Faktische Anerkennung oder einsehbar notwendige Anerkennung?", in: Karl-Otto Apel, Riccardo Pozzo (eds.), *Zur Rekonstruktion der praktischen Philosophie*, Frommann-Holzboog, Stuttgart, Bad-Cannstatt, pp. 67–123.

—— (1990*b*), "Diskursethik als Verantwortungsethik—eine postmetaphysische Trans-formation der Ethik Kants", in: Raúl Fornet-Betancourt (ed.), *Ethik und Befreiung*, Augustinus-Buchhandlung, Aachen, pp. 10–40.

—— (1992*a*), *Diskurs und Verantwortung. Das Problem des Übergangs zur postkonventionel-len Moral*, Suhrkamp, Frankfurt/Main.

—— (1992*b*), "Illokutionäre Bedeutung und normative Gültigkeit. Die transzendental-pragmatische Begründung der uneingeschränkten kommunikativen Verständigung", *Protosoziologie* 2, pp. 2–15.

—— (1993a), "Diskursethik vor der Problematik von Recht und Politik: Können die Rationalitätsdifferenzen zwischen Moralität, Recht und Politik selbst noch durch die Diskursethik normativ-rational gerechtfertigt werden?", in Apel/Kettner, pp. 29–61.

—— (1993b), "Das Problem einer universalistischen Makroethik der Mitverantwortung", *Deutsche Zeitschrift für Philosophie* 41, pp. 201–15.

—— (1993c), *Transformation der Philosophie. Bd. II: Das Apriori der Kommunikations gemeinschaft*, Suhrkamp, Frankfurt/Main.

—— (1994), "Ist die transzendentalpragmatische Konzeption der Diskursrationalität eine Unterbestimmung der Vernunft?", in: Petra Kolmer, Harald Korten (eds.), *Grenzbestimmungen der Vernunft*, Alber, Freiburg und München, pp. 77–101.

—— (1995), "Rationalitätskriterien und Rationalitätstypen. Versuch einer transzendental-pragmatischen Rekonstruktion des Unterschiedes zwischen Verstand und Vernunft", in Axel Wüstehube (ed.), *Pragmatische Rationalitätstheorien*, Königshausen und Neumann, Würzburg, pp. 29–63.

—— (1996), *Karl-Otto Apel: Selected Essays, Volume Two: Ethics and the Theory of Rationality*, ed. and introduced by Eduardo Mendieta, Humanities Press, New Jersey.

—— Matthias Kettner (1993), *Zur Anwendung der Diskursethik in Politik, Recht und Wissenschaft*, Suhrkamp, Frankfurt/Main.

Yoshua Bar-Hillel (1973), "On Habermas's Hermeneutic Philosophy of Language", *Synthese* 26, pp. 1–12.

Michael Baurmann (1985), "Understanding as an Aim and Aims of Understanding", in Seebaß/Tuomela, pp. 187–96.

Jürgen Belgrad (1992), *Identität als Spiel. Eine Kritik des Identitätskonzepts von Jürgen Habermas*, Westdeutscher Verlag, Opladen.

Seyla Benhabib (1992), *Situating the Self*, Routledge, New York.

Alfred Berlich (1982), "Elenktik des Diskurses. Karl-Otto Apels Ansatz einer transzenden-talpragmatischen Letztbegründung", in: Kuhlmann/Böhler, pp. 251–87.

Heide Berndt (1989), "Revolution und Scheinrevolution: Von Horkheimers Angst vor dem autoritären Staat zu Habermas' Sorge um die Legitimation des Spätkapitalismus", in Bolte (ed.), pp. 80–100.

Richard J. Bernstein (1996), "The Retrieval of the Democratic Ethos", *Cardozo Law Review* 17, pp. 1127–46.

Dietrich Böhler (1993), "Diskursethik und Menschenwürdegrundsatz zwischen Idealis-ierung und Erfolgsverantwortung", in Apel/Kettner, pp. 201–31.

Alfred Bohnen (1984), "Handlung, Lebenswelt und System in der soziologischen Theorie-bildung: Zur Kritik der Theorie des kommunikativen Handelns von Jürgen Habermas", *Zeitschrift für Soziologie* 13, pp. 191–203.

Gerhard Bolte (ed.) (1989), *Unkritische Theorie. Gegen Habermas*, Zu Klampen, Lüneburg.

Laurence BonJour (1985), *The Structure of Empirical Knowledge*, Harvard University Press, Cambridge, MA.

Roderick Chisholm (1977), *Theory of Knowledge*, Prentice-Hall, Englewood Cliffs, NJ.

Maeve Cooke (1993), "Habermas and Consensus", *European Journal of Philosophy* 1, pp. 247–67.

—— (1994), *Language and Reason*, Cambridge und London.

Jonathan Culler (1985), "Communicative Competence and Normative Force", *New German Critique* 35, pp. 133–44.

Donald Davidson (1980), *Essays on Actions and Events*, Oxford University Press, Oxford.

Rainer Döbert, Jürgen Habermas, Gertrud Nunner-Winkler (eds.) (1980), *Entwicklung des Ichs*, Athenäum, Königstein/Ts.

Andreas Dorschel (1988), "Is there any Normative Claim Internal to Stating Facts?", *Communication and Cognition* 21, pp. 5–16.

——(1990), "Handlungstypen und Kriterien", *Zeitschrift für philosophische Forschung* 44, pp. 220–52.

Andreas Dorschel (1988), Matthias Kettner, Wolfgang Kuhlmann, Marcel Niquet (eds.) (1993), *Transzendentalpragmatik*, Suhrkamp, Frankfurt/Main.

Klaus Eder (1976), *Die Entstehung staatlich organisierter Gesellschaften. Ein Beitrag zu einer Theorie sozialer Evolution*, Suhrkamp, Frankfurt/Main.

Carolyn P. Edwards (1975), "Societal Complexity and Moral Development: A Kenyan Study", *Ethos* 3, pp. 505–27.

Philippe Forget (1991), "Das 'Gerede' vom performativen Selbstwiderspruch. Zu Habermas' Derrida-Kritik", *Allgemeine Zeitschrift für Philosophie* 16, pp. 47–57.

Forum für Philosophie Bad Homburg (ed.) (1987), *Philosophie und Begründung*, Suhrkamp, Frankfurt/Main.

Dieter Freundlieb (1975), "Zur Problematik einer Diskurstheorie der Wahrheit", *Zeitschrift für allgemeine Wissenschaftstheorie* 6, pp. 82–107.

Peter T. Geach (1985), "Der Askriptivismus", in: Georg Meggle (ed.), *Analytische Handlungstheorie, Band 1*, Suhrkamp, Frankfurt/Main., pp. 239–45.

Richard Gebauer (1993), *Letzte Begründung. Eine Kritik der Diskursethik von Jürgen Habermas*, Fink, München.

Carl Friedrich Gethmann, Rainer Hegselmann (1977), "Das Problem der Begründung zwischen Dezisionismus und Fundamentalismus", *Zeitschrift für allgemeine Wissenschaftstheorie* 8, pp. 342–68.

Anthony Giddens (1982), "Reason Without Revolution? Habermas's Theorie des Kommunikativen Handelns", *Praxis International* 2, pp. 318–38.

Nelson Goodman (1955), *Fact, Fiction and Forecast*, Harvard University Press, Cambridge, MA.

Peter Goodrich (1996), "Habermas and the Postal Rule", *Cardozo Law Review* 17, pp. 1457–76.

Mark Gould (1996), "Law and Philosophy: Some Consequences for the Law Deriving From the Sociological Reconstruction of Philosophical Theory", *Cardozo Law Review* 17, pp. 1239–363.

Horst Gronke (1993), "Apel versus Habermas: Zur Architektonik der Diskursethik", in: Dorschel et al., pp. 273–97.

Logi Gunnarsson (1994), "Diskurs ohne Konsens", *Deutsche Zeitschrift für Philosophie* 42, pp. 313–26.

Klaus Günther (1988), *Der Sinn für Angemessenheit. Anwendungsdiskurse in Moral und Recht*, Suhrkamp, Frankfurt/Main.

——(1996), "Communicative Freedom, Communicative Power, and Jurigenesis", *Cardozo Law Review* 17, pp. 1035–58.

Jürgen Habermas (1973), *Legitimationsprobleme im Spätkapitalismus*, Suhrkamp, Frankfurt/Main.

——(1979), "Aspects of the Rationality of Action", in: Theodore F. Geraets (ed.), *Rationality To-Day*, The University of Ottawa Press, Ottawa, pp. 185–205.

——(1981), *Kleine politische Schriften (I–IV)*, Suhrkamp, Frankfurt/Main.

——(1982), "A Reply to My Critics", in: Thompson and Held, pp. 219–83.

——(1983), *Moralbewußtsein und kommunikatives Handeln*, Suhrkamp, Frankfurt/Main.

——(1984), *The Theory of Communicative Action, Vol. 1: Reason and the Rationalization of Society*, transl. by Thomas McCarthy, Heinemann, London.

——(1985a), "Reply to Skjei", *Inquiry* 28, pp. 105–13.

——(1985b), *Die neue Unübersichtlichkeit*, Suhrkamp, Frankfurt/Main.

——(1985c), "Questions und Counterquestions", in: Richard Bernstein (ed.), *Habermas and Modernity*, MIT Press, Cambridge, MA, pp. 192–216.

—— (1985*d*), "Remarks on the Concept of Communicative Action", in: Seebaß and Tuomela (1985), pp. 151–78.

—— (1986*a*), "Entgegnung", in Honneth/Joas (1986).

—— (1986*b*), "Law and Morality" (The Tanner Lectures), transl. by Kenneth Baynes, http:// www.tannerlectures.utah.edu/lectures/atoz.html#h, accessed on 26 February 2008.

—— (1987*a*), *The Theory of Communicative Action, Vol. 2: Lifeworld and System: A Critique of Functionalist Reason*, transl. by Thomas McCarthy, Polity Press, Cambridge.

—— (1987*b*), *The Philosophical Discourse of Modernity: Twelve Lectures*, MIT Press, Cambridge, MA.

—— (1988), *Theorie des kommunikativen Handelns. Band I: Handlungsrationalität und gesellschaftliche Rationalisierung. Band II: Zur Kritik der funktionalistischen Vernunft*, Suhrkamp, Frankfurt/Main.

—— (1989*a*), *Vorstudien und Ergänzungen zur Theorie des kommunikativen Handelns*, Suhrkamp, Frankfurt/Main.

—— (1989*b*), *Der philosophische Diskurs der Moderne. Zwölf Vorlesungen*, Suhrkamp, Frankfurt/Main.

—— (1989*c*), "Justice and Solidarity: On the Discussion Concerning 'Stage 6'", *Philosophical Forum* 21(1–2), pp. 32–52.

—— (1991*a*), *Moralbewußtsein und kommunikatives Handeln*, Suhrkamp, Frankfurt/Main.

—— (1991*b*), *Erläuterungen zur Diskursethik*, Suhrkamp, Frankfurt/Main.

—— (1991*c*), "A Reply", in: Axel Honneth and Hans Jonas (eds.), *Communicative Action: Essays on Jürgen Habermas's The Theory of Communicative Action*, transl. by Jeremy Gaines and Doris L. Jones, Polity Press, Cambridge, pp. 214–64.

—— (1992*a*), *Nachmetaphysisches Denken*, Suhrkamp, Frankfurt/Main.

—— (1992*b*), *Postmetaphysical Thinking: Philosophical Essays*, transl. by William Mark Hohengarten, Polity Press, Cambridge.

—— (1992*c*), *Autonomy and Solidarity: Interviews with Jürgen Habermas*, ed. by Peter Dews, Verso, London and New York.

—— (1994), *Faktizität und Geltung. Beiträge zur Diskurstheorie des Rechts und des demokratischen Rechtsstaats*, Suhrkamp, Frankfurt/Main.

—— (1995), *Zur Rekonstruktion des Historischen Materialismus*, Suhrkamp, Frankfurt/Main.

—— (1996*a*), "Sprechakttheoretische Erläuterungen zum Begriff der kommunikativen Rationalität", *Zeitschrift für philosophische Forschung* 50, pp. 65–91.

—— (1996*b*), *Die Einbeziehung des Anderen. Studien zur politischen Theorie*, Suhrkamp, Frankfurt/Main.

—— (1996*c*), "Replik auf Beiträge zu einem Symposion der Benjamin N. Cardozo School of Law", *Cardozo Law Review* 17, pp. 1559–643.

—— (1996*d*), "Reply to Symposium Participants, Benjamin L. Cardozo School of Law" (transl. by William Rehg), *Cardozo Law Review* 17, pp. 1477–557.

—— (1996*e*), *Between Facts and Norms: Contributions to a Discourse Theory of Law and Democracy*, transl. by William Rehg, Polity Press, Cambridge.

—— (1998), *Die postnationale Konstellation. Politische Essays*, Suhrkamp, Frankfurt/Main.

—— (1999*a*), *The Inclusion of the Other: Studies in Political Theory*, ed. by Ciaran Cronin and Pablo De Greiff, transl. by Ciaran Cronin, Polity Press, Cambridge.

—— (1999*b*), *Moral Consciousness and Communicative Action*, transl. by Christian Lenhardt and Shierry Weber Nicholson, introduction by Thomas McCarthy, MIT Press, Cambridge, MA.

—— (1999*c*), *Wahrheit und Rechtfertigung. Philosophische Aufsätze*, Suhrkamp, Frankfurt/Main.

Jürgen Habermas (2001a), *Justification and Application: Remarks on Discourse Ethics*, transl. by Ciaran P. Cronin, MIT Press, Cambridge, MA.

—— (2001b), *The Postnational Constellation: Political Essays* transl. and ed. by Max Pensky, Polity Press, Cambridge.

—— (2003a), *On the Pragmatics of Social Interaction: Preliminary Studies in the Theory of Communicative Action*, transl. by Barbara Fultner, Polity Press, Cambridge.

—— (2003b), *Communication and the Evolution of Society*, transl. and with an introduction by Thomas McCarthy, Polity Press, Cambridge.

—— (2003c), *On the Pragmatics of Communication*, ed. by Maeve Cooke, Polity Press, Cambridge.

—— (2003d), *Truth and Justification*, transl. by Barbara Fultner, Polity Press, Cambridge.

Hans Haferkamp (1985), "Critique of Habermas's Theory of Communicative Action", in: Seebaß/Tuomela, pp. 197–205.

Franz J. Hinkelammert (1994), "Diskursethik und Verantwortungsethik: eine kritische Stellungnahme" in: Raúl Fornet-Betancourt (ed.), *Konvergenz oder Divergenz. Eine Bilanz des Gesprächs zwischen Diskursethik und Befreiungsethik*, Augustinus-Buchhandlung, Aachen, pp. 111–49.

Otfried Höffe (1976), "Kritische Überlegungen zur Konsensustheorie der Wahrheit (Habermas)", *Philosophisches Jahrbuch* 83, pp. 312–32.

Horst Holzer (1988), "Kommunikative Rationalität als Basis der Kritik. Zur Theorie des kommunikativen Handelns von Jürgen Habermas", *Deutsche Zeitschrift für Philosophie* 36, pp. 989–1003.

Axel Honneth (1985), *Kritik der Macht. Reflexionsstufen einer kritischen Gesellschaftstheorie*, Suhrkamp, Frankfurt/Main.

—— (1994), "Das Andere der Gerechtigkeit", *Deutsche Zeitschrift für Philosophie* 42, pp. 195–220.

—— Hans Joas (eds.) (1986), *Kommunikatives Handeln*, Suhrkamp, Frankfurt/Main.

Vittorio Hösle (1987), *Begründungsfragen des objektiven Idealismus*, in: Forum für Philosophie Bad Homburg (ed.), pp. 212–67.

—— (1997), *Die Krise der Gegenwart und die Verantwortung der Philosophie*, Beck, München.

Karl-Heinz Ilting (1976), "Geltung als Konsens", *Neue Hefte für Philosophie* 10, pp. 20–50.

—— (1982), "Der Geltungsgrund moralischer Normen", in: Kuhlmann/Böhler (eds.), pp. 612–48.

David Ingram (1993), "The Limits and Possibilities of Communicative Ethics for Democratic Theory", *Political Theory* 21, pp. 294–321.

Hans Joas (1986), "Die unglückliche Ehe von Hermeneutik und Funktionalismus", in: Honneth/Joas (eds.), pp. 144–76.

Rolf Johannes (1989), "Über die Welt, die Habermas von der Einsicht ins System trennt", in: Bolte (ed.), pp. 39–66.

James Johnson (1991), "Habermas on Strategic and Communicative Action", *Political Theory* 19, pp. 181–201.

Immanuel Kant (1987), (ed. by Wilhelm Weischedel), *Kritik der praktischen Vernunft. Grundlegung zur Metaphysik der Sitten*, Suhrkamp, Frankfurt/Main.

Matthias Kettner (1993), "Bereichsspezifische Relevanz. Zur konkreten Allgemeinheit der Diskursethik", in: Apel/Kettner, pp. 317–48.

—— (1994), "Geltungsansprüche", in: Georg Meggle, Ulla Wessels (eds.), *Analyomen I*, pp. 750–60.

Herbert Keuth (1983), "Fallibilismus versus transzendentalpragmatische Letztbegründung", *Zeitschrift für allgemeine Wissenschaftstheorie* 14, pp. 320–37.

—— (1988), "Fehlbarkeit oder Sicherheit?", *Zeitschrift für allgemeine Wissenschaftstheorie* 19, pp. 378–90.

—— (1993), *Erkenntnis oder Entscheidung. Zur Kritik der kritischen Theorie*, Mohr, Tübingen.

Lawrence Kohlberg (1971), "From Is to Ought", in: Theodore Mischel (ed.), *Cognitive Development and Epistemology*, Academic Press, New York, pp. 151–235.

Wolfgang R. Köhler (1987), "Zur Debatte um reflexive Argumente in der neueren deutschen Philosophie", in: Forum für Philosophie Bad Homburg (ed.), pp. 303–33.

Dietmar Köveker (1992), "Zur Kategorisierbarkeit 'verdeckt' und 'offen strategischen Sprachgebrauchs'. Das Parasitismusargument von Jürgen Habermas", *Zeitschrift für allgemeine Wissenschaftstheorie* 23, pp. 289–311.

Wolfgang Kuhlmann (1981), "Reflexive Letztbegründung. Zur These von der Unhintergehbarkeit der Argumentationssituation", *Zeitschrift für philosophische Forschung* 35, pp. 3–26.

—— (1985a), *Reflexive Letztbegründung. Untersuchungen zur Transzendentalpragmatik*, Alber, Frankfurt/Main.

—— (1985b), "Reflexive Letztbegründung versus radikaler Fallibilismus. Eine Replik", *Zeitschrift für allgemeine Wissenschaftstheorie* 16, pp. 357–74.

—— (1993), "Bemerkungen zum Problem der Letztbegründung", in: Dorschel et al., pp. 212–37.

—— Dietrich Böhler (eds.) (1982), *Kommunikation und Reflexion. Zur Diskussion der Transzendentalpragmatik. Antworten auf Karl-Otto Apel*, Suhrkamp, Frankfurt/Main.

Ronald D. Laing (1998), *Self and Others*, Routledge, New York.

Guy R. Lefrancois (1986), *Psychologie des Lernens*, Springer, Berlin, Heidelberg, New York, Tokyo.

Jaques Lenoble (1996), "Law and Indecidability: A New Vision of the Proceduralization of Law", in *Cardozo Law Review* 17, pp. 2901–70.

Steven Lukes (1982), "Of Gods and Demons: Habermas and Practical Reason", in: Thompson/Held, pp. 134–48.

Christoph Lumer (1990), "Argumentation", in: Hans-Jörg Sandkühler (ed.): *Europäische Enzyklopädie zu Philosophie und Wissenschaften*, Meiner, Hamburg, pp. 248 ff.

—— (1997), "Habermas' Diskursethik", *Zeitschrift für philosophische Forschung* 51, pp. 42–64.

Jean-Francois Lyotard (1982), "Beantwortung der Frage: Was ist postmodern?", *Tumult* 4, pp. 131–42.

Ingeborg Maus (1987), "Verrechtlichung, Entrechtlichung und der Funktionswandel von Institutionen", in: Gerhard Göhler (ed.), *Grundfragen der Theorie politischer Institutionen*, Westdeutscher Verlag, Opladen, pp. 132–72.

Thomas McCarthy (1978), *The Critical Theory of Jürgen Habermas*, Hutchinson & Co, London.

—— (1989), *Kritik der Verständigungsverhältnisse. Zur Theorie von Jürgen Habermas*, Suhrkamp, Frankfurt/Main.

—— (1996), "Legitimacy and Diversity: Dialectical Reflections on Analytical Distinctions", *Cardozo Law Review* 17, pp. 1083–125.

Thomas Mirbach (1984), "Das 'Projekt' der Moderne", *Politische Vierteljahresschrift/Literatur-Heft*, pp. 5–16.

Samuel E. Morison (ed.) (1965), *Sources and Documents Illustrating the American Revolution 1764–1788 and the Formation of the Federal Constitution*, Clarendon Press, Oxford.

Willi Oelmüller (ed.) (1978a), *Transzendentalphilosophische Normenbegründung*, Schöningh, Paderborn.

—— (ed.) (1978b), *Normenbegründung und Normendurchsetzung*, Schöningh, Paderborn.

Audun Øfsti (1993), "Ist diskursive Vernunft nur eine Sonderpraxis? Betrachtungen zum 'Verbindlichkeitstransfer' von transzendental-reflexiv (letzt-)begründeten Normen", in: Apel/Kettner, pp. 296–316.

Onora O'Neill (1993), "Kommunikative Rationalität und praktische Vernunft", *Deutsche Zeitschrift für Philosophie* 41, pp. 329–32.

Konrad Ott (1996), *Vom Begründen zum Handeln. Aufsätze zur angewandten Ethik*, Attempto, Tübingen.

Bernhard Peters (1991), *Rationalität, Recht und Gesellschaft*, Suhrkamp, Frankfurt/Main.

Hilary Putnam (1975), *Mind, Language and Reality. Philosophical Papers, Vol. 2*, Cambridge University Press, Cambridge.

William Rehg (1991), "Discourse and the Moral Point of View: Deriving a Dialogical Principle of Universalization", *Inquiry* 34, pp. 27–48.

——(1994), *Insight and Solidarity. A Study in the Discourse Ethics of Jürgen Habermas*, University of California Press, Berkeley and London.

——(1996), "Against Subordination: Morality, Discourse, and Decision in the Legal Theory of Jürgen Habermas", *Cardozo Law Review* 17, pp. 1147–62.

Nicholas Rescher (1993), *Pluralism. Against the Demand for Consensus*, Clarendon Press, Oxford.

Peter Rohs (1987), "Philosophie als Selbsterhellung von Vernunft", in: Forum für Philosophie Bad Homburg, pp. 363–90.

Arno Ros (1990), *Begründung und Begriff: Wandlungen des Verständnisses begrifflicher Argumentationen, Bd. III: Moderne*, Meiner, Hamburg.

Herbert Schnädelbach (1982), "Transformation der Kritischen Theorie", *Philosophische Rundschau* 29, pp. 161–78.

Gerhard Schönrich (1994), *Bei Gelegenheit Diskurs. Von den Grenzen der Diskursethik und vom Preis der Letztbegründung*, Suhrkamp, Frankfurt/Main.

Gottfried Seebaß, Raimo Tuomela (eds.) (1985), *Social Action*, D. Reidel, Dordrecht.

Clifford D. Simak (1992), "Desertion", in: Tom Shippey (ed.), *The Oxford Book of Science Fiction Stories*, Oxford University Press, Oxford, pp. 115–26.

Gunnar Skirbekk (1982), "Rationaler Konsens und ideale Sprechsituation als Geltungsgrund? Über Recht und Grenze eines transzendental-pragmatischen Geltungskonzeptes", in: Kuhlmann/Böhler, pp. 54–82.

Erling Skjei (1985), "A Comment on Performative, Subject, and Proposition in Habermas's Theory of Communicative Action", *Inquiry* 28, pp. 87–105.

John R. Snarey (1994), "Cross-Cultural Universality of Social-Moral Development: A Critical Review of Kohlbergian Research", in: Bill Puka (ed.), *New Research in Moral Development*, Routledge, New York und London, pp. 268–98.

Uwe Steinhoff (1994), "Die Relativität der Gültigkeit von Begründungen", *Conceptus* 27, pp. 239–50.

——(1996a), "Die Begründung der Konsenstheorie. Über das fehlende Fundament der Diskursethik", *Logos*, Neue Folge 3, pp. 191–210.

——(1996b), "Probleme der Legitimation des demokratischen Rechtsstaats", *Rechtstheorie* 27, pp. 449–59.

——(1997), "Truth vs. Rorty", *Philosophical Quarterly* 47, pp. 358–61.

——(2000), "On the Concept, Function, Scope, and Evaluation of Justification(s)", *Argumentation* 14, pp. 79–105.

——(2006), *Kritik der kommunikativen Rationalität: Eine Darstellung und Kritik der kommunikationstheoretischen Philosophie von Jürgen Habermas und Karl-Otto Apel*, Mentis, Paderborn.

Charles L. Stevenson (1965), *Ethics and Language*, Yale University Press, New Haven und London.

Barry Stroud (1968), "Transcendental Arguments", *Journal of Philosophy* 65, pp. 241–65.

John B. Thompson (1982), "Universal Pragmatics", in: Thompson/Held, pp. 116–33.

——David Held (eds.) (1982), *Habermas—Critical Debates*, Macmillan, London.

Ernst Tugendhat (1985), "Habermas on Communicative Action", in: Seebaß/Tuomela, pp. 179–86.

——(1994), *Vorlesungen über Ethik*, Suhrkamp, Frankfurt/Main.

Christoph Türcke (1989), "Habermas oder Wie die kritische Theorie gesellschaftsfähig wurde", in: Bolte (ed.), pp. 21–38.

Max Weber (1964), *Wirtschaft und Gesellschaft*, Kiepenheuer und Witsch, Köln.

——(1978), *Economy and Society: An Outline of Interpretative Sociology, Vol. I*, ed. by Guenther Roth and Claus Wittich, University of California Press, Berkeley, Los Angeles and London.

Johannes Weiß (1983), "Verständigungsorientierung und Kritik. Zur 'Theorie des kommunikativen Handelns' von Jürgen Habermas", *Kölner Zeitschrift für Soziologie und Sozialpsychologie* 35: 108–20.

Albrecht Wellmer (1986), *Ethik und Dialog. Elemente des moralischen Urteils bei Kant und in der Diskursethik*, Suhrkamp, Frankfurt/Main.

Bernard Williams (1973), *Problems of the Self*, Cambridge University Press, Cambridge.

——(1981), *Moral Luck. Philosophical Papers 1973–1980*, Cambridge University Press, Cambridge.

Michael Williams (1996), *Unnatural Doubts: Epistemological Realism and the Basis of Scepticism*, Princeton University Press, Princeton, NJ.

Ludwig Wittgenstein (1953), *Philosophical Investigations*, transl. by G. E. M Anscombe, Basil Blackwell, Oxford.

Allen W. Wood (1985), "Habermas's Defense of Rationalism", *New German Critique* 35, pp. 145–64.

Dieter Wunderlich (1982), "Über die Konsequenzen von Sprechhandlungen", in: Karl-Otto Apel (ed.), *Sprachpragmatik und Philosophie*, Suhrkamp, Frankfurt/Main., pp. 441–62.

Rolf Zimmermann (1985), Utopie-Rationalität-Politik. Zur Kritik, Rekonstruktion und Systematik einer emanzipatorischen Gesellschaftstheorie bei Marx und Habermas, Alber, München.

Index

Marx, Karl 195
Marxism 194, 218
Maus, Ingeborg 214–5
meaning, theory of 61–64
Mirbach, Thomas 236
modernity 197, 198, 236–40
*Moralbewußtsein und kommunikatives
    Handeln* 145
*Moral Consciousness and Communicative
    Action* 145
moral development 183–4
moral discourse, *see* practical discourse
morality 8, 35, 51, 55, 56, 78, 83, 84, 85, 91,
    92, 94, 104, 128, 134, 137, 182–4,
    197–9, 223–5, 225, 232
    of reason (or rational morality) 47, 48,
        49, 67, 128
    see also ethics
moral justification 31, 78–94, 134–53, 238,
    241–2
moral principle (U) 78–94, 96, 129, 137–8,
    153–5, 167–8, 184, 221, 222–5
    and the problem of application 167–80
    as a bridging principle 80, 88–90,
        93–4
    stated 51, 137, 143
    derivation of 143–9, 221
    as inacceptable 149–53
moral norms 44, 47, 51–5, 78–94, 95–6,
    103–5, 150, 180, 223–5
    social currency vs. validity of 87
mutual understanding, *see* understanding

normalcy 184–91
normative context 67, 68, 73, 212–13
norms, *see* moral norms; presuppositions
    or rules of argumentation and
    discourse

Øfsti, Audun 139, 140
ontogenesis 199, *see also* hominization
operational knowledge 89, 100, 101, 106
Ott, Konrad 259 n209

parasitism 56–61, 142–3, 186, 190
particularism 238
Peirce, Charles Sanders 166, 243
performative acts 106, 162
performative attitude 33–4, 43, 46

performative contradiction 78, 100, 102–3,
    104, 107–10, 113, 116, 124, 126,
    128–9, 130, 133, 140, 143, 154, 191,
    228
    characterized and criticized 107–10
perlocutionary acts 32, 38, 57, 58, 59–60,
    61–2, 68, 70, 76
perlocutionary aim 25, 35, 56, 57, 75
perlocutionary effect 56, 57, 62, 71
perlucutionary success 62
Peters, Bernhard 137, 229
Philosophical Discourse of Modernity, The 242
philosophy of history 196, 198, 200
Piaget, Jean 195, 196, 197
pluralism 218, 230, 231, 232–3
Popper, Karl 44, 98
popular sovereignty 232–3
    and human rights 219–20, 226–8
positivism, legal 235
power 211–13, 217, 220–1, 233–4
practical (or moral) discourse 46–50,
    51–4, 78–80, 82, 85–6, 87, 88, 89,
    91, 93–4, 130–1, 140, 144, 148–53,
    177, 220, 222, 223, 235, 248
    aims of 78, 94–5, 147
    see also application of norms;
        argumentation; consensus or
        discourse theory of truth and
        rightness; discourse
pragmatism 243
pragmatist conception of truth 243–48
presuppositions
    existential 67, 70, 73, 74, 206, 207
    of action oriented towards reaching
        understading 57, 187–92, 199, 213
    of communicative action 60, 64–72,
        187–92, 199, 204
    ontological 64–72
    or rules of argumentation and
        discourse 94–143, 144, 146, 147,
        150, 152, 154, 176, 180, 187–92,
        199, 220, 221, 226
        as not constitutive for argumenta-
            tion 102–3, 129, 134, 188–9
    see also identification of presuppositions
        or rules of argumenentation and
        discourse
proceduralist conception of law 228–9, 235
progress 199